Rhetorical Occasions

RHETORICAL

Michael Bérubé | Essays on

OCCASIONS

Humans and the Humanities

The University of
North Carolina Press

Chapel Hill

Designed by April Leidig-Higgins
Set in Garamond by Copperline Book Services, Inc.

The paper in this book meets the guidelines for
permanence and durability of the Committee on
Production Guidelines for Book Longevity of the
Council on Library Resources.

The original publication information for the essays in
this book that have been reprinted follows the index.

Library of Congress Cataloging-in-Publication Data
Bérubé, Michael, 1961 –
Rhetorical occasions: essays on humans and the
humanities / Michael Bérubé.
p. cm.   Includes bibliographical references and index.
ISBN-13: 978-0-8078-3067-3 (cloth: alk. paper)
ISBN-10: 0-8078-3067-4 (cloth: alk. paper)
ISBN-13: 978-0-8078-5777-9 (pbk.: alk. paper)
ISBN-10: 0-8078-5777-7 (pbk.: alk. paper)
1. Humanities — United States.   2. Sokal, Alan D.,
1955 –   3. United States — Study and teaching.
4. Learning and scholarship — United States.
5. Popular culture — United States.   6. Criticism
— United States.   7. September 11 Terrorist Attacks,
2001 — Influence.   8. New Left — United States.
9. Rhetoric — United States.   10. Blogs — United
States.   I. Title.
AZ508.B47   2006
001.3071 — dc22   2006045841

cloth   10 09 08 07 06   5 4 3 2 1
paper   10 09 08 07 06   5 4 3 2 1

Contents

Acknowledgments

Many thanks to the fine editors and generous interlocutors who helped give many of these essays their initial shape: Robin Aronson, Daniel Born, Jo-Ellen Green Kaiser, Alex Star, Marita Sturken, and Karen Winkler. And many thanks to everyone who gave me the opportunity to try out my ideas in one public forum or another: Judith Butler, Jeffrey DiLeo, Jennifer Holberg and Marcy Taylor, Djelal Kadir, David Laurence, Gary Olson and Lynn Worsham, Jennifer Ruark, Alan Sokal, and Curtis White. A special thanks to a pair of savvy and humane friends who helped, directly and indirectly, as I pieced together the arguments that became the essays in part IV of this book: Danny Postel and Leo Casey.

I have had the good fortune to present some of the arguments and essays here to audiences at the American Studies Association, Carnegie Mellon University, Central Michigan University, Central Oregon Community College, the City College of New York, Dartmouth College (the Leslie Humanities Center), Duke University, Emory University, the English Institute, the Federation of State Humanities Councils, Georgia State University, Hanover College, Illinois State University, the University of Miami, the University of Michigan, the University of Missouri, the University of Nebraska, New York University, the University of Northern Iowa, Penn State University, the University of Virginia, the University of Washington, and Wilfrid Laurier University. Thanks to everyone who attended those talks, especially everyone who asked questions about them and led me to see how they could be sharpened.

I have revised some of the essays for publication here. "The Return of Realism and the Future of Contingency," "Of Fine Clothes and Naked Emperors," "Citizens of the World, Unite," and "Idolatries of the Marketplace" have undergone substantial revision and expansion; the rest of the essays in parts I, II, and III have been tweaked and updated with a somewhat lighter touch, except for "The Sokal Hoax for Beginners," which makes its debut in this volume. The essays in part V were posted to my blog, michaelberube.com, but have never appeared in print.

Finally, a heartfelt thanks to Sian Hunter for wonderful editing (in both the tweaking and the substantial-revision categories) and for all manner of kindness. And thanks to Janet, Nick, and Jamie for being the truly remarkable and world-transforming Janet, Nick, and Jamie.

B etween 1997 and 2001, when I served as the founding director of the Illinois Program for Research in the Humanities at the University of Illinois at Urbana-Champaign, I did very little sustained writing. By "sustained," I mean the kind of writing one can do if one has six or eight (or twelve or eighteen) months at one's disposal — the kind of time most people need to conceptualize and begin to work on book-length projects. And in taking that job, I knew I was agreeing not to embark on any major projects for the foreseeable future; instead, I devoted myself to running an institute that would provide other Illinois faculty with released time for *their* major scholarly projects, and I decided that I would spend most of my time learning about academic fields with respect to which I was something between a neophyte and a troglodyte. I wanted, among other things, to build programming bridges between the College of Liberal Arts at Illinois, in which my program was housed, and the College of Fine and Applied Arts, the Krannert Museum, and the Krannert Center for the Performing Arts. Those bridges were eventually built, but I was initially stunned at how easily collaborations between the arts and humanities could be stymied by academic bureaucracies: what is one to make, I wondered, of the fact that art and music are so distant, on the organizational chart, from literature and philosophy, even though most of the forms of human social organization over the past five thousand years have treated these as cognate endeavors that draw on our creative and interpretive energies? How can we make sense of a bookkeeping dispensation in which molecular biology is affianced to English and modern languages under the sign of "liberal arts," while the Department of Theater is as remote from English and modern languages as is the Department of Kinesiology or the College of Business Administration? Is there any defensible rationale behind the parallel curricula governing the arts and humanities, according to which the student artists are to be trained in the practices of representation while remaining largely ignorant of theories of representation in the humanities and the student humanists are to be trained in theories of representation while remaining largely ignorant of the history of art as well as most contemporary artists?

In one respect, my job was a four-year exercise in frustration insofar as I was compelled to ask such questions but proved unable to provide any practical answer to them. I did, however, learn why practical answers are so hard to come by — as I suggest in the fourth essay in this volume, "The Utility of the Arts and Humanities." But I loved the synoptic view of the arts and humanities the job gave me, and (although this will surely sound strange to some academic ears) I relished the office-work aspects of that job. Very rarely does academic life demand that you absolutely, positively have to have your documents in the mail overnight, and in that respect, running a fledgling humanities program took me back to the days when I worked as a word processor at a Park Avenue corporate law firm, flailing away at a primitive IBM keyboard to make sure that the latest draft agreement for the refinancing of Yugoslavia would be completed in time for the 4:00 P.M. DHL pickup. That aspect of my humanities job served, in turn, as the scaffolding for the substantive rewards of the job, a scant few of which I mention in the essay "Speaking of Speakers": hosting presentations by performance artist Joe Goode or Russian émigré artists Vitaly Komar and Alexander Melamid or by political theorist Nancy Fraser and museum director Marcia Tucker; learning about the interdisciplinary conversations between history and anthropology from Richard Handler and Mary Louise Pratt and about the current controversies in art history from James Elkins and Abigail Soloman-Godeau; attending the seminar on early Judeo-Christian ideas of subversion and martyrdom led by Daniel Boyarin or the review of the representational practices of museums conducted by Fred Wilson. At the end of four years as the director of a humanities center, I had learned a great deal about fields of which I had been stunningly ignorant, and I had begun to see — underlying all their disciplinary trajectories and intra-disciplinary distinctions — what constitutes these enterprises as creative and interpretive endeavors.

I wrote about a half dozen of the essays in this book while serving as director of IPRH, but I hope the synoptic view afforded by my experience with a humanities institute informs the rest of the essays collected here as well. That's not to say that these essays embrace a common theme, a single set of concerns, or a distinct topic. On the contrary, they were originally written for a wide range of rhetorical occasions and publication venues — from the annual English Institute conference to the *Common Review* to *Tikkun* magazine to my personal Web log. Some of them represent my "sustained" writing and offer arguments that I have been honing and revisiting for years; others represent more office-work kinds of essays, the kind that have to be done by

4:00 P.M. and sent to copyediting ASAP. For obvious reasons, academe tends to consider the latter kind of writing less valuable than the former — as, for most intellectual purposes, do I. Writing for newspapers and magazines entails dealing with external pressures (constraints of time and space) and negotiating with editors (over specific arguments, paragraphs, and even words) in ways that few writers for exclusively academic journals ever encounter. But that's not the only difference between academic and "popular" writing — and, as it happens, some of the features of "popular" writing are actually conducive to better, sharper writing than one ordinarily does in the course of one's academic work.

Some of the editorial feedback I've received over the years has felt like an "external pressure," like a constraint, but most of it has felt like intellectual stimulation, a matter of learning new modes of address and strategies for revision.[1] And all of my experiences in writing for nonacademic venues — from op-eds to blogs — have taught me to think differently about "public time."

We are not accustomed to thinking about public writing in terms of public *time*. In fact, I'd been doing public writing for a couple of years without realizing what it meant in these terms. Fortunately, however, Bruce Robbins pointed it out to me in the course of a review of my second book, *Public Access*: writing in *Transition* magazine, Robbins noted that "the public is often imagined as a space" (a point on which he elaborates brilliantly in *The Phantom Public Sphere*) but that writing for public outlets also requires a significant shift in how one organizes one's work time:

> If you want to place an op-ed piece that exposes the staggering misinformation purveyed in a televised debate before the newspapers have lost interest in the whole thing, you will not only have to take time away from your teaching and scholarly writing, but you will have to work a lot faster than most academics are used to. Going public (like going professional, which is often taken as its opposite) means an inevitable speedup in work rhythm. (95)

Not all of the essays collected in *Rhetorical Occasions* were written on such an accelerated schedule: some were written in four or five hours, whereas some were stitched and restitched over four or five years. But I think it may be worth saying, in so many words, that "public" rhetorical occasions are not simply a matter of intervening in such-and-such a space in response to this or that debate; they are also a matter of recalibrating work time, especially when one's public writing is required to be *timely*.

It's not just a matter of my time, either. It's also a matter of yours. Writing for newspapers, magazines, online journals, and blogs requires one to capture a reader's attention, to fight for the time it will take one's potential addressees to make their way through an essay of one to four thousand words in the course of an ordinary workday. That doesn't necessarily mean, as too many academics assume, that one has to play to the crowd to get the attention of a public readership; it means, rather, that one can never take one's crowd for granted. As Laura Kipnis argued in an essay cheekily titled "Public Intellectuals Do It with Style," such public writing "poses a request, even a demand, to produce different and enlarged forms of mediation" because it does not, cannot assume a captive audience:

> What it means to be a "public intellectual," then, is not only to be inter-disciplinary rather than disciplinary and surprising rather than fetishistic, but also to seduce an audience that isn't compelled by any particular compulsion (be it requirements of a major or "keeping up" with the profession), and that isn't composed of enablers and co-dependents of the knowledge-fetish (who are non-academics, in other words), into donating its attention. Thus, being a public intellectual demands modes of mediating one's private fascinations and the driven aspects of one's intellectual engagements in order to establish connections and rapport whose terms and publics are not dictated in advance. (195)

This is one reason why my negotiations with editors and other "public" interlocutors (including blog commenters, whom I'll discuss in the introduction to section 5) appear to me to be forms of intellectual stimulation: they involve idiosyncratic work rhythms and enlarged forms of mediation. Sometimes, those negotiations did not work out quite the way I wanted them to: my review essays on Alan Sokal and Martha Nussbaum, for example, were edited rigorously before publication (by *Tikkun* and *Lingua Franca*, respectively). In each case, my editors' responses almost always improved my work, focusing it and requiring me to get to the point for a reading audience that might not have the time to indulge some of my more self-indulgent divagations. Even still, in a couple of instances, my essays for nonacademic journals lost a few sentences, sometimes even a few paragraphs, that felt to me like phantom limbs when I finally saw the published versions. When I finally found the missing sections — usually strewn about in the messy "articles" folder of my hard drive, hiding under long-forgotten names like participants in some First Draft Protection Program — I restored them to what I thought of as their rightful places on the body of these texts. But these newly revised or restored or remastered versions do not quite constitute the original director's cut of these essays, since, as I say, most of the editorial changes that were made to them in the course of their composition turned out to be changes for the better.

In "Teaching to the Six" — an essay I have revised lightly for this collection, an occasion quite different from its original publication in the academic journal *Pedagogy* — I remark that my range of writing experiences and my concomitant range of writing practices has been of some benefit to me in one of my other workplaces, the undergraduate classroom: "My research sometimes enhances my teaching, but not always," I say. "Nor need it. My writing career, on the other hand, almost always enhances my ability to read and comment on student writing, particularly my experience in dealing with editors of journals both academic and generalist, which has taught me all I know about strategies for revision." The idea I was trying to convey in this passage might well stand as the idea that animates *Rhetorical Occasions*: that our lives as academics, as writers and teachers, may be discontinuous in some respects yet coherent precisely in their discontinuity, as we try to address our many interlocutors in their many disparate locations and with their many disparate senses of public time. You don't have to write for newspapers on 4:00 P.M. deadlines or direct a humanities institute to know what I mean: anyone who, in the course of the day, speaks with undergraduates, colleagues, waiters, car mechanics, puzzled parents, mischievous children, or family and friends (let alone journalists and editors) knows what it means to try to find coherence in the discontinuous rhetorical occasions that constitute the time and space of our ordinary working lives. Which is to say, among other things, that I don't expect anyone to read these essays all the way through, front to back. They weren't written that way, and I wouldn't make that kind of demand on your precious time. But I do hope that by the time you've read as much as you care to, dear reader, you will have come to think of *Rhetorical Occasions* not only as a book of essays but as a collection of experiments — in gauging the scope of the humanities, in keeping track of the mechanics of academe and the possibilities of popular cultural criticism, in contributing to the collective determination of how the American left can best respond to the bleak political landscape post-9/11, and in devising new means of public address to accomplish any or all of the above. Whether they first appeared in *American Quarterly*, the *Boston Globe* Sunday Ideas supplement, or my humble Web log, these are essays, as Northrop Frye once put it, "in the word's original sense of a trial or incomplete attempt" (3). Here, in book form, they are meant both as a record of some of my work in the recent past and as incomplete attempts to devise modes of writing that will speak to humans and the humanities in the future.

Notes

1. There have been exceptions, particularly in the early stages of my career as a writer, when I sometimes negotiated badly with editors about space limitations and specific passages. In *The Division of Literature*, Peggy Kamuf calls attention to this (gently) in the course of a brief discussion of my work, asking, among other things, "[H]ow does one plot the correlation between a descending size of the print run and a diminishing constraint on the freedom to print what an author in fact wrote?" (150). The short answer is that the correlation is not directly proportional; the longer answer is that the correlation is not directly proportional and the terms are not quite adequate. Kamuf's question presumes that one writes with less freedom when one is dealing with larger print runs, and I can report that this is not true. More generally, I can suggest that writing (even blog writing, in which I have no editor at all) involves negotiations of every kind at every step of the way. As for print runs and editorial constraints: while *Public Access* gave me a latitude I did not always have in newspapers, my editor at Verso, Michael Sprinker, went over the manuscript with his notoriously fine-toothed comb and objected to numerous passages, many of which were eventually improved by his objections. By contrast, my next book, *Life as We Know It*, was written for a trade press — Pantheon — and was published precisely as I desired it, word for word. My editor at Pantheon, Linda Healey, made my manuscript better but not by challenging or revising specific passages; rather, she habitually directed me to good sources and asked me to extend my argument so that it would be as fresh in 2006 as it had been in 1996. I have been extremely fortunate to have both Sprinker and Healey as editors, but it simply was not the case that the larger print run involved greater concessions to editorial suggestions.

Works Cited

Frye, Northrop. *An Anatomy of Criticism: Four Essays*. Princeton: Princeton University Press, 1957.

Kamuf, Peggy. *The Division of Literature; or, The University in Deconstruction*. Chicago: University of Chicago Press, 1997.

Kipnis, Laura. "Public Intellectuals Do It with Style." *Minnesota Review* 50 – 51 (1998): 193 – 96.

Robbins, Bruce. "The Culture Wars for Grown-Ups." *Transition* 67 (1995): 93 – 101.

———, ed. *The Phantom Public Sphere*. Minneapolis: University of Minnesota Press, 1993.

Part One

PHYSICS

The aftereffects of the 1996 Sokal/*Social Text* Affair have reverberated now for just over a decade: for some cultural journalists, the Sokal Hoax marks the Day Literary Theory Died, whereas for some philosophers, the Sokal Hoax somehow proves that Anglo-American analytical philosophy has been rigorously tested and proven to be true. Yet some of those aftereffects, I've found, have been mere turf squabbles. On one side were scientists, social scientists, and arts and humanities traditionalists for whom the episode demonstrated once and for all that "interpretive theory" was but another name for "obscurantist bullshit" and who believed that Sokal had saved them all from the task of actually reading any twentieth-century Continental philosophy, or queer theory, or science studies — whatever field or fields they considered to be the "real" object of Sokal's hoax. On the other side, some (not all) theorists in the arts and humanities were deeply offended by the hoax and considered it beneath contempt — and certainly unworthy of serious discussion. From the latter group — the constituents of which were and are much closer to me, personally and professionally, than the first cohort — I heard denunciation upon denunciation of Sokal's bad faith and his ridiculous posthoax posturing but not one word (aside from further denunciations) about the actual contents of the essay, not one word about how the hoax had played among literate nonspecialists and general readers, and not one word about how *Social Text*'s initial responses had made things considerably worse for Sokal's critics and considerably easier for his supporters. What those critics (on my side of the academic street) seemed not to understand was that their hauteur and dismissiveness would have been justified if, *but only if, Social Text* had rejected the essay: *then*, perhaps, we post-something theorists could go around snorting about how foolish and underhanded this Sokal character had been. But the Sokal Hoax — and even a few of the other essays published in the "Science Wars" issue of *Social Text* that was conceived partly as a response to Paul Gross and Norman Levitt's 1994 book, *Higher Superstition: The Academic Left and Its Quarrels with Science* — made it much, much harder to make the case that the Gross/Levitt critique was sweeping and indiscriminate and much harder to explain to interested onlookers precisely what, if anything, the humanities could contribute to an informed critique (or a better understanding) of the sciences.[1]

More important than the hoax itself (which, as I show in the first essay in this section, was much weirder than most accounts suggest) was Sokal's second essay, which was published in *Lingua Franca* and centered on Sokal's claim that the political left has always "believed that rational thought and the fearless analysis of objective reality (both natural and social) are incisive tools for combating the mystifications promoted by the powerful — not to mention being desirable human ends in their own right" (*Sokal Hoax* 52). At the center of this claim is a conflation of "natural" and "social" realities and an invitation (or demand) — albeit only an implicit one — to explain why the social-constructionist academic left might resist the conflation. While most of the social constructionists, pragmatists, poststructuralists, and assorted anti-foundationalists I know would simply decline the invitation on the grounds that they feel no need to construct the social-constructionist wheel yet again, I believe they do so at their peril — and that they fail to realize just how attractive the conflation of "natural" and "social" realities remains for some professional philosophers and seekers of certitude in general. It is strange to hear social constructionists say, as did one prominent science-studies scholar who served on a post-Sokal panel with me in 1996, that they have demonstrated once and for all the social character of knowledge. One would think — or, at least, I would submit — that the recognition of the social character of knowledge would prevent one from believing that any proposition about the social character of knowledge could achieve such a permanent status.

Sokal's challenge to the humanities, then, should have been engaged more thoroughly with regard to whether knowledges about the social world should be predicated on knowledges about the natural world, as I argue in the second essay in this section, "The Return of Realism and the Future of Contingency." But another issue lurks here as well, one that was addressed more substantially in 1998 by E. O. Wilson's *Consilience: The Unity of Knowledge*. The humanists at my end of the hallway roundly dismissed this book, too, as a document of disciplinary imperialism so overreaching as to be almost self-parodic: someday, we're supposed to believe, even the disciplines of literary criticism and art history will find their true foundation in physics and chemistry? *Please*. Why waste our precious time debating such bizarre and grandiose claims?

Because they require humanists to explain what's distinctive about the humanities, that's why. Because they ask us to explain how we distinguish between "natural" realities and "social" realities and why we refuse to let the former stand as the bases (or, worse, as the equivalents) of the latter. And because they check our own bizarre impulses to disciplinary imperialism and overreaching in the humanities, which we indulge every time we fail to distinguish between objects whose features are entirely a matter of collective human interpretation — such as, say, justice — and objects whose features, even if they are comprehensible to us humans only by means of collective human interpretation, nevertheless remain untouched by and indifferent to human interpretation — such as, say, photons.

The distinction between natural and social realities is excruciatingly difficult to make, particularly when one considers phenomena such as color, which does not exist independently of our perception of it even though electromagnetic radiation, from radio waves to gamma waves (including the tiny sliver of the spectrum known as "visible light") is indisputably observer-independent. But as I argue in "The Return of Realism," it is possible to be a "soft" social constructionist without giving up a belief in the observer independence of the observer-independent world. Indeed, one can even believe, as I do, that for mere mortals such as ourselves, social realities are the devices by which we understand the distinction between social realities and natural realities. To say this is not to denigrate the physical sciences as mere "social realities"; on the contrary, it is to acknowledge how extraordinary and difficult the disciplines of the physical sciences really are, and to underscore the fact that obtaining reliable knowledge of the observer-independent universe (especially its more recondite and bizarre features, involving quantum mechanics and superstring theory) requires an elaborate — and immeasurably valuable — form of social organization that hominids have only very recently managed to establish. "The Return of Realism" thus sets out, by way of strange bedfellows Martin Heidegger and John Searle, an argument for distinguishing "brute fact" from "social fact" while insisting that the distinction between the two be understood as a question of social fact.

"Of Fine Clothes and Naked Emperors" began life as a review essay of Sokal's sequel to the *Social Text* affair, a book known in the United States as *Fashionable Nonsense* (it was published in France under the title *Imposteurs Intellectuelles*, and Sokal's coauthor was French physicist Jean Bricmont). Vexed by claims that he had built his *Social Text* essay out of random, out-of-context snippets from the work of literary theorists, Sokal responded by publishing a book full of extremely long passages of dreadful, impenetrable, pretentious, and obscurantist work by the likes of Lacan, Baudrillard, Irigaray, and even Julia Kristeva, who was, for a (thankfully) brief period in her career, fond of drawing analogies between psychoanalytic theory and advanced mathematics. (Foucault and Derrida do not appear anywhere in the book, but this has not prevented many readers from concluding that Sokal somehow proved that their work, too, was worthless.) By the time of the book's appearance in 1998, of course, the battle lines had been drawn, and no one on my side of the academic street bothered to read *Fashionable Nonsense*. So much the better for them, in one way: they did not subject themselves to the painful experience of sifting through piles of garbage from the French poststructuralist left at the moment of Jacques Lacan's greatest (and most baneful) influence on French theory. But so much the worse for everyone who failed to notice that *Fashionable Nonsense* doesn't content itself with making fun of French theory: the book also mounts a substantial and thoughtful argument about the status of science studies in the wake of Thomas Kuhn's *Structure of Scientific Revolutions*. There is no question that Sokal followed his spectacular hoax essay (and its immediate sequels) by doing some serious reading in the field of science studies. Both his critics and his cheerleaders would do well to follow his lead.

The last essay in this section is also the most synoptic. Turning from the science-studies end of the Sokal Affair to the humanities, "The Utility of the Arts and Humanities" examines the uses to which the rhetoric of "utility" has been put, not only by university administrations and corporate underwriters but also by cultural journalists and cultural studies theorists. I begin with the pedestrian observation that artists and humanists who work in universities are generally ambivalent about the idea of defending their enterprises in terms of social utility: on the one hand, they do not want to claim that the arts and humanities are such exalted and self-justifying endeavors that no one need bother explaining why such things are worth pursuing; on the other hand, they are rightly skeptical that cost-benefit analyses of academic labor will do justice to disciplines devoted to the varieties of human cultural expression rather than to the research and development of patentable forms of knowledge. The result is that artists and humanists tend to resist thinking about the "utility" of their work except when it comes time to explain what it is they do — when, I argue, the idea of utility turns out to be not merely unavoidable but indispensable. And though my original rhetorical occasion was a post-Sokal reflection on Wilson's *Consilience* (as my conclusion makes clear), I hope the limited defense of "utility" I attempt in this essay remains useful today.

Notes

1. Two examples of "sweeping and indiscriminate" criticism will have to suffice here. In their discussion of Andrew Ross's work, Gross and Levitt very sensibly take issue with some of Ross's calls for a more "democratic" practice of science, such as this passage from *Strange Weather*: "How can metaphysical life theories and explanations taken seriously by millions be ignored or excluded by a small group of power-

ful people called 'scientists'?" (60). When Gross and Levitt cite this passage, they interpolate "[i.e., New Age]" after "metaphysical life theories" (91), but they might have pointed out that Ross's question can just as easily be asked of astrology or the biblical account of creation. In this case, in other words, I believe they had reason to take issue with Ross and actually did not take issue strenuously enough. Earlier in the same paragraph, however, they cite another sentence from *Strange Weather* in which Ross calls for science "that will be publicly answerable and of some service to progressive interests" (29). To this, Gross and Levitt respond, " 'Of some service to progressive interests' seems reasonably clear, if frighteningly Stalinist in tone and root" (91). This, I submit, is sheer hysteria masquerading as a defense of "reason." The idea that medicine or engineering or environmental science might serve "progressive interests" (Ross is not, as I will argue in "The Utility of the Arts and Humanities," calling for a leftist astrophysics) is unremarkable; responding to that idea by calling it Stalinist is, by contrast, altogether remarkable — and far worse than "indiscriminate."

The Gross/Levitt critique of feminism is, if anything, even more remarkable. Gross and Levitt insist that they oppose discrimination against women in scientific fields, and they acknowledge that this discrimination has been real enough in the past. But they also insist that the past is mostly dead and gone, and they brace themselves for battle in the present: "We take a position that is not likely, in the climate described, to endear us to a majority of our colleagues in or out of the sciences, or to the political and administrative avant-garde. It is that sexist discrimination, while certainly not vanished into history, is largely vestigial in the universities; that the only widespread, *obvious* discrimination today is against white males. . . . Of course these remarks violate the feminist metaphysics according to which every institution of this society is irremediably sexist, and every male, even the most sympathetic, ineradicably guilty by association with it. Some positions, even among persons brought up in the logophallocentric West, are well beyond the reach of rational argument. Feminist fundamentalism shares that distinction with other dogmatisms, such as religious fundamentalism; and when all is said and done, similar mentalities give rise to both" (110 – 11). A bit later in the chapter, Gross and Levitt further develop this rational argument against feminist fundamentalism: "Anyone who gives prime-time television a passing glance (we hope none of our readers give it more) is familiar with today's universal spin, for example, on women's careers. Who has not looked sidewise at the screen and seen a beautiful young woman (political correctness in the media does not yet frown upon 'lookism'), high heels, lipstick and all, leaping about with her 9-mm. Beretta held, two-handed, in the approved barrel-up manner, dodging around corners, stalking a murderous criminal? Who has not seen her straddle and handcuff the oaf, toward the end of the show? Who has not seen the impenetrably tough, young woman lawyer face down a crooked male judge in court, and then, as a sop to story line and the *connectedness* of women, make a lonely phone call to her mother, or her sister, late at night? Who, for that matter, hasn't seen the new, standard children's books, in which Mama Bear, like Papa Bear, goes to work or runs a honey-packing business? Who is so asleep as not to have noticed that Dagwood of the funnies, always an amiable dunce, is today a bigger jerk than ever, now that Blondie is a successful businesswoman while he remains under the thumb of his boss?" (123 – 24) To this series of questions, I imagine, one can only reply, "Who, indeed?" while smiling politely and searching the room for the nearest safe exit.

Works Cited

Gross, Paul, and Norman Levitt. *Higher Superstition: The Academic Left and Its Quarrels with Science*. Baltimore: Johns Hopkins University Press, 1994.

Kuhn, Thomas S. *The Structure of Scientific Revolutions*. Chicago: University of Chicago Press, 1970.

Ross, Andrew. *Strange Weather: Culture, Science, and Technology in the Age of Limits*. London: Verso, 1991.

Sokal, Alan. "A Physicist Experiments with Cultural Studies." *Lingua Franca* 6, no. 4 (May – June 1996): 62 – 64. Reprinted in *The Sokal Hoax: The Sham That Shook the Academy*, edited by the editors of *Lingua Franca*, 49 – 53. Lincoln: University of Nebraska Press, 2000.

Sokal, Alan, and Jean Bricmont. *Fashionable Nonsense: Postmodern Intellectuals' Abuse of Science*. New York: Picador, 1998.

Wilson, E. O. *Consilience: The Unity of Knowledge*. New York: Vintage, 1999.

The Sokal Hoax for Beginners

I n 2003 and 2004, I took over the Introduction to Graduate Study course for first-year English graduate students at Penn State, and at some point in each year, I had occasion to refer to the Sokal Hoax — only to find that no more than a handful of people among the two dozen students in each class had the faintest idea of what I was talking about. *These kids today*, I thought, *completely ignorant of the great hoaxes of the past* . . . and then I realized that when the "Science Wars" issue of *Social Text* was published in the late spring of 1996, most of these students were between twelve and fifteen years old. As important as it was, and as powerful as its legacy has been, it's already ancient history to people beginning their graduate careers today. Perhaps, then, a brief review of the hoax is in order here.[1]

NYU physicist Alan Sokal submitted an essay, "Transgressing the Boundaries: Toward a Transformative Hermeneutics of Quantum Gravity," to *Social Text*, a leading journal of the academic left, after reading *Higher Superstition: The Academic Left and Its Quarrels with Science*, Paul Gross and Norman Levitt's free-swinging critique of science studies, cultural studies, feminism, academic jargon, Afrocentrism, Bruno Latour, pretentiousness, New Age medicine, postmodernism, environmentalism, psychoanalysis, and Jeremy Rifkin. Sokal's essay itself is a very strange beast, as I'll show in the course of this discussion, and though as a parody it has many targets, its general object is to demonstrate that some well-respected humanists have published some extraordinarily silly things about the sciences, in some cases presuming to speak critically about subjects they do not adequately understand. And though there are doubtless many reasons why Sokal chose to submit his essay to *Social Text*, a desire to embarrass editors Andrew Ross and Stanley Aronowitz very likely among them (for Ross and Aronowitz were among the figures approvingly cited in the essay), it is safe to say that the essay's publication by a leading journal of the academic left would serve — *if* the hoax succeeded — to demonstrate that a leading journal of the academic left was unable to recognize the work of certain well-respected humanists as scientifically illiterate or obtuse.

The hoax, of course, did succeed, and Sokal made at least his two primary points: that some well-respected humanists have published some extraordinarily silly things about the sciences, and that a leading journal of the academic left was unable to recognize the work of certain well-respected humanists as scientifically illiterate or obtuse. When the essay appeared in *Social Text*, more than a year and a half after Sokal first submitted it in November 1994, Sokal revealed that his article was a spoof. Writing in the May–June 1996 issue of *Lingua Franca* under the title, "A Physicist Experiments with Cultural Studies," Sokal not only named "cultural studies" as the object of his ridicule but insisted that his *real* goal was to oppose "postmodernist literary theory" on behalf of the left: "[T]he results of my little experiment," he wrote, as if summing up a wily lab report, "demonstrate, at the very least, that some fashionable sectors of the American academic Left have been getting intellectually lazy" (52). At the very least, indeed: Sokal claimed that his hoax proved much more.

> *Social Text*'s acceptance of my article exemplifies the intellectual arrogance of Theory — postmodernist *literary* theory, that is — carried to its logical extreme. No wonder they didn't bother to consult a physicist. If all is discourse and "text," then knowledge of the real world is superfluous; even physics becomes just another branch of cultural studies. If, moreover, all is rhetoric and language games, then internal logical consistency is superfluous too: a patina of theoretical sophistication serves equally well.
>
> Incomprehensibility becomes a virtue; allusions, metaphors, and puns substitute for evidence and logic. My own article is, if anything, an extremely modest example of this well-established genre. (52)

The passage not only indicates what Sokal thought he had done but also suggests why the controversy he sparked was so strong and why the counter-Sokal critiques came not just from *Social Text* editors and readers but from academic humanists who "do" (or simply know something about) theory. For it is one thing, a plausible thing, to fault the editors of *Social Text* for exercising a kind of interdisciplinary hubris — of failing to consult a physicist, above all, but perhaps also for treating physics as just a branch of "cultural studies." (Or to fault them, at bare minimum, for publishing the work of a physicist who argued that physics should be so treated. I will leave aside the question of whether Sokal's conception of "cultural studies" was accurate.)[2] It is quite another thing to follow this with the illogical claim that "if all is rhetoric and language games, then internal logical consistency is superfluous." Human "language games" — and Sokal seems not to know that the term is Ludwig Wittgenstein's, not the happy-hour invention of some jejune anything-goes pomos — work partly by means of internal logical consistency, which is why most readers would blink if I finished this sentence with ten igneous rocks that rotate voluptuous velvet ocelots with friendly tomato juice.[3] In other (more internally logical) words, if *Social Text* demonstrated that its editors didn't know enough about science to publish a special issue on "Science Wars," Sokal's explanation of his hoax demonstrated that he didn't know very much about theories of rhetoric and language, none of which requires a suspension of belief in the "real," or phenomenal, world. To many humanists, Sokal's cry, "If everything is language, then everything is permitted" sounded as strange as the cry, "If everything is atoms and chemicals, then everything is meaningless" might sound to a scientist.

But when the Sokal Wars began, the anti-Sokal forces didn't have much of a chance to point out to journalists, colleagues, and interested onlookers that the study of rhetoric and language doesn't entail the denial of the world, because they were regrettably preempted by the initial responses of Ross and Aronowitz, the latter of whom called Sokal "ill-read and half-educated" (76) and the former of whom called the essay "a little hokey" and "not really our cup of tea" (55). Together with Bruce Robbins, Ross wrote a reply to Sokal for the July – August 1996 issue of *Lingua Franca*, "Mystery Science Theater." But Ross's initial (solo) response, which circulated widely on the Internet in May 1996 (at Ross's request), was far worse than the *Lingua Franca* version written with Robbins. Both replies begin with a paragraph of bemused disbelief (the Ross text comes first, followed by the Ross/Robbins version for publication):

> What were some of the initial responses of the journal's editors when we first learned about Alan Sokal's prank upon *Social Text*? One suspected that Sokal's "parody" was nothing of the sort, and that his admission represented a change of heart, or a collapse of his intellectual resolve. Another, while willing to accept the story, was less sure that Sokal knew very much about what or whom he thought he was kidding. A third was pleasantly astonished to learn that the journal is taken seriously enough to be considered a threat to anyone, let alone to natural scientists. At least two others were furious at the dubious means by which he chose to make his point. All were concerned that his actions might simply spark off a new round of caricature and thereby perpetuate the climate in which science studies has been subject recently to so much derision from conservatives in science. However varied the responses, we all believe that Sokal took too much for granted in his account of his prank. Indeed, his claim — that our publication of his article proves that something is rotten in the state of cultural studies — may have turned out to be as wacky as the article itself.

What were some of the initial responses of the journal's editors when we first learned about Alan Sokal's prank on *Social Text*? One suspected that Sokal's parody was nothing of the sort, and that his admission represented a change of heart, or a folding of his intellectual resolve. Another editor was unconvinced that Sokal knew very much about what he was attempting to expose. A third was pleasantly astonished to learn that the journal is taken seriously enough to be considered a target of a hoax, especially a hoax by a physicist. Others were concerned that the hoax might spark off a new round of caricature and thereby perpetuate the climate in which science studies and cultural studies have been subject recently to so much derision from conservatives in science.

All of us were distressed at the deceptive means by which Sokal chose to make his point. This breach of ethics is a serious matter in any scholarly community, and has damaging consequences when it occurs in science publishing. What is the likely result of Sokal's behavior for nonscientific journals? Less well known authors who submit unsolicited articles to journals like ours may now come under needless suspicion, and the openness of intellectual inquiry that *Social Text* has played its role in fostering will be curtailed.

However varied our responses, we all believe that Sokal took too much for granted in his account of his prank. Indeed, his claim — that our publication of his article proves that something is rotten in the state of cultural studies — may have turned out to be as wobbly as the article itself. (54)

The second version is, I think, a shade more diplomatic than the first, though it's hardly fair for *Social Text* to blame Alan Sokal for chilling "the openness of intellectual inquiry that *Social Text* has played its role in fostering" by submitting an essay full of nonsense that could have been spotted, as Sokal admits, "by any competent physicist or mathematician (or undergraduate physics or math major)" (50). Part of the task of fostering open intellectual inquiry, after all, involves making sure that the "intellectual" part of intellectual inquiry is met in journal submissions. Worse still, both versions open by assuming that the rhetorical ball is in Sokal's court and that the editors need merely explain their reactions, one of which (the first mentioned, for reasons that will forever elude me) was premised on the delusional belief that Sokal's exposure of his hoax "represented a change of heart, or a collapse of his intellectual resolve."

From this point on, however, the differences between the Ross/Robbins reply and Ross's solo response become quite stark. The former immediately moves toward an apology; the latter offers nothing of the kind. "Obviously," write Ross and Robbins, "we now regret having published Sokal's article, and apologize to our readers and to those in the science studies or cultural studies communities who might feel their work has been disparaged as a result of this affair" (54). By contrast, when Ross's solo response got around to dealing with Sokal himself, things got downright ugly:

> In sum, Sokal's assumption that his "parody" struck a disreputable chord with the woozy editors of *Social Text* is ill-conceived. Indeed, its status as parody does not alter substantially our initial perception of, and our interest in, the piece itself as a curio, or symptomatic document. . . .
>
> Most of all, what his confession altered was our perception of his own good faith as a self-proclaimed leftist. In the view of our editors, Alan Sokal was now revealed to be either a) a leftist whose self-loathing has been activated by conservative caricatures of the cultural left, or b) a leftist whose genuine sense of commitment led him to a questionable manner of expressing his political point. In either respect, his actions smacked of a temper often attributed to "unreconstructed male leftists." More to the point, the boy stunt pulled by Sokal seemed typical of the professional culture of science education.

It should be an article of faith, I think, that when polemicists try to tar their opponents with the "self-loathing" label, they have effectively admitted defeat (and I say this regardless of whether the alleged self-loather is allegedly self-loathing Jewish intellectual Noam Chomsky or allegedly self-loathing lesbian intellectual Camille Paglia). Egregious as this gesture is, however, it is exceeded by Ross's questioning of Sokal's commitment to the left, followed by the embarrassing more-feminist-than-thou posturing in which Sokal becomes an "unreconstructed male leftist" (unlike the new and improved kind produced by contemporary cultural studies, one surmises) who has pulled a "boy stunt" that is "typical of the professional culture of science education." Finally, Ross follows this caustic skepticism about Sokal's motives and Sokal's sense of self-worth with an absurd challenge: "When Sokal discovers that the cultural left he believes he has outsmarted really doesn't give much of a hoot about what Lacan said about topology in his 1966 seminar, then we can talk turkey." Again, this is the kind of thing one gets to say if one has exposed the hoax prior to the essay's publication; once the essay is out, however, the hoaxee is not at liberty to set conditions for what the hoaxer needs to "discover" before the parties can "talk turkey."

What Ross seemed not to understand was that the rhetorical occasion for his reply took place under conditions far more congenial to Sokal than to Ross and that bystanders were not about to flock to *Social Text*'s side simply because they were outraged at Sokal's "boy stunt." Needless to add, Ross's refusal or inability to realize this made the rhetorical occasion still more favorable to Sokal by dramatically bearing out his claim that "the targets of my critique have by now become a self-perpetuating academic subculture that typically ignores (or disdains) reasoned criticism from the outside" (53). What should *Social Text* have done instead? Simply this: they should have apologized for not sending the essay to a competent referee and then expressed their dismay that Sokal had abused their good faith. They might also have pointed out, far more carefully and modestly, that their publication of the essay did not imply an endorsement of its arguments — which, I gather, what was Ross was trying to say when he high-handedly dismissed the article as "not our cup of tea," a "curio, or symptomatic document" (though "symptomatic document" is a regrettable phrase, since, of course, Sokal too regarded the document as symptomatic and its publication a sign of symptomatic intellectual laziness on the academic left).

Take, for example, the opening paragraph of Sokal's hoax essay, which many journalists cited as proof of the abject foolishness of postmodern cultural studies whateverist humanists:

> There are many natural scientists, and especially physicists, who continue to reject the notion that the disciplines concerned with social and cultural criticism can have anything to contribute, except perhaps peripherally, to their research. Still less are they receptive to the idea that the very foundations of their worldview must be revised or rebuilt in the light of such criticism. Rather, they cling to the dogma imposed by the long post-Enlightenment hegemony over the Western intellectual outlook, which can be summarized briefly as follows: that there exists an external world, whose properties are independent of any individual human being and indeed of humanity as a whole; that these properties are encoded in "eternal" physical laws; and that human beings can obtain reliable, albeit imperfect and tentative, knowledge of these laws by hewing to the "objective" procedures and epistemological strictures prescribed by the (so-called) scientific method. (217)

Let's go over this slowly. The first sentence, unfortunately for all concerned, happens to be quite true, in the sense of "true" commended by proponents of both the coherence and the correspondence theory of truth. The second sentence merely amplifies the first. It is only the third that poses the problem: *Is this guy serious? The idea of an external world is a dogma imposed by the long post-Enlightenment hegemony over the Western intellectual outlook?* This is one of the sentences that was quoted most extensively by journalists and Sokal supporters in the wake of the revelation of the hoax, and it is worth asking (as few journalists bothered to do) precisely what kind of speech act is involved in the publication of such a passage. Did *Social Text*'s editors publish the essay because they believe there is no external world whose properties are independent of any individual human being and indeed of humanity as a whole, or did the editors publish the essay because *they* believed that it was noteworthy that a physicist at New York University would make such a claim? If I had been a member of the *Social Text* collective in 1994–96, on the basis of the first paragraph alone, I would see nothing very terribly out of place — save for the phenomenon of a physicist making rather extraordinary counterintuitive claims about the nature of the physical world. But so what? Since the days of Neils Bohr and Werner Heisenberg, physicists fairly regularly have made rather extraordinary counterintuitive claims about the nature of the physical world. By 1996, surely, one would be forgiven for thinking that making rather extraordinary counterintuitive claims about the nature of the physical world was one of the standard tasks of professional physicists. So on the basis on this paragraph, which so many journalists found so utterly foolish, *Social Text* might well have said, "You know, we gave this guy the benefit of the doubt — and we're sorry. We screwed up, partly because physicists say extraordinary, counterintuitive things all the time."[4]

Allow me to underscore this point: people who refuse to believe that physicists would say anything quite this loopy don't know their twentieth-century physics. The recent history of the field is strewn with the elaboration of theories that seemed to suggest outlandish things, and the fact that some of the outlandish things were initially derived from equations rather than from observable data made them seem only more outlandish. Take, for example, general relativity itself: one of its implications is that the universe is expanding, a possibility Einstein found so ridiculous that he introduced into his equation a "cosmological constant," which he later called the biggest mistake of his life. Then in 1928, roughly a decade after Einstein published his theory of general relativity, Paul Dirac devised an equation that combined Einstein's account of special relativity and the newer quantum theory of matter (so that quantum mechanics would apply to particles moving at relativistic speeds near that of light); Dirac won the Nobel Prize in 1933 as a result, but in his Nobel lecture, he noted that his equation could have two sets of solutions — one for matter as we know it and another for "antimatter," or positively charged electrons and negatively charged protons. "Antimatter," of course, sounds like the stuff of *Star Trek*. But what's really weird is that it exists — although antiprotons and antineutrons were not detected until the 1950s (antielectrons, or "positrons," had been discovered in the early 1930s), and to this day it is not clear why so little of the universe consists of it (that is, why there is such an asymmetry between matter and antimatter). Meanwhile, large-scale physics was having troubles of its own: Edwin Hubble's first calculations of the rate of the universe's expansion, based (in retrospect) on an unrepresentative clump of two thousand galaxies known as the Virgo cluster, produced the nonsensical result that the universe was about two billion years old (this finding came as a great surprise to geologists, working with terrestrial rocks more than twice that age). Hubble doggedly stuck by his findings, with the result that the Big Bang theory of the universe's origins competed for four decades with the Steady State theory, which implied an eternal universe in which new matter was constantly appearing to fill in the gaps, as it were. Steady State did not die until 1963, when Arno Penzias and Robert Wilson discovered cosmic microwave background radiation.

Nothing in the preceding paragraph is obscure or recondite; these stories would be familiar to any undergraduate physics major. Cumulatively, they make a much larger point about our investigations of the natural world: at many points in the past hundred years, it has been exceedingly difficult to tell which theories were capable of being corroborated by experimental data and which theories were simple nonsense. The fact that some theories dismissed as nonsense — of antimatter and an expanding universe — turned out to be backed by stunning empirical data makes the landscape only murkier. Consequently, by the time I was taught the history of the field in my undergraduate astrophysics class, my professor was willing to pass along — without endorsing — Dirac's Large Numbers Hypothesis, a theory Dirac first devised in 1937 and pursued for many years thereafter. The hypothesis is bizarre (and has fallen out of serious consideration), but it's worth a look, not only because it testifies to the degree of bizarreness tolerated in physics but also because it will help me make a point about Sokal's essay (and his later commentary on the essay) a bit later on. Dirac suggested that the ratio of the (estimated) radius of the visible universe to the radius of a hydrogen atom is about 10^{40}. That very large number just happens to be the ratio of the electrical to the gravitational forces between two protons: the electrical force is 10^{40} times stronger than the gravitational force. Is this a coincidence? Dirac thought not, and he further suggested that the gravitational constant, G, therefore varied with time over the evolution of the universe, getting weaker as the universe expanded. While most physicists held the Large Numbers Hypothesis at arm's length, they also remembered that Dirac was the guy who suggested the existence of antimatter and figured that he should be given a fair amount of room for loopy speculations that seem extraordinary or counterintuitive. A temporally variable G obviously would complicate our attempts to estimate the age of the universe and would cause any number of headaches on other fronts as well, but it would also make a palpable connection between gravity and quantum mechanics and possibly a contribution to a theory of quantum gravity. "Quantum gravity" itself sounds too bizarre for belief — more than one journalist assumed that Sokal had simply made up this crazy conceit and that the editors of *Social Text* were too stupid to catch it — but, in fact, it is all the rage these days, as mathematical physicists search for the principles (perhaps involving vibrating super-subatomic strings in eleven dimensions, six of which are curled up in Calabi-Yau space, if you can tolerate *that* degree of nonsense) that will unify general relativity and quantum mechanics.

So, then, let's talk turkey: if a physicist showed up at my door saying, as Sokal did in his second paragraph, "It has thus become increasingly apparent that physical 'reality,' no less than social 'reality,' is at bottom a social and linguistic construct" (217), I'd say, "Hey, sounds like one of those weird physicists being weird." And Sokal knows just how weird they can be, as he notes in the section of his essay devoted to the "hermeneutics of classical general relativity":

> General relativity is so weird that some of its consequences — deduced by impeccable mathematics, and increasingly confirmed by astrophysical observation — read like science fiction. Black holes are now well known, and wormholes are beginning to make the charts. Perhaps less familiar is Gödel's construction of an Einsteinian space-time admitting closed time-like curves: that is, a universe in which it is possible to travel *into one's own past*! (221)

The italics and exclamation point are almost *too much*! Surely Sokal is *putting us on*! But no, this passage is entirely for real, even though, as Sokal notes in a 1998 essay written with Jean Bricmont, "Some Comments on the Parody," it is "rather speculative" (262). When I first read this paragraph, I believed it was part of the hoax — until Sokal set me straight in the course of our e-mail correspondence in June 1996. At that point, I marveled that Sokal knew perfectly well that his field includes people who hypothesize a universe in which it is possible to travel into one's own past but apparently thought that the ancient discipline of "hermeneutics" is so trendy and obscurantist that it was worth including the word in both the essay title and a section subtitle, for ridicule on top of ridicule.

I said at the outset that Sokal's essay is a very strange beast, and this is one reason why: it mocks not only "cultural studies," "postmodernism," and "theory" but also Heisenberg, Bohr, and "popularizations" of real science. In "Some Comments on the Parody," Sokal and Bricmont admitted as much, noting that "the references to physics in [the essay's second and third sections] are, by and large, roughly correct though incredibly shallow; they are written in a deliberately overblown style that parodies some recent popularizations of science" (262). In other words, the object of ridicule here is not postmodernists but popularizers. Sokal and Bricmont also insisted that the essay's first subsection, "Quantum Mechanics: Uncertainty, Complementarity, Discontinuity, and Interconnectedness," was a parody not of Heisenberg and Bohr themselves but of the appropriation of Heisenberg and Bohr by humanists:

> This section exemplifies two aspects of postmodernist musings on quantum mechanics: first, a tendency to confuse the technical meanings of words such as "uncertainty" or "discontinuity" with their everyday meanings; and second, *a fondness for the most subjectivist writings of Heisenberg and Bohr, interpreted in a radical way that goes far beyond their own views (which are in turn vigorously disputed by many physicists and philosophers of science)*. But postmodern philosophy loves the multiplicity of viewpoints, the importance of the observer, holism, and indeterminism. For a *serious* discussion of the philosophical problems posed by quantum mechanics, see the references listed in note 8 (in particular, [David] Albert's book is an excellent introduction for non-experts). (261; first emphasis added)

I agree with Sokal and Bricmont as to the first "aspect" they point to, namely, that humanists — and not just postmodern ones, I should add — have used terms "uncertainty" and "nonlinear" sloppily. In fact, a later section of Sokal's essay makes hay with humanists who seem to assume that "nonlinear" means "complex" and therefore "good" whereas "linear" equations are "straightforward" and therefore "bad." It is as if a literary preference for experimental (that is, "nonlinear") narrative techniques were transposed onto mathematics, with a result that — as Sokal points out — makes no sense at all. But I find the waffle on Heisenberg and Bohr unconvincing, not least because the *Social Text* essay's fifth footnote glosses Heisenberg's principle of complementarity by noting that *Bohr himself* drew social implications from it: "Bohr's analysis of the complementarity principle also led him to a social outlook that was, for its time and place, notably progressive," Sokal writes, proceeding to quote from a 1938 lecture by Bohr:

> I may perhaps here remind you of the extent to which in certain societies the roles of men and women are reversed, not only regarding domestic and social duties but also regarding behaviour and mentality. Even if many of us, in such a situation, might perhaps at first shrink from admitting the possibility that it is entirely a caprice of fate that the people concerned

here have their specific culture and not ours, and we not theirs instead of our own, it is clear that even the slightest suspicion in this respect implies a betrayal of the national complacency inherent in any human culture resting in itself. (232)

The complementarity principle — as applied, for example, to the question of whether light is a particle or a wave — holds that two mutually exclusive definitions are in fact necessary for an adequate explanation of the phenomenon at hand. And why, precisely, should humanists *not* take this as an apt description of cultural and social phenomena as well? Sokal writes, with an audible sneer, that postmodernists like the "subjectivist writings" of Heisenberg and Bohr because "postmodern philosophy loves the multiplicity of viewpoints, the importance of the observer, holism, and indeterminism." But doesn't this sentence dodge the critical question of whether a multiplicity of viewpoints, with regard to electromagnetic radiation or with regard to gender roles, *might in fact be more adequate to the observation at hand*?

There is a legitimate question buried here, and Sokal does nothing to unearth it: when and how is it legitimate or useful to take the lessons of relativity and quantum mechanics as analogies for the state of human affairs? Why *wouldn't* it be legitimate or useful to understand cultural conflicts in terms of "complementarity" or to see complementarity in physics as a principle akin to that of "situated knowledges" in philosophy? Sokal has a great deal of fun tossing around low-hanging fruit such as that provided by Aronowitz, whom Sokal cites approvingly (tongue firmly in cheek) for having "convincingly traced" the "worldview" of Heisenberg's Uncertainty Principle "to the crisis of liberal hegemony in Central Europe in the years prior and subsequent to World War I" (219) and whom Sokal cites at length for the fuzzy-headed claim that quantum mechanics' challenge to "linear causality" will lead us to see that the "segmentation" of time "into hours and minutes [was] a product of the need for industrial discipline, for rational organization of social labor in the early bourgeois epoch" (233). The problem here, and Sokal is not shy about naming it, is that when Aronowitz tries to connect theories in physics to phenomena in the social world, he is severely hampered by the fact that he has no idea what he is talking about. But Sokal deliberately confuses some humanists' misappropriations of Heisenberg and Bohr with claims *made by Heisenberg and Bohr themselves*, some of which — as in Bohr's speculation about cultural difference — do, indeed, seem to bear both on theories in physics and phenomena in the social world.

Admittedly, Sokal hits most of his targets, most often by means of the sneaky tactic of letting them speak in their own words; my point here is simply to remark on how various and disparate those targets actually are. Luce Irigaray, like Aronowitz, is an easy mark, nattering on about how "the mathematical sciences . . . concern themselves very little with the question of the partially open, with wholes that are not clearly delineated [*ensembles flous*], with any analysis of the problem of borders [*bords*]" (225). Robert Markley is scored for calling complex number theory a "postmodern" theory when in fact it dates from the nineteenth century, and for throwing it together with quantum physics, chaos theory, and hadron bootstrap theory, the last of which was abandoned some time ago. And Sokal slyly slips in a number of (admiring) references to the "theory of the morphogenetic field," which he describes as "closely liked to the quantum *gravitational* field" (223), when it is in fact the creation of British biologist Rupert Sheldrake and posits the existence of biological fields that contain information about life forms; it is a theory to be found not in departments of physics but in New Age wellness centers and healing-crystal emporiums. *Social Text*'s failure to catch that one is every bit as bad as it looks.

But then, what are we to make of Sokal and Bricmont's qualified claim about the essay's final section, which, as they write in "Some Comments," "combines gross confusions about science with exceedingly sloppy thinking about philosophy and politics"?

> It also contains some ideas — on the link between scientists and the military, on ideological bias in science, on the pedagogy of science — with which we partly agree, at least when these ideas are formulated more carefully. We do not want the parody to provoke unqualified derision toward those ideas, and we refer the reader to the Epilogue [of *Fashionable Nonsense*] for our real views on some of them. (265)

Oh, well, *now* you tell us you didn't want to provoke unqualified derision. "Some Comments" was published in the United States in December 1998, two and a half years after "Transgressing the Boundaries," long after the parody provoked a great deal of unqualified derision toward leftist ideas on the link between scientists and the military, on ideological bias in science, on the pedagogy of science.

And what are we to make of Sokal and Bricmont's "exposure" of the ludicrousness of the essay's claim that "the π of Euclid and the G of Newton, formerly thought to be constant and universal, are now perceived in their ineluctable historicity" (222)? The claim follows Sokal's citation of Jacques Derrida, which, as Sokal admits later, was a "one-shot abuse, committed orally at a conference" (263). The "abuse" is this:

The Einsteinian constant is not a constant, is not a center. It is the very concept of variability — it is, finally, the concept of the game. In other words, it is not the concept of some*thing* — of a center starting from which an observer could master the field — but the very concept of the game. (221)

This may be opaque or meaningless, but it is also innocuous — and, as Sokal admitted in 1998, utterly anomalous in Derrida's very large body of work. But even though Derrida did not publish anything on physics, Sokal thought this offhand conference remark important enough in 1996 to make it one of his essay's showpieces, most likely because Gross and Levitt had cited and ridiculed it in their book (79). As Sokal and Bricmont explained in 1998,

[T]he primary purpose of this section is to provide a general lead-in to the article's first major gibberish quote, namely Derrida's comment on relativity. . . . The paragraph following the Derrida quote, which exhibits a gradual crescendo of absurdity, is one of our favorites. It goes without saying that a mathematical constant such as π does not change over time, even if our ideas about it may. (263)

This remark is too coy by half. Remember, Derrida is being mocked here for a "one-shot abuse" in which he says that the Einsteinian constant is not a constant, and Sokal and Bricmont are nominating the paragraph that follows as one of their favorites. But while that paragraph is indeed full of gibberish that sounds either like poststructuralism gone wild or like a Kathy Acker – esque take on cyberpunk science fiction ("the putative observer becomes fatally decentered, disconnected from any epistemic link to a space-time point that can no longer be defined by geometry alone" [222]), it did *not*, in fact, "go without saying" in twentieth-century physics that a mathematical constant could not change over time. In citing "a constant such as π," Sokal and Bricmont are — consciously or not — obscuring the little matter of G (the gravitational constant) I mentioned earlier, the question of whether Dirac's Large Numbers Hypothesis had any merit. Though no one today takes seriously the Large Numbers Hypothesis, it is nevertheless disingenuous for Sokal and Bricmont to pretend that the most serious challenge to the idea of a universal and constant G came not from a nutty French poststructuralist but from a brilliant British physicist, one of the century's most distinguished.

THE STORY OF Sokal's reception in academe and the popular press is another matter, and I will not attempt to reproduce it here. Suffice it to say that in the summer and fall of 1996, all hell broke loose, and news of Sokal's hoax traveled at near – light speed through the newspapers and journals of almost every inhabited continent. In the United States, the reaction from the intellectual right was predictable: writing in the *New Criterion*, Roger Kimball (who had been tipped off about the hoax months before the publication of the essay but who was persuaded to hold his tongue) called on deans, students, parents, alumni, college presidents, and trustees to look on Andrew Ross as an emblem of all that is wrong with the world:

> We wonder what the deans overseeing professors such as Andrew Ross will make of this episode. Will they regard it as one more welcome piece of publicity — akin, perhaps, to Professor Ross's declaration in New York magazine a couple of years ago that he had given up on books for television and pop culture? And what about his students — how will they now regard his supervision of their work? And what about his students' parents? After all, they are paying some $30,000 per year for the privilege of having their children educated: how many professors, they might well wonder, share Andrew Ross's views? Alumni, college presidents and trustees: we think that they, too, might do well to ponder the implications of this remarkable episode. What does it tell them about the intellectual health and pedagogical competence of the institutions under their care?

But the reaction from liberal journalists was every bit as vitriolic, as *Salon* magazine's Gary Kamiya demonstrated:

> Absurdly, [Sokal] repeatedly invokes philosophers, psychoanalysts and literary critics like Derrida, Lacan and Jameson to back up his pronouncements about the most rarified and speculative aspects of theoretical physics. But this practice has become so customary in the humanities, where breezy comments to the effect that "Everyone knows that the real world is an oppressive masculinist myth" are heard at every MLA convention, that one scarcely notices.

Such was the verdict of one liberal writer: Sokal's hoax is to be laid at the feet of feminist and feminized oppressive-masculinist-mythmongers at the MLA convention. And in the world of professional journalism, even in the Paper of Record, Sokal was hailed for having punctured … well, just about everything, as Janny Scott suggested in the *New York Times*:

> To a lay person, the article appears to be an impenetrable hodgepodge of jargon, buzzwords, footnotes and references to the work of the likes of

Jacques Derrida and Professor Aronowitz. Words like hegemony, counterhegemonic and epistemological abound. (77)

Surely, I think, it's a bad day for intellectuals of every description when the *New York Times* is chortling in disbelief at the use of words like "hegemony" and "epistemological." (We'll let them have fun with "counterhegemonic" — after all, it has *six syllables*!)

Finally, and for my purposes most importantly, one wing of the left thought it finally had the goods on an academic left it considered inbred, obscurantist, preening, and (as a result) politically counterproductive. In their judgment, as in mine, the response to Sokal's hoax was worse than the hoax itself, and I'll have more to say about that in the essays that follow, in the course of disentangling their judgment from mine. For now, however, I want simply to point out that there is a serious disjunction between the parody itself, which really was a virtuoso piece of work much of which went unread and unappreciated by its biggest fans, and Sokal's subsequent explanations of the parody. Perhaps that's because the parody not only exposed a number of scholars whose writing on science is confused or worthless or both, but also made a serious point about academic subcultures: it *is* possible to get an essay accepted partly because, as Sokal put it, "it flattered the editors' ideological preconceptions" ("A Physicist" 49). (In "Some Comments," Sokal and Bricmont are a bit more cheeky, writing that "the text constantly illustrates what David Lodge calls 'a law of academic life: *it is impossible to be excessive in flattery of one's peers*'" [259], and this is indisputably true as a description of the essay's treatment of Aronowitz and Ross in particular.) The best comments on that disjunction, I believe, came from *Social Text* cofounder John Brenkman and philosopher David Albert (the same David Albert to whom Sokal appealed by calling his book "an excellent introduction for non-experts" with regard to the "philosophical problems posed by quantum mechanics") in a forum convened by *Lingua Franca* in May 1997 and reproduced as the last section of *The Sokal Hoax*, compiled and edited by *Lingua Franca*'s editors in 2000:

> *Brenkman*: The parody itself, it seems to me, was brilliant, but Sokal's explanation in *Lingua Franca* of what he'd done makes two massive claims, neither of which I think is true: On the one hand, that the whole of cultural studies is a morass of relativism and confused logic and lack of interest in empirical reality, and on the other hand, that we should espouse a very narrow realist position on the nature of scientific inquiry — which puts him out of tune with mainstream philosophy of science.
>
> *Albert*: That's right. The character of the opposition (if there is one)

between mainstream analytic philosophy of science and science studies or cultural studies attitudes towards science doesn't seem to me to be helpfully characterized in terms of a disagreement about the philosophical propositions like realism or anything like that. You can find people indisputably within the standard mainstream analytic philosophy of science position, people like Nelson Goodman, whom no one in the poststructuralist camp is going to beat for anti-realism, or relativism, or social constructivism, or what you will. I think the way most people reacted to Sokal's piece was on another level. For them the article pointed to something alarming about standards of scholarship in certain quarters, and standards of argument, and highlighted how much could be gained by simply declaring allegiance to certain kinds of agendas. There was an enormous gap between what he presented himself as doing and what was actually interesting about what he was doing. (253 – 54)

In that gap, Sokal's admirers have projected almost anything they desire: that he showed how many "theorists" write about science despite not knowing very much about it; that he revealed the fatuousness of interpretive theory; that he saved the left from its irrationalist wing; that he struck a blow for plain speech and against obfuscatory jargon; that he demonstrated the vacuity of the humanities as they are taught in American colleges today; that he disclosed the cliqueishness and claqueishness of cultural studies; and that he proved that Anglo-American analytic philosophy is true and that Continental philosophy since Nietzsche is false. I think it's undeniable that Sokal accomplished the first and sixth of these tasks. Sokal's posthoax publications, from "A Physicist Experiments with Cultural Studies" to *Fashionable Nonsense*, suggest strongly that he believes he accomplished the second, third, and fourth; is admirably agnostic about the fifth; and has only a passing interest in the last. But another aspect of Sokal's hoax only looks better and more necessary with the passage of time: his insistence that an indiscriminate skepticism with regard to science not only undermines the left but strengthens the hand of the religious right. At the close of his afterword to "Transgressing the Boundaries" (which was published in *Dissent* in the fall of 1996 because — as Sokal wryly remarks in *Fashionable Nonsense* — *Social Text* rejected it on the grounds that "it did not meet their intellectual standards" [268]), Sokal wrote,

No wonder most Americans can't distinguish between science and pseudoscience: their science teachers have never given them any rational grounds for doing so. (Ask an average undergraduate: Is matter composed of atoms? Yes. Why do you think so? The reader can fill in the response.)

Is it then any surprise that 36% of Americans believe in telepathy, and that 47% believe in the creation account of Genesis? (277)

As Creationism stalks the land once more, this time under the banner of Intelligent Design, Sokal's remarks about Americans' ignorance of science ring true, even if the blame for this state of affairs cannot be assigned solely or even chiefly to academic postmodernists. For one of the most odious developments in the post-Sokal landscape is that the "science wars" are now being conducted not between philosophically realist physicists and partisans of postmodern cultural studies but, as Chris Mooney has recently argued, between scientists who believe in facts and evidence and a wing of the Republican Party whose antipathy to scientific standards of fact and evidence encompasses biology and medicine, climatology and evolution. And in *those* science wars, science studies scholars do indeed sometimes appear on the wrong side of reason, consorting with the Bible-thumpers and faith-based Know-Nothings of the American right. In May 1996, renowned sociologist and philosopher of science Steve Fuller was appearing in *Social Text*'s special issue on the "Science Wars," cheek by jowl with Alan Sokal himself; in October 2005, he was appearing in Dover, Pennsylvania, testifying on behalf of the local school board's religious conservatives that Intelligent Design is indeed a science and that "the main problem intelligent design theory suffers from at the moment is a paucity of developers." For Fuller, the fact that Intelligent Design involves no testable hypotheses and no means of empirical verification is not a problem; rather, the problem is a simple matter of demographics, because the paucity of ID "developers" means that "what you don't have is really a lot of room for theory development, for developing the terms of the argument, and for developing research programs in the area."

In one way, Fuller's Dover testimony provides a compelling example of the possible alliance between science studies and the religious right, an alliance about which Meera Nanda has written compellingly and convincingly in her 2003 book, *Prophets Facing Backward*. Yet Fuller's career is even stranger than that, and not merely because he appears on the back cover of Nanda's book, saying, "This first detailed examination of postmodernism's politically reactionary consequences should serve as a wake-up call for all conscientious leftists." Pro-Sokal scientists and philosophers are fond of blaming our current postmodern malaise on Thomas Kuhn, as if his *Structure of Scientific Revolutions* ushered in an age of rampant relativism in which scientists are understood as merely scampering from paradigm to paradigm without any reference to an empirical world that might serve as a check on their beliefs. But

Fuller is an *anti*-Kuhnian sociologist of science who believes that the Kuhnian view of science somehow unfairly marginalizes smaller "scientific" communities such as those associated with Intelligent Design. In other words, Sokal was right to warn us that a certain kind of skepticism toward science could allow for a meeting of the minds between postmodernists and Creationists but was wrong to imagine that such a skepticism need necessarily flow from an attitude of epistemological relativism: as David Albert pointed out, the epistemological and political ducks just don't always line up that way. In the next two essays, then, I'll suggest some alternative ways of lining up those ducks, and I'll begin with the account of my face-to-face debate with Alan Sokal at the University of Illinois in early 1997.

Notes

1. Useful chronologies and back stories of the hoax can be found in Epstein and *The Sokal Hoax*. Alan Sokal's Web site, <http://www.physics.nyu.edu/faculty/sokal/>, includes hyperlinks to practically every discussion of the hoax accessible by means of the Internet. Jason Walsh also maintains a terrific Sokal Hoax Web site at <http://www.drizzle.com/~jwalsh/sokal/index.html> (accessed 27 November 2005).

2. The editors of *Lingua Franca*, to their credit, did not leave aside this question when they compiled their book on the subject. In the introduction to the volume, they write,

> In many ways, the uncertainty over the identity of *Social Text* reflects the uncertainty surrounding the field of cultural studies itself. In general, cultural studies has come to stand for the interdisciplinary study of how popular culture interacts with its audiences. The discipline's first institutional incarnation was the Centre for Contemporary Cultural Studies, a postgraduate research institute established in 1964 at the University of Birmingham in England. Today, anthologies of cultural studies come out regularly, and with the exception of one or two early Birmingham Centre pieces, they contain none of the same essays. American cultural studies is often said to be characterized by a movement away from the Birmingham school's emphasis on social class toward other aspects of identity, such as race and gender; it has also come to be associated with the ideas of French poststructuralists targeted by Sokal; and it is just as often said to be characterized by a myopic enthusiasm for celebrities. In fact, none of these characterizations account for the bewildering diversity of work done under its name. Such ambiguity lent the Sokal debate an added resonance, since arguments about whether or not his article was a successful send-up of cultural studies could not help but presume what the real thing looked like.

To add to this complexity, discussions of the Sokal hoax have often conflated cultural studies with its cousin, "science studies." Like cultural studies, science studies encompasses an unwieldy collection of interests, methodologies, scholarly backgrounds, and institutional affiliations. The arguments of science studies range from claims that the practice of science is more contaminated by social values than scientists admit to the idea that the pursuit of truth and objectivity is itself a value system and should be analyzed as such, in terms of what it accomplishes and for whom. (3 – 4)

I take this as an admirably judicious discussion of the difficulty of locating the "cultural studies" named in Sokal's "experiment" — a good deal more judicious and more well-informed than Sokal's *Lingua Franca* essay on the subject.

3. Readers familiar with "literature" will realize that poetry and experimental fiction take this kind of liberty all the time and that literary works sometimes make generous use of allusions, metaphors, and puns. As I suggested to Sokal in our June 1996 correspondence, scholars trained in literature may simply have a higher tolerance for this kind of "nonsense" than do working scientists, even or especially when it is applied to the work of working scientists.

4. This is basically what Robbins said in a March 1997 interview: "*Social Text* took Alan Sokal to be a physicist reporting to non-physicists about things that any physicist would know. We saw his article as an act of translation or popularization in which a physicist critical of physics was reporting to non-physicists about material that within physics itself was not controversial. In short, we took him for who he was claiming to be. Thus the idea did not even occur to us that we had to check his physics. We just assumed that any credentialed physicist would get that part right. Our doubts were about the quality of the translation. We thought he was misunderstanding us, his intended audience, and we asked him to remove some of the sillier quotations with which he had amply stocked his article. Obviously he refused, and in retrospect we can see why: he wanted to make us look silly by allowing him to publish these things as if we believed them. We didn't put ourselves behind these authorities or like his way of obsessively citing them. But we were willing enough to have a credentialed physicist express his sort of general idea." (See Ramsamy.)

Works Cited

Albert, David Z., John Brenkman, Elisabeth Lloyd, and *Lingua Franca.* "*Lingua Franca* Roundtable." Reprinted in *The Sokal Hoax: The Sham That Shook the Academy,* edited by the editors of *Lingua Franca,* 253 – 65. Lincoln: University of Nebraska Press, 2000.

Editors of *Lingua Franca,* eds. *The Sokal Hoax: The Sham That Shook the Academy.* Lincoln: University of Nebraska Press, 2000.

Epstein, Barbara. "Postmodernism and the Left." *New Politics* 6, no. 2 (1997): 130 – 44. Available online at <http://www.wpunj.edu/~newpol/issue22/epstei22.htm>. Accessed 27 November 2005.

Fuller, Steve. Transcript of testimony in *Kitzmiller v. Dover Area School District,*

24 October 2005. Available online at <http://www.talkorigins.org/faqs/dover/day15am.html>. Accessed 29 November 2005.

Gross, Paul, and Norman Levitt. *Higher Superstition: The Academic Left and Its Quarrels with Science*. Baltimore: Johns Hopkins University Press, 1994.

Kamiya, Gary. "Transgressing the Transgressors: Toward a Transformative Hermeneutics of Total Bullshit." *Salon*, 17 May 1996. Available online at <http://www.salon.com/media/media960517.html>. Accessed 28 November 2005.

Kimball, Roger. "Notes and Comment: Professor Sokal's Transgression." *New Criterion* 14, no. 10 (June 1996): 1–4. Available online at <http://newcriterion.com/archive/14/june96/june-nc.htm>. Accessed 29 November 2005.

Kuhn, Thomas S. *The Structure of Scientific Revolutions*. Chicago: University of Chicago Press, 1970.

Mooney, Chris. *The Republican War on Science*. New York: Basic Books, 2005.

Nanda, Meera. *Prophets Facing Backward: Postmodern Critiques of Science and Hindu Nationalism in India*. New Brunswick, N.J.: Rutgers University Press, 2003.

Ramsamy, Edward. "Interview with Bruce Robbins." *Common Purposes Journal* (Rutgers University), 6 March 1997. Available online at <http://www.drizzle.com/~jwalsh/sokal/ articles/rbbnstrv.html>. Accessed 4 December 2005.

Robbins, Bruce, and Andrew Ross. "Mystery Science Theater." *Lingua Franca*, July–August 1996, 54–57. Reprinted in *The Sokal Hoax: The Sham That Shook the Academy*, edited by the editors of *Lingua Franca*, 54–58. Lincoln: University of Nebraska Press, 2000.

Ross, Andrew. Untitled mass e-mail. Available online at <http://archives.econ.utah.edu/archives/pen-l/1996m05.d/msg00008.htm>. Accessed 28 November 2005.

Scott, Janny. "Postmodern Gravity Deconstructed, Slyly." *New York Times*, 18 May 1996, 1, 22. Reprinted in *The Sokal Hoax: The Sham That Shook the Academy*, edited by the editors of *Lingua Franca*, 54–58. Lincoln: University of Nebraska Press, 2000.

Sokal, Alan. "A Physicist Experiments with Cultural Studies." *Lingua Franca* 6, no. 4 (May–June 1996): 62–64. Reprinted in *The Sokal Hoax: The Sham That Shook the Academy*, edited by the editors of *Lingua Franca*, 49–53. Lincoln: University of Nebraska Press, 2000.

———. "Transgressing the Boundaries: Toward a Transformative Hermeneutics of Quantum Gravity." *Social Text* 46–47 (1996): 217–52.

———. "Transgressing the Boundaries: An Afterword." *Dissent* 43, no. 4 (1996): 93–99. Reprinted in *Fashionable Nonsense: Postmodern Intellectuals' Abuse of Science*, by Alan Sokal and Jean Bricmont, 268–80. New York: Picador, 1998.

Sokal, Alan, and Jean Bricmont. *Fashionable Nonsense: Postmodern Intellectuals' Abuse of Science*. New York: Picador, 1998.

———. "Some Comments on the Parody." In *Fashionable Nonsense: Postmodern Intellectuals' Abuse of Science*, 259–67. New York: Picador, 1998.

The Return of Realism and the Future of Contingency

One of the questions raised by the Sokal Hoax is this: Do antifoundationalist theoretical commitments undermine progressive politics? And one of the reasons the Sokal Hoax has raised this question is that Sokal himself posed it in his *Lingua Franca* essay (though not precisely in the way I've rephrased it here), answering it with an emphatic yes:

> For most of the past two centuries, the left has been identified with science and against obscurantism; we have believed that rational thought and the fearless analysis of objective reality (both natural and social) are incisive tools for combating the mystifications promoted by the powerful — not to mention being desirable human ends in their own right. The recent turn of many "progressive" or "leftist" academic humanists and social scientists toward one or another form of epistemic relativism betrays this worthy heritage and undermines the already fragile prospects for progressive social critique. (52)

I find this passage problematic on a number of fronts: I object, for example, to the equation of antifoundationalism with "epistemic relativism" and the bald assertion that the left has simply been "identified with science." But the problem I want to focus on in this essay is Sokal's elision of two forms of "objective reality (both natural and social)," which, I think, confounds every important question in dispute — both in science studies and in political theory.

First, however, I want to establish a few basic terms. Leftists, progressives, and liberals may, to varying degrees, "identify" with science, and they generally pursue, with varying degrees of reformism or radicalism, projects they believe will advance the cause of social justice. (I am trying to keep this definition of the political left as ecumenical as possible.) Some believe that those projects, and the more general idea of social justice, can be advanced only if the participants share a belief in a theory of justice that is independent of any observer — a theory of what is often said to be "objectively" true, right, and just. Such people would argue, for example, that the death penalty is *objec-*

tively wrong, according to a uniform moral code that renders it wrong in all circumstances and in all parts of the world, and not merely *contingently* wrong. Others would argue that the belief in the wrongness of the death penalty is a belief that humans have only recently begun to hold and is therefore "contingent" in a historical sense; some of these people might advocate the universal abolition of the death penalty all the same, and some might argue that abolition of the death penalty needs to be weighed in the balance along with other cultural beliefs and historical conditions. But all those who reject the idea that the death penalty is "objectively wrong" would agree that its wrongness is a matter of human deliberation and consensus rather than a matter in which human minds somehow came to intuit or reason their way to a principle that is independent of all human minds. In this essay, I will call the first group, the group that appeals to "objective" moral truths, "foundationalists," and the second group, the group that appeals to "contingent" moral truths, "antifoundationalists." (And I will add the crucial proviso that the second group, in which I include myself, does not believe that moral truths are contingent *on* anything; they are simply contingent, in Richard Rorty's [1989] sense of the word.)

The Sokal fallout is so critical, I think, precisely because it has forced a confrontation between these two theories of justification for political belief and action. (Such a confrontation is imaginable among conservatives as well but seems not to have occurred for two reasons: one, Sokal addressed his posthoax essays explicitly to the left, and two, there does not yet seem to be a significant cohort of conservative antifoundationalists — a phenomenon I am inclined to attribute to conservatism's attachment to beliefs about the importance of tradition and authority.) And in the decadelong aftermath of the Sokal Hoax, there has emerged on at least one wing of the left something like a consensus that human consensus alone is an insufficient ground for thought and action in human affairs. If I'm right about this, then antifoundationalist progressives find themselves in the intolerable position of either (1) believing that social deliberation is the basis for beliefs about social reality even though they seem to be repudiated by a vast majority of the people doing the deliberating, who believe instead that something *else* — God, natural law, objective moral certitudes — must serve as the basis for both social deliberation and beliefs about social reality, or (2) insisting in the face of (1) that critics of antifoundationalism (left or right) are simply *wrong*, in a foundationalist sense, about the necessity of a noncontingent ground for thought and action and that antifoundationalism simply *is true* regardless of anyone's espousal or denial of it.

To explore this paradox further, I will first tell the story of my extended encounter with Alan Sokal, which occurred when I agreed to debate him before what turned out to be a standing-room-only audience of roughly a thousand people at the University of Illinois in late January 1997. The title of the event, unfortunately, was "Fraternizing across the Culture War Trenches: Alan Sokal and Michael Bérubé Search for Common Ground." Although Sokal had kindly asked whether he could debate me rather than simply deliver a stump speech, since we had exchanged some lengthy e-mails in the summer of 1996, at no point had he or I claimed that we would search for common ground, and I was especially uncomfortable with the idea of fraternizing, which implied either a homosocial bonding in the no-man's-land between the trenches (intimate sharing of cigarettes and complaints about our respective supply lines) or outright treason. I was justly afraid that this forum had been convened as a space in which Sokal and I were supposed to conclude by agreeing with one another. More specifically, I feared that because Sokal had already declared himself to be a leftist and a feminist, the encounter would degenerate into a collective dismissal of recondite theoretical problems about the philosophical foundations (or lack thereof) for political beliefs, such that Sokal and I would be understood as saying *What the hell, foundations or no foundations, we're both in favor of single-payer health care.* You say difference and I say *différance*, let's call the whole thing off.

Nor was that the least of my concerns. In the weeks following the debate, I found that despite my impression that I had made a fairly cogent and intelligible case for antifoundationalist politics, many of my listeners apparently left with the impression that I was in fact the kind of cartoon relativist Sokal had attacked in his original essay: that I had no account, for example, of why the Holocaust might have been wrong or why some theories might be better than others in terms of their predictive value. And since the debate had turned precisely on the status of antifoundationalism in social theory as opposed to the sciences, I found the postdebate spin even more depressing and discouraging than the predebate spin. In response, I returned to my laptop and began to write the essays you're reading now — and to revise and rewrite them again and again over the years — and to read more widely among Sokal's supporters in the departments of philosophy and political science. But I'm getting ahead of myself, and for now I need to visit one of those Gödel-Einstein universes with closed timelike curves — you know, a universe in which it is possible to travel into one's own past.

My initial response to Sokal went something like this. I always assume that the phenomenal world exists, that terms such as "deoxyribonucleic acid" or "cosmic microwave background radiation" describe phenomena that exist independently of human observation. I also establish a working relationship with realism — and I do mean "working relationship" literally — whenever

I am searching for my keys, because I have learned that I do not live in Jorge Luis Borges's Tlön, where everyone who searches for an object finds some version of it (and these versions are called *hrönir*).[1] However, should any of my interlocutors demand philosophical proof of this phenomenal world, I refer them to the history of philosophy and wish them the best of luck. The problem of proof is not merely a problem of distinguishing the real world from the neuron firings that give us our sense impressions of it, though that problem is complex enough to discourage most of us; it is also a problem of accounting for the character of human knowledge of the phenomenal world as *human* knowledge. As Martin Heidegger, looking back over the history of philosophy, argued in *Being and Time*, proofs of the "real world" characteristically pass over the question of what "kind of Being" is doing the asking and the proving:

> The "scandal of philosophy" is not that this proof has yet to be given, but that *such proofs are expected and attempted again and again*. Such expectations, aims, and demands arise from an ontologically inadequate way of starting with *something* of such a character that independently *of it* and "outside" *of it* a "world" is to be proved as present-at-hand. It is not that the proofs are inadequate, but that the kind of Being of the entity which does the proving and makes requests for proofs has *not been made definite enough*." (I.6 ¶ 43[a], 249)

Having thus cautiously (but pragmatically) conceded Sokal the existence of the phenomenal world, I then proceeded to take up John Searle's *The Construction of Social Reality*, which describes two kinds of "real" world — one of which, Searle claims, is susceptible to social construction and therefore is fair game for speech act theory, and the other of which is not. The first he calls "social fact," one crucial subset of which is called "institutional fact," and it concerns phenomena like touchdowns and twenty-dollar bills — items whose existence and meaning are obviously dependent entirely on human interpretation, insofar as their properties could be redefined tomorrow by human fiat. The second he calls "brute fact," and it concerns phenomena like Neptune, DNA, and the cosmic background radiation.

As far as ordinary language is concerned, I largely agree with this division of labor on pragmatist grounds. It makes little sense to say that we are constructing Neptune by looking at it; that kind of language will not answer to the need to understand Neptune as an entity whose existence precedes that of any conscious observer. However, following the argument Heidegger develops at the end of the first section of *Being and Time*, we could also say that the discovery of Neptune in 1846 could plausibly be described, *from a strictly human vantage point*, as the "invention" of Neptune. For up to that point, the planet "Neptune" did not exist in human consciousness, just as "gravity" had never meant "a universal force of nature" until Newton invented — or, if you prefer, discovered — it. And yet once humans had invented (from their standpoint) the concept of gravity and the existence of Neptune, they understood these things precisely *as* things that were not susceptible to mere human invention:

> Newton's laws, the principle of contradiction, any truth whatever — these are true only so long as Dasein *is*. Before there was any Dasein, there was no truth; nor will there be any after Dasein is no more. . . . To say that before Newton his laws were neither true nor false, cannot signify that before him there were no such entities as have been uncovered and pointed out by those laws. Through Newton the laws became true; and with them, entities became accessible in themselves to Dasein. Once entities have been uncovered, they show themselves precisely as entities which beforehand already were. (Heidegger I.6 ¶ 44[c], 269)

Once entities have been uncovered, they show themselves precisely as entities which beforehand already were: this, I think, is the critical insight to bring to bear on any post-Sokal discussion of relativist shilly-shallying and fashionable nonsense. The basic physical processes of the universe clearly precede us; they have literally *constructed* us; they do not depend on our understanding or belief. To maintain any other position is to live in the world of that Monty Python housing project in which tenants are required to believe in the buildings they inhabit — and when their belief in the building falters or they begin to think they would do better to live elsewhere, the building topples over. In that sense, then, brute fact is unquestionably prior to social fact, both in a chronological and a logical sense.

Having granted the priority of brute fact to social fact, however, I then proceeded to invert the terms, arguing that there's a compelling sense in which social fact is prior to and even constitutive of brute fact. I had said as much to Searle, who had visited the University of Illinois in the spring of 1996. (Some of the attendees of the Sokal debate at Illinois had also attended Searle's lecture.) Over the course of delivering an entertaining fifty-minute talk about twenty-dollar bills and performative utterances, Searle explained and expanded on the social fact/brute fact distinction for a large (and largely appreciative) general audience. I had not planned on giving Searle a hard time when I showed up at his talk, but he sounded (to some listeners) so much like the soul of sense and (to other listeners) so much like a social constructionist that I thought I should open the question/answer period with the most germane — if the most abstract — possible question: Is the distinction between social facts and brute facts a social fact or a brute fact?

In my naïveté, I figured I had posed a difficult question. If Searle had replied by saying that the distinction between the two is a brute fact, I would have been entitled to ask him in return where the distinction lies exactly, and how he might know this. If, by contrast, he had replied by saying that the distinction is a social fact, then he would have effectively admitted that social fact is the thing that determines how we draw the distinction. In an important sense, social facts would then be philosophically prior to and certainly more immediately available to us humans than the world of brute fact, although there would still be lively commerce between the two domains, especially at that troubled border between them. And had Searle given this answer, the history of science would have borne him out strongly, since the difference between the ancient understanding of the universe and most modern scientific views is partly a difference concerning where that line gets drawn. It is simply the case — and has been ever since hominids first started talking to each other — that we are always and everywhere debating where social fact ends and brute fact begins, and that alone suggests that the realm of brute fact, *as we understand it* (and I have to keep stressing this proviso, without which my argument does not make sense), depends on the workings of complex social processes, some of which happen to go by the name "scientific investigation."

Because Searle is relatively alive to such difficulties, I thought he would be a good postlecture interlocutor; he is also, of course, justly famed for his wit. In *The Construction of Social Reality*, he leans considerably further to the side of social constructionism than do many of his critics in the realist tradition, not to mention many scholars in the life sciences. Notably, Searle assigns to "social fact" any and all attributions of *function* on the grounds that "functions are never intrinsic to the physics of any phenomenon but are assigned from outside by conscious observers and users. *Functions, in short, are never intrinsic but are always observer relative*" (14). Thus, to take Searle's example, it is a brute fact that the heart pumps blood, but when we start talking about whether the heart has a *purpose*, we are speaking from within the realm of social fact, the realm of constructed social reality:

> [W]hen, in addition to saying "The heart pumps blood" we say "The *function* of the heart is to pump blood," we are doing something more than recording these intrinsic facts. We are situating these facts relative to a system of values that we hold. It is intrinsic to us that we hold these values, but the attribution of these values to nature independent of us is observer relative. . . . If we thought the most important value in the world was to

glorify God by making thumping noises, then the function of the heart would be to make a thumping noise, and the noisier heart would be the better heart. (14–15)

For many purposes, therefore (and for all discussions of "purpose"), Searle sounds more like a social constructionist than like the kind of realist who insists that natural objects have natural functions. And for that reason, the metaquestion about the distinction between social fact and brute fact seems altogether relevant to Searle's work. Likewise, Searle acknowledges that many phenomena, such as color, have been assigned both to the category of objects intrinsic to the natural world and the category of objects that exist only from the perspective of conscious observers — and he judiciously refrains from deciding the status of color as either brute or social fact (11).

Searle replied to my question, however, by saying that the distinction between social fact and brute fact was neither a social fact nor a brute fact; it is merely, said he, a procedural question, a matter of logic. But is "logic" a social or a brute fact? Or is a nebulous, intermediate thing, like color? How do we know that the "logic" we're discovering or observing is not, in fact, susceptible to human construction? In asking this question, I'm not thinking of something as arcane and as limited in its application as Heisenberg's Uncertainty Principle, which I will not elide with the banal observation that people behave differently when they know they're being watched; I'm thinking about something much closer to home.

My second child, Jamie, was born in 1991 with Down syndrome. His chromosomal abnormality is a brute fact, and if we don't understand it as such, then we open the door to a number of unsavory political conclusions, one of which is that it becomes possible to "blame" parents of children with Down syndrome for having done "something wrong" during pregnancy. Astonishingly, as late as 1959, Down syndrome was still thought to originate during fetal development, perhaps in the eighth gestational week. (Down syndrome was not understood as resulting from a chromosomal nondisjunction during meiosis until Jerome Lejeune established this in 1959; transfer RNA was not isolated until 1961. In other words, not until eight years after the discovery of DNA did scientists finally began to understand the specific transcription mechanism by which DNA base-pair sequences code for the production of amino acids.) But even though it is distinctly and clearly a genetic phenomenon, Down syndrome is also a profoundly social phenomenon. In fact, thanks to the early intervention policies and federal legal initiatives of the 1970s, whereby children with Down syndrome in the United States are — you should pardon the expression — *constructed as* being entitled to physical, occupational, and speech therapy from birth, it is now beginning to look as if many of the mental and behavioral characteristics long attributed to children with Down syndrome are the result of pre-1970 social policies of institutionalization rather than to the molecular biochemistry of trisomy 21.

That understanding—the contemporary understanding of Down syndrome—was not won easily. It involves much of the history of genetics since Watson and Crick and, equally importantly, much of the history of disability policy since the heyday of eugenics in the early decades of the twentieth century and the landmark 1927 Supreme Court case, *Buck v. Bell*, which legalized involuntary sterilization and helped pave the way for two decades of Nazi "science." The lack of clarity in the historical record is quite clear: genetics, disability, and intelligence have proven to be three crucial areas of human inquiry in which we are *constitutionally* unsure of how to draw the line between social fact and brute fact. But for James Bérubé and for every other human with Down syndrome, social facts will be crucial to the brute facts of their lives both politically and physically, and it is likewise by means of those social facts that we will understand what's a brute fact and what's not—about Down syndrome and about everything else. It is for this reason, then, though not for this reason alone, that I find myself compelled to defend the theoretical projects launched by antifoundationalism, without which life as we know it would not be possible.

This is not a merely local point about my child, about developmental disability, or even about genetic anomaly in general. Rather, it goes to the heart of why leftists and liberals have done well to entertain a healthy skepticism about discourses of biological determinism. For the past hundred years or so, it seems that every time politically powerful humans have tried to extrapolate to the social realm what they thought they understood of genetics, the impulse behind and the results of the extrapolation have been politically reactionary in the extreme. From Social Darwinism to falsified twin studies to Herrnstein and Murray's *The Bell Curve*, the biochemical template has been misread time and again—and I want to stress *mis*read—as the sanction for the naturalization of the social. Genetics has in this sense served as the vehicle for ideology *as such*, the mystification of contingent and historically bounded social formations as the expressions of "natural" constraints and "natural" forces. So every time we hear that infidelity or criminality or religiosity is "in our genes," antifoundationalists are right to defend the proposition that although humans may not be *infinitely* malleable, human variety and human plasticity can in principle and in practice exceed any specific form of human social organization. Moreover, in no sense are we limited to only those forms of social organization or condemned to only those forms of social behavior that can conceivably be traced to our evolutionary history. It should be no surprise, then, that contemporary leftist theorists are skeptical about every kind of genetic determinism, in however mild or mediated a form: when we hear the word "genome," we reach for our social-constructionist guns.

Nonetheless, I want to argue that leftist intellectuals have mistakenly defended two forms of antifoundationalism as if their linkage was necessary, when in fact it is not. There is no necessary connection between realism with regard to observer-independent matters and moral foundationalism with regard to social affairs, and the sooner the theoretical left manages to decouple the one from the other, the better off we will be — theoretically *and* politically. Let me put this another way: if it were somehow proven tomorrow that every politically significant form of human variation from race to gender to sexual orientation to *political* orientation were somehow indelibly inscribed in our double-stranded genetic fibers, it would not affect my antifoundationalist approach to human rights and social justice in the least. At present, what we have is an intellectual dispensation in which every time a conservative suggests a biological basis for human behavior, he or she claims that the antifoundationalist basis for claims to egalitarian social justice has been dealt a mortal blow: Aha! Sickle-cell anemia! Race *is* real! This proves that the left is wrong and that we can now eliminate affirmative action and Head Start! In such a climate, it looks as if every narrative that concedes ground to evolutionary theory is perforce a narrative that delivers us into the hands of the Social Darwinist oppressor, and that therefore to defend an antifoundationalist account of human political belief and moral action we need to defend at all costs a fully antifoundationalist account of what it means to be human.

This need not be the case. To return to the realm of brute fact: James Bérubé is genetically Other. The meanings of Down syndrome and the life prospects of persons with Down syndrome differ widely from culture to culture, but the brute-fact chromosomal nondisjunction is the same across every human culture. Can we allow ourselves to tie human rights to an "antifoundationalist" account of Down syndrome? I want to claim that James is as human as any of you and that as your fellow human he has a right to shelter, sustenance, health care, education, political participation and representation, reciprocal recognition, and respect. I believe that this claim is contingent and that it depends for its realization on specific forms of social organization we have only lately begun to realize, but its contingency as a rights claim has no necessary relation to our understanding of Down syndrome as either a brute fact or a social fact.

By no means am I suggesting that antifoundationalists should stop asking what's fungible in the human condition; certainly, any dreams of political possibility should contain some faith in human possibility. But more crucially, antifoundationalists should insist on the distinction between reading the genome and reading the social text — a distinction dutifully observed by Richard Dawkins in the closing pages of *The Selfish Gene* but, in the past decade, most often honored in the breach by evolutionary psychologists working in Dawkins's wake.[2] I want to insist on this decoupling for two reasons: first, because the biochemical or social status of crucial human traits, like "intelligence," is not likely to be resolved in our lifetime or any other, and second, because the determination of basic human rights, *whatever we consider these rights to be*, should not be predicated on the biochemical or social status of human traits. Innatist theories can and should be debated on their scientific merits, but in no case should they be taken as the basis for crafting social policy; what matters for a democratic political praxis is the creation of social spaces for noncoercive public deliberation, not the scientific determination of potential neurobiological bases of linguistic communication. And thus, as I argued in *Life as We Know It*, we should conceive of social justice in social-constructionist terms regardless of the biochemical status of individual humans or individual human properties.

What astonishes me about the Sokal Hoax, then, is not that so many progressive thinkers want to hold onto an understanding of brute fact as an understanding of noncontingent, asocial phenomena like Neptune and photons; in the qualified terms I've laid out so far, that's an argument I'm willing to concede. (I'm also willing to regard various elements of human behavior, from aggression to language use, as lying at the interstice of social and brute fact.) Rather, what's astonishing is that that so many progressive thinkers seem to want an ironclad, noncontingent account of the bases for social justice. One voluble Chomskian at Illinois, in fact, went so far as to insist to me, in the question/answer session after Sokal and I had made our opening remarks, that the left must entertain the possibility that there are moral imperatives the content of which we do not yet know, for to believe anything else is to open the door to fascism. My reply was that the door to fascism will be closed only when no one on the planet conceives of fascism as a possible thing, and that in the meantime, the belief that there are moral imperatives the content of which we do not yet know leaves that door as wide open as anything does — especially insofar as it holds out the possibility that we have not yet discovered the moral truth of fascism.

Yet I have to add that this line of argument sometimes makes me too angry to argue rationally. You would think, from listening to antifoundationalism's antagonists, that the Crusades, the Spanish Inquisition, the extermination of the native populations of the Americas, the massacre of the Armenians, the Stalinist purges, and the Holocaust are all to be laid at the feet of a handful of jejune postmodern latte-drinking relativists. I find it outrageous that foundationalists proceed in this debate as if their side, the side that appeals to objective facts and secure moral grounds, has nothing to answer for in the world's long and sorry history of civil butchery. I also find it astonishing that the antifoundationalist left now has to start from the defensive when speaking about the social goals of science studies, as if no one but a credentialed scientist should inquire into the convoluted processes that gave us Tuskegee, thalidomide, and plutonium experiments on unsuspecting citizens and mental patients. But at the time, when I was challenged by this Chomskian questioner, I did not answer the Chomskian question angrily; I merely said to the questioner and to Alan Sokal, "Let me put it this way. I have good news and bad news for you. If you want noncontingent, transhistorical grounds for social justice, the bad news is that you can't have them — and the good news is that you don't need them." This reply then provoked another question: If that's really what I think, then if I were the only person on earth who believed in the human rights of my son, James, would he still have those rights after I died?[3]

At the time, I said simply that it would do James a fat lot of good if he "had" rights that no one on earth recognized. But of course, I have to admit, I would like to believe otherwise; I would like to believe that my son's humanity is somehow independent of any form of social recognition. I thought of the poignant moment toward the end of Rorty's introduction to *Consequences of Pragmatism*, where he writes that it is "morally humiliating" to be an antifoundationalist:

> Suppose that Socrates was wrong, that we have *not* once seen the Truth, and so will not, intuitively, recognize it when we see it again. This means that when the secret police come, when the torturers violate the innocent, there is nothing to be said to them of the form "There is something within you that you are betraying. Though you embody the practices of a totalitarian society which will endure forever, there is something beyond those practices which condemns you." This thought is hard to live with, as is Sartre's remark: "Tomorrow, after my death, certain people may decide to establish fascism, and the others may be cowardly or miserable enough to let them get away with it. At that moment, fascism will be the truth of man, and so much the worse for us. In reality, things will be much as man has decided they are." (xlii)

Crucially, Rorty does not claim that his vision of postphilosophical culture expresses at last the real truth of humankind; he asks us merely to entertain the notion of a world in which no one makes appeals to the Truth with a capital T and to decide whether such a notion is true in the pragmatist sense — that is, good in the way of belief: "The question of whether the pragmatist view of truth — that it is not a profitable topic — is itself *true* is thus a question about whether a post-Philosophical culture is a good thing to try for. It is not a question about what the word 'true' means, nor about the requirements of an adequate philosophy of language, nor about whether the world exists 'independently of our minds,' nor about whether the intuitions of our culture are captured in the pragmatists' slogans" (xliii). Yet for many of us mortals, it appears that the answer is simply no: when the secret police arrive, these people want to be able to tell them that fascism is wrong, and they want to be able to point to something more authoritative on the subject than *Consequences of Pragmatism* — just as I sometimes want to believe, despite my theoretical commitments, that my child has "intrinsic" value, whatever the world might think.

Naming this desire, I have found, is dangerous. It invites realists and their friends to say, *Aha, you see, this Bérubé has been to graduate school and has been indoctrinated by Richard Rorty, and yet down deep, in his heart, he wants to have an objective, noncontingent moral philosophy after all.* But this is just a realist's version of wishful thinking. I do not have one desire that resides more deeply than another; I have lots of desires, one of which entails the vain hope that someday we will no longer need to make the case for the human rights of every human born. Yet another of my desires runs directly contrary to that one, for it entails the imperative to keep arguing with moral foundationalists to try to convince them somehow that it is the sheerest folly — politically and theoretically — to think that such an argument about human rights can ever be "won" once and for all in such a way that no one need ever again worry about fascism or eugenics. Still another of my desires entails the recognition that no argument about the impermanence of argument can ever be won once and for all, either, and that therefore I should make my arguments with great patience and an antifoundationalist's sense that I just can't always be right about everything, despite my many other desires to be just that.

Naming all these conflicting desires takes me to my final point as well as to the basis for this essay's title, both of which have to do with a fascinating passage in the final chapter of Barbara Herrnstein Smith's *Contingencies of Value: Alternate Perspectives for Critical Theory*. *Contingencies of Value* occupies a crucial place in the recent intellectual history of the academic left, simultaneously looking back over the debates about canons and representation and forward to debates over relativism, strategic essentialism, and the disjunctions between interpretive theory and political practice. The question at hand in this passage is a practical and recursive one: if "truth" is understood as "what it is best to believe," then what if it's best for us to believe in a noncontingent basis for moral action to mobilize important political constituencies, form coalitions, and get things done? Smith writes,

> It is sometimes objected . . . that one cannot live as a nonobjectivist because, in the real world of real peasants, politicians, and police, one must deal with people for whom only objectivist-type considerations and justifications — appeals to "fundamental rights" and "objective facts," not just to contingent conditions — will be acceptable and effective. Two replies may be made here. One is that it would be no more logically inconsistent for a nonobjectivist to speak, under *some* conditions, of fundamental rights and objective facts than for a Hungarian ordering his lunch in Paris to speak French. . . . The other and equally important reply, however, is that the power, richness, subtlety, flexibility, and communicative effectiveness of *a nonobjectivist idiom* — for example, forceful recommendations that do *not* cite intrinsic value, or justifications, accepted as such, that *do* cite contingent conditions and likely outcomes rather than fundamental rights and objective facts — are characteristically underestimated by those who have never learned to speak it or tried to use it in interactions with, among others, real policemen, peasants, and politicians. (158)

Here, one answer suggests that when we're among objectivists, we should temporarily talk objectivist; the other suggests that we should try talking nonobjectivist first and that we shouldn't knock it until we've tried it. This formulation has the advantage of putting the antifoundationalist/nonobjectivist in a position where she can never be "wrong," but it leaves the uneasy impression that the objectivist idiom is a language of last resort, to be employed only if nonobjectivist language does not (literally) pay its way.[4] I want to suggest that recent schisms in the left have strained the tension in this passage to the breaking point. What, indeed, should we do when claims to contingency fail to persuade policemen, peasants, politicians — and the press? Do we simply mumble an apology and order dinner in French? Does this passage even earn its analogy between national languages and ethical discourses of justification? My answer to this last question is simply no, on the grounds that there is no sense in which nonobjectivism is to Hungarian as objectivism is to French. (Though these languages come from thoroughly different linguistic roots, I know of no study that suggests that French is less contingent than Hungarian.)

What this passage invites, in other words, is what Amanda Anderson calls the "double gesture" — a theoretical conviction that antifoundationalism does in fact describe the truth of human affairs but that foundationalist claims will get us what we want and need in the meantime. And here the double gesture leads us to a double impasse. After Sokal and I had finished debating, one listener pointed out that we had seemed to exchange places: the self-professed realist, Sokal, was arguing pragmatically that science seems to get things done and therefore serves as a good model for distinguishing fact from mere belief, and the self-professed pragmatist, Bérubé, was arguing quite emphatically, in the realist tradition, that we did not have access to noncontingent, transhistorical grounds for social justice because they simply did not exist. All I could say in response was that I was trying my best to persuade people to adopt my position in this debate and that I did not mean to be making any metaphysical claims about *what is really the case*. I hoped to convince my listeners that the world would be a better place, all around, if fewer humans operated as if noncontingent, transhistorical grounds for social justice existed and if (as a result) fewer humans were sure that their beliefs about and actions in the social world were objectively and transhistorically right. Could I honestly have said anything else? I really believe that we humans would do better not to appeal to objective grounds for belief and action in social matters — and for me to say otherwise is not just to order in French when in Paris but to pretend to convictions I do not have. At which point I ask myself, with a Wittgensteinian surmise, what it would be like to have deep convictions but only for a moment, only for as long as those convictions will serve some pragmatic end. For Wittgenstein surely would say that the idea of having deep convictions only for a moment involves a misunderstanding of what people mean by the phrase "deep convictions." To put this another way, Sokal and I were not simply ordering lunch.

But I think I know why I believe that objectivism is a bad idea in the world of moral values and social policies: as I suggested earlier, I think of objectivism as a *temptation*, an invitation to construe one's beliefs as unassailable by people who do not speak objectivist. It is a temptation to which a great many religious believers have succumbed; more interestingly, even a few aggressive secularists have felt its pull. Take, for example, this passage from Sam Harris's recent book, *The End of Faith: Religion, Terror, and the Future of Reason*:

> Pragmatism, when civilizations come clashing, does not appear likely to be very pragmatic. To lose the conviction that you can actually be right — about *anything* — seems a recipe for the End of Days chaos envisioned by Yeats: when "the best lack all conviction, while the worst are full of passionate intensity." I believe that relativism and pragmatism have already done much to muddle our thinking on a variety of subjects, many of which have more than a passing relevance to the survival of civilization.

In philosophical terms, then, pragmatism can be directly opposed to *realism*. For the realist, our statements about the world will be "true" or "false" not merely in virtue of how they function amid the welter of our other beliefs, or with reference to any culture-bound criteria, but because reality simply is a certain way, independent of our thoughts. Realists believe that there are truths about the world that may exceed our capacity to know about them; there are facts of the matter whether or not we can bring such facts into view. To be an ethical realist is to believe that in ethics, as in physics, there are truths waiting to be *discovered* — and thus we can be right or wrong in our beliefs about them. (180 – 81)

What's especially striking about Harris's defense of "realism," his insistence that moral truths are out there in the ether — just waiting to be discovered, like new planets — is that it occurs in a book whose purpose it is to argue against every form of religious faith, every form of belief that is not based on empirical evidence (except for certain forms of Buddhism). But Harris's antipragmatism establishes him as a very distinct kind of philosophical secularist: the kind who believes in freeing people from the shackles of religion but who doesn't quite trust people to adjudicate moral values on their own, particularly if they believe they're inventing rather than discovering those values. In effect, Harris's book demands that we get rid of all religious beliefs while handing ultimate interpretive authority in moral matters over to the philosopher-kings who will "discover" the way morality "really" operates out there in the universe. This, I submit, is a temptation worth resisting. I see the prospect of treating moral edicts as nothing more than good ideas, dreamed up by well-meaning humans, as a guard against the powerful temptation to think that in propounding our ideas, we are propounding something more or other than human ideas.

Rorty suggests as much in the final words of his essay "Trotsky and the Wild Orchids," which speak not of moral humiliation but moral humility:

Despite my relatively early disillusionment with Platonism, I am very glad that I spent all those years reading philosophy books. For I learned something that still seems very important: to distrust the intellectual snobbery that originally led me to read them. If I had not read all those books, I might never have been able to stop looking for what Derrida calls "a full presence beyond the reach of play," for a luminous synoptic vision.

By now I am pretty sure that looking for such a presence and a vision is a bad idea. The main trouble is that you might succeed, and your success might let you imagine that you have something more to rely on than the tolerance and decency of your fellow human beings. The democratic community of Dewey's dreams is a community in which nobody imagines that. It is a community in which everybody thinks that it is human solidarity, rather than knowledge of something not merely human, that really matters. The actually existing approximations to such a fully democratic, fully secular community now seem to me the greatest achievements of our species. (50)

Here, antifoundationalism is presented precisely as a means for avoiding temptation: Rorty's suggestion that one "might succeed" in discovering immutable moral laws is ironic, of course, for what he means is that one might *think* one has succeeded. And what follows from that "success"? Rorty suggests that the consequence would be a kind of complacency: you might think you have the luxury of relying on something more than merely human tolerance and decency. But there is another, nastier possible consequence as well: you might think that you have exclusive access to those extrahuman sources of truth, and you might conclude that people who disagree with you are not simply working from different moral premises but rather are alien — or *opposed* — to morality itself. It then becomes all the easier to exclude them from the conversation, from all forms of human community.[5]

✓ In a long footnote to his discussion of pragmatism in *The End of Faith*, Harris makes the same point I encountered at the end of my debate with Sokal: Harris insists that pragmatists are realists in denial and that pragmatism is not itself pragmatic. The first claim runs as follows: "[T]he pragmatist seems to be tacitly saying that he has surveyed the breadth and depth of all possible acts of cognition (not just his own, and not just those that are human) and found both that all knowledge is discursive and that all spheres of discourse can be potentially fused" (272). This is a construal of pragmatism that some pragmatists will not recognize; some of us believe that it is possible to have discursive knowledge of nondiscursive phenomena such as Neptune and photons, and that it is possible for a pragmatist to deny that all spheres of discourse can be potentially fused. But I'd like to focus instead on what Harris takes the pragmatist to be "tacitly" saying: for here, he takes the pragmatist to be making claims about *what is really the case*, and when he does that, he renders the pragmatist something other than a pragmatist. On this count, Harris and his imaginary pragmatist are simply talking at cross-purposes. But the second claim, that pragmatists are not pragmatic, is more damaging:

> [T]he approach here would be to show that [pragmatism] serves neither our ends of fashioning a coherent picture of the world nor other ends to which we might be purposed. It may be, for instance, that talking about

truth and knowledge in terms of human "solidarity," as Rorty does, could ultimately subvert the very solidarity at issue. (272)

The simple truth — and I hope the irony of the phrase is evident — is that Harris may be right about this. I have admitted as much earlier in this essay: when the secret police come, when the torturers violate the innocent, many of my fellow humans seem to want to say, "Though you embody the practices of a totalitarian society that will endure forever, there is something beyond those practices that condemns you." Having declared my allegiance to contingency and to pragmatism, I have no honest recourse but to believe that rhetorical strategies of persuasion, and nothing else, are the bases for human moral codes; it is, therefore, incumbent on me to devise rhetorical strategies of persuasion that will convince people of the usefulness of this proposition. Those strategies might fail. Humans may not want to become fully secular in the sense that they take full responsibility for having created the moral and political frameworks under which they live. So much the worse for us. Yet the challenge of pragmatism, the challenge of being a pragmatist, lies in believing — despite all — that we might yet do better.

Notes

1. Borges's account of *hrönir* is infinitely superior to mine, even though it is the original: "Centuries and centuries of idealism have not failed to influence reality. In the very oldest regions of Tlön, it is not an uncommon occurrence for lost objects to be duplicated. Two people are looking for a pencil; the first one finds it and says nothing; the second finds a second pencil, no less real, but more in keeping with his expectation. These secondary objects are called *hrönir* and, even though awkward in form, are a little larger than the originals. Until recently, the *hrönir* were the accidental children of absent-mindedness and forgetfulness. It seems improbable that the methodical production of them has been going on for almost a hundred years, but so it is stated in the eleventh volume" (29). I do believe I will love "Tlön, Uqbar, Orbis Tertius" for as long as I am capable of thought.

2. I argue this at length in chapter 5 of *Life as We Know It*.

3. There are more problems with this question than I know how to discuss here, and many of them were called out immediately when I delivered this paper at the English Institute in 1997. First, there is the question of what "human rights" means in this context; second, the question presumes a monolithic model of humans who are never internally inconsistent, who never change their minds, or who could never be compelled by Jamie to rethink their understanding of human rights; third, it suggests that an account of human rights could be sustained merely by one person's belief. Though all these caveats have merit, I still think of the question as a variation on Sar-

tre's vision of fascism being established "tomorrow, after my death" (hence my segue to this passage in the body of the essay) and take it as a thought-experiment challenge in the same vein. Under that heading, the specific content of "human rights" matters less than the mere existence of rights claims in the world: that is, whether health care is included as such a right is immaterial to the question of whether, in general, Jamie will continue to possess any "rights" that only I recognize as valid. Nevertheless, in the world we inhabit, where such thought-experiments are, for now, nothing more than philosophical brain teasers, it does matter what kind of rights I imagine Jamie to possess — such as the rights enumerated in the 1948 United Nations Declaration of Human Rights and the enforceable rights vouchsafed to him in the U.S. Individuals with Disabilities Education Act and the 1990 Americans with Disabilities Act.

4. My thanks to Amanda Anderson, Joe Valente, Idelber Avelar, Peter Garrett, Simon Joyce, and Stephanie Foote, who participated in a Unit for Criticism and Interpretive Theory seminar on "theories of value" (organized by Valente, Joyce, and Foote) in the spring of 1996. This seminar's discussion of *Contingencies of Value* foregrounded the tensions in Smith's text in such a way as to impel me to the argument with which I close this essay.

5. I elaborate this argument (opposing Rorty to Harris) in chapter 6 of *What's Liberal about the Liberal Arts?*

Works Cited

Anderson, Amanda. "Cryptonormativism and Double Gestures: Reconceiving Poststructuralist Social Theory." *Cultural Critique* 21 (1992): 63–95.

Bérubé, Michael. *Life as We Know It: A Father, a Family, and an Exceptional Child.* New York: Vintage, 1998.

———. *What's Liberal about the Liberal Arts?: Classroom Politics and "Bias" in Higher Education.* New York: Norton, 2006.

Borges, Jorge Luis. "Tlön, Uqbar, Orbis Tertius." In *Ficciones*, translated by Emecé Editores, 17–35. New York: Grove, 1962.

Dawkins, Richard. *The Selfish Gene.* 2nd ed. London: Oxford University Press, 1989.

Harris, Sam. *The End of Faith: Religion, Terror, and the Future of Reason.* New York: Norton, 2004.

Heidegger, Martin. *Being and Time.* Translated by John Macquarrie and Edward Robinson. New York: Harper, 1962.

Herrnstein, Richard, and Charles Murray. *The Bell Curve: Intelligence and Class Structure in American Life.* New York: Free Press, 1994.

Rorty, Richard. *Consequences of Pragmatism: Essays, 1972–80.* Minneapolis: University of Minnesota Press, 1985.

———. *Contingency, Irony, and Solidarity.* Cambridge: Cambridge University Press, 1989.

———. "Trotsky and the Wild Orchids." In *Wild Orchids and Trotsky: Messages from American Universities*, edited by Mark Edmundson, 29 – 50. New York: Viking Penguin, 1993.

Searle, John. *The Construction of Social Reality.* New York: Free Press, 1995.

Smith, Barbara Herrnstein. *Contingencies of Value: Alternate Perspectives for Critical Theory.* Cambridge: Harvard University Press, 1988.

Sokal, Alan. "A Physicist Experiments with Cultural Studies." *Lingua Franca* 6, no. 4 (May – June 1996): 62 – 64. Reprinted in *The Sokal Hoax: The Sham That Shook the Academy*, edited by the editors of *Lingua Franca*, 49 – 53. Lincoln: University of Nebraska Press, 2000.

I'm not supposed to say a good word about Alan Sokal and Jean Bricmont's *Fashionable Nonsense: Postmodern Intellectuals' Abuse of Science*. Ever since Alan Sokal pulled off his hoax, the party lines have been drawn, and reviews of the hoax and Sokal's subsequent (more serious) essays have been fairly predictable. In the pro-Sokal camp, an odd assortment of querulous scientists, cultural conservatives, and leftist thinkers who dissent from postmodern or social-constructionist beliefs about what it is to be a human person with political agency. In the anti-Sokal camp, an equally odd assortment of science-studies scholars and theoretically minded leftists who really hate being called jargon-spouting academic-careerist pseudoleftists but who can't quite bring themselves to defend *Social Text*'s decision to publish the piece — let alone the journal's far worse decision not to publish Sokal's follow-up.

Over the years, I have remained largely unsympathetic to Sokal's general aim, an aim shared by leftists of goodwill and fine political credentials, from Noam Chomsky to Barbara Ehrenreich to Barbara Epstein (the first two of whom have kindly blurbed *Fashionable Nonsense*). As I've described it in the preceding essay, this aim involves getting leftists to abandon certain allegedly relativist strains of contemporary theory (even the ones that provide formidable intellectual grounds for resisting racism, imperialism, eugenics, and the like) in favor of forms of thought that rest their claims to truth on appeals to objective fact (as that term is understood by its proponents). The broadest reason that I oppose this aim is that I do not believe that it is useful, in the realm of social theory, to seek an account of "fact" or "objectivity" that is satisfactory for all possible social, ethical, and historical contexts. Put another way, I believe it is a mistake to appeal to observer independent truths that govern human affairs and that it is better for us to recognize that mutable *humans*, not immutable laws, govern human affairs. Nor do I believe that a purportedly objective account of Truth is even necessary for social change; any theory that speaks of relative probabilities, contingencies, and likely outcomes, I think, will suffice for the job, and depending on what the job is (establishing universal health care, opposing mandatory clitoridectomy), the argumentative and moral strategies will differ from case to case. This, in a very small nutshell, is the idea behind the work of antifoundationalist thinkers such as Richard Rorty and Barbara Herrnstein Smith, and the idea of the idea, as I understand it, is to check the moral and intellectual hubris of people who think that *their* neutral, objective account of the social world is self-evidently right and just.

Having said all that, though, I have to admit being taken aback by *Fashionable Nonsense*. It isn't quite the book Sokal and Bricmont think it is (it's actually two books, one of which is quite thought provoking), but it cannot — or should not — be dismissed by the theoretical left as another snarling broadside after the manner of Gross and Levitt's *Higher Superstition*.[1] Indeed, for the patient readers among us — that is, the people who are inclined neither to burn the book nor to crow yet again that the theory emperor has no clothes (a metaphor that appears three times in the book and is now so common among theory bashers that it should be subject to a user fee) — the book offers a lesson or two worth learning. At the very least, Sokal and Bricmont have made the case that there was something very odd about the French psychoanalytic left in the 1960s and 1970s, and that the oddness varied directly with the influence of Jacques Lacan (who, in his senescence, became unfathomably odd himself). But this half of their book, though it gives the book its title, isn't the half worth learning from. The book's other half consists of a handful of essays on the status of knowledge in the sciences and the humanities; it's here that the book offers something edifying and useful and here that its argument is really worth debating.

THE SECTIONS OF *Fashionable Nonsense* that deal with individual theorists (Lacan, Kristeva, Irigaray, Baudrillard, and so forth) are uneven and sometimes (particularly in the cases of Gilles Deleuze and Bruno Latour) simply crabbed and ungenerous. For the most part, they are also unreadable — not because of Sokal and Bricmont but because of Lacan, Irigaray, Kristeva, and Baudrillard, whose writings are quite vulnerable to reasonable critique. Try as I may, I just can't find any point in defending these theorists once they start writing randomly, omnidirectionally, and incomprehensibly about physics and math.

Of course, sometimes the writers in question are simply looking for a good loopy metaphor, as with Lacan's account of the Möbius strip as an image of subjectivity; no harm there, no foul, though occasionally Sokal and Bricmont get literal-minded, complaining that their targets do not "justify" the relevance or application of their metaphors.[2] And to be sure, the fact that Lacan and Irigaray are clueless about science doesn't invalidate their contributions to poststructuralist psychoanalysis; the important things in that school of thought, after all, have nothing to do with fluid mechanics and everything to do with the social or linguistic construction of the "subject," the critical distinction between the subject and the individual, the radical emphasis on the role of the unconscious, and the insistence on the primacy of desire. These hypotheses remain central to many contemporary accounts (of both the readable and the unreadable variety) of our psychic and social lives, and even if Lacan was a charlatan toward the end of his life, twiddling with knots and holding five-minute sham therapy sessions, who cares?

But whatever defense one might marshal for Lacan and crew, the general impression rendered by *Fashionable Nonsense* is pretty damning by any measure: for whatever reasons, there was a time when certain French thinkers evidently expounded, at every opportunity, on theoretical sciences they barely understood. You'd think it was part of the official job description of the post-'68 French intellectual — except that Foucault, Derrida, and Barthes, interestingly enough, seem to have generally avoided the impulse (not that this has stopped Sokal's cheering section from dismissing Foucault, Derrida, and Barthes). Thus one finds the usually clear-headed Kristeva writing stupefying passages like this:

> [I]n the syntactic operations following the mirror stage, the subject is already sure of his uniqueness: his flight toward the "point ∞" in the signifying [*signifiance*] is stopped. One thinks for example of a set C_0 on a usual space R^3 where for every continuous function F on R^3 and each integer $n > 0$, the set of points X where $F(X)$ exceeds n is *bounded*, the functions of C_0 tending to 0 when the variable X recedes toward the "other scene." In this topos, the subject placed in C_0 does not reach this "center exterior to language" about which Lacan speaks and where he loses himself as subject, a situation that would translate the relational group that topology calls a *ring*. (Kristeva 313, qtd. in Sokal and Bricmont 47 – 48)

Kristeva abandoned this kind of silliness decades ago, as Sokal and Bricmont admit, but it's remarkable nonetheless that someone as incisive as Kristeva obviously felt, upon her arrival in the Lacanian quarter of Paris (from her native Bulgaria), that the way to produce a theory of language was to haul out some of the technical implications of Gödel-Bernays set theory and then casually drop phrases like "Dedekind structure with orthocomplements." And Kristeva, for better and for worse, had some idea of the meaning of the mathematical concepts she played with; Luce Irigaray, by contrast, writing *about* science and not just mining it for metaphors, is a rank embarrassment.

Interestingly, all the mischief and faux erudition centers on math and physics; for whatever reason, the French mode of science envy did not latch onto similarly "foundational" sciences such as biology or chemistry. As a result, the post-Sokal debate on "science studies" has strangely focused on only one mode — arguably the most "objective," observer-independent mode — of scientific knowledge, as opposed to, say, debates about evolution, environmental degradation, medical practice, or genetic determinism.

It is a shame that Sokal and Bricmont, by compiling this book and quoting its subjects at such length (they do so, they explain, to avoid the charge that they are quoting out of context), have given such ready ammunition to our vast legions of English-speaking (and English Department) anti-intellectuals, in the faculty lounge with their frayed copies of *It's All a Bunch of Tommyrot, I Say* or at the city desk with their suspenders, who relish nothing so much as confirmation of their conviction that they need never bother to read what I call "theory" and what one of my senior colleagues at the University of Illinois once called "Froggy nonsense." I will never forget an encounter I witnessed as a graduate student at the University of Virginia in 1987, when a Senior Eminence confronted a newly hired feminist with a report on Paul de Man's World War II journalism for the Belgian collaborationist newspaper *Le Soir* and said, "*Now* we've got you." The newly hired feminist had nothing to do with de Man, or with *Le Soir*, or with de Man's manifestly anti-Semitic musings on what might happen to European literature if the Jews were to disappear from Europe (see Hamacher, Hertz, and Keenan), but none of that mattered to the Senior Eminence. He knew, by gum, that something was rotten in the state of Theory, and anything that confirmed his knowledge was all right by him, regardless of whether this knowledge was relevant to the interlocutor at hand. That's more or less how theory bashers have responded to *Fashionable Nonsense*: "Well," they say, "if Julia Kristeva and Luce Irigaray were so stupid or pretentious as to write all this fashionable nonsense, then clearly I don't have to waste any time worrying about whether deconstructionists had a point when they tried to demonstrate that the literal and rhetorical meanings of utterances like 'What's the difference?' contradict each other." That Sokal effect is regrettable, and I regret it. More to the point, though, it is a shame that *Lacan, Irigaray, Baudrillard, and company* have given anti-intellectuals such ready ammunition; as Sokal and Bricmont repeatedly point out, no one put a gun to their heads and forced them to write gobbledygook about math and physics. So if this book gives aid and comfort to know-nothings, it is hardly the fault of Sokal and Bricmont. One does not want to proceed in this discussion by shooting the messengers responsible for strengthening the hand of people who were looking all along for excuses to dismiss "theory," particularly when the messengers have arrived with such exceptionally damaging evidence.

Besides, there's another reason to give credit to Sokal where credit is due — this time, on political rather than intellectual grounds. When the *Social Text* parody essay was published, the French press was, if anything, even more unanimously and vociferously contemptuous of the American theory left than was the domestic American press; from *Le Monde* to *La Recherche* to *Libération*, the French left had a fine, fine time mocking foolish Americans with their "postmodernism" and their "social constructionism." Ho, ho, ho! Monsieur Sokal, he has shown ze emperor il n'a pas des vêtements, n'est-ce pas? After witnessing such volleys of French ridicule in 1996, I found it oddly gratifying to see fresh volleys of French outrage in 1997, when *Fashionable Nonsense* was first published in Paris as *Impostures Intellectuelles* and the French press rose as one to denounce Sokal and Bricmont as self-righteous ignoramuses who would dare, *dare* to attack accomplished French thinkers. I have to applaud Sokal for following his *Social Text* parody with a book that scandalized an entire nation of people who'd applauded the parody. I think of this aspect of the Sokal/Bricmont collaboration as a delightful example of the *Mars Attacks* mode of intellectual debate, whereby one turns and fires one's disintegration ray on the multitudes who've gathered to cheer you on.

IT BEHOOVES ME, then, to explain where and why I'm not among Sokal's fans. In between the tiny chapters on French thinkers, Sokal and Bricmont have placed two "intermezzi" and then closed with an epilogue. These chapters, I think, are the heart of the book and make *Fashionable Nonsense* considerably better than most complaints about "postmodernism." At the same time, both the strengths and the weaknesses of these chapters suggest avenues for more substantive exchanges between the sciences and the humanities — should anyone still be willing to pursue these.

The reason these chapters seem relatively productive to me, as opposed to the merely negative or debunking function of the rest of the book, is that they broach two questions that are fundamental to the epistemological issues in dispute. First, if Lacan et al. are incompetent commentators on science, what would a *good* sociology of science look like, and why would it help us understand where scientific knowledge is truly "objective" (or, to use a better term, observer independent) and where it isn't? And second, what is the relation between epistemic relativism and ethical relativism, especially if the latter is untethered from the former? That is, if you believe that astrophysics discloses the laws of the universe, why doesn't it follow that moral theory obeys immutable laws as well? Conversely, if you acknowledge cultural differences in moral affairs, should you insist that the physical universe is observer relative as well? I don't think Sokal and Bricmont offer satisfactory answers to these questions; on the contrary, they insist that they are concerned "only with *epistemic* relativism and not with moral or aesthetic relativism, which raise very different issues" (52). But they do the questions the honor of taking them seriously, and their position is less inflexible or dogmatic than their book's title would lead one to suspect.

One way of getting at the distinction between the natural and the social is to ask how we can account for radical change in human understanding, either in the natural sciences or in the social sciences. To what extent are these disciplines dependent on social factors, ranging from funding priorities to the political inclinations of individual researchers? With regard to the natural sciences, the hard-line realist position is that natural phenomena provoke epistemic change by showing that current theories do not fit the facts. The hard-line constructionist (or "postmodern") position is that theories and facts are so intimately interdependent that different interpretive paradigms are "incommensurable," not resolvable by recourse to Nature (or by recourse to reasoned dialogue or anything else). The middle-of-the-road position admits that social factors play a role in how scientific knowledge is generated but insists that the knowledge is nonetheless observer independent. Sokal and Bricmont generally try to hold to the middle position, but they occasionally lapse back into hard-line realism for polemical purposes, as when they fault one science-studies textbook for holding that "a theory is never wrong in the sense that it is contradicted by the facts; rather, the facts change when the theories change" (103). Clearly, if the "facts" change when theories change, then you've opened the door to all kinds of mischief, from radical skepticism to Holocaust revisionism. But as Sokal and Bricmont point out in their careful critique of Karl Popper's argument that scientific theories are susceptible to "falsification" (61–69), it really isn't possible to say that theories can be unambiguously "contradicted" by facts, either:

> If one takes the falsificationist doctrine literally, one should declare that Newtonian mechanics was falsified already in the mid–nineteenth century by the anomalous behavior of Mercury's orbit. For a strict Popperian, the idea of putting aside certain difficulties (such as the orbit of Mercury) in the hope that they will be temporary amounts to an illegitimate strategy aimed at evading falsification. However, if one takes into account the context, one may very well maintain that it is *rational* to proceed in this

way, at least for a certain period of time — otherwise science would be impossible. There are always experiments or observations that cannot be fully explained, or that even contradict the theory, which are put aside awaiting better days. Given the immense successes of Newtonian mechanics, it would have been unreasonable to reject it because of a single prediction (apparently) refuted by observations, since this disagreement could have all sorts of other explanations. Science is a rational enterprise, but difficult to codify. (67)

The example is well chosen: the anomalies of Mercury's orbit, by themselves, did not constitute sufficient justification for tossing out everything physicists had learned between 1500 and 1900. And yet they helped to open the way — just as Kuhn suggested, as a mature paradigm produces anomalies — for the supersession of classical mechanics. Sokal and Bricmont's rebuttal of "falsification" thus winds up sounding like what they call a "moderate" Kuhnian thesis (75): theories can be disputed by other theories, and the protocols by which they are disputed inevitably have recourse to observation and experiment, but at no point in our lives do brute facts simply raise their heads and speak in Nature's own voice to tell us that our dominant scientific theories are wrong, dead wrong.

That's why it's so important for historians and philosophers of science to account for what happens when theories collide: if facts aren't wholly independent of theories, then everything depends on how one theory comes to displace another. What, then, are hard-line constructionists saying when they insist on the "incommensurability" of paradigms? In the realm of science, they're suggesting that theories die only when all their adherents die, because if theoretical paradigms really are incommensurable, then no one ever gets persuaded to adopt a newer theory in place of an older one. In the realm of human affairs, where social constructionism is more plausible, they're sensibly cautioning us against thinking that there is one "objective" moral code to which we can appeal when profound cultural disputes arise. In both realms, though, it may very well be that social constructionists tend to speak too readily about the incommensurability of paradigms without stopping to ask how different paradigms might be made intelligible to each other at all — as must surely happen time and again, whenever anyone, moral philosopher or astrophysicist, experiences a profound change of worldview.[3]

The question of epistemic and ethical relativism, then, entails the question of how theories change and the question of how theories collide. And on this question, Sokal and Bricmont do some waffling of their own. They cite, for example, a 22 October 1996 *New York Times* article about Native American land claims in which British archeologist Roger Anyon was cited for the claim that the Zuni worldview was "just as valid as the archeological viewpoint of what prehistory is about" (195). Sokal and Bricmont maintain, reasonably enough, that the Zuni ancestors did not emerge, as the Zuni claim, "onto the surface of earth from a subterranean world of spirits" (195) and that most scientists place the Bering Strait migration about ten or twenty thousand years in the past (194). The second account, I believe, is unquestionably more scientifically accurate than the first, and it is a stretch, at best, to consider the two accounts equally *valid* in an epistemological sense. (Their incommensurability is not the same thing as their equivalence.) But since the issue at hand had to do with scientists asserting their "right" (or at least their "need") to dig up sacred Zuni burial grounds, why are Zuni beliefs being measured here for their probable "validity"? The effect is to substitute an epistemological dilemma for an ethical one, and that's a suspect move in itself — as if the group with the most plausible scientific account of human prehistory gets to do what it wants with the fossil record other people happen to be standing on. Still, Sokal and Bricmont point out that it's possible to defend native land claims without adopting the belief that Native Americans have always lived in North America, having been sprung from the ground at the dawn of time:

> We can perfectly well remember the victims of a horrible genocide, and support their descendants' valid political goals, without endorsing uncritically (or hypocritically) their societies' traditional creation myths. (After all, if you want to support Native American land claims, does it *really* matter whether Native Americans have been in North America "forever" or *merely* for 10,000 years?) (196)

In one sense, no, it doesn't matter: it is entirely possible to dispute the Zuni account of creation while supporting (with whatever degree of enthusiasm or regret) the Zuni right to stymie archeological research into the settlement of the Americas by humans. But Sokal and Bricmont breeze over this example, and in so doing, they decline to explain how it's possible, or when it's necessary, to decouple epistemic realism about fossils and DNA from moral relativism about other people's creation myths.

This is not an academic quibble. This is a profound intellectual and political impasse, and no matter where your sympathies lie, it is absolutely critical to have a good handle on what kinds of claims are at stake — and on how to think about the impasse *as* an impasse. For when Native American "creationists" come into conflict with scientists studying the history of the earth, the claims of faith meet the claims of reason — just as they do every time an advocate of "Intelligent Design" challenges the teaching of evolution. Indeed, in the *New York Times* essay to which Sokal and Bricmont appeal, Dr. Steve Lekson of the University of Colorado Museum is quoted as saying, "Some people who are not sympathetic to Christian fundamentalist beliefs are extraordinarily sympathetic to Native American beliefs. I'm not sure I see the difference" (C13). Here, the claims of science and the claims of history operate on two different registers for two different parties. In other words, with regard to their status as beliefs that oppose themselves to evolutionary theory, there is no difference between Christian and Native American creationism; but with regard to the historical record of how archeologists have dealt in the past with Native Americans and their beliefs, there is all the difference in the world — as at least one scientist told the *Times*:

> Most archeologists agree with the tribes that historical remains, some taken in wars with the Government and shipped to museums, should be given to their relatives for reburial. But in case after case, Indian creationism is being used to forbid the study of prehistoric skeletons so old that it would be impossible to establish a direct tribal affiliation. Under the repatriation act, who gets the bones is often being determined not by scientific inquiry but by negotiation between local tribes and the Federal agencies that administer the land where the remains are found.
>
> "I can understand the loss of a collection when it relates to the recent past," said Dr. Douglas Owsley, a forensic anthropologist at the Smithsonian Institution's Museum of Natural History, which has been compelled to turn over hundreds of prehistoric skeletons for reburial. "Certain collections should not have been acquired in the first place. But we're seeing irreplaceable museum collections that can tell us so much about the prehistoric past lost and lost forever." (C13)

Let me make my own allegiances clear before I proceed any further: I'm with the scientists on this one. As a fan of Jared Diamond's 1997 book, *Guns, Germs and Steel*, and as someone fascinated with the recent prehistory of humans since the emergence of *Homo sapiens sapiens* roughly fifty thousand years ago, I would love to learn more — or simply to allow others to learn more — about how our ancestors settled the last remaining inhabitable continents after the Bering Strait migration, and I mean "our ancestors" in a specieswide sense. Furthermore, I understand and believe scientists' claims that skeletons nine and ten thousand years old have no meaningful biological relation to the bodies of people now walking the earth. But while I do not endorse Native American creationists' beliefs about the origins of their ancestors, I am unsurprised that Native Americans today would respond to scientists and government officials with skepticism, even intransigence. *Certain collections should not have been acquired in the first place. Some taken in wars with the Government.* There are decades of genocidal violence lying behind these deadpan sentences, and anyone who doesn't hear an ethical difference between the creationist claims of Native American tribes with regard to ancient remains and the creationist claims of Christian fundamentalists about alleged gaps in the theory of evolution has a tin ear when it comes to dealing with humans and human histories.

There is nothing relativist about this distinction; nor am I applying a double standard, tolerating one group of religious fundamentalists and dismissing another. Rather, I am placing two different kinds of creationist claims in what I believe is their proper interpretive context. In the "Intelligent Design" dispute, no one is demanding to unearth any fossil remains from purportedly sacred ground, and there is no sorry history of "Indian removal" and extirpation to account for. Christian creationists bring no such ethical and historical questions to the table. The history of Native Americans' relations with European settlers, by contrast, now serves as a barrier to scientific research on the early history of Native American settlement, and though I find this deeply regrettable, I regard it as a social fact that checks our knowledge of some of the brute facts of our collective existence on the planet. The claims of science and the hope of expanding human knowledge through scientific research should sometimes be trumped by other human considerations. The Native American resistance to archeological exploration in the Americas is, alas, one of those times. I would like Native American creationists to believe archeologists' insistence that skeletons ten thousand years old cannot possibly be the remains of ancestors of a tribe of people who have lived in an area for only a thousand years,[4] but I can understand why Native Americans would refuse on both counts, with regard to the age of the skeleton and with regard to the scientific account of their arrival on the land.

Sokal and Bricmont are right, then, to say that one can take the side of the Zuni or other tribes without "endorsing uncritically (or hypocritically) their societies' traditional creation myths." But they do not say why one would choose that side or how one should go about distinguishing the claims of the Zuni from the claims of Christian, Muslim, or Hindu fundamentalists. I mention Hindu fundamentalists not in the interest of multicultural correctness but because Indian biochemist Meera Nanda has eloquently argued that postmodern critiques of Enlightenment universalism have been mobilized, in India, on behalf of the reactionary religious right. Nanda's work is important and chilling, and should be read by anyone who remains interested in devising theories that will be of no use for fascism. But even Nanda is unclear as to whether every kind of social constructionism necessarily winds up working for the right. In one paragraph she writes, "[D]espite their honorable political intentions, all varieties of social constructivism end up giving aid and comfort to Hindu chauvinists who display many symptoms of fascism"; in the next paragraph she writes, "I believe that disclosing the social structuring of knowledge is a worthy enterprise, but it need not take a relativist turn" (582). What, then, is the difference between "social constructivism," which always gives aid and comfort to fascists, and "disclosing the social structuring of knowledge," which is a worthy enterprise as long as it isn't taken too far?

To answer this question, I need to turn back to *Fashionable Nonsense*, this time to the first "intermezzo" (and, I think, the most important chapter in the book), "Epistemic Relativism in the Philosophy of Science." For it is here that they take on the "Strong Programme" of the "Edinburgh school," as developed by sociologists Barry Barnes and David Bloor. What disturbs Sokal and Bricmont about the Strong Programme — and they are far from alone in this respect — is its insistence on "symmetrical" explanations for beliefs, where the principle of "symmetry" holds in abeyance questions of the truth or falsity of belief. In other words, a "symmetrical" account of two different belief systems does not say, "Group A believes X, group B believes Y, and group B believes Y because Y happens to be true"; rather, a symmetrical account tries to explain why groups A and B have the beliefs they do. The relevance of this methodology to Native American creationists and frustrated American archeologists, I imagine, needs no elaboration.

Sokal and Bricmont quote Barnes and Bloor at some length: "Our equivalence postulate," write Barnes and Bloor,

> is that all beliefs are on a par with one another with respect to the causes of their credibility. It is not that all beliefs are equally true or equally false, but that regardless of truth or falsity the fact of their credibility is to be seen as equally problematic. The position we shall defend is that the incidence of all beliefs without exception calls for empirical investigation and must be accounted for by finding the specific, local causes of this credibility. This means that regardless of whether the sociologist evaluates a belief as true or rational, or as false and irrational, he must search for the causes of its credibility. . . . All these questions can, and should, be answered without regard to the status of the belief as it is judged and evaluated by the sociologist's own standards. (Barnes and Bloor 23, qtd. in Sokal and Bricmont 89)

Barnes and Bloor are sometimes infelicitous and ambiguous, as when they insist that "for the relativist there is no sense attached to the idea that some standards or beliefs are really rational as distinct from merely locally accepted as such" (27). This sentence is bothersome on two counts — first, insofar as it suggests that all local knowledges *are* equal in the eyes of the relativist, and second, for its obfuscatory phrase, "there is no sense attached to the idea that," which makes the relativist's relation to the idea more syntactically complex (and conceptually vague) than it should be. But in the longer passage, Barnes and Bloor seem to me to be as clear as day; they are simply enunciating a principle any sociologist, anthropologist, or ethnographer should take for granted in the investigation of belief systems. *Treat all beliefs as if believers believe they have reasons to hold them* — and try to discover what those reasons are, regardless of whether they accord with *your* idea of "reason."

Sokal and Bricmont reply guardedly,

> [T]he ambiguity remains: what exactly do they mean by "without regard to the status of the belief as it is judged and evaluated by the sociologist's own standards"?
>
> If the claim were merely that we should use the same principles of sociology and psychology to explain the causation of all beliefs irrespective of whether we evaluate them as true or false, rational or irrational, then we would have no particular objection. But if the claim is that only *social* causes can enter into such an explanation — that the way the world *is* (i.e., Nature) cannot enter — then we cannot disagree more strenuously. (89 – 90)

In other words, if "Nature" or "the way the world *is*" gets to be one of the grounds for belief, then Sokal and Bricmont have no quarrel with the Strong Programme; but if social factors determine *entirely* the content — and not just the form — of beliefs about the world, then Sokal and Bricmont see the Strong Programme as a defense of irrationality tout court.

A few years later, in 2001, philosopher Paul Boghossian took to the pages of the *Times Literary Supplement* to sort through the claims of science studies scholars post-Sokal. In "What Is Social Construction?," Boghossian attempted to walk the same moderate line laid out by Sokal and Bricmont, admitting that "social values" play a part in how scientific research is conducted while denying that such values inform the content of research findings. And in the course of walking that line, Boghossian took issue with the view that, as he paraphrased it, "although social values do not justify our beliefs, we are not actually moved to belief by things that justify; we are only moved by our social interests":

> This view, which is practically orthodoxy among practitioners of what has come to be known as "science studies," has the advantage of not saying

something absurd about justification; but it scarcely any more plausible. On the most charitable reading, it stems from an innocent confusion about what is required by the enterprise of treating scientific knowledge sociologically.

The view in question derives from one of the founding texts of science studies, David Bloor's *Knowledge and Social Imagery* (1976). Bloor's reasoning went something like this: If we wish to explain why certain beliefs come to be accepted as knowledge at a given time, we must not bring to bear *our* views about which of those beliefs are true and which false. If we are trying to explain why they came to hold that some belief is true, it cannot be relevant that we know it not to be true. This is one of the so-called "Symmetry Principles" of the sociology of knowledge; treat true and false propositions symmetrically in explaining why they came to be believed.

It's possible to debate the merits of this principle, but on the whole it seems to me sound. As Ian Hacking rightly emphasizes, however, it is one thing to say that true and false beliefs should be treated symmetrically and quite another to say that justified and unjustified ones should be so treated. While it may be plausible to ignore the truth or falsity of what I believe in explaining why I came to believe it, it is not plausible to ignore whether I had any evidence for believing it. (568 – 69)

But Boghossian's apparent acceptance of the Symmetry Principle is undermined by the terms of the acceptance: *we are to treat beliefs symmetrically unless one of them is unjustified.* I hope I will not be accused of using Western logic as a tool of oppression if I point out that this formulation begs the question at issue — that is, whether a belief *is* justified. Barnes and Bloor had argued that "the incidence of all beliefs without exception calls for empirical investigation and must be accounted for by finding the specific, local causes of this credibility." Boghossian renders this, whether deliberately or through simple misunderstanding, as the principle that the incidence of all beliefs calls for empirical investigation as to the specific, local causes of their credibility, *with the exception of unjustified beliefs.*

Worse still, Boghossian's attempt to negotiate the claims of the natural and the social makes mishmash of Ian Hacking's work on the subject, for Hacking did not, in fact, "emphasize" that justified and unjustified beliefs should be exempted from the Symmetry Principle; on the contrary, Hacking realizes that treating a belief as unjustified violates the principle at the outset. In his 1999 book, *The Social Construction of What?*, Hacking was considerably more agnostic on the question of how to deploy the Symmetry Principle. In the course of a sinuous discussion of the history of interpretations of dolomite (yes, dolomite), Hacking detours for a few pages to remark explicitly on the assumptions of the Edinburgh school:

> Members of the Edinburgh school were often thought to imply that interests affected the actual content of a science. *I am not sure about the extent to which this accusation is justified.* Interests have a lot to do with the questions that are asked, with the direction of research, and the resultant form, as opposed to the content, of the science. The enormous commercial importance of dolomite, as a container and cap for petroleum, has had an obvious effect on how questions about dolomite are answered, given that the questions are asked.
>
> The Edinburgh school is also famous for its strong thesis of symmetry. . . . The idea is that an explanation of why a group of investigators holds true beliefs should have a very similar structure to an explanation of why another group holds false beliefs. The early days of dolomite serve us well to illustrate this doctrine. There is what we now take to be the correct account, furnished by [Giovanni] Arduino, and the incorrect account furnished by [Nicolas-Theodor von] Saussure and accepted by [Déodat de] Dolomieu. Arduino thought he had a magnesium compound, while Saussure thought it was an aluminum compound and claimed to prove this by chemical analysis. The two cases seem symmetric. Arduino did not reach his belief *because* it was true (in Chapter 3 I inveighed, on logical and linguistic grounds, against saying anything of the sort). The explanation of why Arduino reached his correct conclusions will be of very much the same sort as the explanation of why Saussure reached his mistaken conclusions. (202 – 3; emphasis added)

Hacking then goes on to endorse Bruno Latour's theory of scientific networking to explain why the Saussure-Dolomieu theory of dolomite initially attracted more adherents. Arduino's theory eventually won the day, as Hacking acknowledges, but in his narration of the story of dolomite since its discovery in the late eighteenth century, Hacking never resorts to the claim that dolomite itself decided the dispute simply by being the kind of thing that it is.

But who cares about rocks, you ask? It's one thing to invoke the principle of symmetry when two groups of scientists disagree about the chemical composition of dolomite. It's quite another when you're dealing with legitimate scientists on one side and a bunch of befuddled creationists (of whatever religious conviction on the other), as Boghossian seems to suggest. When you're dealing with the conflict between reason and faith, it surely makes sense to suspend the Symmetry Principle and declare religious arguments to be "unjustified," doesn't it? Well, it depends on what the meaning of "dealing with" is. If you're arguing that Intelligent Design is not a science and should not be taught in science classrooms, nothing I've written here will challenge or obstruct you, and much of what I've written should help. But if you want to account for why it is that people reject evolutionary theory in favor of religious or other non-scientific beliefs about the origins of life, then you're duty-bound to adopt the principle of symmetry — *if* you want to understand why people think they have reason to believe the things they believe.

These questions are important for obvious reasons; they sometimes involve the fates of entire societies. But I'd like to close by pointing out a less obvious reason for the importance of symmetry and skepticism: when we leave the realm of math and physics for more dicey sciences like genetics, ecology, or primatology, it actually becomes quite difficult to specify the point at which we can be sure that the phenomena we observe are not of our own making and consequently difficult to distinguish epistemological relativism from its more innocuous cultural cousins. What's at stake here, as I argued in the previous essay, has to do with the status of the boundary between "brute fact" and "social reality" — a boundary that, for Sokal and Bricmont as for many others, provides the distinction between where it's unreasonable to be a relativist (with regard to the existence of atoms, say) and where it's often ethically necessary (when moral claims are advanced in radically different registers). While I want to suggest that Sokal and Bricmont are right to insist on brute fact (hydrogen, gravity, globular clusters) as an observer-independent realm, I also want to suggest that it is considerably harder to distinguish between brute fact and social reality than Sokal and Bricmont care to admit. This point, however, will remain obscure as long as these disputes are played out over math and physics; if the science in question were bioengineering or climatology, by contrast, it would be quite clear to many laypeople and scientists alike that the realm of "observer-independent objectivity" is harder to attain than Sokal and Bricmont — and their supporters — are letting on.

But since the Sokal – *Social Text* affair has usually generated more heat than light, it's gratifying that *Fashionable Nonsense*, in its best moments, raises the debate to this level of complexity. Readers who take the intermezzi and epilogue seriously will find the book capable of repaying their interest with interest, and those who hanker after good popularizations of quantum physics, advanced math, and science studies can consult the book's copious and helpful suggestions for further reading: for unlike the notes in Sokal's parody essay, all the footnotes in *Fashionable Nonsense* are real and are offered in good faith.

Notes

1. On occasion, the snarling not only obscures but undermines a serious point. For example, Gross and Levitt take aim at a rhetorical question posed by Tim Dean: "What are we to make," Dean wrote while still a graduate student at Johns Hopkins, "of the fact that the development of topological science is historically coincident with the emergence both of 'the homosexual' as a discrete ontological entity and of psychoanalysis?" My reply — and I say this as one of Tim's friends and former colleagues — is, "Not much, I think." But here's what Gross and Levitt make of it: "It is also, we note, coincident with the era in which people played football without a helmet. Would it be too cruel of us to wonder whether Dean is overly fond of some similar activity"? (266). "Cruel" does not seem to be le mot juste here. "Juvenile," perhaps.

2. "Some people," Sokal and Bricmont note at the outset, "will no doubt think that we are interpreting these authors too literally and that the passages we quote should be read as metaphors rather than as precise logical arguments. Indeed, in certain cases the 'science' *is* undoubtedly intended metaphorically; but what is the purpose of these metaphors? After all, a metaphor is usually employed to clarify an unfamiliar concept by relating it to a more familiar one, not the reverse" (10). Not only am I one of the people who think that Sokal and Bricmont are interpreting some of these authors too literally, but I am also one of the people who think that Sokal and Bricmont interpret *the function of metaphor* too literally. Quite often, after all, metaphor is not employed to "clarify an unfamiliar concept" but to defamiliarize familiar concepts. And sometimes a metaphor is just a metaphor.

3. I develop this argument further in chapter 6 of *What's Liberal about the Liberal Arts?*

4. See Johnson: "The 10,600-year-old skeleton of a woman found in a gravel quarry near the town of Buhl, in southern Idaho, was reburied in December 1991 after the Shoshone-Bannocks — believed by many scientists to have occupied the area for less than a thousand years — claimed the remains were those of a dead ancestor. Although tribal officials had given permission for carbon dating to determine the skeleton's age, they forbade archeologists to perform DNA tests and chemical analyses that would have given clues about the origin of the skeleton, its diet and other matters" (C13).

Works Cited

Barnes, Barry, and David Bloor. "Relativism, Rationalism, and the Sociology of Knowledge." In *Rationality and Relativism*, edited by Martin Hollis and Steven Lukes, 21–47. Oxford: Blackwell, 1981.

Bérubé, Michael. *What's Liberal about the Liberal Arts?: Classroom Politics and "Bias" in Higher Education*. New York: Norton, 2006.

Bloor, David. *Knowledge and Social Imagery*. London: Routledge and Kegan Paul, 1976.

Boghossian, Paul A. "What Is Social Construction?" In *Theory's Empire: An Anthology of Dissent*, edited by Daphne Patai and Will H. Corral, 562–74. New York: Columbia University Press, 2005.

Diamond, Jared. *Guns, Germs, and Steel: The Fates of Human Societies*. New York: Norton, 1997.

Gross, Paul, and Norman Levitt. *Higher Superstition: The Academic Left and Its Quarrels with Science*. Baltimore: Johns Hopkins University Press, 1994.

Hacking, Ian. *The Social Construction of What?* Cambridge: Harvard University Press, 1999.

Hamacher, Werner, Neil Hertz, and Thomas Keenan. *Responses: On Paul de Man's Wartime Journalism*. Lincoln: University of Nebraska Press, 1989.

Johnson, George. "Indian Tribes' Creationists Thwart Archeologists." *New York Times*, 22 October 1996, A1, C13.

Kristeva, Julia. *Polylogue*. Paris: Éditions de Seuil, 1977.

Nanda, Meera. "Postcolonial Science Studies: Ending 'Epistemic Violence.' " In *Theory's Empire: An Anthology of Dissent*, edited by Daphne Patai and Will H. Corral, 575–84. New York: Columbia University Press, 2005.

Sokal, Alan, and Jean Bricmont. *Fashionable Nonsense: Postmodern Intellectuals' Abuse of Science*. New York: Picador, 1988.

The Utility of the Arts
and Humanities

B ad news first. In a material sense, the arts and humanities are not going to contribute significantly to what will be, over the next century, the true "growth" areas of higher education in the United States and United Kingdom: business, science, and technology. But before educators in the arts and humanities get too skeptical and self-righteous about "growth" and all the filthy lucre it entails, we should remember that the coming advances in biotechnology are not only potentially extremely lucrative for possible patent holders but also intellectually exciting and world-transforming in their own right. Our incipient (and current) debates over cloning, over the mapping of the human genome, over genetic therapy and prenatal testing, and over the corporate ownership of life forms surely will challenge our sense of what it means to be human just as sweepingly and thoroughly as any artifact, ancient or modern, from the arts and humanities. So we needn't be too smug about not participating in "growth," for although much of this growth will be tied directly and narrowly to the next stage of capitalism (which its exponents will doubtless call "cybercapitalism" or "business at the speed of thought" and its Marxist detractors will call "*really late* late capitalism"), some of it will in fact provoke remarkable and vexing questions about the circulation and substance of our cultural values. And if I say nothing else of any utility in the course of this essay about utility, I want at least to insist that artists and humanists should not come to those questions as so many of us have come to new technologies, as befuddled end users.

A Delightful Dessert

The University of Illinois at Urbana-Champaign, where I taught for twelve years (1989 – 2001) and administered a humanities program for four (1997 – 2001), is one of the best public research universities in the United States. In engineering and the physical sciences, especially, it outranks its "public Ivy" competitors such as Virginia, Michigan, and Berkeley and is comparable instead to private science-intensive institutions such as MIT and Caltech. Indeed, the university's profile is so well established in these fields that upon arriving at UIUC in 1998, provost and vice chancellor for academic affairs Richard Herman (now chancellor) declared that if Illinois were to compete effectively in national rankings with Virginia, Michigan, and Berkeley, it would need to undertake a ten- to fifteen-year capital campaign to enhance the arts and humanities on campus.

No artist or humanist on campus at the time could recall any high-level administrator having said such a thing, and we could only conclude that Herman had been insufficiently socialized into the local culture, where it was far more common to hear administrators wonder aloud why the university would need a philosophy department. Indeed, only a few years earlier, Illinois had created a Critical Research Initiative ostensibly designed to enhance "interdisciplinary work" across the campus by means of grants as large as two hundred thousand dollars. The CRI prospectus, however, spoke of "sundown provisions" and the need to "encourage interdisciplinary efforts to explore the meaning for society of the new computing and communications technologies." The "initiative" was, in other words, primarily a supplement for projects proposed to or undertaken under the auspices of the federal National Science Fund, and the university provided it with only the barest of fig-leaf pretenses that it was open to all faculty members in all disciplines. One strains to imagine how to craft a "sundown provision" for a study of the history of the Balkans or how to draft a proposal that explores the "meaning for society" of something other than computing and communications technologies, such as Foucauldian accounts of governmentality or postconventional theories of ethics and justice. Sure enough, over the first four years of its existence, the CRI funded no proposal in the arts and humanities, not even those from faculty members working in new computing technologies in the arts. Its motto could have been and probably unofficially was, "Putting our money where the money is." Two hundred thousand dollars may not sound like much to a scientist, but it equaled my humanities program's budget for an entire year.

The other indignity is more or less self-inflicted. Most of the university-affiliated artists and humanists I know are profoundly ambivalent about the idea of justifying their disciplines in terms of their social utility; they tend to regard self-justification as a dubious enterprise best left to the writers of admissions brochures and back-patting liberal-arts mission statements. The arts enrich life, the humanities teach us what it is to be human, the arts deepen our spirit, the humanities preserve our common cultural heritage, bleat, bleat, bleat, surely we can all utter such phrases in our sleep, even or especially if we believe some of them. By contrast, scientists are relatively unconflicted about defending their disciplines in terms of social utility, even when they reach for *their* bromides, which usually have to do with humankind's unquenchable thirst to know and explore. I'll draw out this argument in a moment, and then I'll get around (in the final section) to arguing that the arts and humanities do enrich life and teach us what it is to be human, but for now I want simply to note that artists and humanists unfortunately tend to think that all sciences are somehow socially useful and that they cannot possibly compete on that score. As Joanne Trautmann Banks writes, with regard to the subdiscipline of literature and medicine, "[I]f we can show that literature *works* in the context of such a basic, life-enhancing as well as life-threatening endeavor as medicine, then we can ameliorate our otherwise self-centered desire to bask in the philosophical and aesthetic pleasures of superb texts" (98). As long as the issue of utility is framed like this, surely the study of literature is doomed. For literature does not "work" with regard to medicine, in the sense that no infusion of Jane Austen will send stomach cancer into remission and no IV drip of Martin Amis's latest will combat renal failure, and if the study of the humanities is defined as the "self-centered desire to bask in the philosophical and aesthetic pleasures of superb texts," then there is little chance that scientists will see the arts and humanities as anything better — or more consequential — than a delightful dessert.

At Illinois the image of arts as dessert took a horribly literal form. The University of Illinois boasts the Krannert Center for the Performing Arts, a world-class facility by any measure, led by a smart and energetic director in Mike Ross, with whom I had the pleasure of collaborating in bringing figures such as choreographer Merce Cunningham and performance artist Joe Goode to campus. The Krannert's generic advertising in town usually took the form of abstract billboards featuring cellos or dancers and bearing the slogan, "Spirit Matters": fair enough, since no one in her right mind would think of making a case for Cunningham's computer-generated and -coordinated choreography in "BIPED" or Goode's threnody of grief and ritual in "About What's Underneath" in an advertising campaign conducted on billboards along highways and city streets in central Illinois. But the advertising directly outside the Krannert seemed to me to speak to what *really* matters. Alongside the many posters announcing upcoming performances were large ads touting the virtues of the Krannert's lunch/coffee shop, Intermezzo; the ads featured a mustachioed man of indeterminate race looking quite pleased about a torte. And that's basically how all too many administrators, trustees, and retired-faculty Krannert subscribers understood the arts: as a delightful dessert. After a hard day of working with supercomputers or scanning human bodies with nuclear magnetic resonance imaging, you can come to the arts and humanities to take in a lovely symphony, hear some soothing poetry, and have a delicious piece of cake.

Not all sciences are quite as useful as supercomputing and MRI, but I cite these for a reason: in different ways, each is strongly associated with the University of Illinois. Paul Lauterbur, the developer of magnetic resonance imaging, is a longtime faculty member in Illinois's physics department, and many years before his arrival, Illinois's John Bardeen invented the transistor. Bardeen, the only two-time Nobel laureate in physics, can justly be said to have ushered us into the electronic age, and there are few people in the industrialized world who do not pay him unwitting homage every day. But surely the more speculative sciences, from astrophysics to evolutionary theory, do not have quite the same claim on practical utility; surely some endeavors in pure mathematics or cosmology contribute no more than does the study of medieval tapestry to the economic or physical well-being of the general citizenry. Nonetheless, at Illinois and countless other universities, it often seems nearly impossible to make this rather obvious point. The dialogue between scientists and humanists on this front tends to run something like this. I go to the Physics Department and look around for a mathematical physicist who will take the time to explain some of the propositions of Brian Greene's "popular" explanation of eleven-dimensional string theory in *The Elegant Universe*. "It seems to me," I say after finding so generous an interlocutor, "that this staggeringly complex resolution of certain anomalies attendant on the application of the principles of quantum mechanics to distances shorter than that of the Planck length doesn't really have any social utility. It attempts an 'elegant' solution — hence the book's title — to the problem of the 'quantum foam' produced by a point theory of space at distances under 10^{-33} centimeters and attempts a unified theory of forces that reconciles quantum theory with general relativity by basically suggesting that there are no spaces smaller than 10^{-33} centimeters and that the various 'vibrations' of these Planck-length strings, wound up in six dimensions in Calabi-Yau space and four-dimensional spacetime (and one extra dimension I don't understand), account for all the strong and weak forces in the universe. But, hell, this is even more useless, socially speaking, than Roland Barthes's poststructuralist narratology in *S/Z*, which at least has some implications for the understanding of narrative." And the mathematical physicist replies, "See here, son, don't you realize that one of my colleagues down the hall once invented the transistor? G'wan, kid, you bother me."[1]

In recent years, exchanges between humanists and scientists have been at once defined and short-circuited by the Sokal Hoax, which apparently demonstrated (among other things) that C. P. Snow had it exactly right in that humanists are woefully illiterate when it comes to fairly basic scientific information that any first-year college physics major would know. As I've argued in the three preceding essays, Sokal's hoax did not, in fact, show that "social constructionism" is so much poststructuralist hogwash, nor did it make any serious case for Sokal's posthoax argument that culturalist modes of understanding in the humanities are depriving the political left of cogent and effective forms of thought and action. But it did prove, prima facie, that whoever read the essay for *Social Text* did not catch and thus did not ask Sokal to explain the various howlers and deliberate misstatements regarding the physical sciences. And if one of the essay's "gotcha" targets was Andrew Ross, who edited the special "Science Wars" issue of *Social Text* in which Sokal's article appeared, then it's worth pointing out that something quite odd happened in this contretemps between scientists and humanists: whatever else one might want to claim about Andrew Ross, one would be hard-pressed to construe him as an important commentator on new developments in mathematical physics. When Ross has called for more "democratic" forms of scientific practice and review (*Chicago, Strange*), he has concentrated on ecology and on that perennial whipping boy of the cultural left, sociobiology; when he asked for science "that will be publicly answerable and of some service to progressive interests" (*Strange* 29), he was not, in fact, calling for a leftist astrophysics or for a People's Theory of Consecutive Prime Numbers. To date, Ross has not presumed — as has, for example, Andrew Pickering — to speak of the "constructedness" of fundamental particles such as quarks. Yet some of the most vocal and trenchant critics of *Social Text* and of "science studies" more generally have come from the most theoretical and speculative subfields within physics: Norman Levitt, Steven Weinberg, and Edward Witten, to name three, are all mathematical physicists whose work, like Brian Greene's, is inconceivably remote from the kinds of science and medicine that the cultural left actually cares about. And the reason that so few cultural leftists in the humanities care about new developments in theories of matter or of the evolution of the universe is precisely that such theories have no social utility whatsoever. The 1963 discovery of the cosmic microwave background radiation and the rough determination of the age and "size" (and therefore, possibly, the fate) of the universe are triumphs of human intelligence; they are among the achievements of our species of which I am most proud. But they will not increase the peace and they will not fight the power; nor, for the cultural right, will they enhance trust in established authority or shore up traditional forms of identity and sexuality. Nor, for that matter, will they contribute a spare dime or a plugged Euro to the gross domestic product of any gross domesticity. For the conduct of human affairs, the statement that "the identity between the string energies in a universe with a circular dimension whose radius is either R or $1/R$ arises from the fact that the energies are of the form $v/R + wR$, where v is the vibration number and w is the winding number" (Greene 403 n.3) has neither implications nor consequences.

Still, for the most part, physical scientists do not have to defend their disciplines as being somehow useful to taxpayers and trustees. And by means of the Sokal Hoax they have even managed to promote the physical sciences' model of "objective" knowledge, a knowledge of facts and entities indifferent to the vagaries of human cultures and human history, as a basis for understanding truth and justice in human affairs. All we can offer in response is dessert.

In the Service of Service

In 1993, Tony Bennett chided humanities faculty for refusing to defend their enterprise in terms of utility. Writing in the *Southern Review*, Bennett opined that "the readiness of cultural studies intellectuals to fall into line behind traditional defences of the humanities as a form of education which exceeds the mundane calculus that the notions of skills, trainings and competencies imply is most disappointing" (235). The implication was clear: cultural studies intellectuals should not go around sounding like F. R. Leavis or writers of college admissions brochures. By now they would surely know better than to try to peddle sweetness and light or to propose the utopian and disdain the mundane.

Bennett was right to suggest that humanists shouldn't consider "skills, trainings, and competencies" as obviously beneath the high destiny of our calling. But the logic of Bennett's position was — and remains — dangerous: should you insist that the arts and humanities deliver something more or other than deliverable skills and competencies, then you're an old-school, brandy-snifting, meerschaum-chomping elitist snob who probably believes that the arts and humanities are their own reward. But if you take Bennett's scolding seriously and try to justify the humanities in terms of their contribution to the economy or to job training, you wind up (1) serving as one of the service disciplines devoted to servicing the service economy, perhaps by means of English for Technical Writing, French for Finance, or German for Engineering (all real and increasingly prevalent courses designed to increase undergraduate enrollments and promote advanced literacy and language study), (2) inviting a backlash as soon as the next economic downturn hits, insofar as your rhetoric of justification works only as long as the people whom economist and former U.S. Secretary of Labor Robert Reich calls "symbolic analysts" are getting good jobs, and (3) placing at a fire-sale discount whatever arts and humanities knowledges are considered to involve skills, trainings, and competencies for which the economy has no immediate use.

Compare Bennett's argument, then, with that of George Yúdice, who argues that cultural workers have tended all too readily to defend their enterprise in terms of skills and competencies. "Universities and arts organizations have increasingly resorted to a pragmatic defense of the humanities and culture," writes Yúdice. "They characterize the arts as tools that enhance employability in the academic setting, junior partners to the science faculties where profitable intellectual property is produced. On the other hand, in the cultural sector, the arts become part of a social service rationale or of economic development plans for communities, thus justifying subvention by corporations and foundations" (24–25). Yúdice points to a pair of late-1990s reports on the arts and humanities in the United States, *Creative America* (produced by the President's Committee on the Arts and Humanities) and *American Canvas* (written by Gary Larson for the National Endowment for the Arts). In the latter report, writes Yúdice, "skilling is a major aspect of the arts," and he cites a passage in which we are told that the arts

> build the specific workplace skills needed to ensure [students'] own employability and their ability to make a solid economic contribution to their communities and the nation. The arts teach and enhance such skills as the ability to manage resources, interpersonal skills of cooperation and teamwork, the ability to acquire and use information and to master different types of symbol systems, and the skills required to use a variety of technologies. (qtd. in Yúdice 29)

It is hard to see why Bennett would find it "disappointing" that cultural studies intellectuals would fail to fall into line behind arguments such as this. Cooperation and teamwork: Man Ray, Anton Webern, and Jenny Holzer can prepare you to manage resources for the Century 21 real estate development team!

Despite my desire to enhance students' skills and competencies in the arts of textual interpretation, when I read texts like *American Canvas* I cannot resist the compulsion to argue that the arts and humanities also introduce students to many varieties of beauty and technical virtuosity that do nothing to enhance their interpersonal skills of cooperation or their ability to make a solid economic contribution to their communities and the nation. It happens to be true, for example, that we professors of English literature have access to some of the most extraordinarily beautiful and conceptually complex things ever written in our language, even though we tend not to want to lead with this argument when we're asked to justify our existence to the chamber of commerce. I will cite but one example from my own undergraduate education —and I will not take the easy route and capitalize on that Shakespeare fellow's long history of success in American popular culture. The lines below are from the beginning of book 2 of *Gawain and the Green Knight*, and even in that poem they serve no immediate purpose but to narrate the passing of the year between the time Gawain decapitates the Green Knight in Arthur's hall and the time Gawain is compelled to ride to the Green Knight's castle to receive a similar blow:

> A yere yernes ful yerne, and yeldes never lyke;
> The forme to the fynisment foldes ful selden.
> Forthi this Yol overyede, and the yere after,
> And uche sesoun serlepes sued after other:
> After Crystenmasse com the crabbed Lentoun,
> That fraystes flesch wyth the fysche and fode more symple.
> Bot thenne the weder of the worlde wyth wynter hit threpes,
> Colde clenges adoun, cloudes uplyften,
> Schyre schedes the rayn in schowres ful warme,
> Falles upon fayre flat, flowres there schewen.
> Bothe groundes and the greves grene ar her wedes,
> Bryddes busken to bylde, and bremlych syngen
> For solace of the softe somer that sues therafter
> > bi bonk;
> > And blossumes bolne to blowe
> > Bi rawes rych and ronk,
> > Then notes noble innoghe
> > Ar herde in wod so wlonk.

> After, the sesoun of somer wyth the soft wyndes,
> Quen Zeferus syfles hymself on sedes and erbes;
> Wela wynne is the wort that waxes theroute,
> When the donkande dewe dropes of the leves,
> To bide a blysful blusch of the bryght sunne.
> Bot then hyyes hervest, and hardenes hym sone,
> Warnes hym for the wynter to wax ful rype;
> He dryves wyth droght the dust for to ryse,
> Fro the face of the folde to flyye ful hyghe;
> Wrothe wynde of the welken wrasteles with the sunne,
> The leves laucen fro the lyne and lyghten on the grounde,
> And al grayes the gres that grene was ere;
> Thenne al rypes and rotes that ros upon fyrst.

And thus yirnes the yere in yisterdayes mony,
And wynter wyndes ayayn, as the worlde askes,
   no fage,
Til Meghelmas mone
Was cumen wyth wynter wage.
Then thenkkes Gawan ful sone
Of his anious vyage. (ll. 498 – 535)

I have always loved this passage — and I love it especially for its opening couplet, which the footnotes of my Cawley and Anderson edition render as "A year passes swiftly, and events never repeat themselves; the beginning is very seldom like the end" (178) — true enough, but it loses something in translation, we might say. For the couplet does not merely tell us that you can never tell what a year will bring; it couches this cliché in the language of the forme *folding to the fynisment*, thus at once revivifying and literalizing our sense of how, indeed, the events of our lives don't quite fit our plans. The couplet *makes the stone stony*, as Viktor Shklovsky would say. What's more, the syntax makes the most of the potential relation of the forme to the fynisment, leaving the verb hanging for a moment — and "seldom," a discouraging word, for the very end of the sentence — while we imagine that maybe, just this once, the forme will fit the fynisment just fine. And need I add that the language of *Gawain* is a kind of English we just don't hear these days? Even if you're familiar with Middle English and are inclined to line up this sumptuous rendering of the seasons with the much more famous opening eighteen lines of *The Canterbury Tales* to give your students a little compare-and-contrast on the topos of the passing year, it remains the case that the language of *Gawain* is even wilder, thicker, and more richly textured than Chaucer's, from the exuberant bursting and burgeoning of "Bryddes busken to bylde, and bremlych syngen" to the alien "wod so wlonk." All in all, great stuff, even for a theory-addled postmodernist like me. But for those who prefer to speak of how the arts teach students to master different symbol systems, perhaps I should try to suggest that the study of medieval English literature might help a American television weathercaster tell us that a low-pressure system is developing over the Pacific Northwest such that *colde clenges adoun, cloudes uplyften, schyre schedes the rayn in showres ful warme.*

Nonetheless, should we take our distance from the language of utility by pinching our noses at the filthy lucre of the applied sciences, by insisting on the sublime irrelevance of the theoretical sciences, or by quoting *Gawain and the Green Knight* at length and droning on about the eternal verities of the fine arts, we will find ourselves politically very vulnerable very fast. I sometimes think this is why the cultural right has urged us so often in the past two decades to return to the eternal verities of the fine arts: it's part of a two-step plan to eliminate the arts and humanities from any serious social or curricular consideration. For when it comes to defending the utility of the arts and humanities, the cultural right is every bit as and ambivalent and divided as is the cultural left of Tony Bennett and George Yúdice, yet is far more coordinated: one bunch of conservatives — we could call them the Allan Bloom Consortium — wants us to return to the canon, to aesthetics, to the pursuit of beauty instead of all this queer theory and multicultural pabulum. These are the conservatives one finds clustered around the *New Criterion* and the *Hudson Review*, the ones who line their shelves with volumes from the Loeb Classical Library and decry the mediocrity of contemporary American theater. The other bunch of conservatives — let's call them the Tom DeLay Gang — doesn't see any reason why taxpayers should support public universities or why parents and trustees should support private universities in which faculty and students fritter away their time pursuing pointless things like "beauty" when there's important work to be done and people need to see a return on their college investment. These are the conservatives who, in alliance with economic libertarians, declaim from the editorial page of the *Wall Street Journal* that the "important work" to be done consists of eliminating estate and capital gains taxes, gutting workplace regulations, and shredding environmental standards. They like to have a few Allan Bloomers around to talk about the cultural superiority of the West and the depravity of Western academic intellectuals, but as long as those estate taxes are repealed, they really don't care whether college students are reading Cicero or comic books. The two-step plan, then, consists of this: the first group will urge arts and humanities faculty to return to beauty, whereupon the second group will come along and cut all funding for the frivolous aesthetic pursuits of the arts and humanities.

Of course, it is always possible to make the case for the usefulness of arts and humanities *education*, if not exactly the arts and humanities themselves, by pointing to the conditions of labor and teaching in universities: instruction in the arts and humanities usually involves what administrators call inefficient modes of instruction delivery, which sounds undesirable until you talk to people who understand this to mean low faculty/student ratios, in which case they're very desirable. Justifying arts and humanities education thus involves convincing administrative and legislative bean counters that "costly" small-student interactions have always been among the strengths — and attractions — of education in the arts and humanities, whether you're talking about studio classes with sculptors or cellists, advanced honors seminars with a dozen undergraduates, or the direction of dissertation research. At Illinois, there were quantifiable measures of the teaching strengths of the arts and humanities: every semester the student newspaper published an "Incomplete List of Teachers Ranked as Excellent by Their Students," and every semester, the departments most strongly represented on this list were English, art, music, and history, where small class sizes and close individual attention to student work were far more common than in the "profitable" departments across the campus. Ever since the days of the pre-Socratics, the irreducibly idiosyncratic and individualized nature of our teaching has been valuable in and of itself as a pedagogical mode, and ever since the rise of the University of Phoenix it has stood out as the one thing that distance education and for-profit cyberuniversities will never quite be able to offer.

The advantage of stressing the labor conditions of arts and humanities education is that doing so allows cultural workers in universities to highlight modes of learning in which knowledge is produced rather than transmitted, and in which students are participants in the creation of that knowledge rather than merely consumers thereof. The disadvantage is obvious: in universities where teaching is either disdained or merely tolerated as a kind of benign loss leader at the front of the store, paid for by the patent-generating activities in the labs that constitute the real heart of the enterprise, all such talk about small faculty/student ratios and personal attention to student work will be heard as special pleading and fatuous self-congratulation on the part of "service" disciplines. As my university president at Illinois, James Stukel, said when I spoke to him in the late 1990s about the importance of maintaining small classes and tutorials in the arts and humanities, "Yes, well, it's important to think about the warm and fuzzies." (I marveled not only at the fact that he said this but also at the fact that he said it *to me* — that is, to someone who would be sure to repeat it as often as possible.) Teaching, for such administrators, is associated with service, which is associated with women, who are associated with "feminized" fields like English and art (even though the English and Art Departments may house only a handful of tenured women between them), which are associated in turn with warm and fuzzies, down comforters, Paddington bears, herbal teas, and cats curled up by the fire.

Interpretation as a Way of Life

It is no wonder that most of us in the arts and humanities have been content to speak suggestively and vaguely about the social utility of our disciplines, usually by insisting that the arts and humanities enhance students' capacities for creative expression and/or critical thinking. The alternatives are staggeringly worse: sterile aestheticism masked as moral virtue, Rotarian insistence on how the arts bring us together and help us make economic contributions to our communities, cultured appreciation of a fine Sacher torte. Humanists like me are thus especially grateful for university administrators who argue for expanded programs in the arts and humanities to compete more effectively in the national rankings against other universities: such an argument assumes that there is some value in the arts and humanities (after all, there must be, if other universities are ranked highly because of their strengths in those product areas) without bothering to inquire or to specify what that value might be. The argument could, under other circumstances, be applied just as well to jugglers and fire-eaters: if Berkeley and Yale are ranked highly because of their advanced programs in chain-saw juggling and atomic fire-eating, why, then, we've got to have some excellent jugglers and fire-eaters of our own, and we don't much care whether they're poststructural-postcolonialist juggling fire-eaters or liberal-humanist juggling fire-eaters, just so long as they win prizes and are cited often.

Before I am accused of insufficiently appreciating the talents of jugglers and fire-eaters, let me hasten to add three things: first, I believe that for some administrators, trustees, and elected officials, contemporary work in the arts and humanities is indeed indistinguishable from dazzling if sometimes tasteless circus acts. Among those who look upon us benignly, the attitude is something like this: *I don't get it myself, and I don't care to, but people seem to be applauding, and even though some people seem to be throwing rotting fruit, hey, at least there's a commotion here, and that can't hurt.* Second, I believe that there is absolutely nothing wrong with an academic environment in which some activities, be they feminist readings of Lacan or mathematical speculations about the properties of an eleven-dimensional universe, are understood by almost no one who actually funds the enterprise. In the industrialized world, universities have been responsible for so much basic technical research and development in the past hundred years, have employed so many people in every job description, and have contributed so much to the economic well-being of their immediate communities that they need make no apologies for having a bunch of fire-eating jugglers on staff. And third, I believe that it is, on balance, good to have administrators, trustees, and elected officials who care about universities' national rankings and/or international reputations if nothing else; surely it is better than the alternative — that is, powerful people who are determinedly parochial and who don't see why they really have to have a philosophy department just because serious universities do.

Perhaps the argument would seem less facetious if it involved performing arts somewhat more challenging and moving than juggling — arts such as jazz, gamelan, flamenco, juju, and odissi, all of which combine jaw-dropping technical virtuosity with extraordinary emotional range (and, yes, some element of "cooperation and teamwork" as well), and all of which can inspire in audiences various and powerful forms of aspiration and awe with regard to the varieties of human cultural expression. This is not to say that such forms of art lead us to forget Auschwitz or that they provide soothing balm to people who associate "humanity" more with opera than with weapons systems, but it is to suggest that there is, finally, something awry with the idea that such activities need to be justified with regard to their social or economic benefits to colleges or communities. As one moves further and further away from propositionality, into the realms in which art aspires to the condition of music and one cannot tell the dancer from the dance, it becomes increasingly difficult to specify the utility of, say, the complex quintuplets and stunning guitar playing of flamenco or the modal and melodic experiments in postwar jazz. Though the appreciation of such arts on their own terms always threatens to turn into the pseudoargument that they constitute their own justification, any attempt to "appreciate" such arts on the grounds that they enhance skills and competencies will always threaten to sound desperate and/or ridiculous.

The humanities, however, are another matter, largely because they rarely venture far from propositionality (the salient exceptions are the forms of experimental and avant-garde writing produced in the past 150 years) and because they are rather harder to defend in terms of affect and beauty (though this has not prevented legions of litterateurs from trying). For the humanities, I imagine the kind of defense and justification I offered in my 1997 review of David Denby's *Great Books*, in response to Denby's extravagant (and probably counterfactual) claim that "men and women educated in the Western tradition will have the best possible shot at the daunting task of reinventing morality and community in a republic now badly tattered by fear and mistrust" (461): "Why not," I asked,

> say simply that people who hope to think seriously about their place in
> [the] world have a positive obligation to verse themselves in the history of
> human thought and achievement, and that at this time, in this country,
> Plato-to-the-present courses in "Western thought" are as good a place as
> any (and better than most) to start? Perhaps this is not as effective a tactic
> as claiming that the course will prepare you to become one of Tomorrow's
> Leaders, but still, I'd like to propose that it's worth a shot anyway. (111)

I meant (and mean), of course, that it is entirely possible to argue that no one is fit to serve in public office or at the head of a major corporation who has not met our Western philosophy, modern language, and cultural diversity requirements, but that it is more than likely that such an argument will be heard, by actual politicians and CEOs, as one of those grandiose and delusional claims to which embattled humanists resort when they are told that their departments will shrink 10 percent over the next five years. "Ah, yes," they surely say in my own state capital, "we have planned some severe budget cuts for the humanities, so we might as well brace ourselves for a raft of letters about how poets are the unacknowledged legislators of Pennsylvania."

Moreover, it has become increasingly difficult to argue that the humanities are essential to wise and enlightened political leadership when all too many humanists cannot even agree on how to run a humanities department. It is both more modest and more plausible to argue that an informed, literate, and culturally competent citizenry is the very substance and condition of possibility for democracy. But even when we make this argument, and we need to make it at every opportunity, we haven't necessarily made a case for the humanities — since, after all, education in science and economics is also essential for an informed, literate, and culturally competent citizenry. So how then can we claim specifically that an education in the humanities might enhance one's capacity to understand the world — leaving aside, now and forever, the question of whether greater understanding necessarily brings with it greater wisdom, peace, suffering, or cynicism?

I can answer — and conclude — by way of returning to the sciences one final time. In his 1998 book, *Consilience*, famed naturalist E. O. Wilson argues that all human knowledge can and eventually will be unified under the rubric of the natural sciences; early on, he writes that "we have the common goal of turning as much philosophy as possible into science" (12) without specifying who "we" are who have this allegedly common goal. *Consilience* has already become something of a standard reference for humanists and cultural leftists who want to decry the pandisciplinary arrogance of scientists, so before I decry its pandisciplinary arrogance I should point out that Wilson and I have some common goals: both of us would like very much to see public policy with regard to the planet's natural resources carried out by informed, scientifically literate people, and both of us would like to see the liberal arts revivified so that universities require all their students to take courses in the sciences and the humanities. We are similarly impatient with departmental territorialism on campus and with backward, fundamentalist local school boards for whom evolutionary theory is the work of Satan: "[S]urely a loving personal God, if He is paying attention, will not abandon those who reject the literal interpretation of the biblical cosmology. It is only fair to award points for intellectual courage" (Wilson 6). Strong words, these, coming from a man raised on the Southern Baptist worldview.

But before very long our common ground ends, and Wilson's project of fostering consilience among all branches of learning begins to look as if it's missing something:

> Given that human action comprises events of physical causation, why should the social sciences and humanities be impervious to consilience with the natural sciences? And how can they fail to benefit from that alliance? It is not enough to say that human action is historical, and that history is an unfolding of unique events. Nothing fundamental separates the course of human history from the course of physical history, whether in the stars or in organic diversity. Astronomy, geology, and evolutionary biology are examples of primarily historical disciplines linked by consilience to the rest of the natural sciences. History is today a fundamental branch of learning in its own right, down to the finest detail. But if ten thousand humanoid histories could be traced on ten thousand Earthlike planets, and from a comparative study of those histories empirical tests and principles evolved, historiography — the explanation of historical trends — would already be a natural science. (11)

I focus on this passage because it purports to answer the precise objection I would raise — namely, that human action is historical. But I do not proceed from this premise to the argument that history is an unfolding of unique events; rather, I proceed from this premise to the hermeneutic conclusion that our history must always be interpreted anew with each passing year, with each passing generation. Wilson and I must be operating according to two very different senses of "history," one in which astronomy is a historical discipline (!) and one in which history is a human science and an interpretive discipline of very recent invention, dating either from the advent of the Holocene epoch ten thousand years ago or from the work of Gibbon and Hegel, whichever you prefer. Wilson's sense of "history," in other words, is quite deliberately antihermeneutic; indeed, to gauge by this passage, it can be quantified and subjected to "empirical tests" by a kind of *Star Trek* version of *Middlemarch*'s Dr. Casaubon, devoted to compiling a galactic guide to all humanoid historiographies.

And here's where the humanities suddenly seem to be indispensable: nothing in the natural sciences, despite Wilson's dreams of consilience, will tell us what the Glorious Revolution or the American Civil War or the rise of the caliphate or the fall of feudalism have *meant*. The sciences, particularly cognitive neuroscience, may indeed help to tell us how humans interpret signs; in this respect, it may be possible someday to imagine a conversation, if not consilience, between scientists and semioticians. But when it comes to grappling with the larger social process by which cultural meanings are established and challenged, the tenuous understanding of what a "meaning" *is*, our endless debates over specific attributions of meaning, over our methods of interpretation and our interpretations themselves, our struggles to grasp *how* things mean as well as *what* they mean — this is where the humanities are uniquely useful. I do not know what the "usefulness" of hermeneutics and semiotics will mean, for I cannot determine or predict the causes they will be asked to serve: I am proposing a form of utility in which "use" itself is indeterminate and indeterminable. But I cannot honestly do anything else. Common to all the enterprises of the humanities — whether we talk about textuality or about performance and whether we use "performance" in Judith Butler's sense or Madonna's or Martha Graham's — is the recognition that we are in the business of deciphering, of trying to construct and deconstruct meanings that make intelligible to us some aspects of this social world we sometimes think we know. It is a noble and undervalued business, to be sure, yet we do not do well to represent it as the work of unacknowledged legislators and voices crying in the wilderness. It is merely the business of interpretation, of understanding the meaning of meaning, and it is useful only to the extent that humans need to know the meaning of human affairs, past and present.

I don't want to be misunderstood here. I know full well that any decent astrophysicist asks herself *what it means* that the universe is clumpy rather than smooth, even though it appears not to contain enough matter to generate the gravitational forces that would create a clumpy universe. But that's not a question about "meaning" in the sense that I'm using the term. When I talk about "meaning" with regard to human affairs, I want to know, for example, whether the American Civil War was fought over slavery, or states' rights, or the economic conflict between an industrialized North and an agrarian South; and I want to know what its legacy *means* for theories of nationalism, for American identity, for the history of racial segregation, for the history of warfare, for the theory of democracy. And I know that if we understand human history in its historicity, there will be no final answers to any of the questions we might pose about the American Civil War or the fall of the caliphate or the Edict of Nantes or the emergence of homo/hetero classifications for sexuality or any other significant historical event or process; no final interpretations in literature, anthropology, dance, philosophy, or music; no answers that cannot be challenged and answered again from fresh social and historical perspectives. This is what we humanists do: we try to determine what it all means, in the broadest sense of "it" and "means," and just as important, *how* it all means. Every time you converse, every time you think about what the good and just life might consist of, every time you debate the "root causes" of the events of 11 September 2001, every time you try to understand the relation between disability and democracy or domesticity, and every time you wonder why certain films just seem to encapsulate their historical moment, you're putting hermeneutics and semiotics to use — the nuts and bolts of the humanities, useful tools whose uses cannot be specified.

Admittedly, there's a way of saying all this that simply skirts the theoretical debates and developments of the past fifty years emerging from structuralism and poststructuralism; it bypasses the question of undecidability in interpretation, as if deconstruction just never happened, and it seems to ignore the inconvenient fact that structuralism, as imagined by Lévi-Strauss, never wanted to be a theory of meaning at all. But I don't mean to suggest, as so many of my humanist colleagues have done in recent years, that we can justify the enterprises of the humanities only if we jettison this unseemly theory gunk and revive the old-school humanist rhetoric that never should have gone out of style in the first place. I *do* mean to suggest that we should adopt the long view on this — and by "long view" I mean the view of the past five thousand years or so, the view from which disputants like Immanuel Kant and David Hume, Paul Ricoeur and Claude Lévi-Strauss, or, closer to home, Jürgen Habermas and Jean-François Lyotard, can be seen to be working opposite sides of the same street. They may have what appear to be fundamentally opposed projects with regard to the means and ends of interpretation, but if you line them up against E. O. Wilson or your local superstring theorist, you'll see, I think, that even to oppose such figures and their intellectual traditions to each other entails interpretive questions that elude Wilson's reductionist utopia of consilience.

One final point. I've defined artists and humanists as practitioners and theorists of the fine arts of interpretation, and I've implied that the arts of interpretation enhance humans' capacities for critical self-reflection. I may even have suggested, with a few modest caveats, that individuals with enhanced capacities for critical and historical self-reflection might prove useful to emergent democracies or perhaps to democracies that are currently degenerating into plutocracies. All very well, or all very bad enough to begin with. But I have to admit that academic intellectuals are not the only people who are skilled in these fine arts. There are, on the contrary, thousands of professional interpreters, hermeneuts and semioticians, practitioners of cultural studies, employed in mass media. Some of them are our former students, gruntled or disgruntled; some of them are very smart general readers who've plucked a few dozen university-press monographs from the shelves for their background reading; some of them are arrant fools who couldn't interpret a Skinner box if B. F. Skinner himself were alive to help them do it. Mass media, like academe, offers a mixed bag of semioticians and hermeneuts, some quite brilliant, some altogether edifying, some barely literate, all with variously useful talents and competencies and interpersonal skills of cooperation and communication. Accordingly, then, I will close by suggesting that it's precisely by thinking of education in the humanities as a competitor with and potential stimulus for forms of criticism practiced in mass media that we can get the clearest focus on how the disciplines and intellectual traditions of the humanities can realize their potential social utility — and how humanists can get the clearest focus on how our sense of "meaning" means in the world.

Notes

1. This is not actually true. On the contrary, I'm happy to report, my conversations with physicists have generally been lively and wonderfully informative. I want especially to thank Michael Weissman of the Department of Physics at the University of Illinois at Urbana-Champaign, who was always a gracious and stimulating interlocutor, and Sean Carroll, currently of the Enrico Fermi Institute and the Kavli Institute for Cosmological Physics at the University of Chicago, who reviewed my accounts of twentieth-century physics in this section and made a number of very helpful suggestions. I should also thank Alan Sokal, who not only replied generously to my e-mail queries about his hoax in June 1996 but who then followed up the conversation — at considerable length — in the spring of 1999 after my review of *Fashionable Nonsense* was published.

Works Cited

Banks, Joanne Trautmann. "Life as a Literary Laboratory." *Literature and Medicine* 21, no. 1 (2002): 98 – 105.

Bennett, Tony. "Being 'In the True' of Cultural Studies." *Southern Review* 26, no. 2 (1993): 217 – 38.

Bérubé, Michael. "Great Books and Good Intentions." *Dissent*, Spring 1997, 107 – 12.

Denby, David. *Great Books: My Adventures with Homer, Rousseau, Woolf, and Other Indestructible Writers of the Western World*. New York: Simon and Schuster, 1996.

Gawain and the Green Knight. Edited and introduction by A. C. Cawley and J. J. Anderson. London: Dent, 1962.

Greene, Brian. *The Elegant Universe: Superstrings, Hidden Dimensions, and the Quest for the Ultimate Theory*. New York: Norton, 1999.

Pickering, Andrew. *Constructing Quarks: A Sociological History of Particle Physics*. Edinburgh: Edinburgh University Press, 1984.

Ross, Andrew. *The Chicago Gangster Theory of Life: Nature's Debt to Society*. London: Verso, 1995.

————. *Strange Weather: Culture, Science, and Technology in the Age of Limits.* London: Verso, 1991.

Sokal, Alan. "A Physicist Experiments with Cultural Studies." Reprinted in *The Sokal Hoax: The Sham That Shook the Academy*, edited by the editors of *Lingua Franca*, 49 – 53. Lincoln: University of Nebraska Press, 2000.

Wilson, E. O. *Consilience: The Unity of Knowledge.* New York: Vintage, 1999.

Yúdice, George. "The Privatization of Culture." *Social Text* 17, no. 2 (1999): 17 – 34.

Part Two

POSITIONS

If you were to read the first essay in this section, "There Is Nothing inside the Text," from back to front, its connection to the Sokal essays in the preceding section would be obvious. But I don't actually recommend that anyone read the essay back to front, so I'll spell out the link in so many words. The essay revisits a debate far removed from the one initiated by Sokal: the Stanley Fish/Wolfgang Iser exchange in *diacritics*, conducted more than a quarter of a century ago. That exchange, I argue, had profound and not entirely beneficial consequences for the direction of literary theory in the 1980s and 1990s. What's more, I find in Fish's decisive rebuttal of Iser the seeds of a pseudo-Kuhnian argument that would prove troublesome for Fish once it left the domain of the humanities and was deployed in the public sphere as an attempt to dismiss what Fish called, in his *New York Times* op-ed, "Professor Sokal's Bad Joke."

In the course of his 1981 reply to Iser (which decisively exposed the incoherence of Iser's theory of "gaps"), Fish made the dubious argument that "the only thing you can't say is that there is distinction, at least insofar as it is an *absolute* distinction, between a world that 'lives and functions independently' of interpretive activity and a world that is produced by interpretive activity" (12). At the time, Fish was responding to Iser's befuddled and befuddling argument that the "words of the text" are, in his scheme of interpretation, analogous to the "real world" in that they have the status of the "given" (whereas, as I point out, most readers would assume instead that the words of texts are themselves interpretations or representations of the world). But if you go around casting doubt on the distinction between a world independent of interpretive activity and a world produced by interpretive activity (even if you try to give yourself some wiggle room by disavowing an "absolute" distinction), you may just wind up in the pages of the *New York Times* fifteen years later, insisting that the laws of physics can be understood in terms of the rules of baseball. Fish's rhetorical strategy served him reasonably well in the pages of *diacritics*, where Iser was weighed in the scales and found wanting, but Fish's blurring of the distinction between observer-dependent and observer-independent reality in response to the Sokal Hoax, I believe, played right into the hands of Sokal — and into the hands of philosophers like Sam Harris, who, as I've argued in part I, blur the distinction precisely to construe observer-independent reality as the basis for "ethical realism" with regard to observer-dependent realities.

I originally wrote "There Is Nothing inside the Text" for a collection devoted to Fish's work, a collection I saw as an occasion to take issue not merely with one or another of Fish's recent positions on professionalism, pragmatism, or politics in academe but with a tendency in his thought that spans at least two phases in his career. The following essays address subjects that have nothing to do with Fish's career, but they were written for similar reasons: to invite critical responses from their imaginary interlocutors (Martha Nussbaum, Frances Stonor Saunders, George Lipsitz, and Thomas Frank, in order) and to provoke the readers of the journals in which these essays first appeared. In other words, I chose both subject and venue for maximum frisson, but not with the aim of provoking people for the sake of the provocation alone. Rather, I tried to publish each essay in a venue some of whose readership could reasonably be expected to be skeptical of or hostile to my line of thought. "Citizens of the World, Unite!," for example, originally appeared in *Lingua Franca*; I might conceivably have had the chance to write a denser, more academic review in a scholarly journal, but *Lingua Franca* gave me the opportunity to write more than five thousand words in a forum in which I could expect that a good number of my readers would balk at any defense either of Nussbaum or of the postmodernism she dismisses. I figured I just couldn't miss.

Likewise, my essay on American studies and its relation to the state appeared in a special 2003 *PMLA* issue devoted to international American studies — just the right place and time, I thought, for an essay that challenges the New Left critique of American studies during the Cold War and calls for American studies scholars to reverse field, so to speak, and "think more dialectically and less aversively about their relation to the state." I know perfectly well, of course, why scholars in American studies have worked so assiduously in recent years to internationalize the field: not only to combat the field's long and sorry history of American exceptionalism (and even American apologism, though this aspect of American studies is perhaps overstated by people who discount the liberal and socialist traditions of earlier generations of American studies scholars) but also to offer more capacious, more adequate accounts of an "America" whose national boundaries cannot contain the hemispheric and global flows that have constituted the American subject for the past five hundred years. Nonetheless, somebody has to step up and say that forms of American studies that take the state as their object of analysis are not necessarily in thrall to Patrick Buchanan's Fortress America, and I thought that somebody might as well be me — in a special issue on international American studies, no less.

Finally, my review essay on Thomas Frank's *One Market under God* was written in 2000 as an attempt to bury a hatchet and take up a cudgel. The review was commissioned for the inaugural issue of the *Common Review*, the quarterly journal of the Great Books Foundation. As with *Lingua Franca*, I believed that the *Common Review* would provide me with access to general readers, many of whom would have to be persuaded simply that my essay would be worth reading. The *Common Review*'s editor, Daniel Born, has this much in common with Alex Star, *Lingua Franca*'s former editor: both are smart, widely read, and keen-eyed fellows who have no patience with certain forms of academic defensiveness or special pleading. Even better, for my purposes, the Great Books Foundation was (of course) located in Chicago, the home of Frank's journal, the *Baffler*, which had published a baffling attack on me and sundry other professors and graduate students who wrote essays in support of the Yale graduate student grade strike of 1995 – 96 (see Lehmann). I saw this review essay as a chance to open hailing frequencies both with the readers of this new journal and with the Chicago intellectual left — the latter of which did, in fact, respond in kind in a subsequent issue of *In These Times*, graciously crediting me with trying to "to bury the hatchet on the left's longstanding internecine feud over the excesses of pomo cultural studies" and politely passing over the fact that my essay had gently suggested that Frank was unaware of most of the history of cultural studies (see Knowles).

Again, I didn't write these essays simply to provoke or to be a pain in the ass to as many people in as many places as possible. I actually had more substantial goals in mind: the essay on Fish and Iser represents my attempt to account for the strange disappearance of reader-response criticism in the 1980s and to narrate a small but important slice of the recent intellectual history of literary theory; the essay on Nussbaum takes up the question of how the humanities can foster a critical cosmopolitanism, while the essay on American studies serves as a reminder of how the humanities can be deployed (for good and ill) by the machinery of the state; and the essay on *One Market under God* responds to Frank's challenge to disarticulate cultural studies from the excesses of the "active audience" and "consumption as empowerment" branches of the field, which by the late 1990s had come to sound indistinguishable from technolibertarian celebrations of the so-called New Economy. These are, then, four very different essays on humans and the humanities, and I hope their republication here will engage a readership I do not yet know in ways I cannot yet imagine.

Works Cited

Fish, Stanley. "Professor Sokal's Bad Joke." *New York Times*, 21 May 1996, A26.

Knowles, Joe. "A Little Help for Our Friends." *In These Times*, 26 November 2001. Available online at <http://www.inthesetimes.com/site/main/article/a_little _help_for_our_friends/>. Accessed 2 December 2005.

Lehmann, Chris. "Popular Front Redux?" *Baffler* 9 (1997): 19–29.

There Is Nothing inside the Text; or, Why No One's Heard of Wolfgang Iser

In 1980, reader-response criticism was considered a major school of contemporary literary criticism. Two important collections were published that year — Susan Suleiman and Inge Crosman's *The Reader in the Text: Essays on Audience and Interpretation*, which consisted of essays commissioned specifically for the volume and which suggested strong connections between reader-response criticism and French narratology, and Jane Tompkins's *Reader-Response Criticism: From Formalism to Post-Structuralism*, which consisted of previously published work and which explicitly set out to construct a developmental narrative of recent reader-response work (moving from Michael Riffaterre and Georges Poulet through Gerald Prince and Norman Holland and David Bleich and Jonathan Culler, Stanley Fish threading his way through the volume early and late), the conclusion of which was Tompkins's magisterial history of theories of affect and literary response since Plato. Fish, of course, published the landmark *Is There a Text in This Class?* in the same year. But 1980 was no stand-alone *annus mirabilis*; the momentum behind reader-response had been building for more than a decade — indeed, arguably since Fish's *Surprised by Sin* (1967). Both in *Structuralist Poetics* (1975) and *On Deconstruction* (1982), theories of reading were integral to Jonathan Culler's account of contemporary theory. Wolfgang Iser's work was everywhere throughout the 1970s, and *Critical Inquiry* staged debate after debate on the determinacy of meaning. It seemed to some observers at the time as if reader-response had engaged if not assimilated every other major form of criticism, from narratology to structuralism to psychoanalysis to feminism, and was now poised to take on deconstruction and Marxism on matters concerning *différance* and determination.

By 1990, however, any informed observer of the academic scene would have to have wondered where in the world reader-response criticism had gone. Yes, Steven Mailloux had done notable work in the decade, with *Interpretive Conventions: The Reader in the Study of American Fiction* (1982), an explicitly

Cullerian book, and *Rhetorical Power* (1989), a book seasoned by a few more rounds of *Critical Inquiry* debates; Peter Rabinowitz's *Before Reading: Narrative Conventions and the Politics of Interpretation* (1987) and Jon Klancher's *The Making of English Reading Audiences* (1987) had made valuable efforts to negotiate reader-response and reception theory; and Janice Radway's *Reading the Romance: Women, Patriarchy, and Popular Literature* (1984) had set a new standard for feminist readings of women's readings of popular cultural forms. But by 1990, reader-response had fallen off the Major Theoretical Positions chart, obliterated by new schools associated with figures such as Stephen Greenblatt, Catherine Gallagher, Nancy Armstrong, Eve Sedgwick, and Judith Butler; postcolonial theory had achieved critical mass; and Radway, for her part, had become associated more closely with the Birmingham school of cultural studies than with theories of reader-response, even though, as she notes in the introduction to her 1991 edition of *Reading the Romance*, this would have come to a surprise to her when she was an assistant professor in University's of Pennsylvania's American Civilization Department in the late 1970s: "I was wholly unaware of this body of work when I was writing, but it now dominates the context within which *Reading the Romance* is read" (2). (Nor was she alone: "Apparently, no one in my department knew at that time of the work carried out at the Birmingham Centre" [242].) As for Wolfgang Iser, poor Iser had disappeared so completely that some worried theorists of reading wondered if he would ever be seen again save on milk cartons.

To some extent, reader-response criticism expired of its own success, particularly those branches of it that involved hypotheses of what it might mean to read "like" or "as" a woman; at some point in the past three decades, clearly, the women of the profession stopped hypothesizing about what their readings might be like and simply set about doing them. And to some extent, the "success" of reader-response criticism should be measured not on the Major Theoretical Positions chart but by reference to the practical and pedagogical influence it has had throughout the wider K – 16 system, in precincts where Louise Rosenblatt is a justly renowned figure and where professors in composition and writing studies have been talking about "transactional" reading processes regardless of whether the police ever find that Iser fellow. But the fact remains nonetheless that in the annals of critical theory, reader-response criticism was once a major player, a contender, and now it is not. And one of the reasons it is not, I will argue, is that one of its most important American exponents, Stanley Fish, killed it the day he published his *diacritics* review of Wolfgang Iser's 1978 book, *The Act of Reading: A Theory of Aesthetic Response*, under the title, "Why No One's Afraid of Wolfgang Iser."

I do not mean this literally, of course. But in retrospect, I think it is hard to overstate the importance of this review, to the trajectory of Iser's career and, to a lesser extent, of Fish's. Indeed, Fish opens the review by remarking on Iser's exceptional status in the profession. For readers who do not remember a time when Iser was considered a leading figure in literary theory, Fish's initial assessment might sound a bit odd, even hyperbolic:

> *The Implied Reader* and *The Act of Reading* outsell all other books on the prestigious list of the Johns Hopkins Press with the exception of *Grammatology* [*sic*] (a book that is, I suspect, more purchased than read). Iser is, in short, a phenomenon: he is influential without being controversial, and at a moment when everyone is choosing up sides, he seems to be on no side at all or (it amounts to the same thing) on every side at once. (2)

Fish comes not to praise but to bury, of course, and before I explain the details of Iser's interment, I should note that even the circumstances of Fish's review deserve comment. "Why No One's Afraid of Wolfgang Iser" appeared as the lead essay in the March 1981 issue of *diacritics*, but the journal had already published Rudolf Kuenzli's review of *The Act of Reading* in June 1980. Kuenzli's review was highly laudatory, closing with no uncertain praise of Iser's project:

> The unquestionable merit of *The Act of Reading* consists precisely in its making us aware of our own reading process. In focusing our attention on our own act of producing the meaning of a text we will become more aware of the textual strategies, of our own dynamic relations to those strategies, and thus of the importance of analyzing the reading process for the study of literature and literary theory. Iser's working model of the interaction between the reader and norm-breaking literature presents us with a compelling outline of the intersubjective structure of such a reading process — an outline to which we can appeal for contextual support as we pursue the analysis of our own reading experiences. (56)

Historians of recent literary theory will be able to place this praise squarely in the context of the debates of the 1970s, in which theorists such as Culler and Iser forwarded both of the claims Kuenzli presses here: reader-response criticism makes us more self-aware about the processes by which readers (including ourselves) construct patterns of meaning, and it serves especially well as means of reading the avant-garde or experimental ("norm-breaking") narrative works of the past 150 years, since these require readers to engage in explicitly self-reflexive deliberation about textual patterns of meaning.

Fish, however, will have none of it. The June 1980 issue of *diacritics* was supposed to follow Kuenzli's review with an extended (twenty-seven-page) interview with Iser, conducted by Kuenzli, Norman Holland, Wayne Booth, and Stanley Fish. But Fish pulled out of the interview, as Kuenzli notes in his introduction: "Stanley Fish, who had complied with my original request for concise, pointed questions, was dissatisfied with the form that the interview — with the extended questions elaborated by Holland and Booth — had taken; he indicated that he would prefer to withdraw" (57). The result was *diacritics'* second full-dress review essay on *The Act of Reading* within two years, a review essay that refused all the assumptions common to Kuenzli, Holland, Booth, and Iser — and that, in retrospect, helped to change the direction of Anglo-American literary theory. After the Fish-Iser exchange, it became possible for professional literary critics to operate as if there were nothing inside the text and as if this were a good thing, too.

Fish spends the first four pages of his review faithfully summarizing Iser's work to date, and then comes the devastating pivot paragraph:

> And yet, in the end [Iser's theory] falls apart, and it falls apart because the distinction on which it finally depends — the distinction between the determinate and the indeterminate — will not hold. The distinction is crucial because it provides both the stability and the flexibility of Iser's formulations. Without it he would not be able to say that the reader's activities are constrained by something they do not produce; he would not be able at once to honor and to bypass history by stabilizing the set of directions the text contains; he would not be able to define the aesthetic object in opposition to the world of fact, but tie its production securely to that world; he would have no basis (independent of interpretation) for the thesis that since the end of the eighteenth century literature has been characterized by more and more gaps; he would not be able to free the text from the constraints of referential meaning and yet say that the meanings produced by innumerable readers are part of its potential. (6)

Fish is right to argue that Iser's work depends on the distinction between determinacy and indeterminacy, and he's right — though I will qualify this point later in this essay — to argue that the distinction will not hold. The problem with Iser's account of reading, in other words, is that it presumes that some features of texts exist prior to or beyond any scheme of interpretation, while other features are variable and therefore susceptible to interpretation. "Iser insists on the brute-fact status of the text," writes Fish, "at least insofar as it provides directions for the assembling of the 'virtual object.' Thus he declares in one place, 'the stars in a literary text are fixed; the lines that join them are variable'" (6). Readers are thereby assigned the tasks of filling in the "gaps" between the fixed points, and Iser accommodates or licenses a certain degree of critical pluralism by acknowledging that different readers will fill those gaps in different ways. But what counts as a "gap" worth filling? Iser's work answers this question by examining textual phenomena as disparate as "stylistic patterns" in *Ulysses* and "the nondescription of Lady Booby's surprise" in *Joseph Andrews* (*Implied* 224, 38). A theory of "gaps" that can include everything from the presentation of moral hypocrisy in *Tom Jones* (which the reader must perceive by filling the "gaps" in Squire Allworthy's perception of Captain Blifil) to the paradoxes of "unmasked fiction" in Beckett's *The Unnamable* (in which the reader is led to realize that "the usefulness of fiction cannot be dispensed with" [268]) to the facial expressions of individual characters is a remarkably amorphous theory, so much so that one is led to suspect that when it comes to texts, everything's a gap, and when it comes to gaps, *pace* Iser's attempt to provide a firm foundation for distinguishing literary from nonliterary texts, there are finally no important distinctions between fiction and nonfiction.

Fish makes this point as well, not by questioning the embarrassing shapelessness of Iser's examples but by forwarding a condensed version of the argument he'd advanced in the final four chapters of *Is There a Text in This Class?* Hypothesizing a reader of *Tom Jones* for whom "perfection in humankind" is not "incompatible with being taken in by a hypocrite" and who therefore sees "no disparity between the original description of Allworthy and his subsequent behavior," Fish drives home the point that the perception of "gaps" in a text depends on what Kuhn called the priority of paradigms:

> [I]f the "textual signs" do not announce their shape but appear in a variety of shapes according to the differing expectations and assumptions of different readers, and if gaps are not built into the text, but appear (or do not appear) as a consequence of particular interpretive strategies, then there is no distinction between what the text gives and what the reader supplies; he supplies *everything*; the stars in a literary text are not fixed; they are just as variable as the lines that join them. (7)

For Fish, what follows from the possibility that "gaps" are everywhere is the conclusion that "gaps" are only where you — that is, where your interpretive assumptions — find them. But (and by 1981 Fish had already practiced and perfected this closing gymnastic sequence) this does not mean that textual interpretation is a chaotic and hopelessly subjective enterprise; on the contrary, "there is no subjectivist element of reading, because the observer is never individual in the sense of unique or private, but is always the product of the categories of understanding that are his by virtue of his membership in a community of interpretation" (11).

Iser, for his part, did not help his cause by severely misconstruing Fish's challenge to his position. Iser apparently believed that Fish did not grasp the determinate meaning of his (Iser's) definition of determinate meaning, and so, in his September 1981 *diacritics* reply to Fish's review essay, Iser patiently explained that

> Professor Fish's confusion is caused by the fact that he has telescoped three ideas into two. I draw a distinction between the given, the determinate, and the indeterminate. I maintain that the literary world differs from the real world because it is only accessible to the imagination, whereas the real world is also accessible to the senses and exists outside any description of it. The words of a text are given, the interpretation of the words is determinate, and the gaps between given elements and/or our interpretations are the indeterminacies. The real world is given, our interpretation of the world is determinate, the gaps between the given elements and/or our interpretations are the indeterminacies. ("Talk" 83)

This is a string of terrible, terrible arguments. As if it were not bad enough that Iser insists on *two* kinds of determinacies, the given and the determinate, Iser further insists that interpretation is determinate (where one might have thought, in the most naively realist terms, that the text was determinate and the interpretations were variable) *and* that the "the words of the text" have the same ontological status as "the real world" — namely, that of the "given," the brute-fact raw material for interpretation (where one might have thought, in the most naively realist terms, that the words of texts were themselves interpretations of a real world). It is not a pretty moment for Iser, who had opened his reply by praising Fish's précis of Iser's work but condemning Fish's critique, clearly failing to see that Fish's précis was every bit as damning as the critique. Let it not be said that Stanley Fish booted Iser off the top of the Johns Hopkins Press best-seller list all by himself.

Still, Fish's readers — and I imagine that many of the readers of this essay are likely to belong to a loosely knit interpretive community designated by the term "Fish's readers" — are no doubt familiar with all these aspects of Fish's modus operandi. The denial of determinate meaning, the insistence on the ubiquity of interpretation, and the antivoluntarist, strong-constructionist account of "communities" that constrain any individual's activity of interpretation: these are features of nearly everything Fish has written after "Interpreting the Variorum," the 1976 essay in which Fish announced his turn to the fully Kuhnian position that every ostensibly obvious "feature" of texts is actually produced by interpretation (the turn comes, appropriately, in the subsection of the essay titled "Undoing the Case for Reader-Response Analysis"). I am aware, by the way, that I have used the word "feature" twice in the previous sentence, the first time to suggest brute-fact attributes of Fish's texts that are familiar to the loosely knit interpretive community designated by the term "Fish's readers," the second time (in "quotation marks") to suggest that the first usage is, in Fish's terms, problematic. I do so to suggest another path down the antiformalist road, the road not taken by Iser's reply. For the way to debate Fish on textual "features," it seems to me, is not to claim that some aspects of texts precede interpretation and others are produced by interpretation; rather, the counterargument should be that Fish uses "interpretation" in two different senses, just as Kuhn used "paradigm" (as Kuhn admitted, distinguishing between "the entire constellation of beliefs, values, techniques, and so on shared by the members of a given community" and "the concrete puzzle-solutions which, employed as models or examples, can replace explicit rules as a basis for the solution of the remaining puzzles of normal science" [1970, 175]), with appropriately obfuscatory effects. Yes, every feature of a text is interpretive and indeterminate — not just with regard to what Molly's final "Yes" means but even with regard to apparently neutral or submeaningful items such as line endings, chapter headings, and book titles. But as any practicing member of any interpretive community knows, some interpretations are so widely agreed upon as to be indistinguishable from brute facts: "facts," on this reading, are simply interpretations that have won nearly unanimous consensus. Interpretations that designate certain textual features as "characters," "line breaks," "dangling modifiers," and even "scare quotes" are therefore qualitatively and pragmatically quite different from elaborate literary-critical interpretations that see *Paradise Lost* as a poem whose object is "to bring [the reader] to the realization that his inability to read the poem with any confidence in his own perception is its focus" (Fish, *Is There* 21) or that render the Trueblood episode as an exemplum of the relation between commerce and the performance of blackness in *Invisible Man* (see Baker). To put this another way, I know of no reader who is willing to dispute that the title of *Is There a Text in This Class?* is *Is There a Text in This Class?*, but I know of many readers who are willing to dispute Fish's claim that he has repudiated the sentence (in "Interpreting 'Interpreting the *Variorum*'" [1978]) in which he had claimed that his form of criticism "relieves me of the obligation to be right (a standard that simply drops out) and demands only that I be interesting (a standard that can be met without any reference at all to an illusory objectivity)" (180). Such readers are perfectly willing to grant that the line breaks in *Paradise Lost* or *Lycidas* or *Il Penseroso* are where Fish says they are, but they persist in reading Fish's ostensibly "repudiated" sentence as a useful gloss on his career since publishing *Is There a Text in This Class?*

It would have been possible, in other words, to contest Fish's reading of Iser not by stubbornly insisting on the determinacy of the determinate and not, good lord, by insisting on two separate varieties of determinacy and assigning "interpretation" to one of them, but by acknowledging that all forms of reading are interpretive but that some involve the kind of low-level, relatively uncontestable cognitive acts we engage in whenever we interpret the letter "e" as the letter "e" and that some involve the kind of high-level, exceptionally specific and complex textual manipulations, transformations and reconfigurations involved whenever someone publishes something like *S/Z* — or *Surprised by Sin*. (And, of course, that there are any number of "interpretations" that fall between these extremes and that the status of each of them is — what else? — open to and dependent on interpretation.) But the Fish-Iser exchange did not take this form, and no plausible "interpretation" of it can claim that it did. As a result, Fish's interpretive modus operandi is as familiar to us as it is: interpretation is the only game in town, yadda yadda, but there is no such thing as interpretive self-consciousness, yadda yadda, and what's more, interpretive theory has no consequences, yadda yadda yadda. The very familiarity of Fish's antiformalism, and of Fish's deliberately counterintuitive declarations thereof, makes my point: because the Fish-Iser exchange took the form it did, we (and by "we" I mean the even more loosely knit interpretive community designated by the term "Fish's readers and everyone who knows anything about Fish's readers") have long regarded these questions as definitively settled. Interpretive communities determine what's determinate and what's not, so the focus of critical theory clearly should be on the workings of those interpretive communities and not on "texts themselves"; there is no such thing as the "text itself," anyway, and even if there were, there would be nothing inside the text.

I concentrate on Fish's *diacritics* exchange with Iser, then, because I see it as the moment after which Fish largely stopped concerning himself with people who made claims about the grainy details of literary texts. After this point, Fish devoted himself increasingly to the critical metaproblems produced by his work, as in the essay "Change," which opens by asserting — or simply recognizing — that interpretive communities are now the only game in town:

> The notion of "interpretive communities" was originally introduced as an answer to a question that had long seemed crucial to literary studies. What is the source of interpretive authority: the text or the reader? Those who answered "the text" were embarrassed by the fact of disagreement. Why, if the text contains its own meaning and constrains its own interpretation, do so many interpreters disagree about that meaning? Those

who answered "the reader" were embarrassed by the fact of agreement. Why, if meaning is created by the individual reader from the perspective of his own experience and interpretive desires, is there so much that interpreters agree about? What was required was an explanation that could account for both agreement and disagreement and that explanation was found in the idea of an interpretive community. (*Doing* 141)

Very well, then, now that *that's* settled, we can move on to the question of how these seemingly monadic interpretive communities manage to change, and once we've asked that question, we can move briskly to Fish's answer — namely, that an interpretive community is in fact "an engine of change" (146). But these engines are more complicated than they seem, for "to put the matter in what only seems to be a paradox, when a community is provoked to change by something outside it, that something will already have been inside" (147); thus, "no theory can compel a change that has not in some sense already occurred" (154). On, then, to the meta-metaproposition that "the question of change is therefore one that cannot be posed independently of some such self-description which gives a shape to the very facts and events to which the question is put" (158). Q.E.D. Onward, then, to law and legal theory.

Perhaps Fish's career always contained the seeds of its own change, or perhaps he was induced to change by antagonists, influences, and interlocutors whose outsideness to him was always already inside. But I feel safe in suggesting that there was, at some point in the 1970s, a significant change between the *enfant terrible* Fish, who published jaw-droppingly brilliant and original close readings of brilliant writers (from Milton to Donne to Pater) who had been closely read by generations of the most brilliant readers in the English-speaking world, and the *agent provocateur* Fish, who abandoned dense analyses of the temporal element in reading in favor of high-flying, high-stakes rhetorical performances in legal theory and campus politics, undertaken solo or in tandem with Ronald Dworkin, Roberto Unger, or Dinesh D'Souza. The Later Fish is not a theorist of the reading process; the Later Fish is a purveyor of provocative paradoxes (or of propositions that only seem to be paradoxes), a Fish who would have you believe — or not, it really doesn't matter — that "anti-professionalism is professionalism itself in its purest form" (*Doing* 245) and that there's no such thing as free speech and it's a good thing, too.

I do not want to ask whether the arguments of the Later Fish are right or wrong. Rather, in pragmatist fashion, I want to ask what they have done and whether they are good in the way of belief. The turn from texts to "interpretive communities" has had some salutary effects on the study of literature, insofar as this turn has licensed greater inquiry into the sociology of literary reception and the actual mechanics of literary production and transmission. On theoretical grounds, the term "interpretive communities" has been beset by problems at every point in its existence; these have largely been the same problems attendant on the term "paradigm," problems that have to do with the homogeneity, multiplicity, permeability, and self-reflexivity of the "communities" and "paradigms" to which the theory appeals. All the same, when critical work has been done on specific interpretive communities and their operations, the results have produced interesting cross-pollinations between the sociology of literature and the kinds of "ethnographic" media analysis undertaken in cultural studies. Janice Radway's work with the romance readers of Smithton and the editors of the Book-of-the-Month Club is perhaps the best example of the genre. Likewise, when applied to the profession of literary study, the notion of interpretive communities helped to generate greater professional self-scrutiny and perhaps paved the way for the high traffic, throughout the late 1980s and 1990s, in essays and books on the practices of English departments and other institutions of literature. And the canon debates, I imagine, would have been greatly impoverished if not for the theoretical platforms constructed by Fish and by Barbara Herrnstein Smith in *Contingencies of Value*.

Conversely, something was lost in all this talk about interpretive communities and institutions of literature, and by the early to mid-1990s Stanley Fish himself had begun to sense what it was. Lamenting the political and interdisciplinary ambitions of contemporary literary study, Fish reversed field in *Professional Correctness* (claiming in the preface, of course, that he was doing no such thing [x]) and argued that literary study could survive only if it were distinct from other disciplines:

> A conventional activity is one whose possibility and intelligibility depend on a specialized and artificial vocabulary which is generative of the phenomena it picks out, in this case the range of verbal nuances that emerge when one takes up the tools of close reading, semiotics, and poetics. If that vocabulary falls into disuse, the facts it calls into being will no longer be produced or experienced. If no one any longer asks "What is the structure of this poem?" or "What is the intention of the author and has it been realized?" or "In what tradition does the poet enrol himself and with what consequences for that tradition?," something will have passed from the earth and we shall read the words of what was once literary criticism as if they were the remnants of a lost language spoken by alien beings. (70)

To be sure, Fish remains a nominalist; vocabularies create facts and thereby produce experiences. But look at the vocabulary this nominalist wants to preserve: a vocabulary of very basic, introductory-level formalist, genre- and author-based literary criticism. "What is the intention of the author and has it been realized?" indeed. This is the language that Fish fears will become as unintelligible as the postcard from the volcano? Regardless of whether Fish has here decided that in nearly three decades of fighting theory battles with the likes of M. H. Abrams and E. D. Hirsch, he has all along been of the devil's party without knowing it (and remember, for Miltonists, unlike Blakeans, this cannot be a good thing), it is worth pointing out that in the fifteen years between *Is There a Text in This Class?* and *Professional Correctness*, Fish had rarely spoken of the structure of the poem, the intentions of the author, or the traditions in which poets might enroll themselves. If the vocabulary of poetics, semiotics, intentionality, and genre truly is in danger of passing from the earth, Later Fish was partly responsible for hastening its extinction. By contrast, for Wolfgang Iser, that old codger, questions of structure, intention, genre, and poetics were integral to the reading process, to the "intersubjective" enterprise involved in deriving meaning from literary works. But so far as I know, when Fish delivered the 1993 Clarendon Lectures at Oxford, the lectures that became *Professional Correctness*, Iser was not in the audience, and could not ask whether Fish had any regrets about devoting so much more time to elaborating and defending the theory of interpretive communities than to asking "specialized" questions about literary texts.

The most regrettable development of the Fish-Iser exchange, however, has nothing to do with Iser or with the grainy details of literary texts. Rather, it has to do with science. We have already seen that Iser disastrously aligned the "words of a text" with the "real world" as "given." Fish's reply on that score, however, is disastrous in its own way: "The only thing you can't say," he writes, "is that there is distinction, at least insofar as it is an *absolute* distinction, between a world that 'lives and functions independently' of interpretive activity and a world that is produced by interpretive activity" (12). This may sound just fine when you're adjudicating between different interpretations of *Tom Jones*, but it is seriously inadequate when it comes to distinguishing interpretations of *Tom Jones* from the movements of particles in the solar wind. The qualifying caveat about the "absolute" distinction, I propose, is a red herring: this passage really does say that you can't draw a line between brute fact and social fact. It does not make the more modest and defensible claim that distinctions between brute fact and social fact are drawn by social fact, particularly by those "interpretive communities" whose job it is to try to understand the physical phenomena of the universe *precisely* as phenomena that live and function independently of interpretive activity. It does not admit that most responsible theorists who try to devise distinctions between brute fact and social fact rely on blurry distinctions rather than "absolute" ones, as does John Searle when he passes on the question of whether colors "really" exist in nature. And it gives short shrift to the forms of interpretive activity that have so far managed to establish (and make available for further interpretation) those features of our world that do "live and function" independently of the forms of interpretive activity that have disclosed them. Most astrophysicists do not speak of how the cosmic microwave background radiation "lives" or "functions," but all agree that it exists — and that it existed well before and will exist well after the interpretive activity undertaken by the small handful of conscious beings who have been debating the size, age, properties, and fate of the universe since our detection of the radiation in 1963.

For all the problems with the word "paradigm," Kuhn offered an account of how ordinary science produces anomalies that challenge paradigms, and Fish has not; moreover, in the terms he has offered so far, Fish cannot. In the ordinary course of literary study, perhaps, this would not matter, since no one worth attending to believes that literary texts, like rocks and stars, precede interpretive activity. (The day Fish chased the last lingering textual positivists out of the debate club was a good day.) But when Fish tried to defuse the scandal that grew out of the Sokal Hoax in May 1996, it did matter; it mattered most obviously the day Fish published a *New York Times* op-ed reply to Sokal ("Professor Sokal's Bad Joke") that relied in part on a comparison of the laws of baseball (which clearly do not exist apart from interpretive activity) with the laws of physics (which so clearly do exist apart from interpretive activity that it is a mild anthropomorphism even to call them "laws"). That this argumentative strategy was a mistake is a truth almost universally acknowledged, or at least acknowledged by sufficient numbers of Fish's admirers (including myself) as to make it "true" in a pragmatist sense. To many observers, Fish's reply had the regrettable effect of confirming Sokal's complaint that humanists tend to regard the natural world — not our understanding of the natural world, but the thing itself, with all its carbon and hydrogen and magnetic fields and strong and weak forces — as a "social construction." But it has less often been acknowledged that in denying our capacity to make "any distinction" (or, perhaps, any "absolute" distinction) between the worlds of brute fact and social fact, Fish was, back in 1981 when Alan Sokal was known only to his family and friends, countering one of Iser's worst arguments with one of his own worst arguments.

Just as Iser botched the question of determinacy and indeterminacy, arguing that interpretations were determinate where he should have pointed out the differences between the low-level "interpretation" by which we perceive the letter "e" and the high-level "interpretation" by which we produce the book *S/Z*, so too did he botch the question of how interpretations can attempt to distinguish between social fact and brute fact. The most expeditious way of addressing this point, I suggest, is to argue that interpretations are indeterminate *but* that all interpretations produce "objects." The objects themselves depend, just as Fish (and Kuhn and Rorty) would have it, on the workings of the interpretive communities that produce them. The interpretive communities that are known by the terms "low-temperature physicists" or "oral surgeons" operate by different protocols of knowledge production than do the interpretive communities known as "readers of Stanley Fish who specialize in law or literature," and the different protocols of different communities exist in part to produce different kinds of objects. Some of those objects may go by the name "solar wind," some of them may be theories about the solar wind, some of them may be readings of X-rays of impacted wisdom teeth, some of them may be readings of hypocrisy in *Tom Jones*, some of them may be review essays in *diacritics*, and some of them may be analyses of Fish's career as a theorist of interpretation. But they are all objects, and a small but important set of them must be understood as objects that exist independently of anyone's perception of them, *if* they are to be understood properly as the kinds of objects they are. Those are the objects that belong to the world of brute fact, and because brute fact never gets up and speaks for itself in a language that precedes or exceeds all human interpretive paradigms, humans have to keep redrawing the distinction between brute fact and social fact and interpreting it anew by way of the protocols of those social facts we now call "interpretive communities." Wolfgang Iser did not make this argument, and that's one of the reasons why no one hears very much about him any more. Nonetheless, the terms in which Fish won his argument with Iser, and the very decisiveness of his success, have had lasting effects not only on the careers of both men but on the profession of literary study as a whole. Some of those effects, as Stanley Fish was (characteristically) among the first to realize, are now worth trying to undo.

Works Cited

Baker, Houston A. *Blues, Ideology, and Afro-American Literature: A Vernacular Theory*. Chicago: University of Chicago Press, 1984.

Culler, Jonathan. *On Deconstruction: Theory and Criticism after Structuralism*. Ithaca: Cornell University Press, 1982.

———. *Structuralist Poetics: Structuralism, Linguistics, and the Study of Literature*. Ithaca: Cornell University Press, 1976.

Fish, Stanley. *Doing What Comes Naturally: Change, Rhetoric, and the Practice of Theory in Literary and Legal Studies*. Durham, N.C.: Duke University Press, 1989.

———. *Is There a Text in This Class?* Cambridge: Harvard University Press, 1980.

———. *Professional Correctness: Literary Studies and Political Change.* New York: Oxford University Press, 1995.

———. "Professor Sokal's Bad Joke." *New York Times*, 21 May 1996, A23.

———. *Surprised by Sin: The Reader in Paradise Lost.* Cambridge: Harvard University Press, 1967.

———. "Why No One's Afraid of Wolfgang Iser." Review of *The Act of Reading: A Theory of Aesthetic Response*, by Wolfgang Iser. *diacritics* 11, no. 1 (March 1981): 2–13.

Iser, Wolfgang. *The Act of Reading: A Theory of Aesthetic Response.* Baltimore: Johns Hopkins University Press, 1978.

———. *The Implied Reader: Patterns of Communication in Prose Fiction from Bunyan to Beckett.* Baltimore: Johns Hopkins University Press, 1974.

———. Interview with Wayne Booth, Norman Holland, and Rudolf Kuenzli. *diacritics* 10, no. 2 (June 1980): 57–74.

———. "Talk Like Whales: A Reply to Stanley Fish." *diacritics* 11, no. 3 (1981): 82–87.

Klancher, Jon. *The Making of English Reading Audiences, 1790–1832.* Madison: University of Wisconsin Press, 1987.

Kuenzli, Rudolf. "The Intersubjective Structure of the Reading Process: A Communication-Oriented Theory of Literature." Review of *The Act of Reading: A Theory of Aesthetic Response*, by Wolfgang Iser. *diacritics* 10, no. 2 (June 1980): 47–56.

Kuhn, Thomas S. *The Structure of Scientific Revolutions.* 2nd ed. Chicago: University of Chicago Press, 1970.

Mailloux, Steven. *Interpretive Conventions: The Reader in the Study of American Fiction.* Ithaca: Cornell University Press, 1982.

———. *Rhetorical Power.* Ithaca: Cornell University Press, 1989.

Rabinowitz, Peter. *Before Reading: Narrative Conventions and the Politics of Interpretation.* Columbus: Ohio State University Press, 1987.

Radway, Janice. *A Feeling for Books: The Book-of-the-Month Club, Literary Taste, and Middle-Class Desire.* Chapel Hill: University of North Carolina Press, 1997.

———. *Reading the Romance: Women, Patriarchy, and Popular Literature.* 1984. 2nd ed. Chapel Hill: University of North Carolina Press, 1991.

Smith, Barbara Herrnstein. *Contingencies of Value: Alternative Perspectives for Critical Theory.* Cambridge: Harvard University Press, 1988.

Suleiman, Susan, and Inge Crosman, ed. *The Reader in the Text: Essays on Audience and Interpretation.* Princeton: Princeton University Press, 1980.

Tompkins, Jane, ed. *Reader-Response Criticism: From Formalism to Post-Structuralism.* Baltimore: Johns Hopkins University Press, 1980.

Citizens of the World, Unite:
Martha Nussbaum's Plan
for Cultivating Humanity

The largest private university in the United States does not lie on either of the nation's coasts. Its campus is not punctuated with coffee shops, nose rings, tattoos, or soul patches. In the past twenty years, it has developed a strong football program that occasionally vies for the NCAA championship, but it has no party life to go with its pep rallies — no keggers, no two-for-one Jell-O shot nights, no history of public drunkenness or acquaintance rape. Its graduates have traveled to every inhabited continent on the planet, yet its pedagogical philosophy is anything but cosmopolitan; as Martha Nussbaum reports, in 1993 one of its trustees declared that the three great enemies of its founding principles were (in no particular order) "feminists, homosexuals, and intellectuals" (280). The faculty boasts no tenured radicals: on the contrary, as Nussbaum notes in her 1997 book, *Cultivating Humanity: A Classical Defense of Reform in Liberal Education*, one of its English professors was fired in 1996 because of an alleged absence of "gospel insights" and "spiritual inspiration" in her teaching (288).

The university in question is Brigham Young University, and if you haven't thought about BYU as a major player in the campus culture wars, then maybe you've been missing something important. I'll freely admit that I'd missed it myself: until I read *Cultivating Humanity*, I hadn't given a moment's thought to BYU and its implications for the missions of American higher education. But then, neither had anyone else. *Cultivating Humanity* is exceptional among studies of the American university in that it compares BYU to Brown, business-oriented Bentley College to Harvard, Notre Dame to St. Lawrence University, the University of California at Berkeley to the University of Nevada at Reno. But what's truly distinctive about Nussbaum's approach is that she calls on even the most hidebound of these institutions to create "world citizens" who are conversant with multiple philosophical traditions and diverse cultural practices. Surveying small Baptist colleges and large metropolitan universities, she contends that undergraduate education should be structured to lead students to question traditional or conventional beliefs, whatever their source.

Of course, the Socratic life of rigorous reasoning and constant self-examination often seems at odds with the goals of religious universities and fundamentalist institutions of all kinds. When she gets to Utah, Nussbaum knows she's in unfriendly territory: BYU rejects her thesis that higher education should train citizens who "trust no authority but reason itself" (83). BYU, by contrast, holds that "reason must operate within limits set by revelation" (280). As one faculty member tells Nussbaum, "The 'world citizen' is not the conception here — this is a church of apostles. The question it asks is, What people do we want representing the truth?" (286)

One of the strengths of *Cultivating Humanity* is that it explicitly explores the conflict between authority and reason, even if the book does not entirely resolve this conflict. Nussbaum's untrammeled confidence in both the universality of reason and the diversity of human life makes hers a challenging and curious book, one that strongly endorses multicultural study while distancing itself from nearly everything typically associated with it, including postmodernism, identity politics, and the critique of philosophical universalism. Here, in other words, we have an emphatic humanist who rebukes the ethnocentrism and willful ignorance of her fellow self-described humanists *and* the relativism and irrationalism of her postmodernist colleagues. Who knows? If her book is read as carefully and as sympathetically as it was written, it might just give humanism a good name again. But can it convince readers who don't understand "reason" as she does? That's another question entirely.

MARTHA NUSSBAUM has been a singularly intriguing figure in higher education. A classicist by training, she has written on Aristotle, Hellenistic ethics, the role of luck in Greek tragedy, the therapeutic ethos of the Stoics, and, more recently, law, patriotism, sexuality, literature, and disability. Nussbaum's education has served her well. Her critiques of the academy's detractors are notable for their preference of philosophy to polemics, substance to style: in the 1980s, she got her start as a public intellectual by questioning Allan Bloom's understanding of classical antiquity, and in *Cultivating Humanity*, she takes on Christina Hoff Sommers's *Who Stole Feminism?* by going after Sommers's impoverished reading of John Stuart Mill (215 – 19). (The issue is whether one can legitimately criticize the preferences of one's fellow citizens in a democracy; Sommers mistakenly argues that democrats must honor all their compatriots' desires and, hence, that feminists are undemocratic, whereas Nussbaum insists that "[d]emocratic choice need not be understood as the aggregation of uncriticized preferences, and most theorists of democracy, even those in the Utilitarian tradition, by now do not so construe it" [218].) Happily, Nussbaum embodies many of the intellectual ideals she espouses: this is a writer who quotes Marcus Aurelius, the Pope, the third-century Buddhist emperor Ashoka, and the African National Congress. By the time you finish the book, you've learned that she's a former professional actress, that she converted to Conservative Judaism from Episcopal Christianity, and that she knows a thing or two about music, too.

No one has made anything quite like the case Nussbaum mounts for curricular reform. The academic culture wars usually depict faculty as polarized into two major groups — in one camp, the defenders of rationalism, universalism, and classical learning; in the other, the champions of diversity, innovation, and multiculturalism. But here, Nussbaum deploys the traditionalists' values in the service of the vanguard's cause and vice versa. In the belief that the study of human diversity will help us become more rational beings, and in the belief that reason will bring us to a deeper understanding of other cultures' traditions, Nussbaum proposes a curriculum that doesn't just add on a gender requirement or a single minority studies course but engages with the religious and intellectual histories of Africa, China, India, Rome, the Middle East, and even the West. "Infusing world citizenship into the curriculum is a much larger project than the designing of one or two required courses," she writes. "Its goals can and should pervade the curriculum as a whole, as multinational, minority, and gender perspectives can illuminate the teaching of many standard parts of the curriculum, from American history to economics to art history to ancient Greek literature" (77). In this sense, the book takes direct aim at Allan Bloom's strikingly ignorant claim in *The Closing of the American Mind* that "only in the Western nations, i.e. those influenced by Greek philosophy, is there some willingness to doubt the identification of the good with one's own way" (Bloom 36, qtd. in Nussbaum 132). Indeed, writes Nussbaum, "one of the errors that a diverse education can dispel is the false belief that one's own tradition is the only one that is capable of self-criticism or universal aspiration" (11).

Of course, there are lots of ways to do cross-cultural study, and therefore lots of opportunities to do it wrong. Attacking what she calls "descriptive chauvinism" (like, say, Allan Bloom's) as well as "descriptive romanticism" (like, say, Paul Gauguin's), Nussbaum insists that we study non-Western cultures in all their plurality rather than assuming that they are monolithically other than (and therefore worse or better than) our own (118 – 30). This means that the study of other cultures is never less than complex. "When we decide to teach 'Chinese values' in a course on comparative philosophy," Nussbaum asks, "what should we be studying? The Confucian tradition? The Marxist critique of that tradition? The values of contemporary Chinese feminists, who criticize both Confucianism and Marxism (often by appeal to John Stuart Mill, whose *The Subjection of Women* was translated into Chinese early in the [twentieth] century)?" (117) These are hard questions, and few American intellectuals have the expertise to answer them. What's more, even if the United States had cross-cultural intellectual expertise in abundance, there's not a lot of money available for faculty hiring or course development. Nussbaum admits as much when she gets to Nevada: "Reno, like many institutions, cannot afford to hire new faculty to create integrative courses or to free existing faculty from many of their other commitments" (70).

Still, though faculty are scarce and funds are scarcer, Nussbaum finds much to praise in her travels from coast to coast. Together with her team of four research assistants, she attends classes, interviews professors, analyzes curricula, and serves as a visiting lecturer. Most importantly, she listens to students — like the young conservative man from Carson City, Nevada, who had to complete a writing assignment in which he adopted the voice of a gay teen coming out to his parents, or like the beefy business major who's reading Plato's *Crito* in the gym when Nussbaum arrives to work out (4 – 5). From SUNY-Buffalo's American Pluralism and the Search for Equality to Scripps College's Culture, Knowledge, and Representation to St. Lawrence University's program in Cultural Encounters: An Intercultural General Education (in which faculty lived for a month in the regions they planned to study, thanks to grants from the Mellon Foundation and the Fund for the Improvement of Post-Secondary Education), Nussbaum glimpses students engaged in careful, critical thinking about other cultures.

All in all, Nussbaum's picture of American academe is one we have rarely seen of late: teachers are energetic and dedicated, inquisitive and stimulating, civic-minded and well-intentioned. And what a picture it would be if all of academe lived up to this ideal. Campuses would be brimming with engaged, versatile faculty who were matched only by the energy and curiosity of their students; perhaps the humanities building would finally get that major facelift it's been promised all these years. The kind of education Nussbaum proposes would make majors such as accounting and finance peripheral to the university's central mission — namely, rigorous training in the cross-cultural disciplines of the liberal arts and social sciences. African American studies would be part of that mission, so that students might contemplate the United States' vexed history with regard to freedom and egalitarianism; women's studies would be prominent as well, on the grounds that "the effort to see women more clearly and to give a more adequate account of their lives has transformed the disciplines; it has also transformed the law and public policy of our nation" (221). Nussbaum does not stop, however, at showing how new work in African American studies and women's studies is necessary to fill gaps in traditional scholarship (noting, for example, that "a recent attempt to study the situation of widows in India . . . found that there were no data on widows' nutritional or health status because the data did not disaggregate households into their members" [189]). More than this, she grounds her appeal in the richest soil of the Western tradition, calling on humanists to be scholars to whom nothing human is alien.

Yet despite her enthusiasm for the classes she visits and the curricular reforms she notes, Nussbaum is no Pollyanna. There are still plenty of things wrong with academe, and *Cultivating Humanity* is not averse to fingering culprits and chastising laggards. She is especially dismissive of postmodernism, deconstruction, and identity politics (which she lumps together and attributes generally to departments of literature). Casual readers could well be forgiven for getting the impression that the salient problem with American universities has something to do with a bunch of posties who don't believe in truth or (as if this were the same thing) "the objectivity of value judgments" (108). *Value judgments?* Are we really being asked to believe that when Nussbaumian humanism is finally the law of the land, everybody will agree that the Beatles are objectively superior to Beethoven and that crunchy peanut butter is superior to smooth?

Nussbaum treats postmodernism far too sweepingly, and I'll explain how and why in a moment. Meanwhile, the more powerful opponents of her brand of cosmopolitanism lie elsewhere — and closer to hand. At tiny Randolph-Macon College in Virginia, Nussbaum points out that "the greatest enemies of Socratism . . . are vocationalism and indifference" (43). Since Randolph-Macon is surely not alone in this respect, Nussbaum's observation raises a number of questions. Why should American college students aspire to the condition of the critical "world citizen" in the first place? Isn't it infinitely easier to get some professional training and a chance at a good career? And why should American universities bother to expand drastically their offerings in cross-cultural studies and the humanities? Isn't the "national interest" better served by the training of patriotic citizens than by the production of millions of cosmopolitan-minded intellectuals? Last but not least: if we do sometimes require college graduates who can make their way in the world at large, do those graduates really need to be autonomous, free-thinking agents, or can they simply be missionaries (Monetarist or Mormon) sent by the United States to develop new markets and enlighten the heathen abroad?

Nussbaum has two sets of answers to these questions, principled and pragmatic. The principled answers concern democracy and deliberative justice, and they employ that curious, noble language that universities like to invoke when the subject is the life of the mind (rather than, say, the profitability of patents) — a language that, to her credit, Nussbaum takes quite seriously. "It would be catastrophic," she writes in her book's penultimate paragraph, "to become a nation of technically competent people who have lost the ability to think critically, to examine themselves, and to respect the humanity and diversity of others. . . . It is therefore very urgent right now to support curricular efforts aimed at producing citizens who can take charge of their own reasoning, who can see the different and foreign not as a threat to be resisted, but as an invitation to explore and understand, expanding their own minds and their capacity for citizenship" (300 – 301).

These sentences ring true to my ears; they seem good in the way of belief. But are they persuasive, such that they can become true in a pragmatist sense to everyone else as well? Every once in a while, I find, it's possible to convince administrators, trustees, alumni, and state representatives that universities should be places where reasoned inquiry into every aspect of the known and yet-unknown universe takes precedence over profit, patriotism, and party politics. But it's only possible every once in a while. The rest of the time, you run into powerful people who think they have a vested interest in producing university graduates who will identify with U.S. national interests; you run into people who are interested in whether college students will become good employees; you even come across people who believe that unchecked reason is the enemy of sound religious instruction. Point being, if you're going to advocate educational cosmopolitanism as an ideal, you need not just a carrot but a shtick.

Nussbaum doesn't really have a shtick, but she does have some pragmatic answers to go along with her principles. These have less to do with democracy and self-examination than with how to get things done in a global village (although there is, inevitably, some overlap here): "Whether we are discussing the multinational corporation, global agricultural development, the protection of endangered species, religious toleration, the well-being of women, or simply how to run a firm efficiently, we increasingly find that we need comparative knowledge of many cultures to answer the questions we ask" (115). Indeed we do, but there's something curious about this list: Macroeconomic interests show up here twice, in the first and last positions — three times, if you count "global agricultural development." The pragmatic rationale for a cross-cultural curriculum seems to depend heavily on how the business community wants to do business.

Interestingly, Nussbaum's chapter titled "Citizens of the World" opens with the story of Anna, a political science major who graduated and "went into business, getting a promising job with a large firm" but ran into trouble dealing with the cultural consequences of being reassigned to the company's "newly opened Beijing office" (50). Anna found she had to learn about Chinese labor history, gender relations, and child-care practices if she (and her firm) were to thrive in Beijing. Nussbaum's point is that Anna's education had not equipped her to live as a world citizen, that "her imaginative capacity to enter into the lives of people of other nations had been blunted by lack of practice" (51). No doubt this is so. But surely the challenge of creating world citizens, if you're interested in something other than bringing souls to Jesus or opening new markets, lies in convincing people that they have good reason to become world citizens even if their firms don't reassign them to the recently opened Beijing office.

One of the imperatives that drives Nussbaum's view of the world is, as she puts it, "the Kantian demand to treat humanity, wherever we encounter it, as an end and not a means" (220). Presumably, after a few years in China, Anna learned not to take her own cultural traditions for granted, but it's unclear whether her firm regarded her education as an end or as a means. Global capitalism doesn't necessarily entail a global citizenry dedicated to relentless, free-ranging inquiry; sometimes the two can be positively antithetical — as they are in China, where multinational businesses have little sympathy for demonstrating students or organizing workers. Nussbaum does acknowledge elsewhere in the book that "if we become a population who can relate, as citizens, only on the narrow parched terrain of financial interest, we will have lost much that makes us fully human" (172). But by not grappling explicitly with the antagonism between capitalism and cosmopolitanism (or with their complex interdependence), Nussbaum fails to mount a persuasive attack on the McWorld version of her internationalist ideal.

CULTIVATING HUMANITY appeared at a time when many liberal-leftist theorists had nearly given up on the idea of education for citizenship. Bill Readings's posthumously published *The University in Ruins*, to take the most cogent example, argues that the idea of the university as producer of citizens is dead and gone, thanks to the passing of the nation-state. The old university, which had its roots in German idealism, Readings calls "the University of Culture"; the new university, which was first theorized in Clark Kerr's description of the "Multiversity" (in Kerr's *The Uses of the University*), Readings calls "the University of Excellence," and it's devoted mainly to producing professionals and experts. There's a lot of Jean-François Lyotard in *The University in Ruins*, especially Lyotard's distinction (in *The Postmodern Condition*) between the "emancipationist humanism" of the old, Cardinal Newman – style university, and the technocratic "performativity" of the postmodern university. For Lyotard and Readings, there's no turning back to the days when we could hope to produce citizens; all we can do now is struggle to keep knowledge from being measured, quantified, and reified.

Nussbaum isn't buying it. If indeed the nation-state is waning as a political and economic force (and it's still an open question as to whether this is quite as true as Readings believed), then Nussbaum will simply up the ante and call us to produce world citizens instead of U.S. citizens. And as for the postmodern condition, well, Nussbaum isn't buying *that*, either. Even Nussbaum's defenses of women's studies and gay/lesbian studies proceed partly by selling off the literary wing of the campus, where all that postmodernist and poststructuralist shilly-shallying is going on. Women's studies, we hear, is doing well in fields such as history, philosophy, anthropology, and the like, but literary studies are turbid waters — sometimes offering "imaginative and innovative teaching" (214) but too often contaminated by heavy French minerals. "Literary theory inspired by deconstruction does produce empty jargon and argument lacking in the rigor that one should demand of humanistic argument," Nussbaum writes. "Scholars influenced by it teach some bad classes — empty, windy, and contemptuous of argument" (214 – 15). Of whom is Nussbaum thinking, precisely? Deconstructive feminists such as Barbara Johnson, Cynthia Chase, and Peggy Kamuf (just to name a few) are anything but careless as readers and as writers, and as for their teaching, I see no evidence that Nussbaum visited their classes or any classes taught by feminist deconstructionists anywhere. Likewise, with regard to the study of sexuality, Nussbaum writes that "faculty in Philosophy, Religious Studies, and Medicine have had to keep pressing for an emphasis on rigorous scholarly argument and traditional methods of inquiry, alongside approaches influenced by postmodernist literary theory" (248). And although she professes a limited admiration for Foucault's work ("the only truly important work to have entered philosophy under the banner of 'postmodernism'" [40]), her blanket dismissal of Derrida is little short of remarkable: "Derrida on truth is simply not worth studying for someone who has been studying Quine and Putnam and Davidson. In other parts of the humanities, however, they exercise a large influence (in part because their work is approachable as the technical work of philosophers frequently is not), causing students to think that those in the know have disdain for Socrates and his goals" (41). This is a stunning passage. Quite apart from the idea that anyone could come away from, say, "Plato's Pharmacy" with the notion that Derrida has "disdain for Socrates and his goals" (calling a real disdainer: Friedrich

Nietzsche, white courtesy phone!), there is the truly novel suggestion that Derrida is popular because his work is so *approachable*.

Well, all right, so there are a few odd sods cavorting about, giving campy, in-your-face titles to their MLA papers, spewing windy jargon, and chattering blithely about how everything is socially constructed. But the only bad, empty classes *I've* ever seen — or taken — were taught by intellectually incurious faculty who didn't know or care what deconstruction or postmodernism might be. And sometimes, Nussbaum's rhetorical sallies lead her to collapse categories the way my incurious teachers used to do, lumping her antagonists into one mushy, undifferentiated mass. Nowhere is this tendency more pronounced than when Nussbaum pronounces that "much teaching of literature in the current academy is inspired by the spirit of identity politics" (110) — not long after she's noted that literary study is infected by decons and pomos. There are, after all, some serious arguments taking place among deconstructionists and postmodernists, and neither group looks very kindly on identity politics in any case. In fact, if you're worried about identity politics — and Nussbaum certainly is, as a cosmopolitan who's skeptical of all forms of unreflective groupthink — then you might someday find those decons and pomos, with *their* identity-politics solvents, to be of some use to you. And depending on who you run into, you might even come across a few who like to argue rigorously.

So if Nussbaum's neglect of global capitalism poses a problem for her project, so too does her blanket dismissal of postmodernism. Though I get impatient with Jean-François Lyotard and with all who cite him as a bringer of Higher Truths, I find him impossible to dismiss completely — if one is going to be a responsible citizen of the world. For Lyotard surveys the world's different ways of thinking and believes that to bring them to "consensus" — or even to try to get them communicating reciprocally — is to do irreparable harm to the integrity of others. More than this: for Lyotard, the effort to negotiate the heterogeneity of language games amounts to a kind of terror. This view is badly mistaken, I think. Try to imagine that our world is beset by too much communicative rationality, desperately in need of more monads and monologists, and you'll see what I mean. And yet Lyotard's idea of the "differend," or the nonnegotiable difference, strikes me as absolutely essential to an understanding of education and cultural conflict. If you pursue Lyotard too far, of course, you wind up unable to criticize other cultures' practices of female circumcision or widow burning, but if you don't pursue Lyotard at all, you risk succumbing to the fantasy that all disputes between "reason" and "unreason," or between different varieties of reasoning, can be mediated by a double dose of reason.

The prospect of a nonnegotiable difference is extremely troublesome for Nussbaum, and not only because she extends her analysis of education to places such as BYU. It's also a problem because she advocates the study of all forms of human sexuality on the grounds that "a liberal democracy such as ours is built on mutual respect and toleration among citizens who differ deeply about basic goals and aspirations" (249). I couldn't agree more — but I have the funny feeling that not everyone agrees with her about what follows from the premise of "mutual respect." Disarmingly (or disingenuously), Nussbaum repeatedly asks why anyone would oppose gay and lesbian studies: "It is not clear why learning about a subject should be associated with the erosion of moral judgment on that subject," she writes (223), for "it is unclear why learning how different people think about sex should erode any moral judgments that are well founded" (224).

But what counts as a "well founded" moral judgment? A belief, based on the reading of Holy Scripture, that one must hate the sin of homosexuality but love the sinner? A belief, on pragmatic (but conservative) secular grounds, that gay marriage will somehow undermine the foundations of heterosexual marriage? Or a belief that the state has no business regulating sex acts between consenting adults? Nussbaum notes that the study of sexuality may have some practical benefits: "As jurors, we may be asked to reach fair and impartial verdicts in cases dealing with child molestation, spousal abuse, recovered memory, rape and sexual violence, sexual harassment. We may be asked to evaluate testimony on gay parenting, on the 'homosexual panic' defense for manslaughter, on the battered-woman syndrome, on marital rape, on the relative claims of adoptive and biological parents" (225–26). Certainly, our system of justice cannot thrive if our jurors are simply ignorant of the issues presented by the cases before them. But there are those among us who believe that the best way to serve as a juror in such cases is to base one's judgment less on new evidence than on old-fashioned authority, whether the authority of Scripture or the authority of legal precedent. After all, many intelligent people, from Thomas Aquinas to Oliver Wendell Holmes, have deferred to the textual authority of their forebears, at least in part because they thought this authority operated with reason.

Nussbaum's eloquent defense of gay and lesbian studies should provoke a searching debate among religious and political conservatives. But I know too well — and I suspect Nussbaum does also — that the study of sexuality (among many other things) is opposed both by those who rely on faith and by those who regard their position as altogether rational. Faith, of course, is a matter for concern not only at BYU but at every Catholic university in the world, each of which has its own tentative relation to papal decrees forbidding the "promulgation" of homosexuality in the curriculum. And reason, unfortunately, is easily invoked by those who oppose not only gay studies but also antidiscrimination laws. To take an illustrative (and vile) example, consider E. L. Pattullo's 1992 article in *Commentary*, "Straight Talk about Gays," which argues that because society has a compelling interest in discouraging people from becoming gay, "reason suggests that we guard against doing anything which might mislead wavering children into perceiving society as indifferent to the sexual orientation they develop" (22).

When she's faced with illiberal and inhumane sentiments like these, Nussbaum has only one card to play: what these people (Mormon trustees, say, or *Commentary* essayists) need is more reason. She concludes her report on BYU in this vein: "In the areas of gender and sexuality, dialogue, which at present is discouraged, would considerably enhance the lives of people who suffer low self-esteem and ostracism; to encourage such dialogue seems morally essential" (292). But *to whom* does it seem morally essential? Here, then, is where a skeptic of rational consensus such as Lyotard is useful, even though he's more usually invoked by the academic left on behalf of the "language games" of disabled lesbian sex workers of color than those of *Commentary* magazine editors or the elders of the Church of Latter-Day Saints. It is quite difficult, unfortunately, to appeal to reason when confronting discourse in which "reason" is understood as synonymous with "deference to established authority." It's also quite difficult to imagine a universal table of reason that will rule out of court other people's appeals to reason when they clash with our own. As much as I yearn for a decisive criterion by which my own progressive, humanitarian principles are correct and those of my opponents are either nutty or mistaken, I have met just enough people in my travels to know that in this sublunary sphere, "reason," like God, works in ways I do not always understand.

Nussbaum tries to dodge these impasses by means of a kind of rhetorical jujitsu, taking her preferred elements of various religious intellectual traditions and trying to use them against each religion's worst anti-intellectual tendencies. Bypassing the Vatican's strictures on the study of homosexuality, for example, Nussbaum quotes instead Pope John Paul II's October 1995 address to the United Nations General Assembly, in which his holiness said, "To cut oneself off from the reality of difference — or, worse, to attempt to stamp out that difference — is to cut oneself off from the possibility of sounding the depths of the mystery of human life" (257). Similarly, despite the history of friction between Catholic universities and secular ideals of academic freedom, Nussbaum claims that "Roman Catholicism is well placed theologically to establish a religious university that is both truly religious and truly a university" (265). About BYU she has less to say in this vein, since the intellectual tradition of Mormonism is not quite as rich as that of Rome, but she does try to combat Mormon deference to church authority by citing BYU's motto, "The glory of God is intelligence" (290).

Yet Mormonism — and, for that matter, any form of Christianity that subordinates reason to revelation and insists on a "literal reading" of Scripture — is not about to be finessed by Nussbaum's (or my) appeals to the liberating aspects of Socratic self-examination and the humanizing effects of world citizenship. Some forms of religious belief, of course, are entirely compatible with the dictates of reason and the demands of intellectual rigor. I remember very well that, during my four years in a Jesuit high school (during which I was trained in things like Latin, political philosophy from Plato to Nietzsche, groundbreaking biblical exegesis, and doctrinal history since Nicea and Chalcedon), I was impressed time and again with how my instructors in this branch of Catholicism could lead lives in which religious faith and keen intellect worked to the enhancement of each other. But the Jesuits are famous troublemakers in the intellectual history of Catholicism, partly because of their love of learning and disputation. Where my former Jesuit teachers may very likely welcome Nussbaum's critique with open arms (and many legal pads of further commentary), the leaders of other faiths, including the Mormon elders, may very likely see it as precisely the thing their faith was meant to warn them against.

I said that Nussbaum has only one card to play in this position, but then again, in Nussbaum's deck of cards, reason always trumps, and all those holdouts who don't like the rule of reason must ultimately be persuaded to reason differently — that is, similarly to us reasonable folk. Personally, I find this eminently reasonable. But I'm less sanguine about what reason can and can't do when it's confronted with political and religious opposition to gay and lesbian studies; fundamentalist Muslim clerics, evangelical Christian preachers, and even popes have so far seemed unmoved by Nussbaumian appeals to our common humanity and our shared capacity for reason. It seems prudent, then, at the very least, to entertain reasonable doubts about the reach of reason. In *Cultivating Humanity*, Nussbaum tries to make the best of America's major religious traditions, tracing even the most intolerant among them back to their roots in *caritas*, *agape*, and the fostering of compassionate love. Hers is a canny and admirable effort, but it remains to be seen whether Nussbaum's ecumenical appeal to the human spirit will carry the day against ignorance, fear, identity politics, parochialism, fundamentalism, authoritarianism, and — last but not least — vocationalism. For secular intellectuals like me who agree that the unexamined life is not worth living, it seems only human to hope that Nussbaum's vision of higher education will guide American universities in the twenty-first century; and yet it is only reasonable, given the current composition of the human race, to fear that it will not.

Works Cited

Bloom, Allan. *The Closing of the American Mind: How Higher Education Has Failed Democracy and Impoverished the Souls of Today's Students.* New York: Simon and Schuster, 1987.

Kerr, Clark. *The Uses of the University.* Cambridge: Harvard University Press, 1963.

Lyotard, Jean-François. *The Differend: Phrases in Dispute.* Translated by Georges Van Den Abbeele. Theory and History of Literature, vol. 46. Minnesota: University of Minnesota Press, 1988.

———. *The Postmodern Condition: A Report on Knowledge.* Translated by Geoff Bennington and Brian Massumi. Theory and History of Literature, vol. 10. Minneapolis: University of Minnesota Press, 1984.

Nussbaum, Martha. *Cultivating Humanity: A Classical Defense of Reform in Liberal Education.* Cambridge: Harvard University Press, 1997.

Pattullo, E. L. "Straight Talk about Gays." *Commentary* 94, no. 6 (December 1992): 21–24.

Readings, Bill. *The University in Ruins.* Cambridge: Harvard University Press, 1996.

Sommers, Christina Hoff. *Who Stole Feminism?: How Women Have Betrayed Women.* New York: Simon and Schuster, 1994.

I n this essay, I'll ask about the relations between American studies and the state; in so doing, I'll also ask about the relations between American studies and the corporate multiversity, since I think these sets of relations are mutually implicating. I will focus more on the former than on the latter, however, partly because at first blush the corporatization of the university does not seem to have had much impact on the substance of intellectual work in American studies. For in one sense, American studies is peripheral to the "productive" work of the U.S. university in the wake of the Bayh-Dole Act of 1980, insofar as nothing written or taught in American studies, under any description, generates a form of knowledge that can be patented, owned, and sold. In the world of nanotechnology and bioengineering — two of the substantial growth areas of higher education in the United States — American studies promises no deliverables, offers no opportunities for research and development, and produces no profit-generating products. To the extent that American studies is a creature of the arts, humanities, and social sciences, it tends to fly under the radar, so to speak, of Monsanto and Microsoft; thus, it does not generate any indirect cost recovery funds — or National Institutes of Health funds, or National Science Foundation funds, or private subventions — for the rest of the campus, and for that reason you do not often see glistening new high-tech campus buildings devoted to American studies cheek by jowl with dilapidated and inadequate facilities for supercomputing and genomics. Also for that reason, it really does not matter to most campus administrators whether your local American studies program is turning out critiques of the cultures of U.S. imperialism, studies of the possessive investment in whiteness, or evocations of the virgin land and the machine in the garden. Regardless of its content, the work of American studies is in a financial sense immaterial to the corporate multiversity, its fate inseparable from that of the arts, humanities, and social sciences in general.

But in another sense, this argument is quite wrong, for two potentially contradictory or complementary reasons. The first has to do with the place of the nation-state in the production of knowledge. Here I want to take issue with Masao Miyoshi, who writes,

> The basis of national literatures and cultures is very much hollowed out, as the nation-state declines in the hegemonic imaginary. The humanities as they are now constituted in academia are no longer desired or warranted. There is a decisive change in the academic outlook and policy to de-emphasize the humanities and to shift resources to applied sciences. (18)

Miyoshi is right, here and elsewhere, to note the increasing disparity in prestige and resources between the humanities and the applied sciences, a disparity that has grown geometrically since 1980, partly as a consequence of the Bayh-Dole Act. But I doubt that he is right to ascribe this to the decline of the nation-state in the hegemonic imaginary. It would appear, on the contrary, that the hegemonic imaginary is one place where the nation-state has been doing just fine, on campus and off, in part because of Americans' and American universities' possessive investment in Americanness. To take just one odd example, the most recent National Association of Scholars survey of English departments in the U.S. reports that since 1964, a decisive Americanization of the college literature curriculum has occurred — and, make no mistake, this is something the NAS laments.[1] But because the group has largely failed to get journalists and think tankers to join them in ruing the Americanization of the humanities, the NAS has tended instead to publicize it under the banner "English departments have turned away from Shakespeare." The NAS report is fascinating testimony against the proposition that the basis for U.S. national literatures and cultures has been "hollowed out," and it constitutes a kind of old-guard, paleoconservative dissent from the *rise* of the nation-state in the hegemonic imaginary. Perhaps it suggests, moreover, that there is a residual sense, in Raymond Williams's sense of "residual sense," in which the knowledges produced in American studies might matter even to those administrators and trustees who see in them no potential for enhancing the university's portfolio or for building "partnerships" with key "stakeholders" in private industry.

The other reason for the potential importance of American studies in the multiversity concerns not the residual nationalism of U.S. universities but their emergent internationalism. Higher education is, after all, one of the few product areas in which the United States finds itself with a trade surplus; international students now constitute one of our significant constituencies, as the FBI has lately learned, and American studies, for its part, is without question more internationalist in scope than it was in the days of Henry Nash Smith and Leo Marx. If then the corporatization of the university is one aspect of the ongoing globalization of capital, as Miyoshi rightly suggests, then what are the actual and potential intellectual functions of an increasingly internationalist American studies in an increasingly transnationalist economic environment? And how are we to understand the emergent internationalism of American studies in conjunction with the residual nationalism that still justifies this enterprise to many university administrators?

During my four years as a humanities-program administrator at the University of Illinois at Urbana-Champaign, a public Research I university at which research and development in the applied sciences has indirectly subsidized the humanities for half a century, I learned that two key terms were most likely to secure funding and generate excitement at the highest administrative levels: "new technologies" and "international studies." The "international studies" heading accommodated a wide variety of intellectual initiatives, ranging from programs to enhance the university's international standing in the applied sciences to the Ford Foundation Seminar in Identity and the Arts in Diaspora Communities, in which my humanities program had a minor role. If faculty at Illinois were to propose a new program in American studies, interestingly, it is possible that they would be more successful if they pitched it as an explicitly international concern: an area of study invested in the understanding of what it is to be American, in the residual nationalist sense, but also an area of study devoted to the "production" of postnational American identities and cultures in transnational exchanges. The result could be a determinedly progressive and anti-imperialist and anti-isolationist program in American studies, but curiously, it could also be a program perfectly of a piece with the university's roles as partner to corporate management and stimulant to financial growth, under the auspices of which "internationalism" is understood as an important development area, as the titles of most of Illinois' international units indicate: the Center for International Business Education and Research, the Center for International Education and Research in Accounting, the International Programs in Engineering, the International Soybean Program (INTSOY), the Office of International Strategic Management, and the International Trade Center. Though it is unlikely that AMSTUD will ever be constituted as an adjunct to INTSOY, the point remains that internationalism is no guarantee of any political or intellectual tendency in U.S. universities or in American studies — at Illinois, at Penn State, or anywhere else.[2]

I will come back to what this international nationalism might mean for what John Carlos Rowe and others have called "post-nationalist American studies" and George Lipsitz calls "American studies in a moment of danger," but first, to get a handle on the present, I want to turn to the no-longer-recent past, to a time when the concordance between American studies, the nation-state, and private industry was perhaps somewhat clearer than it is now. "During the height of the Cold War," writes Frances Stonor Saunders in the opening paragraph of *The Cultural Cold War*,

> the US government committed vast resources to a secret programme of cultural propaganda in western Europe. A central feature of this programme was to advance the claim that it did not exist. It was managed, in great secrecy, by America's espionage arm, the Central Intelligence Agency. The centrepiece of this covert campaign was the Congress for Cultural Freedom, run by CIA agent Michael Josselson from 1950 to 1967. Its achievements — not least its duration — were considerable. At its peak, the Congress for Cultural Freedom had offices in thirty-five countries, employed dozens of personnel, published over twenty prestige magazines, held art exhibitions, owned a news and features service, organized high-profile international conferences, and rewarded musicians and artists with prizes and public performances. Its mission was to nudge the intelligentsia of western Europe away from its lingering fascination with Marxism and Communism towards a view more accommodating of "the American way." (1)

Much has already been said of Saunders's work, particularly by those who are shocked, shocked, to find the CIA involved in the cultural front of the Cold War and by those who, like the late *Partisan Review* editor William Phillips, continued to insist, in spite of clear and convincing evidence to the contrary, that they were never the beneficiaries of covert Congress for Cultural Freedom (CCF) support (see Sharlet). And I must admit that the level of denial among such people really is remarkable: in the morning they emerge from a meeting with the rest of the American Committee for Cultural Freedom with fresh funding for a high-level conference of writers and artists committed to the anticommunist cause, and by mid-afternoon they can't seem to remember where exactly the money came from. Still, whatever the degrees of duplicity and/or self-delusion of many of the principals involved in the CCF, I want to insist that in a perverse yet entirely unremarkable sense, the Cold War years were the good old days for American artists and intellectuals — the days when, despite the "pernicious consequences of having a clandestine government agency act as the Ministry of Culture" as Michael Rogin's review of Saunders in *The Nation* put it, "the CIA was the NEA" (18, 16). Imagine if you will, if you can, a time when the work of abstract expressionists and twelve-tone composers was considered vital to national security, a time when the establishment of the pax Americana required the funding and nourishment of a noncommunist left with high-modernist cultural tastes in arts and letters. It is hard to tamp down a sense of nostalgia.

In a way I say this to be contrarian and to emphasize the counterintuitive in the CCF's mission. But in invoking the CCF as the index of a halcyon time when American intellectuals had a well-defined function for the state and for crucial segments of the private sector that identified freedom with free markets, I do not mean to gloss over the many brutal contradictions of the cultural cold war. As Saunders's work makes clear, the project of the CCF produced a series of political conundrums that in retrospect makes the landscape look like an M. C. Escher print. First and most obviously, there was the potentially (and eventually) fatal contradiction involved in promulgating the virtues of the open society by covert means. The rationale underlying this contradiction held that "the most effective kind of propaganda" was that in which "the subject moves in the direction you desire for reasons which he believes to be his own" (National Security Directive, 10 July 1950, qtd. in Saunders 4). One of the corollaries of this contradiction was the minor paradox that many CIA fronts based in the United States did not in fact need to take direction from the CIA, since they were staffed by cold warriors who were if anything all too eager to serve the state: these willing partners had to present themselves, sometimes unwillingly, as independent intellectuals, lest their association with the U.S. government taint them in the eyes of their British and western European counterparts. Such subjects, it was clear, were happy to move in the direction the state desired for reasons they believed to be their own, yet they had to pretend that they were acting on their own. "The joke," writes Saunders, "was that if any American philanthropic or cultural organization carried the words 'free' or 'private' in its literature, it must be a CIA front" (135 – 36).

Such is contradiction 1 and its odd corollary; contradiction 2 is somewhat more complex. Because the CCF's chief purpose was to contrast Western cultural freedom with Stalinist tyranny, the artists and intellectuals most useful to the CIA were precisely those whose works had been banned or labeled degenerate by the Soviet Union. Hence the curious nature of the CCF's emphasis on composers such as Stravinsky, Schoenberg, and Alban Berg and artists such as Pollock, Motherwell, and Rothko — figures for whom you could not expect to find any significant support in the U.S. Congress but who served the purpose of championing abstraction and experimentalism as cultural practices acclaimed and supported by Western democracies. Embedded in that contradiction, however, was a still nastier one, contradiction 3: the proposition that Western democracies tolerate and even foster dissidents in arts and letters was the one proposition from which CIA-supported artists and intellectuals could not dissent. Under this heading, dissent is possible in an open society and for that reason unnecessary; it follows, then, that for the cold warrior, dissent in the United States is not an index of freedom but a form of treason. Or, as Saunders more pithily puts it, "[T]o promote freedom of expression, the Agency had first to buy it, then to restrict it" (90). After 11 September 2001, needless to say, this cultural contradiction returned once again, in full force — in the White House and in the country at large — as the "war on terrorism" allowed U.S. patriots both to champion America as the home of the free and to turn with fury on anyone who presumed the freedom to dissent from the premises of the war. Thank goodness we are on familiar ground.[3]

Both of these contradictions — involving on the one hand the freedom to dissent from the Cold War construction of the free world and on the other the relation between the forms of art touted as uniquely Western and the widespread indifference or repulsion most Americans expressed for such art — would flare at the height of McCarthyism, which was for the CCF a profound cultural embarrassment. (As Saunders points out, Josselson cabled Eisenhower to plead for clemency for the Rosenbergs for the same reason: the U.S. willingness to traduce its own principles did not go over well with its European allies [183 – 84]). The appropriate analogy in the 1990s culture wars, for example, would be a high-ranking CIA official's securing covert funding for Karen Finley, Andres Serrano, and Robert Mapplethorpe over the objections of Jesse Helms because the propaganda value of such artists in international courts of opinion outweighed the domestic outrage their work provoked. Since the events of 11 September, U.S. internationalists have argued that we need to demonstrate to the Islamic world — and perhaps even more urgently to our Western allies — that we are not simply SUV-driving, Big Gulp – guzzling, Enron-scheming yahoos, and if Josselson were leading the charge today he would no doubt be trying to sign up Laurie Anderson, Tony Kushner, Bill T. Jones, Joe Goode, Philip Glass, Anna Deavere Smith, and — just to strengthen our new friendship with Vladimir Putin — former Soviet émigrés Vitaly Komar and Alexander Melamid. Saunders quotes art critic Philip Dodd:

[T]here is a perverse way of looking at this question, which is to say that the CIA took art very seriously.... The great thing about politicians when they get involved in art is it *means* something to them, whether it's the Fascists or the Soviets or the American CIA. So there may be a really perverse argument that says the CIA were the best art critics in America in the fifties because they saw work that actually should have been antipathetic to them — made by old lefties, coming out of European surrealism

— and they saw the potential power in that kind of art and ran with it. You couldn't say that of many of the art critics of the time. (259)

The rest of the contradictions of the CCF are at once fairly familiar, as Saunders shows, and uglier. Most have to do with the agency's willingness to overlook an artist's prior associations with fascism and Nazism if the artist could be made to serve a useful propaganda purpose. This is of course the central contradiction of the U.S. conduct in the Cold War, not only with regard to client artists but especially with regard to client states in Iran, Guatemala, Chile, and elsewhere, and I need not rehearse it here. Suffice it to say that when the fate of the free world was in the balance, American studies had a critical and unambiguous role: "[L]ike foreign-area studies," Doug Henwood has written, "this new discipline was of clear imperial import, in that it allowed us to understand our unique fitness for our postwar role as the world's governor, and encouraged a finer appreciation of our cultural sophistication among the ruled" (qtd. in Saunders 238). But the astonishing thing about American studies in the Cold War, in this light, is not that it was supported by the state but that it was hardly supported enough. For two decades, the field examined the "special American conditions" that differentiated American class mobility from European class stratification and produced book after book differentiating the American romance from the British and French and Russian novel of society. The Cold War years in American studies are practically defined by the field's investment in American exceptionalism; indeed, the field did a kind of double duty, exempting the United States from Marxist analysis even as it "served," as Michael Denning has famously written, "as a substitute for a developed marxist culture" (357). It seems almost a shame, in retrospect, that the American Studies Association didn't get more substantial CCF funding for all this important work undertaken by independent intellectuals in leading American universities.

That is not to say that intellectuals in leading American universities were left out in the cold. The career of Arthur Schlesinger is exemplary in this regard; to this day, few of the prominent American liberals involved in the CCF are so undeceived about the CCF's relation to the CIA as is Schlesinger, who stood in the vital center of the enterprise from the start. In his 1996 interview with Saunders, Schlesinger admitted, "I knew because of my intelligence links that the original meeting of the Congress in Berlin was paid for by the CIA. ... It seemed not unreasonable to help the people on our side. Of all the CIA's expenditures, the Congress for Cultural Freedom seemed its most worthwhile and successful" (91). To do justice to Schlesinger's remarks (as Saunders does not), it should be noted that it was far better for the CIA to provide funding for Motherwell than to lead a coup against Mossadeq. And it is worth repeating, I hope, that the Soviet Union was an enemy worth defeating; that its policies with regard to artists, intellectuals, and assorted dissidents were indeed totalitarian and murderous; and that opposing Stalinism by trumpeting intellectual freedom in the West seemed — and to me still seems — one of the best uses of public funds I can imagine for an agency of the state. There were very good reasons for the United States to promote the growth of a noncommunist left in western Europe, and I wish only that the United States had not done so while simultaneously trying to infiltrate and destroy the noncommunist progressive left at home. One of the reasons I am revisiting the history of the CCF is not to register some ludicrous loss of innocence — either mine or the nation's — involved in coming to terms with the relations between intellectuals and the state but to remind us how difficult it is, in the wake of the contradictions I have just enumerated, for contemporary American intellectuals on the cultural left to think of incorporation by the state as anything other than cooperation with evil. It is as if, when the CIA's support of the CCF was first uncovered in 1967, we had somehow obtained decisive proof that Arthur Schlesinger himself had participated in the murder of Patrice Lumumba.

Over the next two paragraphs, then, I would like you, gentle reader, to take part in a thought experiment that will be thoroughly counterintuitive and counterfactual. I want you to imagine an ideological state apparatus in the Cold War that was not defined by all the contradictions I have mentioned, an apparatus in which the promulgation of the values of the open society takes place openly, by means of a national endowment rather than under the auspices of central intelligence; in which the open society harbors no ex-Nazis and fascists under the cloak of anticommunism; where dissent is welcomed even when it does not toe the party line. Imagine for a moment that the United States had fought the cultural cold war on those terms, that there was no House Un-American Activities Committee, no COINTELPRO, no contradiction between American democratic ideals abroad and American apartheid at home; imagine that Joseph McCarthy never came close to holding elected office; imagine no plutonium experiments on unsuspecting citizens; imagine no possessions — I wonder if you can. And hear in that rarefied spirit the words of George Kennan, addressing the Council of the Museum of Modern Art in 1955, and take them at face value:

> We have . . . to show the outside world both that we have a cultural life and that we care something about it. That we care enough about it, in fact, to give it encouragement and support here at home, and to see that it is enriched by acquaintance with similar activity elsewhere. If these impres-

sions could only be conveyed with enough force and success to countries beyond our borders, I for one would willingly trade the entire remaining inventory of political propaganda for the results that could be achieved by such methods alone. (qtd. in Saunders 272)

I am asking you to imagine a world in which U.S. national leaders are actually and genuinely anxious to show the rest of the world that we have a cultural life and that we care something about it — enough even to be internationalist in outlook, "to see that it is enriched by acquaintance with similar activity elsewhere." And I ask you to imagine this not merely because Kennan's words were betrayed by actual U.S. conduct in the Cold War but more immediately because it is so difficult to imagine Kennan's counterparts today saying any such thing. That is not merely because our current foreign policy elites are significantly less brilliant or less cosmopolitan than Kennan. It is primarily because, since the fall of the Soviet Union, it has become harder and harder for Americans to imagine a time when geopolitical competition did not revolve solely around the availability of consumer goods; since 1991, liberal democrats and free-market conservatives alike have widely accepted that the U.S. economy simply outperformed the Soviet economy and that our standard of living — what former White House spokesman Ari Fleischer called our "blessed" way of life — is its own argument for American hegemony. The idea that Nixon did not simply bury Khrushchev in the kitchen debate, the idea that the United States could not just point to Chevrolets and Frigidaires and Oxydol but also had to compete with Tolstoy and the Bolshoi — this idea is increasingly foreign not only to the Bush administration but to American self-representation in any area, which is why American political elites feel so little national anxiety about how U.S. arts and letters are perceived abroad, whether in Paris or in Islamabad. When American culture is touted to the world today, the standard citation is not, say, a work of art like *United States I– IV* but a TV show like *Baywatch*; in the home of the brave and in the court of world popular culture, Pamela Anderson beats Laurie Anderson every time.

Back to the present and to the imagined community of Pamela Anderson. Since there is little likelihood in the foreseeable future that CIA officials — or, for that matter, university presidents and provosts or the chief executive officers of major multinational corporations — will decide that American studies is so central to the national interest that George Sánchez and Mary Helen Washington must be given security clearance and the American Studies Association should be simultaneously funded and infiltrated, how can we think about American studies in its relation to the state? Fifty years ago, the picture was rather clearer: even if the ASA itself was never on the payroll of the CCF,

American studies' elaborations of theories of American exceptionalism were broadly in concordance with the overall Cold War program for the American intelligentsia, and the new field, as Henwood says, was of clear imperial import. Today, by contrast, American studies is defined emphatically by its wholesale rejection of exceptionalism, its success at putting American race relations at the center of cultural analysis, its increasing willingness to expand its intellectual interests beyond the borders of the U.S. nation-state, even to consider changing its name to reflect its geopolitical concerns more adequately, as Janice Radway suggested in her 1998 presidential address to the ASA convention. As I remarked at the outset, this shift in American studies takes place at a time when the field is not generally seen, either by the state or by multinational capital, as an area of vital interest that requires official forms of encouragement and support. But is it perhaps possible that the fitful globalization or hemispherization of American studies somehow coincides with the globalization or hemispherization of American capital? And if so, might American studies not have a more complex and tangled relationship to corporatization on campus and in the Uruguay Round than most commentators have imagined?

American studies is currently an enterprise at once nationalist and internationalist, at the same time that the dominant discourse of American identity and American mission is at once nationalist and internationalist. And just as surely as Cold War American studies spoke to its historical moment, so too did American studies in the crucial decade between the fall of the Berlin Wall and the fall of the World Trade Center speak to its historical moment, mixing U.S. traditions of affirmation and dissent in ways that can conceivably be construed (though they usually have not been) as reinforcing precisely those traditional affirmations of American dissent that marked American studies in the Cold War. Of course, it is always possible, as American studies scholars have lately noted, that "invocations of the post-national by U.S. intellectuals can function as disturbing disavowals of the global reach of U.S. media and military might" (Curiel et al. 2); the danger in such invocations is not that American studies might be replaying an old script but that it might not be reading a new one. But I have a different, though related, question: What if the relation of American studies to the state turned out, in the next few decades, to be uncomfortably similar to the relationship between Cold War American studies and the apparatus of central intelligence, such that American studies scholars found the cultural activities of a noncommunist left funded and encouraged by enlightened multinationals and their supporters in government, who were interested in the propaganda value of a critical, anti-imperialist, internationalist American studies?

It is an uncomfortable question. Everyone who works in a college or university in the United States is already, of necessity, woven into the fabric of the nation-state, and some of us are even reconciled to or pleased about the fact, but it seems another matter altogether to work for Philip Morris International's office in Curitiba or to occupy the distinguished Dole Banana Chair in Asian American studies. Such a state of affairs calls to mind an unpleasant passage from Richard Rorty's *Achieving Our Country* — unpleasant because all too accurate: "[T]his frightening economic cosmopolitanism," writes Rorty, "has, as a byproduct, an agreeable cultural cosmopolitanism. Platoons of vital young entrepreneurs fill the front cabins of transoceanic jets, while the back cabins are weighted down with paunchy professors like myself, zipping off to interdisciplinary conferences held in pleasant places" (85). This is a seating arrangement Rorty maps, two pages later, onto a dystopian vision of what globalization will mean for members of what he calls, after Orwell, the Inner Party ("the international, cosmopolitan super-rich," who will "make all the important decisions") and the Outer Party ("educated, comfortably off, cosmopolitan professionals — [Michael] Lind's 'overclass,' the people like you and me") (87). "The job of people like us," according to Rorty,

> will be to make sure that the decisions made by the Inner Party are carried out smoothly and efficiently. It will be in the interest of the international super-rich to keep our class relatively prosperous and happy. For they need people who can pretend to be the political class of each of the individual nation-states. (87)

I believe that many American studies scholars would find this to be a less than desirable fate for American studies, and I believe that many of them would prefer to imagine the place of American studies in the corporate multiversity rather differently. I believe that most American studies scholars might prefer to imagine, on the contrary, a dissident American studies that served neither as an apologist for U.S. adventurism in Haiti, in Grenada, in El Salvador, and throughout Central and Latin America nor as the intellectual wing of the United Fruit Company, flying around the hemisphere to pleasant places in coach.

But if anyone is to imagine such a dissident American studies, an American studies of the loyal opposition, if you will, American studies scholars will need to think more dialectically and less aversively about their relation to the state. I draw this lesson in large part from a leading American studies scholar from whom I've learned more than I can fairly acknowledge in one essay, George Lipsitz. Lipsitz's book of essays, *American Studies in a Moment of Danger*, is not only an exemplary text of the new American studies, especially in its theorization of the relation between American studies and dissident social movements, but also an exemplary text for the new American studies' profound reluctance to imagine the nation-state as anything but a vehicle for racism and repression. Indeed, one would be hard-pressed to find a book more suspicious of the state than *American Studies in a Moment of Danger*. In his first chapter, Lipsitz writes,

> The hegemony of the nation-state as the ultimate horizon in American studies (and other nationally based inquiries in the humanities and social sciences) has deadly consequences. It encourages us to confine politics to the realm of the citizen-subject, to view emancipatory movements for social change as primarily efforts to reform the state and its privileged institutions. This emphasis on the state as the primary (and often exclusive) site for political action occludes the unity of politics, culture, and economics in social life, leading us to an idealist and inaccurate view of culture as the site where economic and political exclusions become neutralized by the purported inclusiveness of cultural practices and stories. These acts of cognitive mapping leave us poorly prepared to understand the ways in which culture functions as a social force or the ways in which aesthetic forms draw their affective and ideological power from their social location. (17)

However nativist and particularist "nationally based inquiries in the humanities and social sciences" may be at their very worst, this seems an excessive string of crimes with which to charge them. Surely it is a mystification to see culture as the site where economic and political exclusions become neutralized by the purported inclusiveness of cultural practices and stories, and it is even worse to fail to understand how culture functions as a social force or how aesthetic forms draw their affective and ideological power from their social location, but does all that really follow from thinking about the nation-state? Can people not have idealist, formalist, and even misty-eyed views of culture without subscribing to nationalism? Likewise, there are any number of sins of omission and commission I would lay at the feet of American studies scholars who took the nation-state as the ultimate horizon of their work (such as their willingness to serve as literal agents of the nation-state in the covert cultural operations of the Cold War), but those enumerated in Lipsitz's list are not among them.

Two pages later, Lipsitz goes further, arguing that "scholars may still have the luxury of thinking in exclusively national terms, but workers, citizens, migrants, artists, and activists do not" (19). This opposition between scholarly luxuries and political exigencies looks plausible enough, since the unfinished and uneven globalization of capitalism, together with the new new world order after 11 September, requires everyone to think globally and act globally as well. But one could easily reverse this formulation and argue that scholars may have the luxury of thinking in postnational terms but that workers, citizens, migrants, artists, and activists do not, since nation-states' actions and policies structure these people's lives in obvious and immediate ways. Lipsitz admits as much elsewhere in the book, where, in his discussion of the state's promotion of consumer capitalism, he argues that "the seeming contemporary eclipse of the state by the power of private capital and transnational corporations hides the crucial role of the state in promoting, protecting, and preserving the technologies, social relations, and economic interests of corporate capital and finance" (241). Whereas earlier an emphasis on the state as the site for political action occluded the unity of politics, culture, and economics in social life, had deadly consequences, and was a luxury only scholars could afford, now it is imperative to understand the state's crucial role in underwriting the growth of the private sector and the evisceration of public goods and services since 1945, for the state has only *seemingly* been eclipsed by the power of private capital and transnational corporations.

Lipsitz is not wrong about the role of the state as the structural support for so-called private enterprise; on the contrary, when he theorizes the state in his essay "In the Sweet Buy and Buy: Consumer Capital and American Studies," he does a wonderful job of showing how the postwar U.S. state has diverted public funds to private interests and how a "'free market' for business requires enormous amounts of state intervention and invention" (241). Lipsitz's critique of official state neoliberalism recalls Dick Cheney's obscene claim, during his October 2000 vice presidential debate with Joe Lieberman, that he had made his fortune at Halliburton without any help from the federal government — and this after swelling Halliburton's coffers (and his own estate) by means of federal contracts so generous that one is compelled to wonder whether the recipients of state handouts do not, after all, experience a profound personal moral decay. Nevertheless, despite the merits of Lipsitz's critique, the point remains that there is something of a disjunction between the nation-state Lipsitz dismisses in chapter 1 and the nation-state Lipsitz excoriates in chapter 10, as if his form of American studies cannot decide whether the state is irrelevant or insidious. And it should be said as well that the state Lipsitz theorizes in these passages is not the state of the Food and Drug Administration, or the Occupational Safety and Health Administration, or the minimum wage, or the National Labor Relations Board, or the Clean Air and Water Acts, or the Individuals with Disabilities Education Act, or the Voting Rights Act — each of which testify to the myriad ways in which workers, citizens, migrants, artists, and activists have changed the state's composition and public functions.

I close this brief discussion of Lipsitz's work by returning to the argument with which I started — that is, to admit that it may not matter at all to the state whether I am right to suggest that Lipsitz's treatment of the state is consistent only in its hostility to the state. The state is a complex and conflicted sets of institutions and practices, and I am not going to try to predict what kinds of knowledges in American studies will someday be of use to it and why; all I will say is that the potential uses and misuses or our work are not entirely ours to control. At the moment, surely, there is no real danger that the State Department will make any attempt to make George Lipsitz's work the centerpiece of a new propaganda offensive intended to show our European and Middle Eastern critics that the United States is an open and pluralistic society that fosters critical knowledge about the Knights of Labor, the musicians of Miami, and the Movimiento Chicano; the state that finds Lipsitz's work congenial to its domestic or international politics is a state I do not currently live in and cannot currently envision. For all that I have said about those good old days when the CIA was the NEA, I do not imagine that the relations between leftist intellectuals and the state, or between leftist intellectuals and global capitalism can be anything other than conflicted. But if leftist intellectuals in American studies want to be something other and better than what Rorty calls the paid political class of the international superrich, then I propose that they must undertake some hard thinking about American studies' relation to the nation-state. Only then can academic intellectuals, however compromised and corporatized their academic institutions may be, begin to realize their commitment to the ideal of a vital and contentious public sphere, and — as if this phrase had never been abused in our lifetimes — to the ideal of a free society.

Notes

1. "The biggest change since 1964," according to the NAS study, "has been the relative de-emphasis of classic British and Irish authors, the group comprising the most important single component of the English literary tradition. While 47% of the names cited in 1964 course descriptions were authors found in the third edition of the *Norton Anthology of English Literature*, that figure fell to 33% by 1989, and 28% by 1997" (16). The phrasing suggests that even in 1997, the NAS was gauging the literature curriculum against the third edition of the *Norton Anthology*. For statistical purposes, I presume, the NAS's list of "standard British authors" must remain static, the better to make the contrast between 1964 and now. Indeed, at certain points in

the report, the language suggests that any change since 1964 is ipso facto change for the worse, as in the following: "Our statistics also clearly confirm the reality of 'race' as a driving factor in revamping literature programs. The fact that the United States has produced many more 'authors of color' than the British Isles is another reason for the English curriculum's increasing Americanization. Many African-American writers have gone from little or no notice in 1964 to substantial visibility in 1997. Among the better known, Langston Hughes, Frederick Douglass, and Ralph Ellison — each unmentioned in course descriptions in 1964 — accounted for 0.3%, 0.4%, and 0.4%, respectively, of all author citations by 1997. Richard Wright went from 0.1% in 1964 to 0.6% in 1997" (19). There is nothing in the NAS report to suggest that the process by which major African American writers began to appear in U.S. college courses between 1964 and 1997 might be either justifiable or salutary, and there is accordingly nothing in the report to defend "the reality of 'race' as a driving factor in revamping literature programs" on nationalist or intellectual grounds.

2. In "Resituating American Studies in a Critical Internationalism," Jane C. Desmond and Virginia R. Domínguez report that their survey of American studies program descriptions in the 1995 American Studies Association directory found one only program that "includes an international orientation: the result of a new initiative to internationalize all aspects of education at that university." But they immediately follow this observation with the argument that "the lack of an international thrust" in U.S. American studies programs "is all the more troubling and paradoxical, given the current globalization of economic, cultural, and informational flows and the amount of cultural studies scholarship devoted to charting them" (481). Here, the argument for critical internationalism would seem to depend on the idea of an international American studies as a kind of supplement, in the Derridean sense, to global capitalism.

3. The proposition that dissent is unnecessary because possible also animated much of the most heated rhetoric of the culture wars, with their ritual denunciations of unpatriotic faculty on U.S. campuses. Indeed, one of the most striking features of the deployment of that rhetoric was that Cold War liberals engaged in it every bit as eagerly and unreflectively as did Cold War conservatives. Witness Jason Epstein in his 1994 interview with Saunders: speaking of the 1949 Cultural and Scientific Conference for World Peace held by communists and American fellow travelers at the Waldorf-Astoria, in New York, Epstein says, "[T]he Stalinists were still a very powerful gang; they were like the political correctness lot now. There was good reason, therefore, to question the Stalinists' right to culture" (Saunders 48). Accordingly, in the early 1990s, Epstein's *New York Review of Books* was often friendlier to figures like Dinesh D'Souza than to figures like Stanley Fish, presumably on the grounds that assorted multiculturalists and poststructuralists were basically warmed-over Stalinists and that there was therefore good reason to question literary theorists' right to culture.

Works Cited

Curiel, Barbara Brinson, et al. Introduction. In *Post-Nationalist American Studies*, edited by John Carlos Rowe, 1 – 21. Berkeley: University of California Press, 2000.

Denning, Michael. " 'The Special American Conditions': Marxism and American Studies." *American Quarterly* 38, no. 3 (1986): 356 – 80.

Desmond, Jane C., and Virginia R. Domínguez. "Resituating American Studies in a Critical Internationalism." *American Quarterly* 48, no. 3 (1996): 475 – 90.

Fleischer, Ari. Press briefing, Washington, D.C., 7 May 2001. Available at < http://www.whitehouse.gov/news/briefings/20010507.html. > Accessed 29 July 2002.

Lipsitz, George. *American Studies in a Moment of Danger*. Minneapolis: University of Minnesota Press, 2001.

Miyoshi, Masao. "Ivory Tower in Escrow." *Boundary 2* 27, no. 1 (2000): 7 – 50.

National Association of Scholars. *Losing the Big Picture: The Fragmentation of the English Major since 1964*. Princeton, N.J.: National Association of Scholars, 2000.

Radway, Janice. "What's in a Name?: Presidential Address to the American Studies Association, 20 November 1998." *American Quarterly* 51, no. 1 (1999): 1 – 32.

Rogin, Michael. "When the CIA Was the NEA." *Nation*, 12 June 2000, 16, 18, 20.

Rorty, Richard. *Achieving Our Country: Leftist Thought in Twentieth-Century America*. Cambridge: Harvard University Press, 1998.

Rowe, John Carlos, ed. *Post-Nationalist American Studies*. Berkeley: University of California Press, 2000.

Saunders, Frances Stonor. *The Cultural Cold War: The CIA and the World of Arts and Letters*. New York: New Press, 2000.

Sharlet, Jeff. "Tinker, Writer, Artist, Spy: Intellectuals during the Cold War." *Chronicle of Higher Education*, 31 March 2000, A19 – 20.

Idolatries of the Marketplace:
Thomas Frank, Cultural Studies,
and the Voice of the People

T he 1980s were a fine time to be rich in America — but the 1990s were fabulous. And if you were a CEO or a nose-ringed dot.com entrepreneur, you were a figure of world-historical proportions, not merely a wealth magnet but a very example of the New Man to whom the New Economy was giving birth. Here's the view from the top: in 1990, average CEO "wages" were 85 times those of the average blue-collar employee. In the next decade, that ratio went from merely staggering to truly astronomical, winding up at 475:1 in 1999 — greater than a fivefold increase in nine years. The CEO/worker income ratio in Japan, meanwhile, held steady at 11:1, and in Britain — "the country," writes Thomas Frank in *One Market under God: Extreme Capitalism, Market Populism, and the End of Economic Democracy*, "most enamored of New Economy principles after the U.S. itself" (7) — it was 24:1.

The New Economy and its CEO speedwagon were fueled by the long Dow boom, but they got a few crucial pushes from the U.S. federal government, so that every so often, American free-market ideologues had to take a twenty-second time-out from their ritual attacks on government to count all the bundles of money government policies had dumped in their laps. And after the passage of the Telecommunications Act of 1996, media moguls really had to bundle up: as Frank points out, when the act became law, the telecommunications industry "promptly embarked on a spree of buyouts and monopoly building, with telephone and cable systems merging and converging in a whirling tangle of free-market ebullience that continues to this day" (x). Transferring public ownership of $70 billion worth of digital frequencies to private interests, the Telecommunications Act presented what Frank calls "one of those tableaux of greed, legislative turpitude, and transparently self-serving sophistry that American culture ordinarily delights in exposing and deriding" (x). But there was little public protest about metastasizing CEO compensation — and nary a peep from anyone with any meaningful access to state or corporate power.

Why such silence, and why so little gagging? Two reasons come to mind.

One, cultural critics on the left were not significant campaign contributors and could only fume on the sidelines while corporate dollars bought one major American political party and three-quarters of the other. Two, the expansion of the stock market to middle-income Americans, largely by way of 401(k) mutual funds, allowed market apologists to claim that what was good for General Motors was now good for the country's retirement portfolios. Frank quickly exposes the speciousness of this claim, noting that because "the vast majority of shares are still held by the wealthy . . . the booming stock market of the nineties did not democratize wealth; it concentrated wealth" (96 – 97). The economy as a whole thus followed the logic of right-wing tax cuts — namely, an extra ten bucks each for you and your friends, another ten billion for John Malone, Rupert Murdoch, Jack Welch, and Bill Gates. And, as we know, this strategy apparently worked sufficiently well in the last decade to allow the right wing to pass new and even more amazing rounds of tax cuts in this decade.

One Market under God, however, is not primarily concerned with such piecemeal, partial explanations as these. To his credit, Thomas Frank seeks bigger game: not the specific people, laws, or campaign contributions that secured neoliberalism's current stranglehold over public policy but the broader cultural formation (though Frank doesn't call it that, for reasons I'll get to later) that made it all possible. Frank calls this market populism, "a curious but ideologically potent cultural hybrid bringing together the antiauthoritarian strains of traditional populism with the most orthodox faiths of classical economics" (111 – 12). In one sense, market populism is nothing more than the traditional libertarian equation of free markets with free societies, according to which humans are most free from persecution when corporations are most free from government regulation. This equation, notes Frank, has been "part of the cultural wallpaper for years" (xiv) but has become standard-issue wallpaper only very recently:

> Market populism began in nearly all its varieties as an ideology of business, as a PR scheme for this industry or that, as a simple management tactic, as a dream of the media conglomerates, as an official slogan for the New York Stock Exchange. What makes it worth studying, though, is its recent triumph in the larger world of American culture, the process by which even non-bankers, non-CEOs, and non-Republicans learned to accept the logic of the market as the functional equivalent of democracy. (57)

The triumph of market populism thus renders it something other than garden-variety libertarian social theory, since to become hegemonic, market populism has to appeal somehow to people who don't subscribe to *Reason* magazine or

Investor's Business Daily. In explaining this triumph, Frank has a twofold task: to describe market populism and its apologists, and to account for the relative collapse of other ways of thinking about the world.

Much of *One Market under God* is devoted to parsing out and exposing the remarkable idiocies of what passes for "management theory" these days, and one of the delights of the book is surely the dexterity and élan with which Frank skewers the genre and its gurus — Tom Peters, George Gilder, Peter Senge, and company. Here are the business world's paeans to the soulful corporation, glassy-eyed treatises on the Tao of Dow, and hymns to the cosmic rightness of free trade, all of which give Frank his title and all of which earn his well-deserved scorn. Frank's reaction upon reading Thomas Friedman's fatuous *The Lexus and the Olive Tree* pretty much sums up his relation to most of the material in which he'd immersed himself for the previous few years:

> Enthusiasm for the "rebranding" of Britain, pointless ponderings about the physical weight of each country's GNP, facile equating of Great Society America with the Soviet Union. Each of them is preposterous in its own way, but thrown together they make a truly dispiriting impression, a feeling akin to the first time I heard Newt Gingrich speak publicly and it began to dawn on me that *this is what the ruling class calls thinking*, that this handful of pathetic, palpably untrue prejudices are all they have to guide them as they shuttle back and forth between the State Department and the big think tanks, discussing what they mean to do with us and how they plan to dispose of our country. (67 – 68)

For readers like me, this is a seductively satisfying account of Newthink; it (almost) lulls me into thinking that They have all the power but We have all the brains. I like Frank's pun on "dispose," and I find it pleasing to believe that the people who dispose of our country are as shallow and as easily disposed of as this, even or especially if that's not quite true. But these moments of sublime superciliousness are not the best things about Frank's book; they are merely moments of sublime superciliousness, something like a consolation prize offered to liberal readers who like to think of themselves as the smartest kids in the room. Instead, what makes Frank worth studying is his unerring eye not only for the pomposities of market populism but also for their consequences.

Opening the book by noting that free marketeers treat union supporters as dupes and automatons, "people lacking agency of their own, empty vessels filled with the wills of others" (xiii), Frank teases out perhaps the most important feature of market populism — that is, its strategic confusion of who counts as an "agent." According to market populists, people can only act freely and rationally in a free market; thus, anticorporate activists are really Stalinoid puppets, duped by the discourses of collectivism. Furthermore, the globalization of the free market is inevitable, and resistance is the work of flat-earthers and fools. The first proposition — that trade unionists are dupes — is prima facie absurd, since it entails the ancillary claim, as Frank shows, that "workers weren't *victimized* by downsizing and job insecurity; these were things they *wanted*, things they fought for, things they needed to realize their full humanity, to escape from the corporate conformity of yesterday" (199 – 200). But the second proposition — that completely free markets are inevitable — is not merely absurd but (in tandem with the first) incoherent, for it undermines the notion that free markets free people: "How," asks Frank, "can we really be 'free agents' or 'empowered' or 'liberated' if we are in the tight grip of inevitability?" (240)

Something at once odd and odious masks this contradiction, a cultural shift that has drawn Frank's fire before — namely, the corporate "conquest" of cool. Appropriating the language of populist revolt and postpunk Bad Attitude, corporate America has managed to define itself precisely against what most people think of as corporate America, and the terrain of cultural criticism has been transformed accordingly. The symbolism runs like so: twentysomethings with interesting hair configurations are revolutionizing the culture of the corporation. The new Wall Street's attitude toward the old, pinstriped Wall Street is like unto the Sex Pistols' attitude toward, say, Elvis. And the Internet? Dude, the Internet changes *everything*. So pervasive is this self-representation of the financiers of the New Economy that Frank is hard put to lampoon it. Take, for example, Jonathan Hoenig, P.O.V. columnist, NPR commentator, and author of *Greed Is Good*: "A dramatic shout is being heard in America these days. *It's the voice of new money*. It's young people who are determined to be themselves" (qtd. in Frank 143). The best Frank can muster in response, alas, is mere paraphrase: "It's the George Gilder model of social conflict — righteous new money vs. snooty old — only spiced up in this telling with a few tired slogans from the sixties, as filtered through decades of TV commercials." Even his attempt to parody Hoenig falls a bit flat: "So disgusted are we by the materialism of our wealthy elders that we must break with them altogether and become . . . wealthy!" (143). Nevertheless, Frank does not lose sight of the political reality driving this symbolic shift — namely, Wall Street's ideological investment in inducing Americans to think of themselves as shareholders rather than as citizens and thus, as in the passage of the Telecommunications Act, refashioning privatization as an enhancement of the public good. This is surely the main point of the enterprise of private enterprise, the force behind not only the dot.com bubble but also the related and perhaps incipient privatization of Social Security.

I admire Frank's project in *One Market under God*. And I'll admit to having learned a good deal from it — particularly about the transformation of American business culture and the millennial pretensions of management theory. The book does, however, have some flaws. Among the most minor of these is the indiscriminateness of its outrage: on one page, Frank insists that "there is no social theory on earth short of the divine right of kings that can justify a five-hundred-fold gap between management and labor" (250); on another page he's complaining about the Nortel ad in which an executive recites the lyrics of "Come Together" (172). Well, yes, it's annoying that the surviving Beatles don't control the rights to their own oeuvre and that Lennon's trippy exhortation to simultaneous orgasm be rewritten as the script of the company meeting, but it has been more than sixty years since Walter Benjamin warned us of the amazing conscriptive powers of the bourgeois apparatus. Surely the next Nortel commercial will find some visually arresting way to quote Benjamin on the amazing conscriptive powers of the bourgeois apparatus. Likewise, you can only fulminate once per book about the smug self-congratulation of the movie *Pleasantville*. Three times bespeaks either poor editing or repetition compulsion. And you shouldn't still be defining "market populism" on page 111. But then, there's a lot of repetition here, too many management theorists and not enough workers, too much about TheStreet.com and not enough about government.

These, as I say, are minor flaws. For *One Market under God* attempts to chart a new cultural terrain — the details by which "making the world safe for billionaires has been as much a cultural and political operation as an economic one" (15). The book is, in other words, a cultural studies intervention into the hegemonic language of neoliberalism; and yet these are "other words" indeed, for if there is one intellectual tradition with which Frank does not want to align himself, it's the tradition of cultural studies. The book's chapter on cultural studies as a result will prove nettlesome for some of Frank's academic readers, and though it will win him admirers and blurb suppliers among those who (1) know nothing more about cultural studies than what Frank tells them or (2) know just enough about cultural studies to hate, hate, hate Andrew Ross and his earring too, it will also cost him some credibility among precisely those cultural critics who need most to read this book.

Frank's argument is that the cultural studies wing of the academic left has aided and abetted the spread of market populism by undertaking analyses of "subcultures" in which consumers of mass culture turn out to be empowered by the practice of consumption. In Frank's parlance, "cult-stud" scholars are little more than cheerleaders for the New Economy, endlessly burbling about how people use products in ways their makers never intended and thereby perform the important cultural work of "resistance." To this Frank adds a loosely related bill of particulars: cultural studies is too insular; it's too preening and faux hip; it's too invested in its own European lineage, not sufficiently aware of American sociologists such as Herbert Gans; it's too proud of its opposition to the Christian right; it was badly embarrassed by the Sokal Hoax; it did not attend to the crisis in academic labor; and it has been co-opted by neoconservatives as well as libertarian economist Tyler Cowen and the irascible, incoherent advertising critic James Twitchell.

But most annoying about Frank's attempt to cast cultural studies as the academic wing of Market Populists Inc. is that he has a point. He's not always sure how best to make it, and he keeps fingering the wrong suspects and missing the easy openings, but still, I have to give him his due: he must be among the very few nonacademics in North America who's read all of Larry Grossberg's *We Gotta Get Out of This Place*. When Frank goes after the consumption-as-empowerment school, though, he doesn't mention its leading exponent, John Fiske, whose scholarly career is basically that of the austere Adorno scholar who one day discovered that wow, hot dogs really taste *good* and has since devoted himself to the celebration thereof. Similarly, Frank seems to score a point against "cult studs' strange fantasy of encirclement by Marxists at once crude and snobbish" (304), but he misses the real antagonists at stake in subcultural analyses of World Championship Wrestling — not the League of Adornian Marxists, certainly, but the tweedy, Moynihan-liberal faculty who DJ the Mozart show on public radio every second Sunday and who just happen to be the distinguished senior colleagues whose scholarly sensibilities cultural studies is supposed to offend. In this academic economy, of course, the critic with the coolest, most transgressive subculture wins, which is why you don't see many cultural studies essays on the Amish.

Yet here, in roundabout fashion, is where Frank lands his most palpable hit. Cultural studies, whatever its other real or imagined failings, has not said boo about the cultural formation Frank describes in *One Market under God*, and that's one reason why Frank won't use the phrase "cultural formation": "for all its generalized hostility to business and frequent discussions of 'late capital,'" he writes, "cultural studies failed almost completely to produce close analyses of the daily life of business" (290). There's simply no disputing this claim. Of all Frank's complaints about cultural studies, this is the one cult studs should take most to heart: with few exceptions (such as the work of Michael Denning and Richard Ohmann and, more recently, Andrew Ross's *No-Collar*), American cultural studies has indeed broken with the Hall-Williams-Thompson tradition of British cultural studies and devoted itself instead to the unearthing of "counterhegemonic" practices of TV watching. Subcultural analysis has too often proceeded by way of a kind of political ventriloquism (as John Frow argued in *Cultural Studies and Cultural Value*, a book not cited by Frank, though it should have been), and cult studs who promote the model of "the intellectual as fan" (also not addressed by Frank, though it should have been) usually manage to forget that fans are often quite critical of their objects. (Perhaps what is required here is a model of the intellectual as Chicago Cubs fan.) Overdrawn and partial as Frank's case may be, his main charge has too much merit to ignore: all the while the New Economy was building us a house of cards, most cult studs were churning out Gramscian readings of MTV's *House of Style*.

Frank is more than smart enough to know, and honest enough to admit, that some of the most trenchant critiques of cult-stud populism have in fact been launched by cult studs themselves (and here he should have cited Judith Williamson's classic "The Problems of Being Popular," now more than twenty years old), but he occasionally lets his penchant for polemic get the better of his judgment. Early in the chapter on cult studs, Frank cites a fairly innocuous sentence I wrote in 1992 about how cultural studies tries "to discover and interpret the ways disparate disciplinary subjects *talk back*" (Bérubé 10, qtd. in Frank 283) and proceeds to make this out to be a refrain for the market populism of cultural studies professors everywhere, as if we're all chirpy proponents of town meetings and focus groups in the mode of GOP pollster Frank Luntz. This is great fun, no question, but anyone remotely familiar with the practice of anthropology since Lévi-Strauss, let alone the history of prisons and mental illness, knows that the question here is a profoundly ethical one. And Frank knows it, too: the idea that people can talk back to the institutions and discourses that structure their lives is absolutely essential to any populism — and any theory of democracy — worthy of the name.

This is why Frank closes his book with, of all things, the ringing cadences of people *talking back*:

> And in the streets and the union halls and the truck stops and the three-flats and the office blocks there remained all along a vocabulary of fact and knowing and memory, of wit and everyday doubt, a vernacular that could not be extinguished no matter how it was cursed for "cynicism," a dialect that the focus group could never quite reflect, the resilient language of democracy. (358)

But strangely, there is no evidence of this language anywhere in the book, no union halls or truck stops or three-flats or office blocks. On the contrary, Frank repeatedly argues that the public itself is part of the problem: "[A]ll through the nineties the public had seemed to shrink ever further from any actual embrace of democratic power" (44). But then, why shouldn't Frank avail himself of the same rhetorical strategy he mocks in others? The very idea of market populism would have no political purchase, no sting, if it did not assume the possibility of a real populism of which the "market" version is an obscene corruption. If Frank did not believe in the language of popular consent to begin with, there is no way he could write of a market-populist "consensus in which *massive abuse of the language of popular consent* masked a repugnant politics of enrichment for some and degradation for millions of others" (274; emphasis added). Ironically enough, people familiar with the history of cultural studies will surely hear in "market populism" a deliberate echo of Stuart Hall's famous descriptions of Thatcherite "authoritarian populism" in *The Hard Road to Renewal*; and at the heart of both "market populism" and "authoritarian populism" lies the indispensable belief that these cultural formations deploy populist sentiment to mobilize social policies that work viciously against the ordinary people in whose name they fraudulently speak. The question of whether the people are actually "talking back" is not a trivial matter of market research. It should be central to the project of cultural studies, and it should be central to Frank's work: for if the people *aren't* really speaking the language of market populism, then they are being ventriloquized and betrayed by Tom Friedman and Tom Peters and all their fellow travelers.

Frank insists that the management-theory targets of his wrath are directly responsible for the relaxation of Americans' gag reflex at the further enriching of the superrich:

> That America was able to endure the wrenching upward redistribution of wealth that it did in the nineties with only small, localized outbreaks of social unrest must be chalked up, at least in part, to the literature that explicitly sought to persuade the world of the goodness and justice of that redistribution. (180)

But this is sloppy economics, sloppy ethnography, and even sloppy literary criticism (the "at least in part" hedge covers any number of sins). Frank offers us no evidence that New Economy literature performed this function, and no evidence against the argument that social unrest was actually *blunted* by the expansion of the economy, by record-low levels of unemployment, and by Clinton's progressive tax initiatives, such as the expansion of the Earned Income Tax Credit (the most progressive form of taxation since the days of LBJ and a form of taxation about which Frank says nothing). If Frank is to be believed, Americans were pacified not by the ancillary benefits of Clinton-era economic policy but by the "literature" produced by Tom Peters, Spencer Johnson, and company. But then again, if Frank is to be believed, Americans were not pacified at all; on the contrary, they continued to speak a vernacular that could not be extinguished no matter how it was cursed for "cynicism," a dialect that the focus group could never quite reflect, the resilient language of democracy.

By the time *One Market under God* appeared, the god of the New Economy was looking very much like a god that failed: in early 2001, TheStreet.com was trading at $2.72 a share, down from its high of $71; the dot.com explosion was beginning to look like it was founded on the film *Boiler Room*; and the *Wall Street Journal* was reporting incredulously that younger Americans think that unions are cool. Even before 9/11, the cracks in the market-populist foundation were becoming obvious not only to leftists and progressives but also to people who don't think of themselves as either leftist or progressive. Maybe Frank helped that process along. And maybe Frank's work will help to shake American cultural studies out of its complacency, its institutional insularity, its inattention to public policy. Perhaps then cultural studies will resume doing the kind of tactical, engaged cultural criticism it always claims to do, the kind Thomas Frank might someday want to claim as an ally of — and an influence on — his own.

Works Cited

Bérubé, Michael. "Pop Goes the Academy: Cult Studs Fight the Power." *Village Voice Literary Supplement* 104 (April 1992): 10 – 14.

Frank, Thomas. *One Market under God: Extreme Capitalism, Market Populism, and the End of Economic Democracy*. New York: Doubleday, 2000.

Friedman, Thomas. *The Lexus and the Olive Tree: Understanding Globalization*. New York: Farrar Straus Giroux, 1999.

Frow, John. *Cultural Studies and Cultural Value*. London: Oxford University Press, 1995.

Hall, Stuart. *The Hard Road to Renewal: Thatcherism and the Crisis of the Left*. London: Verso, 1988.

Ross, Andrew. *No-Collar: The Humane Workplace and Its Hidden Costs*. New York: Basic Books, 2003.

Williamson, Judith. "The Problems of Being Popular." *New Socialist*, September 1986, 14 – 15.

Part Three

PROFESSIONS

T his section is devoted to some of the more quotidian (but critical) features of academic life and work—teaching classes, grading papers, living as a member of a campus community. "When I think of the future of literary studies," I write in "Days of Future Past," "I deliberately try to concentrate on the mundane bookkeeping matters of the profession, out of the conviction that if the profession offers its aspirants good material and intellectual working conditions, the shape and the range of the knowledges produced in the profession will eventually take care of themselves." In my accounts of the profession of literary study, I do not want to be prescriptive about what literary criticism and theory should and should not do; indeed, laments about the state of criticism and theory seem to me to be one of the most tiresome varieties of academic complaint, and in their revanchist mode they take the unwittingly self-aggrandizing form of the assertion *Nobody treats literature correctly except for me.* But my approach to such matters is not completely laissez-faire. I do, for example, want to warn my colleagues against self-flagellating (or self-aggrandizing) disciplinary narratives, and I do want to be prescriptive, in a meta kind of way, in my disdain for prescriptive accounts of literary criticism and theory.

I believe that the profession would be better off, on balance, if more professors of literature (and many more of our critics outside the academy) were to recognize that literature is an extraordinarily capacious field of endeavor, quite capable of sustaining all manner of approaches to it. I myself do not "do" queer theory, and I am largely innocent of Gilles Deleuze and Giorgio Agamben, but the fact that other scholars work in queer theory or pledge allegiance to Deleuze and Agamben does not harm me, or literature, in the slightest. I care far more about disparities in the basic working conditions of my fellow scholars—between tenure-track positions that afford time for reading and research, and adjunct positions that include neither a living wage nor health insurance—than about intellectual disparities between scholars who develop an epistemology of the closet and scholars who study medieval lives of the saints. And I refuse to believe that the relation between the epistemology of the closet and the lives of the saints is that of a zero-sum game. Only petty academic territorialism leads us to think so, and as this section demonstrates, the only thing that wearies me more than laments about the state of criticism and theory is the petty academic territorialism that infects so much of our professional lives.

Starting, then, with an essay about the dismaying prevalence of decline-and-fall narratives in contemporary accounts of literary studies, this section proposes an introductory curriculum in literary theory for graduate programs; surveys the conditions and challenges of teaching undergraduate literature surveys; casts a cold eye on the discourses of institutional affiliation and professional prestige; and offers a series of brief takes on some of the mundane but often misunderstood aspects of academe — campus policies and politics with regard to child care; the workings of the invited-speaker circuit; the mysterious mechanics of paper grading; and, last but not least, the encroachment of corporate culture on every corner of campus. These brief takes were originally published in the *Chronicle of Higher Education*, as were the final two essays in the section — companion pieces, as I like to think of them, on popular culture and its critics. The first takes up some of the function(s) of nonacademic cultural criticism at the present time, and tries to assess how the discourses of popular evaluation have implications for cultural studies: Top 5 love songs, greatest one hundred sports figures, worst ten movies of all time. The section's final essay names and analyzes the Elvis Costello Problem in teaching popular culture, the curious phenomenon whereby professors in cultural studies, who keep aging every year even as their undergraduates stubbornly remain in their late teens and early twenties, have to find ways of negotiating both the ephemerality *and* the longevity of popular culture. On the one hand, the early albums of Elvis Costello — or the Clash, or the Ramones, or the Talking Heads — recede infinitely into the distance or remain in professorial memory (in my case) as the signpost of one's own late teens and early twenties, even as they become, like the sitcoms and advertising jingles of decades gone by, less and less intelligible to one's students. But on the other hand, the culture industry has, in recent years, developed a powerful "retro"-generating apparatus which, far from being limited to stock representations of innocent 1950s "happy days," now touches every kind of cultural production up to and including those of the 1990s. The runaway neo-neoism involved in this development should not be underestimated. If, as Fredric Jameson once pointed out, 1977's *Star Wars* represented an attempt to evoke without irony the era of Saturday-morning serials, satisfying "a deep (might I even say repressed?) longing to experience them again" (116), what are we to make of the phenomenon of fans who are nostalgic for the original *Star Wars*? Imagine, if you will, a culture whose inhabitants include television viewers who long for the era of *Happy Days* — that is, the good old days of the 1970s, when nostalgia for a still earlier time was still fresh and immediate.

The problem of temporality (and neo-[neo-]temporality) structures these two essays more than the others in this section. Because they deal with popular culture and with the question of teaching ephemeral aspects of popular culture, they require an update and an upgrade since their original publication in 1999 – 2000: the cultural phenomena that were fresh then — *Dawson's Creek*, *The Matrix*, "Show me the money" — have become relics, and new figures, from 50 Cent's "Candy Shop" to VH1's *Twenty Most Awesomely Bad Songs of 2004*, have taken their place. Though I've brushed up these essays so that they look back on rather than speak from the bygone, innocent days of Britney Spears's first tentative forays into sexual commerce, I think I have been faithful to the spirit of each essay precisely to the extent that I have been willing to tweak its flesh.

Ars longa, VH1 brevis, and all we are is dust in the wind.

Works Cited

Jameson, Fredric. "Postmodernism and Consumer Society." In The Anti-Aesthetic: Essays on Postmodern Culture, edited by Hal Foster, 111 – 25. Port Townsend, Wash.: Bay Press, 1983.

E very so often I am asked, either by reporters on slow news days or by people three seats down the bar looking for an argument, for my opinion on the Next Big Thing in literary studies. Now that cultural studies, postcolonialism, and queer theory have joined New Historicism and deconstruction as established subfields of theoretical study complete with courses, book series, major figures, keywords, and well-worn avenues of debate over the efficacy of those courses, book series, major figures, and keywords (such that any schoolchild can now recite the seven reasons why *hybridity* is a problematic term), inquiring minds want to know: what's next? What are trendy, supercilious, finger-to-the-wind folk like me cooking up in our basement theory labs for the rest of the twenty-first century? What should I be reading to stay ahead of the curve? And will there be a conference?

But even though the phrase "the future of literary studies" makes up part of the subtitle of one of my books, I didn't care then and I don't care now what the Next Big Thing might be. I do try to conduct myself like a responsible citizen of the profession, but I'm not a groundbreaking theorist and never will be, and with each new development in the world of theory, from Agamben to *Antigone* to *Empire*, I lose even more of my ability to paraphrase and review the work of other groundbreaking theorists. It's true that I do care about the intellectual and institutional status of the emergent body of work known as disability studies, but I have serious doubts that disability studies will ever become the profession's Next Big Thing and serious misgivings about what it would look like if it did. After all, one of the things that make emergent bodies of work so exciting and surprising is precisely that, being *emergent* bodies of work, they don't yet have a settled terrain of courses, book series, major figures, keywords, and well-worn avenues of debate: it hasn't been decided yet just what counts as disability studies, what counts as a theoretical position in disability studies, what kind of account of the body or of the built environment is relevant to disability studies, or what the possible relation(s) might be between disability studies and disability law or disability activism. Disability studies will surely grow and mature over the next ten years, and will be an exciting and surprising area of study not only because its terms are still up for grabs but also because its terms (whatever they turn out to be) can potentially speak to everything from dyslexia to dystopia, from prosthetics to aesthetics. Still, one of the things that happens to academic fields as they grow and mature is that they become predictable and routinized. Or, to put this as sourly as possible: you know an emergent area of study has really begun to establish itself once it starts to produce mediocre and derivative work — that is, once search committee members can say of job candidates, as did one such committee member in the late 1980s, "This person is without question the best of this year's Greenblatt clones."

Instead, when I think of the future of literary studies, I deliberately try to concentrate on the mundane bookkeeping matters of the profession, out of the conviction that if the profession offers its aspirants good material and intellectual working conditions, the shape and the range of the knowledges produced in the profession will eventually take care of themselves. But in the couple of years since I published a collection of essays under the title *The Employment of English*, I've read many similar assessments of the status and the future of the profession, and I've come to believe that perhaps those bookkeeping matters are not quite as simple or as mundane as I had thought. Indeed, it is a bit ridiculous to ask English professors to gauge the future of their profession when so many of us are so unreliable when it comes to gauging the past.

Take, for example, the crisis of student enrollment in English, as a specific index of the more general crisis of student enrollment in the humanities. What crisis is this? Why, it's the crisis remarked by everyone from Alvin Kernan to Andrew Delbanco to Russell Jacoby to John Ellis: since 1966 or 1970 or thereabouts, students have been leaving the humanities in droves, and English enrollments accordingly have plummeted. The result is that English, once the queen of the disciplines, is now the campus court jester. Thus Delbanco, writing in the *New York Review of Books* in 1999: "[E]veryone knows that if you want to locate the laughingstock on your local campus these days, your best bet is to stop by the English department" (32).

Let me say first that I have all kinds of respect for Andrew Delbanco's work as a literary and cultural critic and that I even agree with his complaint, voiced much later in the essay, that "English has come to reflect some of the worst aspects of our culture: obsessing about sex, posturing about real social inequities while leaving them unredressed, and participating with gusto in the love/hate cult of celebrities" (38). But I don't have any respect for the claim that "everyone knows" that English departments are the laughingstocks of their local campuses. For one thing, it sounds parochially unaware that there are major universities in Kansas, Wisconsin, Nebraska, Pennsylvania, Virginia, and Illinois where English departments are actually the largest and most highly ranked departments in their colleges. I've traveled widely in this business, visiting campuses from Duke to Drury College, from Princeton to Central Oregon Community College, and I know that for every insane, dysfunctional, rancorous English department I've seen, there are another four whose on-campus reputation is that of the best department in the liberal arts, a department that upper-level administrators can trust to exercise good judgment, a department with a solid base of majors and a stellar record of teaching, a department that can be counted on to hire exciting and productive new faculty, host important conferences, and maybe even invite an interesting speaker or two. On one campus I know of, that of the University of Illinois at Urbana-Champaign, you could have looked up the director of the Illinois Program for Research in the Humanities, the director of the Campus Honors Program, the director of the Unit for Criticism and Interpretive Theory, the dean of the Graduate College, the director of the Drobny Center for the Study of Jewish Culture and Society on the week that Delbanco's essay was published — and you'd have found that all five were English professors. In fact, Delbanco's essay earned its opening claim by citing Carol Christ's monitory injunction that "on every campus there is one department whose name need only be mentioned to make people laugh; you don't want that department to be yours" (55) and contending that "everyone knows" that Christ means English although "she does not name the offender" (32). But this is a strange conclusion to draw from the example of Christ, an English professor who was, at the time her essay was published in *Profession*, the provost of the University of California at Berkeley. Perhaps, then, Berkeley's English Department is not nearly as risible as Delbanco suggests.

I do not mean to suggest that the crises at Columbia, which prevented the department from undertaking senior hires for some years, and similar crises at any number of the top twenty Ph.D.-granting departments of English, were not real. On the contrary, the fact that so many of those departments dissolved into incoherence and factionalism in the 1990s is noteworthy, and is an important sign of structural crisis in a profession whose intellectual parameters are roughly as fluid and as volatile as liquid helium. Nonetheless, and speaking only for myself, I am really quite tired of having my profession and my department called a laughingstock because the faculty at certain elite universities cannot agree on new hires, on new departmental leadership, or even on what hors d'oeuvres to serve at the fall faculty reception.

It may be objected that Delbanco's indictment of English as laughingstock does not depend primarily on enrollment figures; this much is true. Furthermore, Delbanco is careful to historicize the figures he cites, placing them in the context of the postwar economy and the professionalization of higher education and thus departing significantly from the Alvin Kernan/John Ellis model — the account of literary study in which our apparently steady decline since 1967 is to be attributed to theory, feminism, queer folk, politicization, jargon, solipsism, or postmodernism (unless indeed "postmodernism" itself includes all the other usual suspects). Since Delbanco's essay is a review of books by Kernan and Ellis (and, inter alios, me), this distance from the Kernan/Ellis model is noteworthy. Still, it's worth taking a look at the numbers Delbanco does cite, taking these from "a 1999 MLA report on Ph.D. placement and production, and from the statistical appendix to *What's Happened to the Humanities?*, Kernan's collection of essays by twelve leading scholars" (33):

> During the unprecedented expansion of American higher education in the 1960s, in my own department at Columbia, scores of candidates registered each year for the MA degree, and many went on for the Ph.D. Today, all this has changed. The number of Ph.D.s in English awarded annually in the United States peaked in the mid-1970s at nearly 1,400. Since then, the number has dropped by almost one third — a trend consistent with the contraction of the humanities (literature, language, philosophy, music, and art) as a whole, which fell as a percentage of all Ph.D.s from 13.8 percent to 9.1 percent between 1966 and 1993. In the same period, the percentage represented by the humanities of all BAs granted in the United States dropped from 20.7 percent to 12.7 percent. (33)

But the problem here, as with all statistical assessments of the humanities since the mid-1960s, is that the mid-1960s represented a high-water mark for study in the humanities in the United States, a period unmatched in the history of the republic. It is impossible to construct a narrative of anything *but* precipitous decline in the humanities when one starts from the mid-1960s, and I imagine that we habitually do so for two complementary reasons: first, to flagellate and abase ourselves, and second, to glorify ourselves in our self-abasement. That these rationales are in fact complementary has been deftly suggested by Bruce Robbins, who noted in his reply to Delbanco's essay that such decline-and-fall narratives

> will always be suspected of secret self-aggrandizement. These narratives can take paradoxical pleasure in how low their subject has fallen because

their real aim is to insinuate, often against the evidence, that once upon a time their subject used to soar high over other, more pedestrian fields, and still deserves that lost eminence. (91 – 92)

What, then, would the story of decline and fall look like if we began it elsewhere? Using the same statistical base as Delbanco and Kernan, we could, if we wanted to, point out that humanities enrollments have *increased* in terms of the percentage and number of degrees awarded to American undergraduates since 1980. A remarkable decline indeed occurred between 1970 and 1980, partly impelled by the rise of professional schools and partly impelled by the fact that some of the students in these professional schools were, for the first time, women (see Oakley). Since 1980, the humanities have returned to their pre-1960s levels, and English, for its part, has seen a 63.3 percent increase in degrees awarded between 1980 and 2002, according to the December 2004 edition of the National Center for Education Statistics' *Digest of Education Statistics*. In 1950, English accounted for 3.99 percent of all bachelor's degrees awarded in the United States (17,240 English degrees); in 1968, in the midst of the wonder years, 7.59 percent (47,977 degrees); in 1980, 3.50 percent (32,541 degrees); in 1993, 4.82 percent (56,133 degrees); and in 2002, 4.115 percent (53,162 degrees). To take a somewhat larger perspective: between 1974 and 1985, humanities enrollments did, in fact, decrease by 18.2 percent. But enrollments in the social sciences fell much further, by 33.7 percent, and even in the physical sciences the drop was a considerable 19.4 percent. Where did those students go? To business (a 65.3 percent increase), engineering (up by 92.2 percent), and computer science (a staggering but altogether historically appropriate increase of 627.3 percent). Interestingly, between 1986 and 1997, business majors underwent a dramatic decline: in 1986 they accounted for 24 percent of all degrees awarded (237,319 out of 987,823), whereas in 1997 they had slipped to 19.3 percent of all degrees (226,633 out of 1,172,879). In 1997 business degrees still outnumbered English degrees (49,345) by four and a half times, but still, a 20 percent drop in market share in only one decade? Where, one wonders, were the *New York Review of Books* jeremiads on the decline and fall of business education?

Let me be clear about this post-1980 story and my desires for it: I am not trying to supplant the story of decline but to supplement it, in both the deconstructive and predeconstructive senses of that word. I am not trying to claim that the English glass is really 4.115 percent full rather than 95.885 percent empty, nor am I trying to mask the disciplinary crises of English by claiming that everything must be all right if we still have paying customers. I am only trying to point out that if you start either from 1950 or 1980 rather than the mid-1960s, *there has been no significant enrollment decline in English at all.* Quite the contrary. It follows, of course, that post-1980 phenomena such as theory, feminism, queer folk, politicization, jargon, solipsism, and postmodernism cannot plausibly be blamed for a decline that did not happen on their watch — though they cannot reliably be credited for the increase in enrollment numbers, either.

What's truly curious about this story of the relative stability of English enrollments, I've found, is that so few English professors believe it. I have recited these numbers to faculty members in the humanities throughout the various precincts of the profession, and I almost always meet with denial and disbelief. And this disbelief itself, I now believe, is an important sign of the state of the profession — namely, that we continue to talk of an enrollment crisis even though there is no enrollment crisis. Obviously, we must be clinically depressed. We continue to tell ourselves, our readers, and our administrations that we've fallen, fallen utterly into despair and disrepair and that we are being justly punished by undergraduates deserting en masse. We therefore deserve — so "we" say — to have full-time faculty lines cut still further and to have our declining enrollments serviced instead by legions of just-in-time adjunct laborers. It would seem that if we call ourselves laughingstocks often enough, the truth value of the claim will eventually be beside the point, since it will have taken on all the qualities of a performative utterance.

Again, I am not trying to claim — and I do not believe — that the humanities are doing just fine in the world at large. If our crisis is not a crisis of student enrollment or intellectual degeneration, it is still a crisis of purpose and self-definition. Many humanists feel that they have lost direction and lost prestige, largely because, to gauge by whatever instruments might agree on such a thing, they have; and in that narrative, events like the PC media hype of the early 1990s or the Sokal Hoax of 1996 are just symptoms of a larger phenomenon, in which, as I pointed out in the first section, it has become increasingly difficult to *justify* the humanities. My point is simply that the degradation of working conditions in the profession — what I have called, clumsily but accurately, the "adjunctification of the professoriate" (afterword) — has nothing to do with undergraduate enrollment numbers, and we should argue strenuously with any pundit, colleague, or administrator who claims otherwise.

The statistics relevant to graduate education and enrollment, however, tell another story. For here is where the profession's relative decline in funding and prestige is felt most acutely, and where the profession's various *real* crises — in publishing, hiring, graduate program policy, and disciplinary self-regulation — radiate outward like so many spokes from a shopworn wheel metaphor. From the angle of the prospective graduate student, for example, the conditions of the profession look something like this: graduate enrollments are down, partly due to a decrease in applicants and partly due to a decrease in the size of graduate programs; students who do earn the Ph.D. enter a job system in which about half of the available jobs are part-time positions or otherwise off the tenure track; new Ph.D.s trying to place a first book with an academic press find a severely depressed market for monographs in the humanities. Tenured and tenure-track faculty members, for their part, find hiring and tenure decisions rendered excruciatingly complex by the intellectual breadth of the field(s) of English and the austerity policies of many colleges and universities with regard to new hiring in the humanities, which together compel English departments either to pit disciplinary subfields against each other by reallocating faculty lines, or to devise new hybrid positions that will speak to multiple faculty and curricular interests, such as "rhetoric/cultural studies with an interest in postcolonialism." Surely it is the rare English department that has been able to say in the past decade, "It's quite a boon that the field of literary and cultural studies has expanded so vertiginously, because it's given us the opportunity to expand our faculty by 20 percent." And as if the expansion of the field together with the contraction of tenure-track lines weren't bad enough as a one-two punch, add to this the extraordinary degree to which many faculty members at major institutions devote their disciplinary energies to the task of intellectual self-replication, and you've got a toxic — but, I submit, altogether recognizable — professional environment.

Having so little interest in my own intellectual self-replication in junior faculty or in graduate students, I confess to being somewhat clueless about some of the things that animate my colleagues so ferociously when new faculty lines are approved. (In twelve years at Illinois I chaired four dissertations and served as a committee member on twenty-five others, and none of them bore any resemblance to my work. Similarly, I served on only three search committees — one in anglophone African literature, one in Latino and Latina literature, and one in African American literature.) And having interests in multiple fields inside and outside literary studies, I am always dismayed by the profession's subdisciplinary identity politics, by which faculty in film or media are supposed to represent the interests of faculty in film or media, faculty in late early modern are supposed to represent the interests of faculty in late early modern, and so forth. This kind of territorialism is among the least attractive features of academic life, and it is doubtless exacerbated by the shrinking of faculty lines and resources in English. I do not imagine that it can be eradicated by mere goodwill. But whenever search committees are paralyzed or curricular innovations stymied, I think faculty members would do well to remember that the examined life — the life worth living — offers more than the possibility of enhancing one's perceived intradisciplinary interests among one's perceived intradepartmental allies in debates about the maintenance and upkeep of one branch of the English division of the liberal arts subsector of the university enterprise.

About graduate education I have more specific suggestions and more tangible concerns for the future: two of these have to do with graduate unionization and the graduate curriculum. They are not necessarily related, except by my desire that graduate education in English involve as much intellectual edification and as little economic exploitation as possible. I support unionization because I think it is the best available solution to the problem of undercompensated graduate teaching assistantships, particularly when those assistantships are occupied by graduate students who have no reliable academic grievance procedure and no recourse to adequate health insurance and health care. I also support unionization for more, shall we say, psychological reasons: all too much of the experience of graduate school is infantilizing, and I support anything that aids and abets the process of deinfantilization. Thus, while I share John Guillory's opinion that the profession should be wary of inducing its graduate student aspirants to adopt a mode of "preprofessionalism" in which they attempt to contribute to the discipline before they've learned very much about what it entails, I also try to discourage my colleagues from thinking of graduate students as baby birds whose attempts to fly will likely be fatal unless they wait until the dissertation stage (or until after earning the Ph.D.) before sending out that first essay or conference paper.

I should explain that I belong to a small (and, in the United States, stigmatized and oppressed) religious sect known as agnostics, who believe that the fetus is viable by the time it turns thirty-five or by the time it completes a doctoral degree and undergoes various pretenure reviews and the final tenure review, whichever comes first. This faith-based approach, for which I intend to seek appropriate federal funding from the Bush administration, also informs my outlook on the academic content and protocols of graduate programs. When I attended the University of Virginia in the 1980s, I noted that the preliminary Ph.D. oral exam was administered in an especially old-school manner: students were required to name a major author, a major field, and a major genre (fair enough) but were not permitted to select their examination committee. Indeed, they were not permitted to know the identities of the members of their committee until three weeks before the exam. This system did have the advantage of making me even more antiauthoritarian and anti-infantilization than I'd been in my early twenties, but I did not fully understand the rationale behind it until I was a newly tenured associate professor at Illinois and served for four consecutive years on the English department's

M.A. exam committee. The department had, in 1990, revamped its comprehensive M.A. exam, which purported to cover all literature written in English since *Beowulf* (complete with a close-reading section of fifteen unidentified lines of verse), in favor of a system in which students devised four questions relevant to a literary-historical period, spent six to eight months preparing the questions, and were then asked, on a day of their choosing, two of their four questions (as determined by the committee). At first students were given one day to respond, which turned the exam into a typing test with notes. The exam was further modified to give students one week's notice as to which questions would be asked and one day to compose answers. The exam was further modified and further modified, and . . . you get the idea. Every year I served on the M.A. exam committee, the faculty complained about the poor quality of the exams and about the fact that even our best students were turning in mediocre responses and thus making it more difficult to distinguish stronger students from weaker ones.

"Well, then," I suggested in my third year of service, "if the purpose of the exam is to help us distinguish among students, and that's a significant 'if,' why don't we allow them two months to write answers, so that students who've read more widely and can address secondary materials more fluently have a chance to distinguish themselves?"

"But," came the almost unanimous reply, "if we gave students two months in which to work, we wouldn't be giving them an exam — we'd just be asking them for another term paper, really."

"And what would be the problem with that, if you want your best students to do their best?" I asked, innocently enough. "I mean, seriously — what are we worried about? That they'll cheat?"

Illinois has since eliminated its master's exam, but at the time, I learned three things from this exchange. The first and most immediate is that it is a bad thing to name and to ridicule your colleagues' anxieties in one breath, however innocently and unwittingly you do so. The second, more retrospective, is that too many such testing systems, like the one I completed at Virginia and the one I administered at Illinois, are indeed driven by anxieties that the children will cheat — by playing to their professors' interests, by peeking at the instructor's Norton Critical Edition of *The Mill on the Floss*, or by cutting corners on American poetry 1912 – 45 (and here cheating anxieties become coverage anxieties). The third and most important for the future of English is that graduate programs should, to the greatest degree possible, train students for the actual intellectual demands and pedagogical tasks of their profession.

Under this third heading, it is not enough to redesign graduate programs to eliminate needless or counterproductive forms of testing. More than this, if we want to think seriously about graduate programs as institutions of professional training, we should, I believe, be concentrating on the current status of literary theory. I say this with many caveats, one of which is that the term "literary theory" has now been all but superseded by the catchall "theory," which is taken to include not only latter-day staples Michel Foucault and Jacques Derrida but also Judith Butler, Gayatri Spivak, Eve Kosofsky Sedgwick, Gilles Deleuze, Felix Guattari, Maurice Merleau-Ponty, Giorgio Agamben, Emmanuel Levinas, Jürgen Habermas, Alain Badiou, Teresa de Lauretis — and of course, for those of you involved with autopoesis and trees of knowledge, Humberto Maturana and Francisco Varela. The radical dereferentialization of the term is something of a historical irony, for (to mention another of my caveats) literary theory was once thought — and this would be back in the heady days of high structuralism — to be the device by which the field of literary studies would become internally coherent and self-reflective as well (see Culler). As the past three decades have played out, however, it would appear that disciplinary self-reflexivity comes precisely at the price of internal coherence. And yet I would insist, at minimum, even in the hour of our fragmentation into sixty-six subspecialties, that training in contemporary literary theory should be one of the central purposes of graduate education in English. I want to emphasize the *literary* in that theory: I mean, more or less, the history of twentieth-century theories of literature and of textuality, beginning with the work of Viktor Shklovsky and his fellow Russian Formalists (including Mikhail Bakhtin's and V. N. Volosinov's replies thereto) and running through Marxism, psychoanalysis, New Criticism, structuralism, poststructuralism/deconstruction, feminism, reader response, New Historicism, postcolonialism, and queer theory — in other words, from the origins of a discipline-founding theory of the literary (this discipline-founding aspect is what would distinguish Shklovsky from Samuel Taylor Coleridge or Matthew Arnold or, for that matter, John Crowe Ransom or Northrop Frye from Sir Philip Sidney) to the moment of the breakdown of the idea of the specifically literary text under the pressure of structuralism and poststructuralism. I believe more firmly with each passing year that this history of twentieth-century theories of textuality should be something like a lingua franca shared by advanced graduate students, not only because it gives them access to myriad ways of reading literary and social texts but also because, if it's taught in a sufficiently historically and institutionally grounded way, it gives entrants into the discipline a good general idea of the history of the discipline as we can plausibly claim to know it. And I have tried to put this principle into practice at Penn State, where I've taught the Introduction to Graduate Study along the lines I've sketched out here.

I recall—to invoke one last episode of my institutional history at Illinois—a yearlong debate with a colleague over precisely this question. It was a debate I more or less lost, in the sense that the department never did devise anything like a "theory" requirement for its graduate program but did manage to put together something like an introductory "reading methods" course as part of its overhauled undergraduate English major (as part of its first revision to the English major since 1969). To reduce a year of exchanges to anecdotal form, I could say that my colleague's primary concern was that "theory" changes with every year (I believe the words "with every passing fad" may have been put in play at some point) and that there would be no consensus, for example, on whether Judith Butler should be on a required syllabus. My reply was first, that Judith Butler already *is* on the de facto "syllabus" of the profession by any reasonable measure; second, that "literature" changes with each passing year as well but that the department continues to offer courses in literature written since 1945; and third (in which I finally got around to addressing the substance of my colleague's real argument), if one wanted one's graduate students to be well read and well rounded rather than trendy, supercilious, finger-to-the-wind disciplinary subspecialists who saw no need to read anything written before 1980, one could hardly do better than to introduce them to Shklovsky's "Art as Technique" and Austin's *How to Do Things with Words*, both of which would surely deepen anyone's reading of *Gender Trouble*.

I suggest, therefore, that we try to see the intellectual challenges of contemporary literary study as enriched by rather than in competition with knowledge of the history of literary theory. In the same spirit, I suggest that we cultivate a determined antagonism to disciplinary territorialism, whether in faculty hiring, curricular design, or graduate admissions. While I have numerous complaints about the profession and various critiques of its mode of conducting business, I have not forgotten that literary study truly is a remarkable field whose appeal lies in its ceaseless intellectual delights and debates. I am surrounded as I write by new work on the origins and the locations of modernity; on the history and contemporary meaning of gender and sexuality; on the relation between telecommunications conglomerates and popular cultural forms; on the role of narrative in medicine and law; and on the invention of the human—by William Shakespeare, perhaps, as Harold Bloom would have it, but also by emergent discourses of disability and biotechnology. For all the crises that define the advanced study of literature and culture in our time, English remains, for me, a field worthy of a lifetime of study, and regardless of the practices of individual departments or the machinery of the job system, it is a field that continues to appeal to the best and brightest and most creative of my students. The central question for them is the question to which I have directed some of my own work and to which people who care about the future of English should want to direct theirs — namely, how to make that lifetime of study a life worth living for the next generation of aspiring scholars and teachers.

Works Cited

Austin, J. L. *How to Do Things with Words*. Cambridge: Harvard University Press, 1962.

Bérubé, Michael. Afterword to *On the Market: Surviving the Academic Job Search*, edited by Christine Boufis and Victoria C. Olson, 348 – 63. New York: Riverhead, 1997.

———. *The Employment of English: Theory, Jobs, and the Future of Literary Studies*. New York: New York University Press, 1997.

Christ, Carol. "Retaining Faculty Lines." In *Profession 1997*, 54 – 60. New York: Modern Language Association, 1997.

Culler, Jonathan. *Structuralist Poetics: Structuralism, Linguistics, and the Study of Literature*. Ithaca: Cornell University Press, 1975.

Delbanco, Andrew. "The Decline and Fall of Literature." *New York Review of Books*, 4 November 1999, 32 – 38.

Ellis, John M. *Literature Lost: Social Agendas and the Corruption of the Humanities*. New Haven: Yale University Press, 1997.

Guillory, John. "Preprofessionalism: What Graduate Students Want." In *Profession 1996*, 91 – 99. New York: Modern Language Association, 1996.

Jacoby, Russell. *Dogmatic Wisdom: How the Culture Wars Divert Education and Distract America*. New York: Anchor, 1995.

Kernan, Alvin. *In Plato's Cave*. New Haven: Yale University Press, 2000.

———, ed. *What's Happened to the Humanities?* Princeton: Princeton University Press, 1997.

National Center for Education Statistics. *2003 Digest of Education Statistics*. Washington, D.C.: U.S. Department of Education, 2004.

Oakley, Francis. "Against Nostalgia: Reflections on Our Present Discontents in American Higher Education." In *The Politics of Liberal Education*, edited by Darryl J. Gless and Barbara Herrnstein Smith, 267 – 89. Durham: Duke University Press, 1992.

Robbins, Bruce. Letter to the editor. *New York Review of Books*, 13 April 2000, 91 – 92.

Shklovsky, Viktor. "Art as Technique." In *Russian Formalist Criticism: Four Essays*, translated and introduction by Lee T. Lemon and Marion J. Reis, 3 – 24. Lincoln: University of Nebraska Press, 1965.

In the course of this essay, I will mount an argument about undergraduate education that will, among other things, explain my title, but first I will open with five talking points inspired by my reading of the journal *Pedagogy* and (just as *Pedagogy* published its first issue) completing my twelfth and final year of working at the University of Illinois at Urbana-Champaign:

One. I have done most of my teaching in undergraduate courses, in mid- and upper-level surveys designed primarily for English majors. At Illinois I offered seven graduate seminars and three undergraduate honors seminars. The rest of my courses were standard 200- and 300-level surveys, aimed at sophomores to seniors. I also offered three versions of English 300, a writing-intensive course developed in 1993 to meet the university's Composition II requirement (imagine that—two courses in which substantial writing is now required at a major institution of higher education) and now also a prerequisite for English majors. Titled Writing about Literature, this course can accommodate any topic or focus (mine have been autobiography, twice, and African American literature, once) as long as it assigns thirty to forty pages of writing in multiple assignments.

I see nothing odd about this kind of teaching record, and I am continually astonished by my colleagues who insist that successful career paths require a studied avoidance of the undergraduate curriculum. George Levine's essay in the inaugural issue of *Pedagogy* is much more careful and thoughtful than most in this genre (no surprise, coming from Levine), and in fact I think of this essay as a continuation of his argument that senior faculty do not, as a rule, write compellingly or seriously about teaching. Still, Levine's essay does contain a few sweeping statements like "The assumption of most new university hires is that they will have little to do with lower-level undergraduate education as soon as their 'work' gets national notice" (16), and I cannot imagine that this generalization applies to very many university hires outside the top fifteen or twenty Ph.D.-granting departments in the United States. Illinois and Penn State rank in the next fifteen or twenty, and cannot accommodate—structurally—any new faculty member who wants to avoid basic undergraduate instruction. (What "lower-level" means here is another matter, one I will come back to at the end of point 5.)

Two. I was hired by Illinois in 1989, just as I was hired by Penn State in 2001, to teach — but also to write. I sometimes introduce myself, in nonacademic social settings, as a teacher of literature, and sometimes as a writer who works at a university. I see nothing odd about this, either. I thought it was an explicit part of the contract: *Here's an annual salary, a low teaching load, and some modest research support. Now go write some stuff that'll bring some attention to this place.* I have not experienced that part of the contract as an imposition or as a distraction from my other duties. Indeed, I wonder what I would have done with my first couple of four-month summer vacations if I had not been reading and writing through most of them. In my first six years at Illinois, I also won released time, in competitions of varying severity, from two campus units that gave me two-course reductions: in 1990 – 91 this enabled me to offer two labor-intensive new seminars, one graduate, one undergraduate (reception theory and postmodernism, respectively) in a 1/1 teaching load, whereas in the spring of 1994 I simply took the semester off. I was turned down for released time twice by another campus unit as well.

From 1989 to 2001 Illinois did not change its character as a Research I institution or lower its requirements for tenure and promotion, but it did scale back slightly its generous awards of released time to humanities faculty: whereas such faculty had been allowed, in the early 1990s, to apply to the Research Board for course reductions every three years, now it is every five, and whereas they had been allowed, in the early 1990s, to combine released time with sabbaticals, now they must make other arrangements so as not to take a full year off from teaching. At the same time, the College of Liberal Arts and Sciences signaled a new emphasis on teaching by various means, good and bad: by expanding and enriching (literally) the campus awards for undergraduate instruction (good); by creating — and rewarding departments for offering — "Discovery Courses" that consist of fifteen-student freshman seminars taught by senior faculty (good); and by developing a liberal-arts teaching institute that most junior faculty seem to experience as something between a corporate seminar and a summer camp (bad). All this time, of course, the College of Liberal Arts and Sciences was doing about 40 percent of the undergraduate teaching on the Illinois campus in return for less than 30 percent of the campus budget. And all this time, of course, there was no "renewed emphasis" on undergraduate teaching in the colleges of engineering, business administration, or the applied sciences, whose research is assumed to be self-justifying regardless of its content. The discourse of undergraduate instruction was disseminated unevenly across the Quad, it would appear, and the faculty who flagellated themselves most vigorously for their department's inattention to undergraduates tended to come from the departments most heavily invested in undergraduate instruction.

Three. My research sometimes enhances my teaching, but not always. Nor need it. My writing career, on the other hand, almost always enhances my ability to read and comment on student writing, particularly my experience in dealing with editors of journals both academic and generalist, which has taught me all I know about strategies for revision. Every time a journalist cites a literature professor's allegedly bad writing, the writing is taken as evidence not only of the profession's low intellectual standards (as if intellectual rigor could be indexed only by journalistic prose) but also of the writer's manifest inability to teach anything to do with writing. Strangely, however, literature professors rarely respond to these routine charges by pointing out that the vast majority of us are quite capable writers — certainly as capable, on balance, as the great mass of journalists, not all of whom are exemplars of precision, clarity, or Kemptonian élan — and are more thoroughly involved with student writing than most of our counterparts in anthropology, psychology, sociology, or geology, not to mention engineering, business, and the applied sciences. My experience is somewhat anomalous, in that I receive more editorial feedback (and make more editorial revisions and compromises) than most of my colleagues, insofar as I publish in more generalist and fewer academic journals. But any English professor who does any writing — I do believe that this includes all of us — has grounds to argue that his or her writing, whether or not it counts as "research" (as some of mine does not), enhances the quality of his or her response to student writing. Indeed, since our extensive engagement with student writing is one of the most salient features of our profession, one might expect us to be less defensive about our own writing (regardless of whether it counts as research, it always takes the form of *writing*) and about how publishing — as individual aspiration or as professional expectation — can be understood as one of the ordinary and beneficial aspects of working in English. Perhaps, in other words, publishing can have a pedagogical value for people who teach writing even when they are not trying to publish essays in journals like *Pedagogy*.

The obvious counterargument is that too few of us — especially among the so-called stars or those at elite universities — engage sufficiently with student writing to make such a case for ourselves. To address this counterargument, I have to return to the first point and say more about what kind of teaching one is expected to do at institutions such as Illinois and Penn State.

Four. Large public research universities are at once elite and utterly ordinary. A place like Illinois is elite in the sense that it affords its humanities faculty a teaching load of two courses per semester (although until 1992 it was the only Big Ten school to assign a 3/2 load to all English faculty from the third year of the tenure track until promotion to full professor) and a good deal of research support, ranging from subventions to travel support to released time. Its English Department ranks in the upper quartile of the 128 that grant Ph.D.s and, like its peers, has a graduate program large enough to free the faculty from the teaching of introductory composition: roughly 200 students when I arrived, roughly 120 when I left (a decline matched and in part impelled by a decline in enrollment generally, as well as by the realization, among both faculty and students, that our Ph.D.s were not faring well on the job market). Illinois thus affords its faculty, though not its graduate students, some of the best working conditions available in the profession.

But in every other way the University of Illinois at Urbana-Champaign is wonderfully unexceptional. The undergraduate student body is drawn almost entirely from Illinois, and the school must compete for the Prairie State's best and brightest with places such as Northwestern and the University of Chicago. About eight hundred of its twenty-seven thousand undergraduates major in English; most of those undergraduates are required to take the introductory rhet/comp course, Rhetoric 105, which is staffed largely by graduate teaching assistants.

Penn State is not significantly different: it, too, is a large public university in the mostly rural middle of an otherwise industrial state, with first-class private institutions (Penn, Carnegie Mellon) competing for local undergraduates. Among English departments, Penn State's is slightly lower in the rankings than Illinois's, but in base teaching load, faculty size, graduate program enrollment, and workplace organization, it is nearly identical to my former department.

Illinois is thus sometimes cited, as it was by Northern Kentucky University Professor John Alberti in *College English*, as being somewhere around the Boardwalk and Park Place corner of the university Monopoly board. Alberti, assessing the impact of multiculturalism in departments of English, notes that "from the beginning, whether in the infamous attacks by Allan Bloom (based on experiences at Cornell and the University of Chicago) or Dinesh D'Souza (Dartmouth), or in the principled defenses of multiculturalism by Lawrence Levine (Berkeley), Cary Nelson and Michael Bérubé (both University of Illinois), and others, focus has been on the elite institutions, for understandable reasons" (566). Alberti is, of course, right to suggest that most of the discussion about multiculturalism, and everything else in higher education, has been dominated by the elite tier of Research I schools, yet there is no sense in which the student body or the undergraduate teaching conditions at Illinois are comparable to those at Cornell, Chicago, Berkeley, or Dartmouth. The competitive liberal-arts colleges, from Bowdoin to Grinnell to Reed, also outrank Illinois and Penn State in this respect, as do some fine-arts colleges like the School of the Art Institute of Chicago or the Rhode Island School of Design; although they are considered "teaching colleges" by the professoriate and are thus lower in the professional pecking order than Research I schools, they typically offer their faculty a more highly motivated and skilled group of undergraduates than the student bodies of places like Illinois, Iowa, Nebraska, Ohio State, and other such ordinary places.

Five. Undergraduate education at places like Illinois and Penn State is thus defined not so much by faculty desires or professional rewards as by the needs of the institution. As I have already noted, it is possible to achieve national prominence and sustain a meaningful writing career at a large public university, but it is not possible to do so by avoiding most of the undergraduate teaching work of the English Department. The numbers simply won't let you do it. The English Department at Illinois caps its course enrollments at thirty-six (at Penn State, forty) for general surveys, at eighteen for honors seminars (at Penn State, fifteen), and at twenty-four for writing-intensive courses. When I left Illinois, only five courses (the two British lit surveys, the early American lit survey, the African American survey, and the rarely offered science fiction course) were conducted in large lectures via the so-called Harvard system (with graduate teaching assistants). All fifty-plus full-time faculty members were teaching everywhere in the curriculum. On a regular basis, senior faculty eminences such as Nina Baym and Jack Stillinger taught the large introductory lecture (American and British, respectively), and rising stars such as Tim Dean taught 101, the poetry course at the very lowest level of the literature curriculum.

As far as I knew, Illinois was not a utopian society composed of magnanimous, well-adjusted faculty members. It was merely an ordinary place from which a great number of the standard in-house complaints about the profession sounded either weird or irrelevant. In this respect, too, it is similar to Penn State, where senior faculty in English teach "first-year seminars" and everyone in English is required to teach a Monday-Wednesday-Friday schedule once a year. I realize, from reading many of the profession's critiques of itself, that somewhere, in the uppermost echelon, somebody is behaving very badly: such is the complaint of various curmudgeonly (at worst) or civic-minded (at best) critics like Yale's David Bromwich, whose fictional trendy tenured radical, Jonathan Craigie, "negotiated early to sever his obligation to teach the department's bread-and-butter surveys" (177); Columbia's David Damrosch, who inveighs against "superstars who avoid every kind of departmental work like the plague" (87); and Damrosch's colleague, Andrew Delbanco, whose 1999 essay in the *New York Review of Books* concludes by noting that "the flight from undergraduate education seems to be slowing," citing new programs at Harvard and Stanford, and hailing the return of Emersonian "evangelical teachers" (38). The English departments of the Ivy League clearly must be harboring all manner of laggard, no-show prima donnas, or perhaps some people are simply convinced that some of their hotshot colleagues aren't carrying their weight.

It is true that senior literature faculty at Illinois and at many other schools do not teach composition. I have had to admit as much on many occasions, usually in response to conversational turns like "Yes, well, you may teach undergraduate literature courses, but surely you don't teach the composition course that justifies your entire departmental budget." (As more of my work has dealt explicitly with the mechanics of English departments, it has become increasingly likely that my conversations with colleagues at other universities will take this turn. In fact, frankly acknowledging that composition courses underwrite most English departments' literature offerings has gotten me into trouble with composition specialists looking to pick a fight, as in Richard E. Miller's essay "'Let's Do the Numbers': Comp Droids and the Prophets of Doom," which rather implausibly casts me as one of those nasty literary types who call the rhet/comp specialists bad names.) Because introductory composition is so important a course, pedagogically and financially; because it involves so insistent and demanding an engagement with undergraduate writing; and because it carries so little prestige or professional reward, it is routinely (1) staffed at every large university by poorly paid graduate teaching assistants and (2) used as the benchmark by which literature faculty, themselves poorly paid in comparison to their peers in law, science, and business, can be cast as pampered, penthouse-dwelling magnates ignorant of the masses who toil under them. But it is hard to see how senior faculty at Illinois or Penn State could teach enough composition courses to make their efforts more than symbolic: six or seven thousand first-year students, fifty full-time English faculty. Let's do the numbers, indeed. Why not reserve senior literature faculty for the jobs for which they are most thoroughly qualified — that is, the teaching of literature to the hundreds of English majors who need courses and credits to graduate? Perhaps the best answer to this structural dilemma is to double the departmental budget so that all three hundred rhet/comp sections are taught by graduate students and faculty (full-time or adjunct) making a living wage of at least five thousand dollars per course. I would strongly support that budget increase. It would be a good thing. And I would hope for your vote in November. But I would still want to teach literature.

WHAT I HAVE sketched out are some of the conditions of teaching (and of talking about teaching) in the kind of institution at which I have worked thus far. Here is what those conditions mean in practical pedagogical terms: Undergraduate honors seminars at Illinois can include some of the most exciting, brilliant, diligent students in the state. The best students at large state universities, flagships or no, compare well to the best students anywhere; some of them have chosen Illinois or Penn State over the more competitive universities and liberal arts colleges for financial, political, or familial reasons, assuming for now a heuristic distinction among these. Consequently, in each of the three "postmodernism and American fiction" honors seminars I offered at Illinois, as in the honors seminar I've offered at Penn State, I've had students who were not merely promising, rewarding, enterprising, and so on but also able to teach me a great deal — about working at Disney World or the best Pixies record (actual examples), fine, but also about how to think about reciprocity, simulacra, performance art, household chemicals, and the conflict between postmodernism and Mormonism (also actual examples).

Honors courses, however, are the exception — filled with exceptional students exceptionally well versed in the ways of literature, criticism, and theory. Many of these students have gone on to graduate school in English (or, having been scared away from the grad-school enterprise by prophets of doom like me, have chosen other textual enterprises in which to hone their skills), so honors seminars are sort of like junior graduate seminars anyway. The English Department's more standard survey offerings — the 200- and 300-level courses (at Illinois) or 200- and 400-level courses (at Penn State) that make up the bulk of the "period" courses in the disciplinary repertoire — draw a far more heterogeneous and modest bunch, many of whom are in your course only because it is offered at an hour that fits their schedule and/or will meet a requirement for graduation.

In my final semester at Illinois, I offered English 352, American Literature since 1945. I taught it as a course on fiction, working backward from Don DeLillo's *Underworld*, and then I offered a similar version of the course at Penn State in the fall of 2001. I wanted to teach the kind of long novel that almost never appears in survey courses; I consider *Underworld* the best work of one of the major writers in the United States; and I did not want to inflict an eight-hundred-page monster on students in April. So I mimicked DeLillo's narrative scheme and taught the course in reverse chronological order, ending with Jack Kerouac's *On the Road* and James Baldwin's *Go Tell It on the Mountain*, neither of which I had taught to undergraduates before. The rest of the syllabus consisted of Sandra Cisneros's *The House on Mango Street*, Toni

Morrison's *Sula*, Thomas Pynchon's *The Crying of Lot 49*, and Ursula K. Le Guin's *The Left Hand of Darkness* (the last three of which I had first encountered in a course at Barnard College taught by Catharine Stimpson and titled Postmodern Fiction — in 1980!). All in all, pretty standard college fare, and my class was made up of pretty standard college students — for the University of Illinois. (At Penn State, I dropped Cisneros, Le Guin, and Pynchon, replacing them with *Lolita*, Octavia Butler's *Kindred*, Maxine Hong Kingston's *The Woman Warrior*, and selections from Flannery O'Connor's *A Good Man Is Hard to Find*.)

I teach such courses not only for their obvious survey content — to offer students an introduction to a small segment of the American literature of the past half century, with only passing reference to the world of "quality fiction" inhabited by Philip Roth, Richard Ford, Madison Smartt Bell, Julia Alvarez, and their ilk — but more generally to teach students about principles of narrativity, the generic and historical dynamics that determine what is written and how. I have found that most students come to class with a fair enough idea of how to critique representations of race and gender, although they often need work on thinking about class, sexuality, and disability (no surprise); in this class, teasing out their reactions to Kerouac's admiration for and exoticization of racial Others was not difficult and not unenlightening, and none of them was oblivious to the gender politics of *Sula* or *The House on Mango Street*. But few undergraduates — and, for that matter, too few graduate students — are formidable formalists, just as few undergraduates are formidable historicists. Here, the trick lies in getting students to see how narrative principles are both embedded in and (in some cases) critiqued by the narratives they generate. Lest this enterprise sound too fusty and high-structuralist, let me take a pivotal example from Richard Wright's *Native Son*: "He [Bigger] knew that the moment he allowed what his life meant to enter fully into his consciousness, he would either kill himself or someone else" (10). It is a knotty moment of narrative irony, in which the narrative lets us know that Bigger knows that he cannot let himself become aware of what he would know if he acknowledged it. Sentences like these dot Wright's text, and they contain the socionarrative key to Bigger's rendering; they are also the source of most criticisms of the novel that follow in the train of Ralph Ellison's (1953) complaint that Wright could imagine Bigger but Bigger could not imagine Wright. Similarly, in *The House on Mango Street*, Esperanza's claim about Earl's "wife" — "we never agree on what she looks like" (71) — is an index of Esperanza's innocence and therefore crucial to her gradual introduction to the world of sexuality and patriarchy. All of my students understood, of course, that Earl brings home prostitutes, but not all of them understood that a principle of narrativity was at stake in Cisneros's deliberate — and, in places, quite severe — circumscription of Esperanza's capacity for reportage.

I began this process of reading with *Underworld*, which offers its readers a series of characters, from the fictional Marvin Lundy to the fictionalized Lenny Bruce, who illustrate or enact the novel's myriad narrative modi operandi. The first and most obvious is New York Giants baseball broadcaster Russ Hodges, who, before the fateful game begins on 3 October 1951, thinks back to his days of doing "ghost games" on Charlotte radio, "the telegraph bug clacking in the background and blabbermouth Hodges inventing ninety-nine percent of the action" (25). As the reverie moves into the narrative discourse proper, DeLillo writes, "When he was doing ghost games he liked to take the action into the stands, inventing a kid chasing a foul ball, a carrot-topped boy with a cowlick (shameless, ain't I) who retrieves the ball and holds it aloft, this five-ounce sphere of cork, rubber, yarn, horsehide and spiral stitching, a souvenir baseball, a priceless thing somehow" (26). Since this passage occurs in the midst of DeLillo's extended re-creation of the third and final Giants-Dodgers playoff game in 1951, the most lit-criterate of my students immediately recognized Hodges as the doubled figure of DeLillo himself (and exactly who is confessing shamelessness here?), and the boy with the cowlick as the intratextual double of Cotter Martin, a fictional boy (African American and cowlickless) who retrieves Bobby Thomson's home run ball after a struggle with the older white man who had befriended him during the game.

So far, so good. This is how narrative works, and how it comments on its own operations. But it was a challenge getting even those relatively advanced students, let alone the other thirty, to understand what is at stake in the wonderful, almost Borgesian series of bizarre lists that drive Marvin Lundy's stories. The lists appear in full as a kind of free indirect discourse, except that they are so loosely organized that they include not only obsessive repetitions ("3. The ship on the dock in San Francisco — don't even bring it up. . . . 13. The ship on the dock — please not now") and unrelated narrative flotsam ("12. Riding up the side of a building in an elevator that's transparent") but also a running metacommentary ("9. The detailed confusion of Marvin's narrative, people's memories mixed with his own, shaped to bending time") (176) that simply makes no sense as something spoken or thought by Marvin. I promised my students that if they could get through Marvin's tangle of condensed story lines, they not only would have a good handle on how *Underworld* works but also would be more than prepared for the series of off-kilter openings that make up *Sula*'s first thirty pages. "In the meantime," I told them, "this man, Marvin Lundy, is clearly not someone you want as your narrative guide. And yet this comic figure who literally can't get from point 1 to point 2 is also the guy who weaves the thread tying the whole novel together, the story of what happened to Thomson's baseball. In a sense he knows more about the novel's principles of composition than any other character. At this point, though, and for the rest of part 2, Marvin can be said to embody the text's narrative principles, which suggests that the novel is seriously flirting with incoherence. And some critics would say 'flirting with' is altogether too kind." The larger question at stake with Marvin and with *Underworld*, in turn, is the question Fredric Jameson famously mapped out in "Cognitive Mapping" and in his every foray into postmodernism: How, if at all, can the social totality, if such a thing exists, be represented?

The rest of my course ran more or less in this vein, but I hope that this example conveys the general idea. My point, however, is not that I did this or did that. My point is that the course really did not go very well in the end. My "best" students — the ones who were best prepared and most intellectually curious — did quite well, and one critic-in-the-making lodged a complaint about how quickly and conveniently Marvin brings up the Cold War in his conversation with Brian Glassic and later argued that Cisneros should not have had Esperanza write, "He's not fat anymore *nor* a boy" (his emphasis) if Cisneros wanted to limit her narrator consistently to a preadolescent mode of expression. But on my bad days I was teaching to the six — the six (or five or seven) students who came to class already caring about literature, criticism, narrative, and history. Of the other thirty, twelve or so were intermittently engaged by the course and will probably remember it fondly for some time, and the remaining eighteen were by turns surprised, stimulated, puzzled, and bored. I can expect that those six will go on to care passionately about writing, their own and others'; that the twelve will keep up something like an active or passing interest in matters intellectual; and that the eighteen needed the course to graduate. Almost twenty of the papers I received, both in March and in May, were terrible, barely college level in any sense; four or five of those were abominable. Another ten were decent, interesting, or quite good. Six were terrific. To quote Esperanza, that is how it goes and goes.

I am not complaining, nor am I forecasting the lives of my students on the basis of four months' acquaintance with them. I am merely remarking what everyone already knows who teaches in schools like these: undergraduate teaching is at once more and less challenging than graduate teaching, for while it is much easier for faculty members to appear brilliant and witty to undergraduates and class prep time is significantly shorter for surveys than for seminars, it is quite impossible to inspire in undergraduates the single-minded attention, the devotion to every professorial train of thought and tangent thereto, that devotees of the old school (of whatever age) expect of their graduate students. Over twelve years, undergraduates at Illinois judged my teaching as just slightly above the departmental average — 4.45 on a scale of 1 to 5, good enough for me to make the campus's "Incomplete List of Teachers Ranked as Excellent by Their Students" every other semester but not good enough for me to be considered for campus teaching awards (at Penn State I have a 6.3 out of 7 thus far). My style is informal (but usually informal with sports jacket) and ranges from patient disquisition to open-ended question-and-answer to manic stand-up, complete with mimicked voices. But even on the happy days when I am at once intelligible, insightful, and interesting, I know that most of these young adults have many other things to do with their lives and that teaching to them will therefore be a more diffuse, tenuous process than the relatively easy, always gratifying prospect of teaching to the six.

I do not lament this state of affairs. On the contrary, most of the time I like it, so long as the number of abominable essays is kept to a bare minimum of three or four. I realize that many students write papers the night before they are due (I certainly wrote my share of such things in my undergraduate years), but only a small percentage of students can compose well-considered arguments under these circumstances. I realize also that many of those students do not value good writing as I do, and that they will either underread or ignore the line edits and the general comments with which I festoon their margins. I tell every class that coherent, compelling writing involves a set of skills they can take almost anywhere in the late-capitalist marketplace, but I know that many of my students will not require coherent, compelling writing either for pleasure or for profit and will therefore disregard most of what I have to say on the subject. So why do I like teaching undergraduates? Because I am not dismayed by the prospect of a world in which at least one-sixth (and as many as one-half) of my auditors-students-interlocutors take seriously the possibility that they will use the critical tools I try to wield and to offer for further use. I'm actually rather cheered by the idea. I think of it this way: On my bad days I teach to the six young adults who just might pursue literary and cultural studies for much of the rest of their lives, but on what scale of values does that constitute failure? Another twelve, maybe another twenty, might be motivated, by me and by my colleagues, to continue serious, critically reflective reading in their adult lives, and how could I possibly hope for a better "rate of response" from anything I might publish in a "public" forum? College teaching is, as many teachers have pointed out in the past decade, a substantial form of "public intellectual" work. And isn't pedagogy, in the end, one of the principal reasons that literary journalists have such complex and conflicted relations with literature professors — because we work the same beat save that they have readerships and we have students?

Teaching to the six is not nearly as elitist or exclusive as it can be made to appear. It entails nothing more than the realization that for half or more than half of the students in an undergraduate-survey classroom, you are a node in their lives just as they are nodes in yours. It's just part of the job at large public universities: the things you say and do in such classrooms will be disseminated, in the Derridean sense, in ways you cannot predict or control. I find this exhilarating, challenging, and depressing every semester, and it induces in me a range of intellectual and emotional responses that at once match and intensify the exhilarating, challenging, and depressing experiences that make up the rest of my diurnal life. For those few deluded faculty members still wedded to the *Doktorvater* mode of education, such a set of expectations may seem dismaying or even appalling: surely, they imagine, the function of the senior faculty at Research I institutions is self-reproduction, whereby one's graduate students/children are schooled in the correct manner of addressing the literary or cultural text so that they can, on attaining maturity, propagate that mode of address throughout the length and breadth of the land — or at least as much of the land as will register in the next National Research Council ranking. Surely, many of us who have worked in doctoral programs know of colleagues who think of these programs as elaborate cloning devices from which students will not be released until they have learned to reproduce — or at least to cite reverently — the work of the mentor under whom they "study." I cannot imagine that this model of pedagogy is widespread in most English departments in North America, but if in fact it is the model of pedagogy on which the profession's incipient "stars" are relying, then perhaps it is time for the reality check that only social reality can provide. One signal virtue of teaching undergraduates, then, is that it serves as a powerful reminder that pedagogy should be understood as a means of dissemination rather than a means of reproduction, even — or especially — on those bad days when you are teaching only to the six.

Works Cited

Alberti, John. "Returning to Class: Creating Opportunities for Multicultural Reform at Majority Second-Tier Schools." *College English* 63, no. 5 (2001): 561–84.

Bromwich, David. *Politics by Other Means: Higher Education and Group Thinking.* New Haven: Yale University Press, 1992.

Cisneros, Sandra. *The House on Mango Street.* New York: Vintage, 1984.

Damrosch, David. *We Scholars: Changing the Culture of the University.* Cambridge: Harvard University Press, 1995.

Delbanco, Andrew. "The Decline and Fall of Literature." *New York Review of Books,* 4 November 1999, 32 – 38.

DeLillo, Don. *Underworld.* New York: Scribners, 1997.

Ellison, Ralph. "Richard Wright's Blues." In *Shadow and Act,* 77 – 94. New York: Random House, 1953.

Jameson, Fredric. "Cognitive Mapping." In *Marxism and the Interpretation of Culture,* 347 – 60. Urbana: University of Illinois Press, 1988.

Levine, George. "The Two Nations." *Pedagogy* 1, no. 1 (2001): 7 – 19.

Miller, Richard E. " 'Let's Do the Numbers': Comp Droids and the Prophets of Doom." In *Profession 1999,* 96 – 105. New York: Modern Language Association, 1999.

Wright, Richard. *Native Son.* New York: HarperPerennial, 1998.

Working for the U:
On the Rhetoric of "Affiliation"

I n 1989, after sending out seventy-three job applications for assistant professorships and getting just under seventy-three rejections, I was hired by the University of Illinois at Urbana-Champaign, in the sense that I began teaching there and receiving paychecks as a member of the faculty. At the time, I did not think of working at UIUC as an "affiliation" any more than I would think of working at *Newsweek* as an "affiliation." Rather, I thought — and I still think — of my affiliations in terms of my relations to intellectual fields that are organized around various forms of identity I do not currently claim as my own: African American literature, disability studies, and feminism. Though my associations with these fields are voluntary, the terms of my affiliation with each are not simply mine to dictate.[1] My affiliations with African American literature, disability studies, and feminism are tangled and tenuous and are worthy of regular scrutiny, yet this is not necessarily sufficient matter for comment, nor is every variety of self-scrutiny worthy of publication. By contrast, my intra-institutional affiliations seemed fairly straightforward, a merely bureaucratic concern: for all of my twelve years at UIUC I was affiliated with the campus's Afro-American Studies and Research Program and its Unit for Criticism and Interpretive Theory. But that was business as usual, I thought. It is, after all, routine for academics to speak in terms of their *institutional affiliation*, as if their relations to their places of work were something other than routine relations to places of work: we think of Fredric Jameson as being affiliated with Duke University more readily than we think of Jameson *working for* Duke University. Likewise, when we describe ourselves as "affiliated with" a college or university, we usually do not think of ourselves as close relatives of our local insurance agents who describe themselves as "affiliated with the companies of United Assurance Amalgamated."

The discourse of affiliation would thus seem to do double duty for academics' self-understanding: it can make our intellectual commitments appear as matters of business routine (signing up for African American studies and theory, joining the relevant organizations or filling out the appropriate numerical codes on the MLA membership form) at the same time that it makes our actual business routine — the business of working and getting paid — appear to be something other than the business of working and getting paid. It would also seem to serve a few ancillary functions as well, one or two of which I'll discuss in this essay.

Affiliation and Aggression

Two stories about aggression: one story deals with a brutally competitive and occasionally vicious sport; the other deals with ice hockey.

In my last year and a half at Illinois, I started playing twice a week in various nonchecking hockey leagues, and I've kept up my playing "career" during my time at Penn State. During one game, I was breaking into the offensive zone and heading for the front of the net, looking for a pass or a rebound, moving reasonably quickly, when Yellow's best defenseman (we were Gray, they were Yellow) ran his stick up and under my arms and rode me away from what's called the "slot," the area ten to fifteen feet in front of the net. Given the speed at which we were moving, it was a slightly dangerous thing to do, and it was certainly illegal — except that, even in nonchecking leagues, it's well understood that if you hang out in front of the net you should expect to draw some hostile physical attention. His idea, I think, was to use my momentum against me and then shove me off behind and to the right side of the net. So I responded in kind: countering one illegal but rarely penalized move with another, I clamped my left arm tightly to my chest, effectively and imperceptibly trapping my opponent's stick and right forearm, and rode him briskly right into the boards. My idea, I think, was to dump *him* behind the net and then work free to do some mischief in the slot, where I belong. But that didn't work either, because as soon as he slammed into the boards, my opponent simply tripped me on my way back out — and that too went unnoticed and unpenalized, for, as luck would have it, the puck had wound up behind the net as well, and no one could see that little trip in the general scramble of four or five bodies.

So Gray's offensive rush dissipated; Yellow picked up the puck in the far corner and started out of their zone. I started down the ice to play some defense, but before I did, I lightly tapped my antagonist on the shin pads and said, "Nice play." What did I mean by this? I think I meant, "OK, neither of us got the upper hand on that one, but you did take me out of the play and your team did strip us of the puck. As for our little encounter, it's always business, never personal, no hard feelings." But of course I didn't have time to say all that.

My opponent's response, however, stunned me. "Nice play my ass," he hissed. "You try that again and I'll take your fucking head off."

Now what exactly was going on here? On one hand, it could simply be that my opponent was a jerk. On the other hand, it could be that my saying "Nice play" was an especially insidious form of aggression — the kind that masks itself as something other than (and nicer than) aggression. Perhaps, even worse, it was an attempt on my part to disavow the competitiveness and adult-ram horn locking that had made the play possible. Did I want to run my opponent into the boards and then have him think well of me anyway? I'm not sure. I do know that I've since had numerous similar encounters with male and female players in other leagues at Penn State, and usually what happens is this: we try to mess each other up in front of the net, skirting the borders of legality, and then when the play ends and/or the whistle blows we each say something like, "Nice play," meaning, more or less, "You did what you were supposed to do, and besides, it's always business, never personal. We're good." "Nice play," in those contexts, serves as a useful marker by which players let each other know that they're not going to get too vicious or weird in the course of the game. But still I wonder about my run-in with that guy from the Yellow team back in Champaign. Maybe sometimes, when you're playing an aggressive sport, you should acknowledge that you're playing an aggressive sport and behave accordingly (within the borders of legality, of course). Because sometimes, saying "Nice play" can be read as an especially aggressive maneuver in its pretense to courtesy and congeniality.

So, then, here's the second story. A cocktail party at the MLA, of course, this one held by the Society for the Study of Narrative Literature. It's the last night of the convention, and earlier in the evening I'd lost my name tag. The Brownian motion of such parties places me suddenly in conversation with a young woman whose tag identifies her as being employed by one of the smaller public schools in the middle of a northeastern state. We make introductions, I apologize for having no tag; she says archly that I must have thought I wouldn't need one. I say I see that she teaches at Midstate and ask how she likes it (both the school and the area), the usual small talk, and I mention that my first MLA interview was with that school and that I met some of her colleagues and so forth.

"That would be before you started flying first class," she says.

I furrow my brow. "You know, I actually did fly first class — once," I reply, attempting to deflect the growing hostility. "It was a mistake on TWA's part, but I didn't correct them, and I'll tell you, I really didn't mind being able to read with my legs crossed for three hours. But there isn't any first class travel out of Champaign, you know. Like you, we're all turboprops."

Well, perhaps the "like you" was too much, but the conversation quickly swooped downhill from there. It was as if I'd said, "Nice play."

For as it is in ice hockey, so it is in academe. What I thought was an ordinary exchange, however tense or contentious, turned out to be high drama: "Ask me how I like teaching at Midstate again and I'll take your fucking head off." I certainly should have been more careful. Not all of us are as competitive as the acquaintance of mine who once said, scanning the name tags (more precisely, the names and their institutional affiliations) at MLA, "Place is *everything*," and not all of us are as creepy and unctuous as the former grad-school acquaintance who called me out of the blue one fine summer day in 1996 and opened the conversation by saying, "It's really been a pleasure to watch your career take off" (and I assure you that I can't even begin to tally all the forms of aggression *that* remark entailed). But I've slowly come to learn, dim bulb that I am, that lots and lots of people in academe gauge themselves and others exclusively by their place in the scheme of academic affiliation, hierarchy, and prestige. I would say, "*imagined* place," but it would be redundant, would it not, as every Althusserian in the room knows.

I remembered this MLA conversation (and a couple of others like it) upon reading Joseph Urgo's *Symplokē* essay, "Affiliation Blues," and his variously nasty encounters with people who asked him how he liked teaching at Bryant College:

> Alas, we are a business college and some things in life, like a facial scar, demand explanation. My experience is that this affiliation indeed may be considered professionally disfiguring but can also become, like a Hawthornesque birthmark, a gauge by which one sees how standards are perpetuated. I stand before my colleagues, at national conferences, as a listing on an editorial board, as a candidate before a selection committee, as a marked scholar. Why does he teach there? Can it be that he could not get hired elsewhere? But look, he has these books and articles, these accomplishments; he has more than some of us. Maybe he is a bastard. . . . Among the questions I have encountered over the years are these: "Have you wondered how much you might have accomplished had you spent this first part of your career at a research institution?"; "How do you manage to teach students who have such strong interests outside your discipline?"; "You have published quite a bit. Why have you stayed there?" One recruitment-minded colleague meant to be pleasantly polite when he said he could only imagine how things might become for me should his institution (a large but mediocre northeast research university) be able to offer me a position some day. (16)

Urgo proceeds to suggest, in a Melvillean vein, that "[I]f I may strike through the mask of such polite, cocktail hour queries, things can get ugly" (16). Is this how my Midstate University interlocutor perceived our encounter, I wonder? Did I seem as arrogant and as clueless as the people Urgo cites? Most likely. I was sincerely asking how she experienced her place of work, and I did not imagine that I was asking from the empyrean heights of the University of Illinois, where we are lords of all we survey. I thought I was asking from the institutional location of a large state school in the rural Midwest, name tag or no name tag. I ask about other English professors' places of work for all manner of reasons, primarily because we're in the same industry and experience a lot of the same pressures and pleasures, and I assume that people teach where they teach for any and every reason I can imagine. Some people want to work in a certain area of the country, some people have partners with other interests, some people (sure enough) wanted something else but it didn't pan out, some people are quite happy where they are, and some people just need jobs. Imagine that: a doctoral student who takes a job someplace because it includes health insurance — just as if it were a *job* or something.

So I think of my awkward MLA encounter this way: it's as if I were from *Newsweek* and was asking someone how they liked working at the *Minneapolis Star-Tribune*. OK, my publication is national and yours is local, and my travel budget is more generous than yours, but I don't infer from this that I am a qualitatively better journalist — or better person — than you are. I'm just asking how you like working at the *Minneapolis Star-Tribune*. You might say, "I hate it, I should never have taken the job, and I'm looking to leave at the first opportunity," as did one of my acquaintances who works at a major private college in the Northeast. You might say, "I couldn't be happier — we've got plenty of money, I like my students, I feel like I landed in the right place," as did one of my acquaintances who wound up in one of the many small, unsung liberal arts colleges that punctuate the Pennsylvania landscape. But whatever you say, your affiliation is not going to stand as the measure of your worth — at least not to any sane person in the business.

Peas and Queues

Yet surely it is a distinctive feature of academe that so few of its inhabitants are "sane" in this sense. Where else but in literature departments could you find hundreds — nay, thousands — of genuinely smart and well-meaning people who have managed to deconstruct every hierarchy and revalorize every kind of stigmatized and degraded cultural practice while somehow remaining enthralled and ensnared by every form of institutional snobbery? (And where would the campus novel be without such characters?) As Urgo cannily writes, "I can't imagine an executive recruiting agent for a Taco Bell playing the blues just because in the fast food business, where hamburgers run the show, tacos and burritos can provide feeding stops for those more suited to beans. Man, I just can't see myself selling soft tacos when I trained for burgers" (8). True enough, precisely because you can't imagine most literature professors imagining themselves as workers in the fast food industry — or even as workers in the industry of print media. Or maybe because you simply can't imagine most literature professors imagining themselves as workers. After all, we don't *work for* anyone; we are *affiliated with institutions of higher education*.

I don't know anything about tacos or burgers, but one of my most valued nonacademic friends likes to keep himself sane by talking about peas — not by talking about peas qua peas, exactly, but by reminding himself that when he worked at Birdseye freezing those "frozen fresh" vegetables, he and his co-workers would occasionally go out for a drink, and their shop talk would take the form of chatter about frozen peas. The chatter could include gossip about other coworkers and complaints about management, but as far as Tom was concerned, it consisted mainly of variations on ways of talking about peas. This is not a homely blue-collar anecdote meant to deflate entrenched and meaningless academic pretensions; it is a *much more complex* anecdote meant to deflate entrenched and meaningless academic pretensions. For my friend Tom was, at the time he told me his peas theory of shop talk, a neonatal intensive care nurse, and a brilliant one at that: his job was far more tense and trying than any literature professor's, and his coworkers' actual shop talk concerned ways of saving babies, not ways of freezing peas. And yes, it included gossip about other coworkers and complaints about management, too. But however dicey, urgent, or emotionally difficult his work became, however daunting the technological or biological or political challenges he faced, Tom reminded himself that his job was, in fact, a job. More hit TV shows are written about doctors, nurses, and medical emergencies than about Birdseye workers and frozen peas, but Tom's not the kind of guy to play up the drama of his workplace. Or mine, such as it is: at various points during the three years I was writing my dissertation, he always took care to ask me how my "book report" was going. "Pretty good," I would say. "How about them peas?" And now every time I go to the MLA and overhear the kinds of conversations you can only hear in such places, I try instead to think about peas: "Did you hear that Walter Benn Michaels moved to Del Monte?" "I can't believe they scheduled three sessions on flash-freezing and the split subject at the same time." "The second reader said I needed to shell the peas more neatly, which makes no damn sense, and now I'm wondering if that second reader wasn't the guy whose broccoli

I criticized in the *Jolly Green Giant Review*." We're all in the same industry, somehow, all talking about peas — but with different affiliations.

Let me not be misunderstood. Of course it matters whether one works at a research university or a business college or a historically black university or a small liberal arts school serving a largely local population. Of course it matters whether one works for *Newsweek* or the *Minneapolis Star-Tribune* or the *Champaign-Urbana News-Gazette*. Of course some utterances are given more institutional weight than others in any institution; of course (to invoke Foucault's work to answer one of Foucault's most famous and unfortunate questions) it matters who is speaking. The politics of academic affiliation are critical to an understanding of how academe works. But at the same time and for the same reasons, I propose that the discourse of "affiliation" is a serious impediment to the rethinking — and the restructuring — of the academic workplace. The discourse wherein professors speak of themselves as loosely, temporarily, voluntarily associated with one university or another is a discourse in which it appears to be next to impossible for professors to think of themselves as workers, let alone workers who *work for* someone. After all, why would we think of ourselves as working for anyone but ourselves? It seems too servile, too abject to think that we might be working for, or even simply *at*, the University of Excellence (and though "working for" might seem somehow harsher and more cynical than "working at," if we're teaching and trying to publish at that University of Excellence, we certainly are working *for* it, to enhance either its internal intellectual quality of life or its external reputation or both); surely, we think, such terms do not capture the nature of the special and almost familial relation that obtains between faculty members and the universities with which they are affiliated.[2]

In an important sense, then, the discourse of affiliation is both more and less pernicious than the discourse of professionalism. For the problem with the rhetoric of professionalism, as it pertains to professors of English, is that the conditions of employment in the humanities are not professional *enough*; we see ourselves as analogous to doctors and attorneys but have no professional apparatus comparable to the AMA or ABA and accordingly far less control over our working conditions. Whereas the discourse of affiliation insists, against all the material evidence, that we are somehow an especially *rarefied* version of professional: your garden-variety megacorporate lawyer might "work for" Simpson Thacher and Bartlett or Cravath Swaine and Moore, but Marjorie Perloff is merely "affiliated with" Stanford and Joseph Urgo "affiliated with" the University of Mississippi. The discourse of affiliation is perhaps less often invoked than the discourse of professionalism as a means of structural self-understanding, hence less of an impediment to thinking about work as work: the MLA Committee on Professional Employment was not, after all, convened as an MLA Committee on Affiliations. But the discourse of affiliation is nonetheless, for all too many people, the primary language in which humanities professors at different workplaces understand their relation to each other, and is therefore a significant obstacle to imagining university employment and mental labor as forms of employment and labor. Ironically, then, the language of academic affiliation seems to be one of the things that prevents academics from thinking of themselves as potentially affiliated with other people who work for a living.

The Only Bands That Matter

"You have published quite a bit. Why have you stayed there?" When I hear — or even when I read — such questions I wonder what universe the questioner is living in. Probably the universe in which planets are merely "affiliated with" the nearest massive clump of hydrogen. The question presumes, of course, the old-school belief that you can publish your way out of anywhere, even though in the current job system there's actually no guarantee that you can publish your way *into* anywhere. And in the old school, of course, place is everything. While I was placement director at the University of Illinois at Urbana-Champaign, from 1993 to 1995, we had one extraordinarily talented and fortunate student with multiple offers from Kansas, DePaul, and Yale. His spouse could easily have found gainful employment in Chicago or the metro New York area, so his choice came down to DePaul and Yale — the one offering him a 3/2 load on the tenure track, the other offering him 2/2 and Ivy League students and some released time and world-class research facilities and a four-year *non*-tenure-track contract and some very, very difficult employment conditions for an assistant professor; the storm that would become the 1995 – 96 GESO grade strike was already gathering, and there was the possibility that he would be asked to stand in opposition to Yale's graduate student union, perhaps even to teach extra classes in the event of a teaching-assistant strike.[3] That student and I agonized for days about what was, given the circumstances, an exceptionally rare and pleasant dilemma for a new Ph.D., and during that time I managed to hear one of my senior colleagues express his outraged disbelief that I would even help a student weigh such a choice: "I will not have it said," he said, and it's important that he would not *have it said*, "that one of our students turned down Yale for DePaul." What universe did this come from? A universe that is composed entirely of what people say, a universe that contains no matter at all. A universe in which faculty don't think, "What are

the best working conditions for this new Ph.D. and his family?" but rather, "How can this new Ph.D. contribute to our sense of institutional prestige?"

Ah, but then, academic affiliation is a competitive sport, and I should probably stop pretending to myself, on the ice or off, that competitive sports are something other than competitive sports. I should also admit that although I don't have much patience with the discourse of affiliation, I do take my work — and my reputation — seriously. My own workplace analogy involves neither tacos nor peas; it comes from my days in my twenties as a mediocre drummer playing various paying and nonpaying gigs, from CBGB on a few Wednesday nights (hardly a desirable thing, for all its retroactive prestige value) to all-ages shows in Norfolk, Virginia, from opening for the Ramones to closing down teenage house parties. For people with and without the affiliation blues, then, I suggest thinking of academic jobs as gigs. They're hard to get, and really fabulous ones are almost impossible to find. When you get a gig you like, whether it's playing somebody's wedding or playing the best club in town, you want to show the booking agent s/he made the right call. You want to get invited back, even if you don't necessarily want to *come* back. If you're the competitive sort, you also want to show all the folks who didn't book you that they screwed up — not as monumentally as Dick Rowe, the guy from Decca who passed on the Beatles, say, but meaningfully nonetheless. I wonder, in this vein, if any working musician has ever described himself or herself as being "affiliated with" the 9:30 Club in D.C. or the Five Spot in New York or the Holiday Inn in Lewiston, Maine.

Or to return one last time to my ice hockey analogy: I was not "affiliated with" the Gray team, I'd been *drafted by* Gray. The previous semester, I'd been drafted in the fifth or sixth round (out of thirteen rounds) by Red, and among the things I wanted to do that semester was show the various team captains that I could plausibly have been drafted higher. Then Gray drafted me in the second round, and I spent my time that season trying to show its captain that he didn't screw up (I thought second was a little *too* high, myself). So, as you can see, there's still plenty of room for competition, envy, resentment, injury, and schadenfreude in my musician/athlete rendition of the academic workplace; musicians and athletes, for all their realism about work, are not always paragons of collegiality and interdisciplinary collaboration (though they often have to work together closely in ways that humanities professors never do). There's also plenty of opportunity, in my version of the workplace, for people to have hostile and contentious conversations about peas at the next MLA convention. But in my language, in which people speak of where they're *working at* or *playing at* or whom they're *playing for*, you don't have all the mystifications and occlusions of material working conditions that you get with the discourse of academic affiliation. We sometimes play the blues, too, but we don't talk about which blues club or which blues tradition we're "affiliated with." Who knows? Maybe if there were fewer academic workers caught up in the mechanisms of disciplinary and institutional snobbery, we could start thinking about what it means to be a member of a musicians' union or a players' union. And then maybe, when we got the workplace blues, we could get together and work it on out.

Notes

1. I've written on disability and African American literature and have various forms of membership in areas of study relevant to each; I have published significantly less work on feminism and have no formal relation to feminist literary or cultural study (I was not, for example, a zero-percent appointee in women's studies at UIUC, though I could plausibly have been). However, I regularly teach feminist work in theory classes, ranging from my reader-response and canonicity seminars to my introduction-to-postmodernism classes, and as a result have been asked on two occasions (by Illinois undergraduates) to conduct individual-study courses on feminist theory. My primary texts for the last such course, in the fall of 1999, were Alice Echols's *Daring to Be Bad*, Judith Butler and Joan Wallach Scott's *Feminists Theorize the Political*, and the Benhabib-Butler-Cornell-Fraser exchanges known to the world as *Feminist Contentions*. Although I am not a dues-paying member of any feminist organization, therefore, I have an informal affiliation with feminism that is every bit as tangled and tenuous as my relations with any other intellectual field organized around a form of identity I do not currently claim as my own.

2. The preceding paragraph contains an implicit tip of the hat — which I'd like to make explicit here — to Kent Puckett and Marc Bousquet for naming their online journal *Workplace*. Puckett, Bousquet, et al. clearly anticipated this argument years ago (*Workplace*'s inaugural issue appeared in February 1998), and indeed it has been a signal feature of graduate student activism throughout North America that it has compelled faculty, administrators, trustees and (on rare and happy occasions) arbitrators and labor relations boards to think of universities as workplaces — workplaces that employ teachers as well as people who serve tacos, burgers, and peas. The resistance with which that activism has met has everything to do with old-school faculty and administrators and paid ideological obfuscators (not to mention, in the case of the University of Illinois, law firms renowned for strikebreaking) who cannot — or who profess to be unable to — imagine university employment as anything other than a genial form of affiliation.

For an apt discussion of "working at" and "working for," see the opening paragraphs of John Marsh's essay, "One Rhetoric Fits All." See also all the succeeding paragraphs of Marsh's essay.

3. For accounts of the 1995–96 GESO strike at Yale, see Nelson.

Works Cited

Benhabib, Seyla, Judith Butler, Drucilla Cornell, and Nancy Fraser. *Feminist Contentions: A Philosophical Exchange*. New York: Routledge, 1995.

Butler, Judith, and Joan W. Scott. *Feminists Theorize the Political*. New York: Routledge, 1992.

Echols, Alice. *Daring to Be Bad: Radical Feminism in America, 1967–1975*. Minneapolis: University of Minnesota Press, 1989.

Marsh, John. "One Rhetoric Fits All: What Graduate Student Unions Have Taught Us about Higher Education and the Public Sphere." *Workplace* 4, no. 1 (2001). Available online at <http://www.louisville.edu/journal/workplace/issue7/marsh.html>. Accessed 13 January 2006.

Nelson, Cary, ed. *Will Teach for Food: Academic Labor in Crisis*. Minneapolis: University of Minnesota Press, 1997.

Urgo, Joseph. "The Affiliation Blues." *Symplokē* 7, no. 1–2 (1999): 7–20.

It's the class of my dreams. We're just beginning a new semester; I'm going over the syllabus, term papers, midterm, final, and so on when suddenly a secretary pops her head in the door to say that the class has been moved to a different building, effective immediately. Puzzled, my students and I gather our bags and belongings and begin the hike to Zzyzzych 304, a room in a building none of us has ever heard of. It's about a twenty-minute walk, and before long, almost half the students disappear. I begin to get worried and start talking to the remaining students about the assigned novelists and poets, trying to keep them entertained; that works for a while, until we enter a construction site and find ourselves shuffling through a makeshift plywood corridor whose ceiling seems to be getting lower as we go. More students bail out. By the time we reach the dank basement entrance to the Zzyzzych Building, I'm left with a class of twelve students, eight or nine of whom leave while I'm discussing the grading policy.

Another tableau: I wander into the English Department office as the semester begins to find that my course on twentieth-century African American fiction, meeting later that day, has been changed to Avant-Garde and Representation: The Problem of the Holocaust. I have no syllabus, nor do I know anything about the topic. Nevertheless, terrified as I am, I manage to bluff my way through the first class meeting by asking students for their reactions to *Schindler's List*. Thankfully, they are less annoyed by my incompetence than by the fact that the classroom has window ledges seven feet high — and no chairs.

Anyone who's had an anxiety dream about teaching knows the psychic landscape: the mysterious building, the spectral students, the surreal classroom, the sheer suffocating terror. *This is the class that will expose me as a fraud*, you think. Or: *This time they'll know I didn't prepare all summer.* Even: *When this is over, they'll fire me on the spot.* From what all my friends and colleagues tell me, it doesn't matter how experienced or accomplished you are: If you care at all about your teaching, you are haunted by teaching-anxiety dreams.

They come in all genres and feature all forms of torment, and they afflict graduate students and emeriti alike. My wife, Janet Lyon, despite having won numerous teaching awards, begins each year with some variation on a dream in which she walks into the room, discovers that she must lecture to five hundred students on a short story she's never read, and promptly pretends to faint at the lectern.

And then there are the related anxiety dreams, so often triggered by the advent of classes, in which you imagine yourself back in college under some terrible dispensation — you have to write a hundred pages by dawn to graduate; you're told on the eve of your Ph.D. orals that your B.A. has been investigated and found to be invalid. *I'm sorry*, intones the lugubrious, sixteen-rpm voice, *you will have to leave the graduate program by midnight tonight.* Bats whirl in the light of the moon as the ancient clock on the quad strikes eleven.

That last nightmare (minus the bats and the tolling bell) was actually related to me by the late W. T. H. Jackson, a renowned medievalist whom few colleagues would have suspected of a moment's doubt about his skills or his credentials. It was May 1982, and I, then a senior at Columbia University, had appeared at Jackson's door in the kind of cold sweat that one associates with . . . well, with nightmares. I was frantically explaining to him that the R (for "residence credit") that he had given me in his class on *Tristan and Isolde* was preventing me from graduating. "I'm not a graduate student," I said, "and I can't take classes for R credit, and the registrar's computer reads it as an F, and my parents are flying in at 4, and . . ." Professor Jackson graciously explained that he had mistakenly given my B+ to some bewildered graduate student and given me her R. Then he told me that, without a doubt, this experience would stay with me the rest of my life if I pursued a career in academe, where I would periodically dream that someone would declare my B.A. invalid and fire me on the spot. He knew. He'd had the dream many times.

In my case, you see, anxiety dreams are kind of like conspiracy theories — every once in a while, they have a basis in fact. Remember that dream about the course you didn't know you were taking and, therefore, didn't go to all semester? That's the Ghost Course dream. I have it three or four times every year, just as classes begin.

About half the time, it's the foreign-language requirement that gets me. Sure, sometimes I dream that I'm supposed to be taking Geology 801 or Intro Entomology or some other subject of which I have remained almost completely ignorant my entire life, but most of the time the Ghost Course concerns a subject close to me — yet not close enough. French is a perfect psychic magnet for my free-floating sense of inadequacy. It doesn't help matters that I really did fail my second semester of French as a college sophomore because I transferred from one section to another without completing the appropriate forms: I signed up for a 9:00 A.M. section, then got a job cleaning a local restaurant from 7:00 to 11:00 A.M. weekdays, then switched to the 11:00 A.M. section without properly dropping the 9:00 A.M. section. I finally got the F removed, although not before spending the spring semester on academic probation.

The experience might have been mildly traumatic — particularly for a nineteen-year-old who had spent most of his conscious life jumping through the requisite academic hoops, usually with the greatest of ease. But why should I replay it over and over in my dreams *to this day*? Why should it be linked to the start of classes? And why do I bother obsessing about little anxieties of twenty years ago instead of about the much greater ones that have dotted my adult life since? I'm actually not terribly worried about academic matters in my waking life. Bad book reviews, rejected fellowship applications, stinging student evaluations — those are annoying or discouraging, no question. But one severely asthmatic, repeatedly hospitalized toddler, then another child with Down syndrome, now *that's* serious.

Or so one would think, in one's waking moments. The unconscious, however, has a mind of its own. And so every semester, when anxiety strikes in the still of the night, I don't dream that I have to cancel a class because of my children; no, I dream that my course descriptions have been changed, that my students get up and drift away as I'm in midsentence, that I'm three hours late to a classroom that doesn't exist — or that I forgot to attend French for Reading Proficiency last term and will not be allowed to teach the novels of André Gide. I've never taught the novels of André Gide. But it doesn't matter; there's something about teaching that rouses all the gnawing fears that have accumulated over our academic lifetimes.

My dreams during the summer of 2001, as I was changing institutions, were particularly intense. For the first time in twelve years, I really *didn't* have any idea where my classrooms would be, and I really *hadn't* filled out the book-order forms for my contemporary American literature courses. I arrived at Penn State with much to learn, threading my way through what seemed to be an especially opaque and unnavigable campus. Many things about Pennsylvania are opaque and unnavigable — it appears to be impossible to register a motor vehicle in the commonwealth, for example, without a blood test and a note from your college French teacher — but my unconscious worries about moving to a new place seemed to concentrate exclusively on what would happen on the first day of classes.

As I prepared my opening handouts, unaware that the English Department was changing my office phone number (they eventually changed it *twice*) and that I'd forgotten to include Flannery O'Connor on the survey syllabus (now how did *that* happen?), I realized why professors have anxiety dreams at the start of the academic year: teaching is really hard to do. If you're doing it in classes of fifteen and forty students, as I am, you're teaching in a setting where the students will find out not only what you think about x and y but also what you are like in some strange and intimate way. They'll get a sense of how thoroughly you prepare, of course, but, even more, they'll see how you respond to the unexpected — to the savvy young woman who wants to know whether you're using the term "postcolonial" in a cultural or an economic sense, to the curious junior who wonders aloud why Don DeLillo gave the name Simeon Biggs to a snappish African American character in *Underworld*. For such moments, you simply can't prepare — except by accumulating years upon years of teaching experience and weathering night upon night of anxiety dreams.

Because on that first day of class, truly anything can happen: your students aren't going to love you just because your last three semesters went well, and it's a fair bet that none of your undergraduates (and almost none of your graduate students) will have come back from the summer freshly impressed by how deftly you handled that ludicrously unfair book review in the June issue of *Crank Quarterly*. Amazingly, none of your students will arrive on the first day having heard anything you've said to other students over the past twenty years; amazingly, you'll have to make a first impression all over again, for the twenty-first time.

If it's a course you've never taught before, you may wind up rewriting or scrapping the syllabus in midstream; if it's a course in a fairly new area of study, you'll have no idea what kind of knowledge base to expect from your students. And, of course, if the window ledges are seven feet high in Zzyzzych 304, how will anyone be able to close the windows when the motorcycle gangs roar by?

Buddhists speak of learning to see the world with "beginner's mind," and that's precisely what you have to do every semester: begin again, from scratch, knowing that anything can happen — seeing those ten, or fifty, or even five hundred students, like the two thousand students you've seen before, with beginner's mind. Our anxiety dreams, surely, are the index of our secret fears of failure and inadequacy. But they're also the measure of how very difficult it is — and how very exhilarating — to begin each semester with beginner's mind.

In the third week of August, the fall 2001 semester started at Penn State. In September, just after Labor Day, the K–12 school year began in the State College Area School District. The deliberately uncoordinated schedules bespeak considerable cultural complexity, especially since Penn State is the largest employer in the area and the K–12 school district the second largest. You'd expect that they'd be on the same page when it comes to putting people in classrooms. But apparently the Grange Fair occupies a two-week period before Labor Day and induces area families to live in tents, eat cotton candy, compete in livestock shows, play music, and generally have a good old time. The reason the grade schools and high schools begin after Labor Day, then, is that town and gown have reached a kind of compromise between the needs of faculty members and students and the desires of local residents who've been attending the Grange Fair for more than a century.

But for me and Janet Lyon, my wife, what all that meant was that we had to find some way of teaching in August with a ten-year-old who was out of summer camp and not yet in school. Baby sitters covered some of the terrain, but eventually I wound up in a position I know all too well, announcing to my students that our next meeting would be my own personal Bring Your Child to Class Day. It didn't disrupt my honors seminar to have Jamie by my side, interrupting me periodically by calling to my students, "Any questions?" On the contrary, my students found Jamie charming and surprising (they hadn't expected him to ask each of them their names), and perhaps on that fine August morning they learned something they didn't know about children with Down syndrome. Still, teaching with Jamie at my side was not ideal for any of the parties involved — especially Jamie himself, who had not planned to spend two fifty-minute sessions drawing at a desk while his father droned on about contemporary American literature.

Twelve years earlier, when Janet and I had first arrived at the University of Illinois, we had only one child — Nick, then three years old and already (alas) an old hand at negotiating the oddities of academic life, like receptions at which everyone eats hors d'oeuvres while standing and holding napkins and drinks. But we couldn't afford full-time day care at ninety dollars a week, so, after jumping through the university's formidable series of hoops (including the wonderfully misnamed Child Care Resource Service, which required you to register for referrals in person but would only give out information about private child-care providers by phone, five providers at a time), we signed Nick up for half-day care in the afternoons. Both my wife and I taught in the morning, but we took what we could get.

I will never forget that semester. Janet taught from 9:00 to 9:50 A.M. and then again at 11:00; I taught from 10 to 10:50 and then again at 12:00. Day care began at 1:00. I would take a Champaign city bus with Nick, getting to school at 9:47, meet Janet in the hall, and hand off Nick with three or four minutes to spare; at a few minutes to 11, Janet would pass him back to me; he and I would grab lunch while Janet taught, and then I'd toss him back to Janet, and she would take him to day care.

The University of Illinois was somewhat anomalous among its peers, many of which have extensive child-care programs for faculty and staff members. (Even for many months after moving to Penn State, I continued to receive e-mail messages from frustrated faculty parents at my old university, notifying me of yet another initiative to "study" the child-care situation. This was impressive news: successive administrations at Illinois had been studying child care for more than thirty years, which must have meant that the institution was by that point among the world's leaders in the creation of task forces on child care.) But it is not at all uncommon at many colleges and universities for married faculty members with children to have great difficulty managing their lives as teachers, scholars, and parents. Commuting couples with children have it worst, of course — financially, physically, and emotionally.

The paradox is that university life can be both terrific and troubling for parents and children alike: the workplace environment is casual and accommodating on the one hand and clueless and hostile on the other. Usually all at the same time.

From day to day, a campus can be a great place for a kid: movies, recreation centers, computers, museums, you name it. What's not to like? At Penn State, Jamie has become especially fond of the swimming pool, the hockey rink, and the tropical aquarium in the student center. Not to mention all the pizza. Throw in parents' reasonably flexible work schedules, and the campus looks infinitely more inviting than the cubicle, the boardroom, or the shop floor.

But academe as an institution isn't always understanding about faculty children. I know of one institution at which important faculty meetings are routinely scheduled for 5 P.M., as if no one lived in a world where kids needed to be picked up, brought home, and fed. I remember a colleague at Harvard complaining to me about the prestigious Saturday Club — a bastion, she said, of unalloyed old-boy privilege. "The fact that they meet on Saturdays says it all," she fumed. I was about to agree when she added, "and everyone knows we need Saturdays to write." "Um, no," I replied, "I haven't written anything on a Saturday in many years."

I also recall a member of a search committee telling me that although my curriculum vitae was strong in most areas, it was clear that I had not sought a sufficient number of external fellowships and awards. "You mean," I asked, "the kind where you go to live at a research institute for a year or serve as a 'visiting professor' for a semester?" Yes. "Well, of course, I'd love the release time and the prestige and all," I said. "But do you have any idea how expensive it is to have your children cryogenically frozen?"

Everything about my life and Janet's is structured by our children and has been ever since our graduate-school days. At first it was a dissertation-writing agreement that I would take care of toddler Nick for three afternoons and Janet would take him for two; then it was a tenure-track agreement that we would split the weekends into half-days and switch off parental duties at 1:00 P.M. And, of course, as every parent knows, when the children are sick, the world literally stops turning and all other obligations are postponed until the earth's rotation starts up again. The spousal contract covering all our comings and goings is long and complicated, full of disputed phrasings and oft-renegotiated subsidiary clauses. But it stipulates quite clearly that neither one of us will leave the other holding the bag for weeks at a time, let alone entire semesters or years.

For me, being an academic parent has also had unexpected benefits, quite apart from the fact that I have two wonderful children.

When Janet first became pregnant, I was agonizing over an incomplete I had taken in Richard Rorty's Heidegger seminar; for three months I had been unable to write the paper, thinking (quite understandably) that there was nothing I could say about Heidegger that Rorty would find valuable or interesting. But the idea of imminent childbirth put Heidegger and Rorty in a wholly different light. I wound up writing a fifty-page paper in four days, not only because I needed to finish the incomplete but also because I knew that Rorty's reaction to my argument, whatever it might be, was not going to matter as much to my life as would the experience of being a parent.

For most academics, however, having a child does not enhance writing skills or reduce professional anxieties. That's why most wait until after tenure to start thinking about babies. It's also why many men in academe (including many men who consider themselves unimpeachably liberal) are wont to belittle their female colleagues who have "too many" children — "too many" often meaning "more than one or two." Janet and I, in having two children before either of us was tenured, were perhaps especially foolhardy; then again, we thought there was something weird, even unsavory, about waiting for a dean or a provost to let us know when it was all right for us to procreate.

Thankfully, many universities are now instituting "rollback" policies for junior, female faculty members who have children, giving them one more year on the tenure clock (and Illinois, to its credit, has been generous and fair here). And the American Association of University Professors, after many years of silence, recently adopted a recommendation that new parents get extra time to prepare for tenure. Some institutions are updating maternity-leave policies, and some are even drafting paternity-leave policies as well. And many more offer on-site day care for faculty and staff members.

However, as family-friendly policies have gone forward, they have met with some resistance — not only from the Old Guard who see women and children intruding on a traditionally male preserve but also from childless academics who think that parent-professors get all the slack, and even from some gay and lesbian scholars, themselves recent arrivals to many campuses, who see "family friendly" policies as aggressively heterosexist. "It's not enough that you have your standard federal child deduction and your child-care tax credit," said one of my gay friends in an exasperated mood. "Now you need campus-subsidized baby-sitting as well? Do you really need to be so amply rewarded just for procreating?"

It's enough to send any garden-variety liberal into a tizzy. Family-leave policies are obviously good, solid, welfare-state progressivism at work, but they're homophobic too? To people who have always supported the right of gay and lesbian couples to adopt, the idea that it is homophobic to support day care must sound rather, well, queer.

It's true that, in mainstream American life, the term "family" is often little more than a code word for antigay politics; that's how so many "pro-family" conservatives can oppose health care, nutrition programs, and subsidized day care for children in poverty and yet call themselves "pro-family." To champion "the family" is to oppose divorce and single motherhood and all such insidious forces of cultural decay, and among the most insidious of those forces, as we learned in the 2004 presidential campaign, are the same-sex couples whose stable "alternative lifestyles" pose such a challenge to myths of gay promiscuity and heterosexual married bliss. Hence the obsessive intensity with which "pro-family" organizations have worked to deny gay and lesbian couples the right to marry (as if Clinton's 1996 Defense of Marriage Act were the only thing protecting my own marriage from being torn asunder by hordes of queer theorists who might make me or my wife think twice about this whole heterosexuality boondoggle). No doubt about it, from the statehouse to the court-house to the White House, the "family" is the first refuge of scoundrels.

And yet it need not be so on American campuses. University policies can support same-sex partner hiring and can recognize same-sex partners in health and insurance plans while providing child-friendly workplace accommoda-tions that will inevitably most often benefit married couples, heterosexuals, breeders, and even those dangerous unwed mothers who get themselves, uh, knocked up. There's no need to set one constituency against another. All that's needed is the political will — though I realize this is a little like saying, "All you need to implement universal health care is the political will." Unfortu-nately, in November 2004, the voters of our neighboring state of Ohio passed ballot initiative Issue 1, decreeing that the state "shall not create or recognize a legal status for relationships of unmarried individuals that intends to ap-proximate the design, qualities, significance or effect of marriage." So much for health benefits — and hospital visitation rights and all private contracts between cohabiting gay persons — for every gay or lesbian student and faculty member in the state of Ohio.

The anti-gay-marriage backlash in the United States is formidable, and for all I know, it may be decades before decent Americans regard homophobia the way they now regard state laws forbidding "miscegenation" (which, after all, survived until the 1967 Supreme Court decision in *Loving v. Virginia*, a deci-sion opposed by the vast majority of the American public when it was handed down). But though the arc of the moral universe is long, it bends toward jus-tice, and savvy campus officials can stay ahead of the curve. Universities can try, with a little imagination, a little nerve, and a little more money, to provide a humane working and living environment for every human being they em-ploy and every human family in every form of human social arrangement. A few are already doing so. And like those universities that have adopted living-wage policies and have negotiated in good faith with campus unions, they are setting an example for the rest of American business culture to follow — and perhaps even an example for which our children and our gay colleagues will someday thank them.

I n my first year as humanities director at the University of Illinois, I invited a well-known filmmaker to campus. Her agent's response came over the fax a few days later, with a list of necessaries: so much per day, first-class air travel, Marriott-quality accommodations or better. "Well," I said to my associate director, Christine Catanzarite, "if you'll float the bond issue, I'll hire the subcontractors — we haven't *got* a Marriott-quality hotel in Champaign." For that matter, we didn't have first-class air travel, either.

It turned out that the filmmaker in question was a gracious and generous woman, nothing like the diva we'd envisioned from her agent's fax. Her tiny turboprop from St. Louis arrived more than an hour late, and she got to her almost-Marriott hotel at 11:00 P.M.; having flown in from Los Angeles and having foregone an airport dinner, she inquired at the desk as to whether the restaurant was still serving. Yes and no, she was told: the kitchen was open until 11:30, but she would have to call from her room for room service. All very well — except that the room into which she was booked turned out to be occupied.

She told me this story the next morning, quite lightheartedly, almost as if she were simply adding a comic chapter to her personal Travails of Travel. And what could I do? Embarrassed and feeling vaguely guilty, I shambled as best I could: "They did ask me whether you wanted a smoking or nonsmoking room," I told her, "but they didn't ask about occupied and nonoccupied. I'll have to speak to the desk about that."

Now, where did I learn such silly banter? At the Catskills in the late 1950s, working two shows a night behind Shecky Greene? No, actually, I learned it in my own travels — like, for instance, my journey just southeast of the Poconos, to Allentown, where I was an invited speaker in the mid-1990s at one of Pennsylvania's small, excellent liberal arts colleges. An undergraduate student aide had apparently done the booking, which explains why I had to hail a cab from the airport at 8:00 P.M. to take me to a godforsaken Hampton Inn twenty miles west of the campus — indeed, twenty miles west of any human habitation. Hampton Inns, as every business traveler knows, are basically upscale motels: free "continental" breakfast but no restaurant; coin-op laundry; indoor pool, "fitness" room consisting of a stationary bike and a treadmill. But I, disdaining the Hampton's options for dial-up dinners delivered from local pizza-and-grinders establishments in forty-five minutes or less, boldly set out on foot across the thigh-high grass of the corporate park into which I had been deposited (noting that my hotel abutted the Keebler Cookie Factory, where surely the elves would keep me up all night), seeking paved roads and the customary commercial dining establishments appurtenant thereto. Clambering over the concrete divider that constitutes PA-100 as a "divided" road, I realized that I had only two options within hailing distance, Burger King and Gyro King. I needn't add that I chose the king I didn't know over the king I did — or that my gyro special was of an order of deliciousness beyond the descriptive capacity of all known written and oral languages.

The next morning, the group of faculty that was supposed to take me to brunch could not find me — not because I had gotten lost in the corporate park or kidnapped by cookie-baking elves, but because no invited speaker had ever been put up in that Hampton Inn before. When at last I was found, about an hour after the scheduled pickup, there were apologies for the lodging, apologies for being so late for brunch, and promises to "speak to" the student who did the booking. "It's perfectly all right," I said, assuring my hosts that I had dined robustly and slept well. "But if it wouldn't be too much trouble, I really would like to stay someplace closer to campus or downtown." Within an hour I was transferred to a gorgeous, rambling old hotel in downtown Allentown, where the desk clerk really did say, "Smoking or nonsmoking?" and when I replied nonsmoking, he followed with "Occupied or nonoccupied?," waiting a crucial half-beat before drily adding, "Kidding, of course."

I PROMISE MYSELF that I will never become the Guest from Hell, partly because I've hosted two or three of these in my life and it's just astonishing how much trouble and nonsense they can cause. The guest who rebooks his own flight at the last minute, bumping his fare from $350 to $1,200; the guest who fails to turn up for dinner; the guest who's too hung over to make the informal coffee get-together at midmorning *and* the lunch with students at 1:00. It's hard enough to schedule a good campus visit in most college towns, threading your guest through the hubs and spokes of the American air travel system, checking to make sure there are no home football games or other major cultural events that will fill the local hotels, double-checking with the desultory and erratic taxi service, watching for dietary restrictions and personality clashes and possible competing events with cosponsors. At Illinois one year I almost had to cancel a small conference upon realizing that it conflicted with Mom's Weekend, a particularly nasty — and *very* popular — piece of Kampus Kitsch brought to you by the same folks who invented Homecoming (yes, Illinois claims, plausibly, to have invented Homecoming). Every hotel within a fifteen-mile radius was full, presumably full of Moms and Dads and Other Family Members, and we faced the prospect of lodging our five guests in faculty homes. (Even Urbana's bed and breakfast was full, and since it goes by the odd, Dr. Seussian name of Hodge Podge Lodge, we had grave reservations, so to speak, about putting any of our guests in it. The long-whiskered concierge in the tall red-and-white striped hat didn't help matters any.) Worse still, the husband-and-wife team we'd invited were no longer husband and wife, which meant that they would need two rooms unless we could somehow get them back together within two weeks (we consulted sitcoms and romantic comedies for possible solutions, to no avail). We were saved by the sudden, unexpected Grand Opening of a place called ExtendedStayAmerica Efficiency Studios, which offered our guests a week's stay for about $200 — less than three nights of lodging anyplace else, as it turned out. And none of our guests, thank goodness, was a Guest from Hell.

FEW PROFESSORS have written seriously about the phenomenon of the Invited Speaker, perhaps because the subject bumps up uncomfortably against the phenomena of academic stardom and professional resentment: apparently it is widely assumed that Invited Speakers routinely fly first class, stay at the Four Seasons, dine on quail, collect 10 or 20K a pop, and spend their free time thinking up ways to break Cornel West's record for Most Speaking Engagements in One Year. The reality, of course, is far less alluring, as I remarked to myself one scary night in a rustic Wyoming bed-and-breakfast whose proprietor had left town for a few days, leaving me, his only guest, alone with instructions on how to feed his three large, lean, feral Dobermans. And for the hosts, University Speakers' Series and Distinguished Lectures can be thoroughly unglamorous, logistical nightmares involving months of putting together itineraries and dealing with difficult "cosponsors" who volunteer to pick up speakers at the airport only to whisk them away for departmental functions that appear nowhere on anyone's itinerary. I have witnessed visits that required the distinguished invitee to conduct three seminars in one day, visits that were derailed by feuding faculty members who could not agree on restaurant reservations, visits on which speakers were delivered to the wrong building by the desultory taxi service and left to wander around the campus at night in search of their lecture hall. Setting up a successful visit requires an almost artisanal attention to minute detail, not only with regard to the quality of the lecture hall and its equipment but also with regard to the bodily requirements of the speakers themselves — from the speaker who must observe Passover to the speaker who requires access ramps to the speaker who needs a ride to the town's only black-owned radio station, where her afternoon interview will generate terrific publicity for her evening's presentation. My own needs as a speaker are few; I'm easy to feed and lodge, but I do like to work out for about an hour a day if I can. Most universities are happy enough to accommodate me whenever I find myself in a hotel without so much as a single stationary bicycle, but I reserve a special place in my heart for hosts above and beyond the call, like Mark Freed, who, when he learned that Central Michigan's gym does not make towels available to guests, simply ripped his own towel in half and handed it to me. So much depends on the minor grace notes of hosts and guests alike.

It is rare that invited speakers complain about traveling or dining or lodging arrangements; the vast majority of them know that it is a privilege and a treat to be invited anywhere, and for someone like myself, who had never seen any of the United States west of Hershey, Pennsylvania (save for a brief visit to Los Angeles), until I was hired at the University of Illinois, traveling to universities in the Far West is especially thrilling. But there is a thriving culture of complaint about the invited-speaker circuit nonetheless, and a host of people (other than the speaker's hosts, of course) who have made a cottage industry out of criticizing, protesting, and on extreme occasions even disrupting public lectures at universities.

The complainants come from all points on the political spectrum, and the complaints run from the deadly serious to the unimaginably trivial. Even in my limited experience as a host, I have handled complaints that one or another speaker was unacceptable because he did not have a theory of subjectivity, because she would attend to Chicano/a literature but not Latino/a literature, or because his account of distributive justice did not include a denunciation of NATO bombing in Kosovo. These complaints, of course, are mere irritations when compared to the kind of political histrionics involved when a speaker turns out to be unacceptable to far-right-wing commentators on the Middle East or to the campus Black Caucus or to the Decency League or to the local Committee of People in Solidarity with People. When political protests on that order take place, the organizers of speakers' series must wonder, first, why any group would expect that all campus speakers or symposia would be "acceptable" to them, and second, whether the intellectual rewards of hosting a speaker are really worth all the logistical and political trouble. Who wants to clean up (in a literal sense) after David Horowitz is hit with a pie, and who wants to clean up (metaphorically) after Ward Churchill has elaborated on his claim that the "technicians" who died in the World Trade Center on 11 September 2001 were little Eichmanns?

The vast majority of the time — that is, when the invited speaker is not a flame-thrower whose work is free of intellectual content, like Ann Coulter — I would argue that it is worth the trouble. A good lecture and a good visit can have ripple effects that go on for months, sparking further exchanges among faculty and students, creating a critical mass of people devoted to a subject, and generally enhancing a campus's intellectual quality of life. I have been so fortunate as to have hosted or cohosted a fair number of such visits, by performance artist Joe Goode and Russian émigré artists Vitaly Komar and Alexander Melamid, by philosopher Nancy Fraser and former museum director Marcia Tucker. In each case, my fellow lecturegoers and I left knowing that we'd learned something new, that we'd been asked to rethink what we thought we knew about our social or affective lives, and that we'd be slightly different people as a result. And in each case, I left thinking that a good lecture can be one of the most edifying and challenging aspects of campus life, for hosts and guests alike.

A s a former humanities-program administrator, I welcome the growing chorus of voices calling for universities to be run more like businesses. For too long now, American higher education has lagged behind most other American industries with regard to innovative cost-cutting, market-expanding, and profit-enhancing strategies. Perhaps the surest sign of American universities' disconnection from the real world of profit and loss is that in 370 years of operations, they have not managed to coin one single AIM-T (Acronym for Implementing Management Techniques) or produce even one self-help guide delineating the habits of highly effective people. Indeed, over the course of twenty years in academe as professor and student, during which I have visited dozens of universities large and small, I have come to the conclusion that many people in academe actually *disdain* management acronyms and self-help guides — the lingua franca of American business discourse.

Amazingly, this disdain for aggressive marketing and self-promotion is matched or exceeded by academe's aversion to the kind of structural, systemic change that has made the American economy so remarkably productive. While it is true that American universities have adopted some of the most constructive developments of the business world — boosting the pay of dynamic executive officers to almost a million dollars a year while maintaining a flexible, "as-needed" workforce for outsourceable tasks such as physical plant maintenance and freshman composition — it is also true that not a single American university to date has shown enough basic business sense to register its name as a commercial trademark. This has had a strongly negative impact on universities' mobility, and therefore prevents them from seeking out optimal wage environments in New Delhi and Singapore. But it also speaks more generally to academe's cluelessness about how the world actually works.

Take, for example, universities' most valuable asset — real estate. How are buildings currently named on American campuses? Occasionally a building will bear the name of a wealthy donor or noted alumnus; too often they are simply called by generic names such as "Physics" or "History." Even colleges of business administration, which should know better, tend to follow this rule. Contrast this medieval practice with that of Dan Snyder, owner of the Washington Redskins, who signed a twenty-seven-year, $205.5 million contract to sell the name of Jack Kent Cooke Stadium to Federal Express. Again, universities have taken a few steps in the right direction in recent years: witness the Taco Bell Distinguished Professorship of Hotel and Restaurant Management at Washington State University, the General Mills Chair of Cereal Chemistry and Technology at the University of Minnesota, and the Federal Express Chair of Information-Management Systems at the University of Memphis. But these are baby steps, particularly when you realize that large state universities are letting *hundreds* of valuable buildings lie dormant and unnamed, even though a single 3Com Material Sciences Building or Burger King School of Animal Husbandry could garner millions in revenue — and thereby enable universities to compete more effectively for the most dynamic executive officers.

Tuition, too, is a problem. At the vast majority of American universities, it is far too low. Public colleges, especially, are prevented from pursuing market-value tuition rates by socialist state legislatures whose regulatory ambitions know no bounds. The absurd result? At a "low-tuition, low-aid" flagship state school like the University of Illinois at Urbana-Champaign, undergraduates who live off campus typically pay more in rent than tuition per annum — usually for cramped, dingy apartments that, unlike college degrees, will do nothing to enhance a student's lifetime earnings potential. Surely a reasonable benchmark for such universities would be to set tuition rates at six to eight times the local rate of a two-bedroom apartment, seeing as how the university is already structurally supporting local real estate development by keeping it primed with thousands of consumers in the all-important eighteen – to – twenty-five age range. At elite schools, tuition should simply be whatever the national market will bear. Once the dead hand of government regulation has given way to the invisible hand of the free market, college-tuition deregulation will ultimately benefit everyone, just as we have learned from key industries like pharmaceutical companies and savings-and-loans institutions.

Of course, it will be objected — rightly — that students are not getting enough for their money even now. This is why tuition deregulation must be accompanied by aggressive curriculum *re*regulation. Many campuses have entire departments that do little or nothing to prepare students for employment, to enhance the university's portfolio, or to develop crucial new products for corporate underwriters. I refer to the arts and humanities, where, according to one conservative estimate, 50 percent of the research currently being conducted is "nonsense."[1] Departments of history, for example, often focus obsessively on the past, when our children need to be prepared for the future. And it's not even worth *talking* about departments of literature.

That's not to say we shouldn't preserve the cultural treasures of our civilization, like Shakespeare. Shakespeare was not only a fine writer of what the *San Diego Union-Tribune* eloquently called "deathless prose" (qtd. in Fish 64);[2] he remains important to the American public — and the American economy — in ways that other writers, whoever they were, do not. His products combine extraordinary cross-demographic appeal with very long shelf life, and perhaps tie-ins are not out of the question, if only McDonald's had had the foresight to offer Happy Meals with action figures from *Shakespeare in Love*. For this reason, the departments of history, anthropology, linguistics, art history, music, philosophy, and the modern languages should be consolidated into a single Department of Shakespeare. Universities will save millions by pruning their rolls of unnecessary and redundant teachers, thereby restoring some of the public's lost confidence in universities' value.

But when it comes to the long overdue task of initiating mass firings of faculty, then we run into the biggest problem of all: tenure. The institution of tenure is profoundly antibusiness, and consequently profoundly wrong. As James F. Carlin, businessman and former chairman of the Massachusetts Board of Higher Education, has perceptively written, tenure offers extraordinary job security, and "lifetime job guarantees border on being immoral." Moral law, in other words, clearly mandates termination-at-will forms of employment, not merely because all forms of healthy growth require regular pruning but also because there is no reason for American society to support anyone who has become unproductive. As Carlin writes, academic freedom will not be in jeopardy when tenure is dismantled, for "numerous state and federal statutes, commissions against discrimination, and the vigilant news media protect anyone — in or out of academe — who wants to expound unorthodox beliefs" (76). Surely faculty members are aware that the American mass media will stand firm in defense of controversial scholars, as has so often been the case in recent memory.

More important than academic freedom, however, is the fact that tenure prevents university presidents and trustees from engaging in the single most entertaining feature of American business: the hiring of external consultants and efficiency experts to fire middle-aged account executives, nurses, editors, and secretaries after making them run a humiliating gauntlet of pointless self-assessment trials. This ritual is vividly (and, I confess, entertainingly) depicted in such contemporary films as *American Beauty* and *Office Space*.

Academe, like business, is rife with anxiety, territorialism, and ill will. But what academe lacks is a mature culture of abjection and groveling. Fiftysomething faculty members with thirty or more years of service to their colleges simply do not live in terror that they may be terminated without cause, and this surely constitutes the major reason why most Americans do not understand the institution of tenure — especially now that new technology has the potential to make many faculty as obsolete as telephone operators. With the judicious use of the Internet and your ordinary household touch-tone phone, in fact, most college courses could be conducted for $4.95 a minute: press one and the pound key if you would like to hear a lecture on the Italian Renaissance, press two if you would like to hear a lecture on the French Revolution. For seminar credit, just log on with a password and a credit card number! If not for tenure, these systems would already be in place — and universities would be richer places of learning for it.

Finally, universities have stubbornly refused to engage in the single most important activity of American business in the 1980s and 1990s — namely, mergers and acquisitions. Think of what a powerful conglomerate like Harvard/MIT/Tufts/BU/BC could do to revolutionize education delivery in the greater Boston area. And why shouldn't a lean, sleek enterprise like Adelphi University attempt a hostile takeover of the entire bloated, mismanaged SUNY system? Not only would this force SUNY to cut personnel costs and close outlying plants in Geneseo, Plattsburg, and New Paltz, it would drive up the value of both SUNY *and* Adelphi, to the benefit of stockholders everywhere.

Yet for mergers and acquisitions to work, needless to say, universities would first have to offer stock. It has long been a truism of academe that a free society requires a free marketplace of ideas. It's about time the products of that marketplace were made available to the ordinary investor. Indeed, this is perhaps the most critical item of all: if American universities truly want to reconnect with the American public, they will have to *go* public. It worked for Martha Stewart. It can work for Sarah Lawrence.

Notes

1. See the Works Cited for just whose "conservative" estimate is being cited here.

2. The relevant context of this citation in Fish reads as follows: "[Louis] Montrose reads an editorial in his local newspaper that attacks new historicism by name and concludes from this attention 'that there is something immediately important at stake in our reading and teaching of Shakespeare' ('Professing the Renaissance,' 29). But what is important to the editorial writer is the opportunity to score a political point at the expense of a few professors without the power to fight back. The newspaper's indifference to the way Shakespeare is interpreted is indicated in its characterization of the bard's work as 'deathless prose.' When the honour of an author is defended by

someone who seems not to have read him, you can be sure that the gesture is directed not at the critical community but at another audience altogether, the audience of those who resent the academy in part because they know so little about it" (64 – 65).

Works Cited

Carlin, James F. "Restoring Sanity to an Academic World Gone Mad." *Chronicle of Higher Education*, 5 November 1999, A76.

Fish, Stanley. *Professional Correctness: Literary Studies and Political Change*. New York: Oxford University Press, 1995.

The first time a student asked me about my "grading system," I was nonplussed — and a bit intimidated. It was an innocent question, but I heard it as a challenge: I was a twenty-five-year-old graduate student teaching my first section in an English literature class at the University of Virginia, and I really didn't know *what* my grading system was. Nor did I feel comfortable saying, "Well, it's like Justice Stewart's definition of pornography, really — I simply know an A paper when I see one."

I fumbled my way through a reply, but I was unsettled enough by the exchange to seek the advice of the professor in charge of the course (and roughly a dozen teaching assistants). He went on a sublime rant that I've never forgotten, though I'm sure I've embellished it over the years. "These students come in here," he fumed, "with the idea that you have to explain yourself. 'You gave me a B-plus,' they say. 'What did you take points off for?' I tell them, 'Your paper was not born with an A. Your paper was born with a "nothing," and I made up my mind about it as I read it. That's what the marginalia are — they're the record of my responses to your arguments.'"

Today I've incorporated versions of that rant into my own teaching handouts: I try to explain the differences among superior, mediocre, and failing papers, and I tell students that my skills as a reader have been honed by my many experiences with professional editors, who attend carefully to paragraph transitions, dangling modifiers, and inaccurate citations. But I've never been able to give my students a visceral idea of what goes through my head as I read their work — until now.

Like many sports fans, I've grown a bit tired of ESPN's twenty-fifth-anniversary hyper-self-awareness of itself as a sports medium. While it's great to see the network poke fun at its early years, when its anchors wore dorky yellow sport coats and weren't always sure when they were on the air, it's really quite tedious to be reminded of how sports-television hype helped hype TV sports.

To me, the show *Around the Horn* has come to epitomize the general decline. Another half-hour program with which it's paired, *Pardon the Interrup-*

tion, gives us two volatile, opinionated sportscasters (Tony Kornheiser and Michael Wilbon) disagreeing with each other in rapid-fire fashion with but a handful of seconds devoted to each topic. *Around the Horn* takes that format and makes a game show of it, offering us sportswriters competing for whose commentary will "win" by the end of the show.

I still play an organized sport — ice hockey — and as an amateur (and aged) player, I have to say that sports talk shows like this make me wonder whether some people don't see sports as simply an opportunity for endless metacommentary . . . and, of course, as gainful employment for an entire entourage of chattering parasites. In all that noise, I think, where are the games themselves?

Imagine my surprise, then, when I watched *Around the Horn* one afternoon and realized that here, at last, was my grading system in practice.

The idea behind *Around the Horn* is simple. There are a host and four contestants, each of whom speaks briefly on a series of up-to-the-moment sports topics. Points are awarded for smart — or merely plausible — remarks, and points are deducted for obviously foolish or factually inaccurate ones. There's a mute button involved, too, and players get eliminated as the show progresses (but those aspects of the game, as far as I can tell, have no counterpart in the world of paper grading). And — of course, for this is the point of all such sports metacommentary — the viewers at home get to disagree with and complain about the commentary as well as the officiating.

My standard undergraduate survey course guide for paper writing tells students things like this: "Assume a hypothetical readership composed of people who have already read the book. That means you shouldn't say, 'In class, we discussed the importance of the clam chowder in chapter 5.' But more important, it *means you don't have to summarize the novel*. We're your readers, and we've read the book. However, we haven't read it in quite the way *you're* reading it. We haven't focused on the same scenes and passages you're bringing to our attention, and we haven't yet seen how your argument might make sense of the book for us."

Not all of my students see the point. Every semester I'm approached by some who don't quite understand why they're being asked to make an *argument* out of literary criticism. Why shouldn't they simply record their impressions of the works before them? When I tell them that an observation is not a thesis, and that their thesis isn't sufficiently specific or useful if they can't imagine anyone plausibly disagreeing with it, they ask me why they can't simply explain *what happens in the novel*.

But in what world, exactly, would such an enterprise count as analysis? Not in any world I know — not even in the ephemeral pop-culture world of sports metacommentary. Can you imagine someone showing up on *Around the Horn* and saying to host Tony Reali, "Well, Tony, let me point out that last night, the Red Sox completed a sweep of the Tigers and crept to within three games of the Yankees."

"And?"

"And nothing. I'm just pointing out that the Sox won, 3 – 1, on a four-hitter by Schilling, while the Yanks blew another late-inning lead."

No one does that, because no one in the sports world confuses summaries with analyses.

I also tell students that an essay of two thousand words doesn't give them all that much space to get going. "You've only got a few pages to make that argument of yours. You don't need a grand introductory paragraph that begins, 'Mark Twain is one of Earth's greatest writers.' It's far better to start by giving us some idea of what you'll be arguing and why. If you like, you can even begin by pointing us to a particularly important passage that will serve as the springboard for your larger discussion: 'Not long after the second scaffold scene in *The Scarlet Letter*, when Arthur Dimmesdale joins hands with Hester Prynne and her daughter, Pearl, Nathaniel Hawthorne asks us to reconsider the meaning of the scarlet A on Hester's breast.'"

On *Around the Horn*, commentators have to make their points in fifteen seconds, which, as people who know me can testify, just happens to be roughly the amount of time it takes me to utter two thousand words. So here, too, the analogy holds up.

Seriously, the sports-talk analogy is useful simply as a handy way of distinguishing between summary and analysis — and, more important, as an illustration of what happens in my grading process when a student paper cites textual evidence so compelling and unusual that it makes me go back and reread the passage in question (good!), suggests that a novel's conclusion fails to resolve the questions and tensions raised by the rest of the narrative (interesting! — possibly good, depending on the novel we're talking about), or makes claims that are directly contradicted by the literary text itself (bad! the mute button for you!).

So in a sense, I do "take off" points as I go — but then I add them back on as well, sentence by sentence, paragraph by paragraph, as I weigh the claims my students advance and the means by which they advance them.

The rules for literary analysis are the same rules in play for any kind of analysis: mastery of the material. Cogency of supporting evidence. Ability to imagine and rebut salient counterarguments. Extra points for wit and style, points off for mind-numbing clichés, and permanent suspension for borrowing someone else's argument without proper attribution.

And yet, every year, I'm left with a handful of students who tell me that if that's what I want, I should simply assign topics to each student. "Not a chance," I reply. "Most of the mental labor of your paper takes place when you try to figure out just what you want to argue and why." As books like Thomas McLaughlin's *Street Smarts and Critical Theory* and Gerald Graff's *Clueless in Academe* have argued (with wit and style), students seem to understand this principle perfectly well when it comes to music, sports, and popular culture. It's our job to show them how it might apply to the study of literature.

My students, too, are often suspicious of what they regard as an idiosyncratic and subjective enterprise that varies from English professor to English professor. But I can tell them there's really nothing mysterious about its mechanics. In fact, if they want to watch it in action, they can tune in to ESPN any weekday afternoon, 5:00 P.M. Eastern.

Works Cited

Graff, Gerald. *Clueless in Academe: How Schooling Obscures the Life of the Mind.* New Haven: Yale University Press, 2003.
McLaughlin, Thomas. *Street Smarts and Critical Theory: Listening to the Vernacular.* Madison: University of Wisconsin Press, 1996.

The Top 10 Contradictory
Things about Popular Culture

On my desk at home, next to my list of the seventy-five greatest love ballads of all time, there's a list of the one hundred best novellas written since Goethe. Having been thwarted in my efforts to persuade the music-video channel VH1 to publish my list of the ten thousand best guitar solos in rock 'n' roll, I have turned my attention to smaller units of measure, in another medium — heroic couplets. I hope to have completed my list of the one thousand best heroic couplets by the end of the year, though Heaven knows, "In human works, tho' labour'd on with pain, / A thousand movements scarce one purpose gain." So says Alexander Pope, the No. 1 Augustan poet, in the 130th-finest heroic couplet ever written.

I used to disdain such lists, thinking them fodder for the fatuous. To my weary ears, litterateurs who blathered on about the five greatest modern novels or the ten most accomplished American writers under the age of forty didn't sound appreciably different from my high-school friends who had once blathered on about the three best lead guitarists or the five most bitchin' drum solos. Such talk had been great for staging arguments about the relative merits of Jeff Beck and Eric Clapton, and it had given my teenage friends and me something to do with all that excess testosterone sloshing around in our brain pans. But I came to doubt that the rankings game could serve any nobler purpose, and so, as I got older, I pretty much stopped talking in lists.

But then in 2000, of all years, my older son, Nick, turned fourteen and began compiling lists of his own. He's always had a keen aesthetic sense; even at the tender age of eight, he had derisively described the dreamy soft-rock group Mazzy Star as "just like Leonard Cohen" — which he pronounced "Ko-han" — "only worse." (My favorite Nickism from that era was his reaction to Kenny Loggins's hideous "House on Pooh Corner": "What, did Winnie the Pooh *die* or something?" To which I could only reply, when I had finally stopped laughing, in a Beavis-and-Butthead voice, "Heh heh — Pooh is dead. Yeah. That would be cool.") Now, however, he's an adolescent, and it's not enough to have an aesthetic sense or, for that matter, a decent working knowledge of college football. You have to have a list. A good part of Nick's enjoyment of the history of film and of rock music, it seems, consists precisely of efforts to understand popular culture in the manner of college-football rankings. In that, as in so much else, Nick is more knowledgeable about the workings of popular culture than I am.

Nick's adolescence was timed nicely for the arrival of the millennium, which gave us lists of everything that could possibly be enumerated: most influential people, greatest historical events, worst weather disasters, most significant inventions. Martin Luther, the cotton gin, Hurricane Camille, Jim Thorpe, the Gutenberg printing press, the Atlantic slave trade, the Six-Day War — all available for your perusal, all sorted, filed, and ranked. And if ESPN's yearlong countdown of the fifty greatest athletes of the century didn't slake your thirst for millennial compilations, you could always check out the issue of *Sports Illustrated* that informed Nick and me of the fifty greatest athletes ever to come out of our home state of Illinois (and the fifty greatest out of each of the other forty-nine states).

Imagine the possibilities if the American Film Institute and the Modern Library had followed suit and broken down their famous, century-ending Top 100 lists by state: the one hundred best comedies about Delaware, the one hundred greatest works of nonfiction written by residents of Minnesota, the one hundred finest twentieth-century novels set in Mississippi (perhaps a Faulkner bibliography). That isn't quite as far-fetched as it may seem. By 2000, VH1 had become a list industry unto itself, churning out compendiums of the one hundred greatest rock songs, the one hundred greatest groups, the one hundred greatest male and female artists, the fifty greatest movie soundtracks, the fifty greatest rock moments ever televised, the fifty greatest chord progressions ever penned.

All right, I made up the last item. But back when Nick was fourteen, VH1 really did air a regular program called *The List* on which various critics, musicians, gadflies, and celebrities tallied their three favorite songs or performers or power ballads or big-hair metal bands (I am not making up any of those) and then sought to convince the studio audience of the cogency of their choices. And VH1 continues to generate lists upon lists of lists, from the definitive "Twenty Most Awesomely Bad Songs of 2004" to the finely honed "Forty Most Awesomely Bad Dirrty Songs . . . Ever." (Number 2: "I Wanna Sex You Up," by Color Me Badd; number 1: "Physical," by Olivia Newton-John. Hard to argue with discerning judgments like those.)

What does it all mean?

Well, for one thing, it's annoying. Not only because all these lists truly are fodder for the fatuous (and who but the fatuous knew that the fatuous were so many?) but also because they tend to disguise the fact that a great deal of popular culture isn't worth ranking or remembering at all.

Day after day, Nick and I would flip through our fifty-seven channels or tune in to commercial radio only to find that Bruce Springsteen (the all-time No. 12 rock-anthem singer/songwriter, by the way) was right: there's nothing on. Nick did help me to distinguish one cookie-cutter mainstream band from another, so that I didn't confuse the Matchbox Dolls with the Sugar Blind 20 or Third Eye Goo Goo. But, for the most part, our conversations ran like so:

"How's this?"

"Unadulterated pap."

"OK, what about this?"

"Mindless drivel."

"This?"

"Soul-crushing swill."

"Maybe this?"

"Self-indulgent flapdoodle."

The really interesting thing about these exchanges was that Nick wasn't always the one asking the questions; sometimes he delivered the verdicts (although, I admit, he rarely used the term "flapdoodle"). Nick was nearly as critical as his father — if not about Eagle-Eye Cherry, whom he once liked, then certainly about Britney Spears, Christina Aguilera, 98°, 'N Sync, and the Backstreet Boys, whose music he justly referred to as "mass-produced, undifferentiated crap." And I am pleased to say that over the past six years, Nick has developed impeccable alt-rock taste, steering me to Ted Leo, Franz Ferdinand, Interpol (I offered him Television's *Marquee Moon* in response, on the grounds that the guitars in "Obstacle 1" sounded like the guitars on "Marquee Moon"), and the Walkmen. But there's still a great deal of crap out there.

That crap, I used to say in bygone years, back when I still disdained lists, is just the price you pay for culture. You want Goethe and Martha Graham and the Independent Film Channel? Fine, then you have to put up with three hundred versions of *Us* magazine at the supermarket checkout. But as I climb into my mid-forties, I find myself less and less willing to tolerate the trade-off. It could be my advancing years; I've checked out the actuarial tables and figured out that in all likelihood, more than half my time is already up. Maybe I shouldn't waste the second half with reruns of *Happy Days* on cable TV. Or it could be simply that most summer blockbusters have gotten so unrelentingly god-awful, useful only for the reflection that the budget for any one of them would provide a year's supply of clean water, antibiotics, and *salade niçoise* to every human being in sub-Saharan Africa. Either way, I knew that I had had enough of pop-culture crap on the day I forbade Nick to see one of those movies on the grounds that it was indeed, without a doubt, from beginning to end, crap.

"Define 'crap,'" said Nick, in intransigent-adolescent mode, as if we had never used the word before.

"OK," I replied. "How about, 'turgid, voyeuristic, gratuitously violent, misogynist,' and if that doesn't do it, 'derivative' and 'unimaginative?'"

That seemed to suffice, at least for the moment. But not long after, I began to realize why lists — even the most trivial of them — perform so many functions in popular culture. Take Stephen Frears's imaginative and nonderivative film *High Fidelity*, starring John Cusack and adapted from Nick Hornby's 1995 novel. The narrator, Rob, is an early thirties, alternative-rock aficionado and record-store owner who experiences the world by means of Top 5 lists, including the all-important list of his Top 5 most painful breakups.

But Rob's lists, like those on VH1, aren't self-explanatory. On the contrary, the real fun of a list — and the intellectual labor that goes into it — is realized only when its creator has to explain and defend its rationale. *That's* where the allure of lists really lies, because, for impassioned devisers of Top 5s, the nakedly evaluative function of the list is underwritten by a mode of popular-culture criticism that is considerably more complex — and more exegetical — than the form of the Top 5 seems to suggest. If you want to argue with any of Rob's Top 5 — or *SI*'s rankings of athletes or the AFI's rankings of movies — you'd better come armed with some convincing exegeses of the texts in front of you. If you're going to argue that Babe Didrikson Zaharias was, in fact, a better athlete than Babe Ruth, for example, you've got to be prepared to argue for the virtues of the multisport athlete (and the pre–Title IX female athlete) over those of a man who utterly changed the national pastime even though he was never in very good physical shape.

Of course, even the nakedly evaluative aspect of lists serves an immediate purpose: obviously enough, people want and need to winnow the wheat from the crap. But that "obvious" observation has some interesting corollaries. First of all, although there are legions of crabs, cranks, and curmudgeons who proclaim that all popular culture is worthless garbage and/or responsible for crime, violence, short attention spans, and disrespect for elders, nobody who knows anything about popular culture has so simple a relationship to the stuff. Nobody says, "I just love all movies," or "I like pretty much every song I hear," or "I'm a fan of every sports team in existence."

On the contrary, as Nick has discovered, developing the faculty of discrimination is part of the fun of immersing oneself in the popular — which means, interestingly, that few fans of popular culture are wholly "immersed" in it. To be a really knowledgeable fan, in other words, you usually have to be a keen critic. Remember this the next time you're accosted by some bloviating, muttonchop-wearing columnist for the *New Criterion* or the *Vocabula Review*: it's the people who can't stand popular culture who are truly indiscriminate. Just say to your muttonchop friend, "If you can't tell the difference between Poison and the Cure, don't waste my time with your worthless denunciations of what you call rock 'n' roll."

The next corollary is important not for readers of the *New Criterion* but for their opposite numbers on the cultural left. Popular culture, even at its silliest and swilliest, is saturated with criticism. Academic modes of cultural criticism, by contrast, are rarely explicitly evaluative (and the exception of that famous outlier, Harold Bloom, only proves the rule). Though this aspect of academic criticism is usually ascribed to the pernicious relativism of postmodernism, it actually has a much more tangled and interesting history. It was not Stanley Fish, after all, but Northrop Frye who, in his 1957 book, *Anatomy of Criticism*, derided evaluative criticism as so much "literary chit-chat" (18). Such an approach may make "the reputations of poets boom and crash in an imaginary stock exchange" (18), Frye wrote, but it has no place in properly professional literary criticism. (Included in his list of inappropriate modes of criticism, sure enough, are "all lists of the 'best' novels or poems or writers" [18].) Barbara Herrnstein Smith's 1988 book, *Contingencies of Value*, actually tried to reintroduce evaluation as an explicit problem in literary studies, partly by arguing that evaluation is ubiquitous and inescapable. But that's not how most people have read her work; instead, people tend to say, "As Smith has shown, value is contingent, and that means we can't talk about it." In fact, she has argued that value is contingent and, therefore, we *must* talk about it. It's actually one of my Top 5 favorite things about Smith's book.

Cultural studies theorists, meanwhile, have widely adopted the model of the "intellectual as fan" — which they've generally taken to mean that you need to establish the fact that you really, really *like* popular culture before you embark on any discussion of popular culture and its relationship to geopolitical hegemony. But such understanding of fans misses half of what fandom is all about — namely, criticism. Although your average cultural studies theorist would sooner go door to door for the World Trade Organization than admit this, one of the most important functions that the culture industries perform is to produce criticism of the cultural artifacts produced by the culture industries. Devising lists is one rather reductive, mechanical way to produce criticism, but the entertainment industry doesn't confine itself to VH1 or AFI lists; it offers up, every day, rafts of critical readings, trenchant observations, and many, many warnings that the latest summer blockbuster is nothing but ... why, self-indulgent flapdoodle.

Normally, we academic critics, whether we read the *New Criterion* or *New Formations*, think of popular-culture criticism as little more than movie or TV reviews, and we tend to discount it as criticism. If you think of the E! channel or shows like *Entertainment Tonight*, you'll see why: much of the reportage about the entertainment industry takes the form of celebration and gossip, so much so that it easily falls under the heading of "promotional material." But, as it happens, lots of smart people work in the entertainment industry, criticism division, and they're often better at evaluating contemporary popular culture than their academic counterparts are. And because they tend to work for "popular" publications, they also tend to have some influence — as most cultural studies theorists do not — on how popular culture is actually consumed by actual consumers.

Take this quick read of *Jurassic Park* and Hammond, the film's visionary entrepreneur/corporate mogul:

> The worst thing about it is that the very idea of Jurassic Park, a place where eye-popping wonders are served up as a megabuck attraction, seems an obvious yet pointless metaphor for the commercialization of Steven Spielberg's empire. Since Hammond's toys and gizmos feature the same logo that's being used to sell the movie (and its many tie-in products), there's no way to separate Spielberg's "satire" of marketing from the marketing itself. (40)

I've scanned many a work of what academics call "cultural studies" looking for punchy, keen wit like that. But it appeared in *Entertainment Weekly*, in Owen Gleiberman's review of the film. *Entertainment Weekly*? Isn't that one of those supermarket glossies, on the rack next to *Us*, *People*, and *InStyle*? Well, yes, but since its first issue, in 1990, *EW* has reviewed bajillions of movies, and the average grade it's given out (yes, it uses grades, not stars or thumbs) has been something like a C-plus. Let the cultural studies professor with a more stringent grade scale throw the first stone.

My own favorite one-paragraph piece of pop-cultural criticism (and yes, I'm working on my list of the Top 100) appeared not in *EW* or any other culture-industry glossy but in the online magazine *Salon*, in a column by James Poniewozik. In a fascinating essay on, of all things, the neglect of the work of German writer and cultural critic Hans Magnus Enzensberger by American practitioners of cultural studies, Poniewozik describes Enzensberger's rebuttal of the argument that (as Poniewozik paraphrases it) "a 'National Entertainment State' is violently and irresistibly depriving us of free thought and volition." Poniewozik writes,

> In 1988's "The Zero Medium; or, Why All Complaints About Television Are Pointless," Enzensberger concisely lays out and coolly demolishes four reading variations on that thesis, namely, that television 1) manipulates our opinions (a belief, he notes, equally attractive to the left and the right), 2) forces us to imitate immoral behavior, 3) destroys our ability to distinguish fantasy from fact, and 4) numbs our critical faculties. Enzensberger nails the condescension underlying these theories, deadpanning that their proponent either "makes no use of the media at all, in which case he doesn't know what he's talking about; or he subjects himself to them, and then the question arises, through what miracle he has escaped their effects . . . unlike anyone else."

Not bad, not bad at all. Yet for some reason, Poniewozik isn't an oft-cited figure in cultural studies, any more than Enzensberger or Gleiberman is. And where is this Poniewozik now, you ask? Why, writing for the very house organ of Conventional Wisdom, *Time* magazine, smack in the epicenter of the Megamerger Culture Industry Apparatus. You can buy *Time* in any supermarket. I think it's right next to *Entertainment Weekly*.

This doesn't mean that we shouldn't evaluate *Time* or *Salon* or *EW* in turn, and it doesn't mean that we can't ask about such issues as the relationship of those publications to geopolitical hegemony. But it does mean that people who call themselves professional critics of popular culture should acknowledge that many millions of amateur critics of popular culture — also widely referred to as "consumers" — experience it partly by reading (and taking issue with) popular-culture criticism of popular culture. Sometimes that criticism takes the form of lists, sometimes it takes the form of grades, and sometimes it's so close to "promotional material" that it hardly merits the name of criticism. And sometimes, no doubt, it is just another form of self-indulgent flapdoodle. But it's an integral element of popular culture, and no one who aspires to produce valuable evaluations of popular culture should ignore it.

About lists themselves I remain ambivalent. Having outgrown the language of lists and Top 5s and Ten Bests, I'm still not sure I'm ready to outgrow my outgrowing. But I've learned to enjoy an important aspect of popular culture that's overlooked by conservative curmudgeons and cult-studies cliques alike: pop-culture criticism, brought to you by the hardworking critics employed by the Popular Culture Industry itself. Next summer's movies and teen-dream hit songs may be even worse than last year's, but Nick and I won't mind wading through the sludge — not as long as we have our wits and our lists and, more important, our savvy, discriminating pop-culture critics writing for their Web sites and their glossy magazines.

Works Cited

Frye, Northrop. *Anatomy of Criticism: Four Essays.* Princeton: Princeton University Press, 1957.

Gleiberman, Owen. Review of *Jurassic Park. Entertainment Weekly,* 18 June 1993, 39 – 40.

Poniewozik, James. "The Man without Principles." *Salon,* 27 January 1999. Available online at < http://archive.salon.com/media/1999/01/cov_27mediab.html >. Accessed 6 March 1999.

Smith, Barbara Herrnstein. *Contingencies of Value: Alternate Perspectives for Critical Theory.* Cambridge: Harvard University Press, 1988.

The Elvis Costello Problem

Popular culture has been a problem for as long as there has been something called popular culture. Our youth have been corrupted, first by Socrates and now by 50 Cent, for three millennia and counting. Each new development in the popular culture industry — from Wordsworth's "sickly German romances" to today's sickly Harlequin romances, from the birth of television to the rise of Jerry Springer — has proved beyond doubt that our culture has never before been so overflowing with garbage, and that the decline of Western civilization is complete and irreversible.

Most of the outcry against teaching popular culture in college courses takes this form: the subject, we are told, is unworthy of serious study, lacking the textual and cultural density that defines the masterworks of the arts and humanities. For some critics, popular culture is also a problem precisely because it is popular. College students are already familiar with the stuff, the argument goes, so the university should therefore provide access to *un*popular cultures — ancient, ethnic, or avant-garde — because students have so little exposure to them elsewhere.

Those caveats against studying popular culture are reasonable, but not sufficient. The complaint that popular culture lacks quality is itself an indiscriminate complaint, usually made by people who know little about popular culture and are unequipped to distinguish among its many textually dense and intellectually rewarding artifacts, on the one hand, and its innumerable, interchangeable Backstreet Boys and Spice Girls, on the other. And as I argued in the previous essay, the argument that popular culture is too popular overlooks the vast difference between being immersed in the stuff and looking at it critically.

There's another reasonable caveat about teaching popular culture, though, that is more complicated. It was given voice by Sanford Pinsker, professor of humanities at Franklin and Marshall College, and Roger Kimball, managing editor of the *New Criterion*, at a 1999 convention of the National Association of Scholars. The problem with popular culture, for Kimball and Pinsker, is that it is inescapably contemporary and ephemeral: regardless of whether we're immersed in it or whether we're looking at it critically, we have no way of reading our contemporary moment in such a way as to figure out which artifacts will eventually prove to be of some historical or aesthetic significance and which ones will wind up as next year's garage-sale fodder alongside the Teenage Mutant Ninja Turtles. As the *Chronicle of Higher Education* reported, Kimball claimed that

> [p]op-culture studies are "an educational disaster area . . . part of an infamous effort to make education relevant" — something too often accomplished at the expense of rigor.
>
> When asked how long it should take before a work is included in the canon, Pinsker suggested 50 years. That seemed fair to Mr. Kimball, although he was unconvinced that pop culture deserved any place in the classroom. "Do we really need classes on Toni Morrison? Our students will read it anyway," he said. (Schneider A15)

The interesting thing about the Kimball-Pinsker proposal is that it would affect all kinds of literature. Sure, plenty of professors could agree to forgo the ambiguous pleasures of teaching and assigning books by Tom Clancy or Belva Plain, but do we really need to protect our students from the blandishments of such world-renowned writers as Don DeLillo, Toni Morrison, Michael Ondaatje, Zadie Smith, and Jeanette Winterson? At this point, that seemingly reasonable argument begins to look silly. It looks even sillier if we apply it to the usual corpus of "modern masterpieces." Imagine, if you will, the literary scene if the world's leading literary critics had agreed not to touch *Ulysses* or *The Waste Land* until 1972, *To the Lighthouse* until 1976, *Invisible Man* until 2002.

In the middle of my life as a graduate student, I had a conversation with a professor who thought much as Pinsker and Kimball do. When this professor invoked his version of the fifty-year rule, I meekly pointed out that he had required me to read Edmund Wilson's magisterial *Axel's Castle*, a book about modernist literature that was published in 1930 — while its subjects were still alive. Indeed, to Wilson's great credit, he discussed even *Finnegans Wake* (then known as "Work in Progress"), the first excerpts of which had been published but two years earlier in the pages of the avant-garde journal *transition*. If Wilson could turn his attention to the literature of his time, I asked, why couldn't we? My professor responded with a strict non sequitur about how Eliot had displaced Stevens, who in turn had displaced Frost. I wondered how that was relevant to my point, and received an answer like Kimball and Pinsker's argument: we simply don't know which of our contemporary writers will turn out, after fifty years, to have survived the Test of Time.

The Test of Time requires the passage of time, does it not? Of course it does. But wait a second — or fifty years. Exactly who is supposed to conduct the test, and why should academic critics be barred from participating in it for fifty years? Just who is supposed to benefit from these sorts of suggestions? Not literary critics, who tend to despise any arrangement that keeps them from doing work they want to do. Not contemporary writers, most of whom prefer to get their critical attention *before* they die. Ah, but journalists would have the field of contemporary literature all to themselves, especially with regard to the job of book reviewing. Academics would have to hold their tongues for fifty years, while the *Washington Post* and the *New Criterion* could comment and critique just as much as they liked.

In my first book, *Marginal Forces/Cultural Centers*, I argued that invocations of the Test of Time, when made by journalists, represent (among other things) a form of competition between journalists and professors for the right to speak and write about contemporary literature. I still think that's true, but since my assistant-professor days I've come to see that the Kimball-Pinsker Principle and its cognates are also more complex than I initially believed. Precisely because the principle does not discriminate between contemporary trash and contemporary treasure, it speaks to purposes that are more pedagogical than aesthetic: that is, by insisting that we cannot pass judgment on *any* cultural work until half a century has passed, the principle seeks to simplify the task of creating a canon — or a syllabus.

During the twentieth century, universities in the United States first created Great Books and Western Civilization courses as part of a larger general-education enterprise, in part to combat the excesses and impermanence of vocationalism and specialization. Amid all the 1990s culture-wars fervor over whether Western Civ courses are hegemonic and oppressive or the bedrock of all that we stand for, academic critics (and journalists) largely forgot that "core" courses were proposed at places such as Chicago, Columbia, and Harvard partly to insure that undergraduate education would have a kind of cross-generational continuity. At Harvard, for example, the landmark committee report of 1945, *General Education in a Free Society* (known more colloquially as the Red Book), argued that the books that "have most influenced the men who in turn influenced others are those we can least afford to neglect.... It is a safe assumption that a work which has delighted and instructed many generations of ordinary readers and been to them a common possession, enriching and enriched, is to be preferred to a product which is on its way to limbo and will not link together even two school generations" (26). No doubt the phrasing may strike some readers today as infelicitous: Are "men" the only readers who count? Who are those "ordinary readers," anyway? And do we really have to keep reading and teaching third-rate drivel like *Pilgrim's Progress* just because the emergent British middle classes kept a copy at their bedsides for the better part of three centuries?

But the cogency of the Red Book's argument will be felt by any teacher who has experienced what I call the Elvis Costello Problem — namely, the difficulty of communicating to students by means of the touchstones of popular culture. If you're reading this in 2006, think of it this way: next year's entering class of college students was born in 1988, by which point Elvis Costello had long since made the transition from punk/New Wave wunderkind to Serious Singer/Songwriter; for those students, the cultural impact of Costello's first three albums — whose remarkable wit and anger helped to puncture the bloated, complacent rock-star scene of the 1970s — is so remote as to be unintelligible. On my bad days in the classroom, even the man's name draws blank stares from twenty-year-olds whose memories barely reach back to the reunion of the Eagles in the mid-1990s, let alone to the breakup of the Beatles in 1970. How many of today's students can recall the punk class of 1977 — the Clash, the Sex Pistols, the Ramones — whose music is now ancient enough, though still not tame enough, to be played on an oldies station? How many students, for that matter, can recall the ephemera of the early years of the previous decade — Londonbeat and Tone-Lōc, Deee-Lite, and Bell Biv DeVoe? Those ubiquitous cries of yesteryear, "Whoomp! There it is!" and "2 Legit 2 Quit," have rapidly become as dated as "Twenty-three skidoo" and "Hubba hubba." "Who let the dogs out?," in turn, will no doubt be unintelligible by 2010, and it'll be a good thing, too.

Popular culture is designed, after all, to move products quickly, and that means short shelf lives for the vast majority of cultural artifacts in any genre, from good-quality paperbacks to eight-track tapes. By the time pop singer Natalie Imbruglia's latest single hits the airwaves, the system is betting that you've forgotten all about last year's Warbling Waif, Heather Nova. And chances are (as Johnny Mathis used to say) that you *have* forgotten — if, in fact, you ever noticed.

I should point out that I say all this not as an aspiring managing editor of the *New Criterion* but as a fortysomething teacher of undergraduate seminars on postmodernism, someone who goes out and sees movies like *The Matrix* (twice! It rocked!) whenever enough students suggest that its references to the French theorist Jean Baudrillard are really worth checking out. I have no desire to invoke a fifty-year rule for my courses (it would, of course, eliminate my entire reading list in postmodern fiction), but I can tell you from a lifetime of immersion in the detritus of popular culture that whereas the subject is often quite worthy of serious study, it's getting harder for an aging body to keep up with it every year, and . . . well, let me put it this way: I simply have no idea who 50 Cent is, all right? I yearn for the good old days of Tupac. (Actually, that's not true on either count. But you see my point, I'm sure.)

Yet that's not all there is, my friends. As it happens, the terrain of popular culture has lately become even more complicated — and therefore has made a pedagogy of the contemporary both more possible and more interesting. It remains true that most of the stuff of the entertainment industry consists of cultural ephemera destined for trivia contests, tent sales, and collectors' bins. But over the past decade, popular culture has also begun to institutionalize its own canons — in oldies radio (and its niche-market offshoots, classic rock and "jammin'" oldies soul), cable-television stations devoted to "the classics" (meaning everything from *I Love Lucy* to *Welcome Back, Kotter*), motion-picture "revivals" and "remakes" of practically every 1960s sitcom save for *Hazel*, and the retrospective *Where Are They Now?* and *Behind the Music* series on the music-video network VH1. The cultural-recycling industry even has its own self-parodying devices, like VH1's *Best Week Ever*, a nostalgic look back at whatever week has just concluded (a show modeled on VH1's only slightly less self-parodic features, *I Love the 70s/80s/90s*), such that it is not unusual to hear — in 2005, say — a call for a "revival" of Sisqo's 2002 "Thong Song." Accelerating and deranging the modernist demand to "make it new," this aspect of popular culture says, *Make it neo- and make it snappy.*

The irony of that last item is itself postmodern, is it not? Music video, once thought to be the *final* final piece of evidence that the decline of Western civilization is complete and irreversible, turns out to be one of the vehicles of cultural memory seeking to combat the Elvis Costello Problem — making, for example, the 1977 divas of disco available to a whole new generation of dancing fools. Who would have guessed it? Though there are still some days when students look at me blankly when I speak of Parliament-Funkadelic, popular culture has actually begun to link the generations more broadly than "high" culture ever could. Thanks to contemporary culture's ravenous appetite for recycling, fans of music video can not only keep up with This Year's Model (oops, a dated Elvis Costello reference) but also get acquainted with twenty-first-century versions of 1970s reggae and 1940s swing. The same economic forces that drive popular culture's high rate of turnover also drive popular culture's high rate of revival. Popular culture creates the Elvis Costello Problem — and affords its partial solution, all at the same time. Hubba hubba. Also, show me the money!

The fitful emergence of a kind of "classic" popular culture is sometimes tedious if not vexatious: if I had known in 1972, being driven to hockey practice by my father along the Belt Parkway in lower Brooklyn, that the droning, mediocre Seals and Crofts song on the radio would *still* be on the radio thirty years later as I drive my son to tae kwon do class, I would have cashed in my chips right there. And surely there's no point celebrating a cultural development that has provided an excuse for Fleetwood Mac to ruminate on the twentieth anniversary of their album *Rumours,* as if that tepid record were the totemic equivalent, for the adult-contemporary radio crowd, of *Sgt. Pepper's Lonely Hearts Club Band.*

But the central point remains: the arguments against teaching contemporary culture in the classroom simply don't take into account how complex and contradictory contemporary culture really is. There's no reason to think that everything in our current historical moment will turn out to be as evanescent as a blush, just as there's no reason to bar ourselves from conducting the first trials of the Test of Time in our own courses — or in our own lives. On the contrary, it should be one of our central obligations to teach our students how to think critically about the present. And teaching students how to discuss ideas in Jean Baudrillard and *The Matrix* — or in the novels of Don DeLillo or Jeanette Winterson — is every bit as legitimate an enterprise, every bit as vital to the projects of the humanities, as teaching them to think critically about the present by marking its debts to and differences from the distant cultural past.

I'm not suggesting that every aspect of popular culture has the pedagogical potential of *Antigone* or the *Aeneid,* and I'm not suggesting that "classic" popular culture can do all of the intellectual work of core courses in Western Civ. The advent of "classic" popular culture means, among other things, that the cultural dreck of your childhood has somehow survived to become the cultural dreck of your children's childhood. But it also means that popular culture is not necessarily ephemeral after all, and that the saga of *Star Wars* and the faux funk of KC and the Sunshine Band may in fact unite the past two generations more effectively than any number of Great Books and Western Civ courses. The curious thing about teaching popular culture these days, then, is really this: while so much of it is transitory and ephemeral, so much of it, surprisingly enough, seems to be here to stay.

Works Cited

Bérubé, Michael. *Marginal Forces/Cultural Centers: Tolson, Pynchon, and the Politics of the Canon.* Ithaca: Cornell University Press, 1992.
General Education in a Free Society. Report of the Harvard Committee on the

Objectives of a General Education in a Free Society. Cambridge: Harvard University Press, 1951.

Schneider, Alison. "At Chicago Meeting, Defenders of Traditional Curriculum Assume Embattled Air." *Chronicle of Higher Education*, 30 April 1999, A15 – 16.

Wilson, Edmund. *Axel's Castle: A Study of the Imaginative Literature of 1870 – 1930.* New York: Norton, 1931.

Part Four

POLITICS

The essays in this section deal with debates and divisions on the American left since 11 September 2001; they were written for rhetorical occasions of some urgency, and they show the strain. While they contain a number of sentences — far too many for my taste — that I now wish I could rewrite or strike, I have chosen to republish these essays almost exactly as they first appeared, warts and all.[1] One essay I've written on post-9/11 politics that is not included here is an account of Christopher Hitchens's debate with Tariq Ali at Georgetown University in April 2002. That essay was, among other things, my attempt to distance myself from Hitchens, who had not yet come out in favor of war against Iraq but who, as I wrote at the time, was clearly displaying some of "the troubles of the liberal internationalist who doesn't say where his commitment to foreign intervention might end, and on what ground." To avoid the slippery slope that would lead to the bombing of Baghdad, I thought, "liberal internationalism will have to think more clearly and speak more loudly about its own limits, and its opposition to imperialism" (B13). The essay takes its distance from Ali as well, in more emphatic terms. But because the same argument informs the conclusion of my September 2002 *Boston Globe* essay ("Can the Left Get Iraq Right?"), I have decided against including both here. The essays that follow are presented, appropriately enough, in the order of their composition.

The first essay in the section is a review of Richard Rorty's *Achieving Our Country*, which I offer here as a point of contrast with the terrain of leftist politics since the attacks of 11 September: in the 1990s, our primary debates concerned multiculturalism (or "identity politics") and domestic social policy, and most leftist and liberal intellectuals staked out one or another position with regard to what Eric Alterman called the "two lefts" of the day or what Nancy Fraser terms the "politics of recognition" and the "politics of redistribution." In those days, it sometimes seemed as if the American left simply had to strike the right balance between progressive tax schemes and liberal positions on hot-button "social issues" to devise an adequate theory and practice of social justice. Accordingly, it appeared to some on the academic left that the proper response to this state of affairs was to reject the notion of *social* justice in favor of a more inclusive — but more nebulous — idea of "cultural" justice (see Ross). Neither camp had much to say about U.S. foreign policy except to decry this or that foul aspect of it, and as a result, when the 11 September attacks were carried out, the tussles between the "reformist left" and the "cultural left" or between poststructuralists and policy makers or between Goreans and Naderites were superseded by a set of questions that almost no one outside the field of international relations had foregrounded. After 11 September, the most important rift on the left had nothing to do with Todd Gitlin versus Robin D. G. Kelley or Martha Nussbaum versus Judith Butler or *Salon* versus *Social Text*. Now it was Michael Walzer and *Dissent* on one side, Noam Chomsky and *Z* on the other, and what had been an acrimonious but internecine debate about Kosovo suddenly reappeared as the dividing line between progressive liberals, who saw in al-Qaeda an enemy worth defeating by military and other means, and hard-core leftists, who saw in Afghanistan an imperialist war and (in Chomsky's famous words) a "silent genocide."

My first foray into post-9/11 politics, "Nation and Narration," was written in January 2002 and offered my statement of allegiance to the Walzer left — the left wing of *Dissent*, if you will, as distinct from *Dissent*'s right wing of figures such as John Patrick Diggins and Paul Berman. But at the time, Chomsky's most prominent critic was Hitchens, who in a *Nation* essay titled "Against Rationalization" had insisted that al-Qaeda and the Taliban deserved no measure of "root causes" sympathy from the international left and that there was no moral equivalence between Islamist fundamentalism and American foreign policy. I mention my "sympathy with" Hitchens in this essay, and it is one of the aspects of the essay I would now like to take back — for well before the end of 2002, it had become clear that Hitchens had moved not from the *Nation* to the position of someone like Michael Walzer but from the *Nation* to the position of someone more like Paul Wolfowitz. But I will let that moment of sympathy stand, as this seems the only intellectually honest thing to do. I will, however, say one prefatory thing about this essay, which was derided on the far left as evidence of (among other things) my craven desire to break into corporate mass media by repudiating Chomsky. I wrote it for *Context: A Forum for Literary Arts and Culture*, which is published by the Unit for Contemporary Literature at Illinois State University. *Context* is not available for purchase anywhere in the country. It is distributed only to independent bookstores, in print runs of five thousand. So I wonder just how much further from the corporate mass media Chomsky's fans would like me to get before I am permitted to disagree with them. Indeed, many of this essay's critics on the left failed even to entertain the possibility that people like me disagree with them not because we're trying to slime our way onto the masthead of some slick glossy but because we sincerely and reasonably believe that they were substantively wrong — wrong to have equated the attacks of 11 September with Reagan's mining of the Nicaraguan harbors; wrong to have claimed that the death toll of 9/11 was far exceeded by the 1998 U.S. bombing of the al-Shifa pharmaceutical plant in the Sudan; wrong to have claimed that the United States deliberately tried to kill millions of Afghans when it temporarily closed down the aid convoys to Afghanistan in September; and wrong to have called the war in Afghanistan a "silent genocide" thereafter.

The problem with these last two claims, of course, has to do with charging the United States with massive human rights crimes before they happen, and then continuing to make the charge even after they do not happen. Accordingly, in "Can the Left Get Iraq Right?," I argue that the real disaster for the American left when it came to mobilizing public opinion against war in Iraq was not so much the Chomskian reaction to 9/11 itself but the hyperbolic and overwrought terms in which the left framed opposition to war in Afghanistan. There were and are good reasons to oppose war in Afghanistan, especially as it was and is conducted by the Bush/Cheney regime and its specialists in torture, though even these arguments must start by acknowledging the danger of leaving the Taliban and its terror camps in place while more nonviolent means of opposition to al-Qaeda are mounted. And it should go without saying — but will not, here — that the events of 9/11 did not give the United States the right to take even one innocent life anywhere around the globe. But those in the Chomsky camp were not content to make plausible arguments; rather, they embellished their plausible arguments with a series of astonishing claims about how the war to remove the Taliban from power was actually, in Cynthia Peters's words, a "calculated crime against humanity . . . many times larger" than that of 9/11. By September 2002, of course, it was clear that for all of Afghanistan's troubles, the United States had not in fact carried out a "silent genocide" in that country (see Weiner; Rozen; Kaufman), and as a result, I argue, the antiwar left's credibility had been severely damaged in the eyes of precisely those mainstream Americans necessary to the building of a broad movement to oppose war in Iraq. And because I believed that war in Iraq could be prevented only by a *very* broad, popular movement in the United States (given the depth and passion of the Bush/Cheney fixation on Iraq), I saw the hard left's position on Afghanistan as something that could — and, I believe, did — damage liberals' and progressives' chances of winning the hearts and minds of people who were uncertain about how best to respond to Islamist bombings and attacks around the world.

By November 2002, the terrain had shifted yet again: the self-appointed leaders of the antiwar movement were making it quite clear that opposition to the war in Afghanistan was a prerequisite for "correct" opposition to war in Iraq, and the major antiwar rallies were being organized by a splinter group so far left as to reside somewhere between neo-Stalinism and Monty Python. Meanwhile, the ranks of the prowar liberals were growing. I therefore tried to write an essay ("For a Better — and Broader — Antiwar Movement") that outlined an antiwar position capable of addressing the prowar liberals' most salient arguments — that it was a betrayal of Iraqi democrats to leave Saddam in power and that the principle of "humanitarian intervention," so critical to discussions of Somalia, Rwanda, and the Balkans, should be applied as well to Iraq — while dissenting from the sectarian extremism of Act Now to Stop War and End Racism (ANSWER). I follow this with a pair of essays written after the war had begun, by which point I had decided that however much credibility the left had lost because of Chomsky's charges of "silent genocide" in Afghanistan, the liberal hawks had lost far more in their support for what turned out to be a nearly unilateral invasion. For not only did the hawks hitch their wagon to Bush's in a way that cannot be undone now, but they were and are considerably more influential than anyone writing for *Z*. This argument forms the backbone of my review essay on Paul Berman's *Terror and Liberalism* (published, like my review of Rorty, in *Tikkun*) and my essay on "The Loyalties of American Studies," which originated in a plenary panel at the 2003 American Studies Association convention and which articulates my current position on the war (while augmenting my earlier essay on "American Studies without Exceptions").

As this book goes to press, roughly 60 percent of the American public has come to believe that the war in Iraq is a mistake. President Bush's approval rating hovers in the mid-30s. Debates about the manipulation of prewar intelligence are rippling through Washington so powerfully that it may seem quaint of me to revisit these debates about how the American left might best have mobilized support against war in Iraq. But I think something quite terrible has happened, apart from all the terrible things that have happened from Fallujah to Abu Ghraib: the ideal of liberal internationalism, the dream of internationalist antitotalitarians from the Abraham Lincoln Brigades in Spain to the advocates of "humanitarian intervention" in Rwanda and the Sudan, has been all but delegitimated by its most prominent advocates, such as Michael Ignatieff. It is devastating to the party of Iraq hawks, I believe, that Human Rights Watch, which judiciously contested some of the Chomskian left's more extraordinary remarks about Afghanistan and 9/11, has repudiated the "humanitarian intervention" rationale for war in Iraq (see Bogert; Roth): this repudiation means, among other things, that the ideal of humanitarian intervention will, in the foreseeable future, need to be wrested from the hands of those who invoked it as grounds for an illegal and counterproductive invasion. How best to go about this I do not know.

Notes

1. The only exception to this rule concerns outright factual errors: for example, my September 2002 *Boston Globe* essay on the march to war in Iraq, published here as "Can the Left Get Iraq Right?," mistakenly identified Michael Walzer as a supporter of war in Iraq when in fact he was about to publish an eloquent essay in the *New Republic* opposing that war and had not — contrary to the rumors then swirling on listservs to my left — written anything in support of an Iraq war to that point. Accordingly, I have substituted Paul Berman's name for Walzer's as an example of a "liberal hawk" with regard to Iraq.

Works Cited

Bérubé, Michael. "Ali v. Hitchens: Battle on the Left." *Chronicle Review (Chronicle of Higher Education)*, 3 May 2002, B13.

Bogert, Carroll. "Noam Needs a Fact Checker" (letter to the editor). *Salon.com*, 22 January 2002. Available online at < http://www.salon.com/people/letters/ 2002/01/22/chomsky/index.html >. Accessed 3 December 2002.

Hitchens, Christopher. "Against Rationalization." *Nation*, 8 October 2001. Available online at < http://www.thenation.com/doc.mhtml?i=20011008&s= hitchens >. Accessed 8 January 2002.

Kaufman, Mark. "Massive Food Delivery Averts Afghan Famine." *Washington Post*, 31 December 2001, A1.

Peters, Cynthia. "It's Simple. It's Not So Simple." *Z Magazine Online (ZNet)*, October 2001. Available online at < http://www.zmag.org/peterssimple.htm >. Accessed 24 October 2001.

Ross, Andrew. *Real Love: In Pursuit of Cultural Justice*. New York: New York University Press, 1998.

Roth, Ken. "War in Iraq: Not a Humanitarian Intervention." *Human Rights Watch: World Report 2004*, January 2004. Available online at < http://hrw.org/ wr2k4/3.htm >. Accessed 17 November 2005.

Rozen, Laura. "Crying Wolf — Or Doing Their Job?" *Salon.com*, 16 November 2001. Available online at < http://www.salon.com/news/feature/2001/11/16/aid/ index.html >. Accessed 3 December 2005.

Weiner, Tim. "Now, the Battle to Feed the Afghan Nation." *New York Times*, 16 November 2001, A1, B6 – B7.

Richard Rorty's *Achieving Our Country* is a much richer and stranger document than many readers have taken it to be. In one sense, it represents the clearest combination to date of Rorty's philosophical pragmatism and his recent defenses of patriotic nationalism; in another sense it is a blueprint for nothing less than the renewal of the American left, a provocative challenge to leftist sectarianism of the past and present. Despite its brevity (three lectures, one hundred pages), the book is broadly ambitious and deeply conflicted. Appropriately, both its ambitions and its conflicts find their strongest expression in Rorty's analysis of (and attempt to repair) the schism that has produced the "two lefts" of American politics in the 1990s — the left that aspires to analyze culture (Rorty's "cultural left"), and the left that aspires to carry out public policy (Rorty's "reformist left"). Unlike all too many books that simply blame academic cultural left elites for the decline of the left since 1968, *Achieving Our Country* does its best to give the cultural left its due, but since Rorty tends to see cultural politics simply as a distraction from "real" politics, the book's rhetorical strategies sometimes run counter to its explicit political goals, and Rorty thereby repeatedly runs the risk of exacerbating the divisions he had sincerely set out to transcend.

Rorty's first lecture attempts to revive a pragmatic patriotism in the spirit of Whitman and Dewey, partly on substantive grounds — which include the belief that the United States remains a valuable democratic experiment — and partly on the instrumental grounds that "the government of our nation-state will be, for the foreseeable future, the only agent capable of making any real difference in the amount of selfishness and sadism inflicted on Americans" (98). The second lecture, "The Eclipse of the Reformist Left," offers a very brief, very idiosyncratic "history" of the twentieth-century American left, one purpose of which, oddly enough, is to persuade us to forget much of the history of the American left. The third lecture is as conflicted as the second, at once ruing and recuperating the rise of the academic left of the past few decades. No one will like the third lecture who doesn't like the second, since Rorty's analysis of the left's future follows directly from his series of proposals for what we should forget about the left's past. And the success of Rorty's enterprise will rest largely on how his readers respond to those two lectures, insofar as the prospects for egalitarian social justice will depend less on our ideas about Whitman and Dewey than on whether leftists, progressives, and liberals can form broad-based coalitions to oppose the forces of privatization and plutocracy.

Unfortunately, though, *Achieving Our Country* is most divisive precisely when it's most concerned with repairing the damage to the post-Vietnam American left. The problem with the discourse of the "two lefts" — the phrase is Eric Alterman's, but the analysis is ubiquitous — is not only that it obscures from view everyone who has applied for membership in both parties but also that it construes leftist thought as a zero-sum game in which the academic/cultural left is not the counterpart to the public policy left but its antithesis. Reading polemics on the two lefts, one is sometimes tempted to think that the United States would have passed a national health-care plan, implemented a family-leave policy, and abolished "right-to-work" laws if only we leftist-liberals in the humanities hadn't been wasting our time writing books on cultural hybridity and popular music.

And Rorty is often tempted to think this way, as the opening salvo of *Achieving Our Country* suggests: "Leftists in the academy have permitted cultural politics to supplant real politics, and have collaborated with the right in making cultural issues central to public debate. They are spending energy which should be directed at proposing new laws on discussing topics as remote from the country's needs as were [Henry] Adams' musings on the Virgin and the Dynamo" (14–15). The passage features everything that's regrettable in the discourse of the two lefts: the disparagement of cultural politics as unreal politics; the dismissal of abstract intellectual "musings" on things like symbols of historical change (which is what that Virgin-and-Dynamo blather was all about); and not least, the incendiary accusation that the members of the cultural left have been "collaborating" — unwittingly, one hopes — with their opposite numbers in the Christian Coalition. The charge is almost certain to provoke the counterallegation that the soi-disant "real politics" left simply discounts every form of cultural activism that doesn't pertain to white men, and thus we will be right back where we started, with two polarized lefts.

But despite all the nastiness that's defined the "two lefts" discourse, I'm not convinced that good, public-minded, left-leaning American citizens can't work both sides of the street, just as the Heritage Foundation works both sides of *its* street, marking or making the connections between cultural politics and public policy. The work of Nancy Fraser is exemplary in this regard (likewise, it's telling that there's no mention of Fraser in *Achieving Our Country*), and her distinction between the "politics of recognition" and the "politics of redistribution" certainly offers a better way of grasping the problem than does the distinction between cultural politics and "real" politics. For as Fraser has repeatedly argued, while the politics of recognition always have an economic component, they are not *reducible* to the politics of redistribution and are not categorically less important than redistributive politics, either. To put this another way, the cultural conditions in which gays and lesbians or people with disabilities or ethnic minorities live in the United States can be dehumanizing in ways that have nothing to do with taxation, federal spending, private investment, and the minimum wage, even though strategies of dehumanization may have broad implications for the distribution of goods; surely any left worthy of the name should mount opposition to strategies of dehumanization without regard to their economic implications. Indeed, there need be no contradiction between "passing laws" and "making cultural issues central to public debate," as our national debates over abortion, gay marriage, and hate crimes legislation amply demonstrate.

In his best moments, Richard Rorty knows all this perfectly well, and even tries valiantly to imagine a set of terms that will reconcile redistributive politics with recognition politics. Especially in his third lecture, he speaks of the necessity of opposing both selfishness (through what Fraser would call a politics of redistribution) and sadism (through Fraser's politics of recognition). Where the opponents of sadism talk about stigma, says Rorty, the opponents of selfishness talk mainly about money. This is a fair enough description of the two fronts on which an activist left should work, and on these fronts Rorty gives the cultural left high marks for its successes in fighting social stigmata and sadism: "The American academy has done as much to overcome sadism during the past thirty years as it did to overcome selfishness in the previous seventy. Encouraging students to be what mocking neoconservatives call 'politically correct' has made our country a far better place. American leftist academics have a lot to be proud of. Their conservative critics, who have no remedies to propose either for American sadism or for American selfishness, have a great deal to be ashamed of" (82). The distance between this characterization of "political correctness" and that of Rorty's nearest political colleagues, Paul Berman and the late Irving Howe, is quite striking — and is one important instance of Rorty's attempts to reconcile the two lefts while maintaining primary allegiance to a politics of redistribution.

The olive branch thus extended to the contemporary cultural left has its counterpart in the second lecture, where Rorty nearly endorses, then subtly modifies, Todd Gitlin's account of the 1964 Democratic National Convention. In *The Twilight of Common Dreams*, Gitlin had written, "[T]his was a time when cross-racial alliances for civil rights were proving unmanageable," citing the challenge Fannie Lou Hamer and the Mississippi Freedom Democratic Party (MFDP) posed to Mississippi's "official white supremacist regulars, who had been chosen without the slightest participation by blacks, and who would not even promise to support the Democratic nominee" (130). To the MFDP, Lyndon Johnson wound up offering a devil's bargain, but in Gitlin's rendition of events, it was a devil's bargain in which historians should have some sympathy for the devil:

> President Johnson orchestrated a compromise, supported by liberals, labor unions, and moderate civil rights leaders, offering the MFDP a token two votes for its leaders, retaining the official delegation, while pledging to change the rules by 1968. The MFDP refused the compromise. The radical position was immortalized in Fannie Lou Hamer's famous statement that it would be wrong for the leaders to take seats because "all of us [in the MFDP delegation] are tired." (130)

The MFDP refused the compromise. In phrasing LBJ's offer as a "compromise" rather than as a "rebuff" or an "insult," Gitlin's account seems to suggest that groups like the MFDP, far from being the kind of radical democrats any American leftist should honor, actually helped to make cross-racial alliances "unmanageable." Rorty, by contrast, steers clear of these waters altogether, refusing even to pass judgment on either LBJ or Hamer; seconding Gitlin's sense that the 1964 convention was a "last straw" for the New Left, Rorty moves quickly to insist that the New Left may have been in the right: "[T]here had to be a last straw sooner or later if American leftism was ever to be revitalized.... By saving us from the Vietnam War, the New Left may have saved us from losing our moral identity" (69, 68). This is not only a significant break from what like-minded writers of Rorty's generation tend to say about the 1960s and their aftermath; it is also a significant revision of the account of post-Vietnam politics Rorty offered in his address to the John Sweeney – inspired intellectuals/ AFL-CIO conference at Columbia University in October 1996, when he simply blamed the New Left for labor's lurch to the right in the 1960s.

In one sense, then, *Achieving Our Country* marks a slightly cultural-leftward move on Rorty's part with regard to how Rorty-affiliated writers (including Rorty himself, one imagines) might hereafter write about the recent history of the American left: the politics of money are the real politics, but don't forget to give the politics of stigma their due. And the reason to hew to real politics, Rorty reminds us, is that since 1973, as casual sexism and stigmatization have declined in American life, economic inequality has dramatically increased. Our liberal campuses, too, have not been immune from the country's general redistribution toward the rich, as Rorty notes when he cites a remarkable 1997 study by the National Council of Educational Opportunity Associations showing that the percentage of degree-earning college students from the wealthiest 25 percent of the population jumped from 31 percent in 1979 to 79 percent in 1994 (86). "It is as if the American Left could not handle more than one initiative at a time," Rorty notes, "as if it either had to ignore stigma in order to concentrate on money, or vice versa" (83). If Rorty is right about this, it would seem to follow that a cogent and useful American left should handle both initiatives at once; only eight pages later, however, Rorty reverts once again to zero-sum thinking, advising that the cultural left will "have to talk much more about money, *even at the cost of* talking less about stigma" (91; emphasis added). This is an important impasse, which is why it's worth emphasizing how Rorty's book positions itself in current leftist debates about the relative importance of stigma and money, sadism and selfishness, recognition and redistribution. And yet the terms in which I've discussed the book so far — friendlier to the cultural left than most "policy-oriented" writers, not as willing to think past the "two lefts" as people like Fraser — amount almost to a betrayal of the book's larger rhetorical purpose, which is precisely to *elide* differences among leftists, progressives, and liberals.

It is in the service of this elision that Rorty's second lecture asks us not only to drop Marxism altogether as a god that failed but also to stop assessing the behavior of members of the left in recent history. His complaint about the current left is not only that it is "spectatorial" but that it is "retrospective" (14). Indeed, history itself is in one sense quite beside the point Rorty wants to make. "Stories about what a nation has been and should try to be are not attempts at accurate representation," Rorty writes in a passage that may be the key to reading the book as a whole, "but rather attempts to forge a moral identity. The argument between left and right about which episodes in our history we Americans should pride ourselves on will never be a contest between a true and a false account of our country's history and its identity. It is better described as an argument about which hopes to allow ourselves and which to forgo" (13–14).

Rorty's housecleaning amounts to what I call his General Amnesty Platform (so, vis-à-vis Vietnam, amnesty for Daniel Berrigan and everyone who evaded the draft, as well as amnesty for Robert MacNamara and everyone who came out against the Vietnam War more than a decade after it ended); in addition, he proposes that "we should abandon the leftist-versus-liberal distinction, along with the other residues of Marxism that clutter up our vocabulary — overworked words like 'commodification' and 'ideology,' for example" (42). If the Marxists agree to come in out of the cold and stop speaking their dead language, in other words, they will be admitted to the Popular Front. And that Front will be capacious indeed: it will drop the term Old Left, replacing it with "the term 'reformist Left' to cover all those Americans who, between 1900 and 1964, struggled within the framework of constitutional democracy to protect the weak from the strong" (43). "To bring this about," Rorty writes at the end of his plea for general amnesty, "it would help if American leftists... emphasized the similarities rather than the differences between Malcolm X and Bayard Rustin, between Susan B. Anthony and Emma Goldman, between Catharine MacKinnon and Judith Butler" (51). The only important division will be this: we will adopt Herbert Croly's argument that the state should aim for "a morally and socially desirable distribution of wealth," and we will agree that "from 1909 to the present, the thesis that the state must make itself responsible for such redistribution has marked the dividing line between the American Left and the American Right" (48). When Rorty asks what side you're on, here are the teams he has in mind, *sub specie aeternitatis*:

> A hundred years from now, Howe and Galbraith, Harrington and Schlesinger, [Woodrow] Wilson and Debs, Jane Addams and Angela Davis, Felix Frankfurter and John L. Lewis, W. E. B. Du Bois and Eleanor Roosevelt, Robert Reich and Jesse Jackson, will all be remembered for having advanced the cause of social justice. They will all be seen as having been "on the Left." The difference between these people and men like Calvin Coolidge, Irving Babbitt, T. S. Eliot, Robert Taft, and William Buckley will be far clearer than any of the quarrels which once divided them among themselves. Whatever mistakes they made, these people will deserve, as Coolidge and Buckley never will, the praise which Jonathan Swift ended his own epitaph: "Imitate him if you can: he served human liberty." (45)

This is perhaps the most eloquent and generous passage in *Achieving Our Country* — and one of the most problematic, for pretty much the same reason that Swift's self-designation as a servant of human liberty is problematic. For on the one hand, Rorty couldn't be more accurate about the left's sectarian purity rituals, particularly in academe; it's as if he's thumbed through the big rolodex on every good leftist's desk that catalogs the many toadies, finks, informers, stooges, turncoats, and objective reactionaries *among our allies* and decided to ask everyone to bury their damn rolodexes. Yet on the other hand, it seems shortsighted, to put it generously, to ask the left to stop trying to learn lessons from its own past. Take 1964, once again. The seating of the all-white Mississippi delegation may have helped Johnson to secure passage of the Voting Rights Act the next year — the most progressive (and federal-interventionist) piece of law to hit the South since Reconstruction. It's worth debating. But if Johnson and his supporters (including Walter Reuther, for whom Rorty also proposes amnesty on this and on Vietnam) were motivated by the desire to keep the South voting Democratic, then (1) Rorty himself notes that this thinking undermined Roosevelt's New Deal thirty years earlier and (2) it didn't even work in 1964, as the Mississippi delegation endorsed Goldwater and the South bolted rightward to Wallace and Nixon in 1968, never to return.

I happen to agree with Rorty that the contemporary left should be less spectatorial and retrospective than it is, so I'm not altogether hostile to the notion that we should be more worried about the state of the left in 2032 than in 1968. But I am skeptical of reading American history as Rorty asks us to, as a repository of stories about what we might become; though this is surely one of the functions of history, I think, it is just as surely only *one* of those functions. For when you lose sight of those other functions, you stop asking grainy-details questions about whose history is more adequate and plausible than whose, and why. The result, in this case, is that *Achieving Our Country* reads as if it were designed (as it was) to defeat questions about the accuracy of its own account of the left. I would suggest instead that it be read as something of a general invitation, seeking not to describe the past but to dictate the terms for the future: we should see Malcolm X and Bayard Rustin, Jane Addams and Angela Davis as engaged in a common enterprise of expanding human liberty not because it would be objectively true to do so but because it would be pragmatically useful.

About the utility of the argument I have little doubt, convinced as I am that nothing will resist the growing corporatization of the world save for a very broad coalition of anticorporatization folks on the left, all the way from the mealiest-mouthed of liberals to the stark-ravingest of Marxists. But I have grave doubts about whether Rorty's "two lefts" analysis of the contemporary scene will further the creation of that coalition: unless we can see the politics of redistribution and the politics of recognition as the double helix of leftist thought — and we should think especially here of issues such as immigration, disability, reproduction and motherhood, and criminal justice, where cultural politics and public policy are woven as tightly as any strand of DNA — no amnesty program for the sectarians of the past will suffice to remedy the two-left sectarianism of the present. The value of *Achieving Our Country*, then, does not lie in its accuracy about the past and present state of the left; it lies, instead, in its willingness to throw down gauntlets for the formation of a future left that can think beyond the impasses with which *Achieving Our Country* would leave us.

Works Cited

Alterman, Eric. "Making One and One Equal Two." *Nation*, 25 May 1998, 10.

Gitlin, Todd. *The Twilight of Common Dreams: Why America Is Wracked by Culture Wars*. New York: Holt, 1995.

Rorty, Richard. *Achieving Our Country: Leftist Thought in Twentieth-Century America*. Cambridge: Harvard University Press, 1998.

Nation and Narration

[January 2002]

I magine the forty-third presidency without Osama bin Laden, the year 2001 with an uneventful 11 September.

It's January 2002, one year after Bush's controversial inauguration, and the White House is a shambles. Having passed the tax bill that was the only rationale for his presidency in the eyes of his financiers, George W. Bush is in deep doo-doo. The post – New Economy recession is in full swing, and working Americans have discovered to their dismay that the three-hundred- and six-hundred-dollar rebates they received back in 2001 will cover a couple of heating bills and winter clothes for the kids, and that's it; over the next fifteen years they'll see another fifteen dollars from the tax cut, having no capital gains or estate tax relief to look forward to, while the executives at Halliburton look to pick up fifteen billion dollars each. The same holds true for the executives of Enron and their sixty-million-dollar severance packages (severance packages for CEOs having been exempted from taxation by a little-noticed rider to the bill), except that Enron's spectacular collapse has fired one House investigation into Bush's and Cheney's financial interests in deregulation, one Justice Department investigation into Enron's role in crafting Bush/Cheney energy policy, and another broader Senate investigation into corruption and influence peddling in the new administration.

All three investigations have been denounced by Rush Limbaugh, William Kristol, and the *Wall Street Journal* as "a monkey wrench in the very engine of prosperity," but nobody is listening to these toadies anymore. They've been discredited not only by their unflagging support for Enron but also by their earlier denunciations of the review of the Florida election returns, which, though ambiguous in many respects, indicated beyond all doubt that more Floridians intended to vote for Gore than for Bush in November 2000 — and that Florida Republicans, knowing well in advance that they were in for a dogfight, deliberately struck thousands of black voters from the rolls while filling out fraudulent absentee and military ballots months before the election. And since more Americans voted for Gore than for Bush nationwide in the first place, the new president's legitimacy hangs by a thread. The Electoral College is soon to be abolished, and sweeping reforms in voter registration and voting tabulation systems are being enacted in every state of the union. It doesn't help matters that 84 percent of Americans think that Bush "isn't working hard enough" as president, largely because he has not yet returned from summer vacation at his ranch in Crawford, Texas. As for Bush's cabinet . . . what cabinet? O'Neill and Rumsfeld have made early departures, as predicted by Beltway insiders from Day 1; Gale Norton has resigned under pressure after having been discovered clubbing baby seals off the coast of Alaska; and attorney general Ashcroft is widely criticized for continuing to hold his controversial "prayer breakfasts" in which he calls on Jesus Christ to "smite the unbelievers."

I think it's safe to say that the events of 11 September changed everything, don't you?

LIKE THE DEADLY particulate matter floating in the air of Lower Manhattan, the political fallout from September's terrorist attacks will have immeasurable toxic effects for decades. The narrative of that fallout remains to be written — indeed, it remains to be lived and experienced. But it's already becoming possible to see several important story lines taking shape in U.S. political culture.

The early days now seem like days of hysteria: there was the justifiable hysteria of New Yorkers who feared that the bridges and tunnels were the next targets, and there was the ugly hysteria of right-wing pundits for whom the attacks changed nothing but the volume of their daily screeds. One unwittingly ludicrous example was provided by celebrated hack Shelby Steele, who was writing an op-ed for the *Wall Street Journal* denouncing the U.N. conference on racism when the planes hit and merely tweaked it into a 17 September column denouncing global crybabies in general — some of whom were apparently flying those planes, although the connection wasn't made quite clear. (News flash: advocates of reparations for slavery kill six thousand in New York!!) More dangerous were the early responses of people like Andrew Sullivan — and Ann Coulter and Rich Lowry of the *National Review*; Coulter went so far as to lose her job at the *Review*, less for the content of her written work (according to editor Jonah Goldberg's 3 October column) than for her public demeanor after her incoherent follow-up essay was spiked. And Goldberg's postmortem has the ring of truth, for Coulter's now-infamous line, "We should invade their countries, kill their leaders and convert them to Christianity," was after all not terribly different from Lowry's plan for "identifying the one or two nations most closely associated with our enemies, giving them 24-hours notice to evacuate their capitals (in keeping with our desire to wage war as morally as possible), then systematically destroying every significant piece of military, financial, and political infrastructure in those cities."

This is strong stuff—so strong, in fact, that in response to Sullivan's vile suggestion that the attacks would bring out a "fifth column" of "decadent" leftists on the coasts (you know, where a lot of those decadent Oscar Wilde types live), any rational person could've replied that throughout September and October, you couldn't do better recruiting work for al-Qaeda in Muslim nations than to distribute free copies of the *National Review*.

Of course, some of the right's hysteria was understandable: remember, they excoriated Arab terrorists for days after the bombing in Oklahoma City, only to be compelled to swallow hard once the white kid with the crew cut emerged as the perp. Think of their tension, their long-unfulfilled desires to rage, rage against the backward cultures of Islam: by 11 September 2001, the right had been waiting more than six years to vent, and some of them simply lost control.

Interestingly, though — and devastatingly for the left — they reined themselves in; after the first few queasy weeks, there would be no more talk of crusades and conversions and infinite justice. For who knew until 11 September that Grover Norquist, longtime tax nut and conservative organizer extraordinaire, had been cultivating Arab American voters for the GOP? (So assiduously, it turned out, that he'd had his president lunching with some Hamas and Hezbollah supporters, as Franklin Foer pointed out in the *New Republic*.) And who knew that the hard right would scotch its plans for systematically destroying the capitals of Muslim nations the minute they realized that they couldn't get to Afghanistan without going through Pakistan?

Prevented by their own president from conducting a hate campaign against Arabs, the harpies of the culture-war right turned to a safer domestic target — students and professors. In a remarkably crude, incompetent pamphlet, the Joe Lieberman – Lynne Cheney outfit, the American Council of Trustees and Alumni, combed college campuses for seditious statements like "Ignorance breeds hate," "Hate breeds hate," "Our grief is not a cry for war," "An eye for an eye leaves the world blind," "Knowledge is good," and "If Osama bin Laden is confirmed to be behind the attacks, the United States should bring him before an international tribunal on charges of crimes against humanity." (All but one of these are actual statements cited by ACTA as evidence of insufficient patriotism on U.S. campuses. Aficionados and adepts will recognize the last item as the words of Joel Beinin, the antepenultimate item as the words of Mahatma Gandhi, and the penultimate item as the motto of Faber College in *Animal House*.) Lynne Cheney has not commented on the pamphlet, and may in fact be in a secure undisclosed location for all I know; Lieberman's office has issued one of those "distancing" statements that stops short of taking the senator's name off the letterhead.

Meanwhile, even as the *New Republic* continued to publish the work of liberal writers, the editorial staff collectively staged what Stuart Hall once called the Great Moving Right Show, and kept right on moving until they passed the *National Review*. Think I'm kidding? Count the number of times each magazine has criticized Ariel Sharon since 11 September, and you'll get some sense of why I respect the *National Review*'s Middle East coverage more. Or read every post-9/11 editorial signed by the *New Republic* editors, like the 29 October clarion call to "weaponize" our courage. (In his bunker in Baghdad, a shaken Saddam Hussein looks up from his copy of the *New Republic*: "Nothing would please me more than to fight American armed forces in the daughter of the mother of all battles — but I cannot face the fearsome senior editors of this weekly magazine.") Or look at their vicious attacks on Colin Powell, who is apparently unfit to run the State Department and should be replaced by someone wiser, someone with a firmer grasp of the perfidy of Arabs, perhaps someone who has attended the Johns Hopkins School of Advanced International Studies, like editor Lawrence F. Kaplan.

THE NARRATIVE OF the left is more tangled and more somber. But before I remark on the ways the Chomskian left has consigned itself to the dustbin of history, let me go back to those early days of hysteria and say a few words in defense of people I now disagree with: it was entirely plausible, in those first few days, to think that the United States had received some kind of global comeuppance. Bless their hearts, the diehards of the anti-imperialist left had always had the integrity and the conscience to say publicly that the United States had too often acted unilaterally and unethically in the post-1945 world, often against its own realpolitik interests as well as against its own democratic ideals. The anti-imperialists were right about Vietnam, they were right about Chile, they were right about El Salvador and Nicaragua, they were right about Indonesia in 1975, and they were right about Iran in 1953. It was not initially unreasonable for any of them to think, as the World Trade Center collapsed five blocks from my best friend's apartment, *Son of a bitch, someone's gotten to us at last*. Such a sentiment, despite the vitriol heaped upon it by the right, implied no sympathy with the attackers; the anti-imperialist left, at its best, despised antidemocratic forces no matter where they came from. It merely registered the sorry fact that the United States had, indeed, too often given the wretched of the earth cause to hate us.

But when the narrative of the attacks became more complex, the Chomskian left did not. It slowly became clear that for all its past crimes, the U.S. government wasn't nearly as proximate a cause of the attack as were the governments of Saudi Arabia and Egypt, U.S. "allies" who'd been dancing a dicey pas de deux with their own Islamist radicals for twenty years to keep the lid on the domestic unrest created in part by their own corruption. And slowly it became clear that Osama bin Laden and al-Qaeda were not animated by any of the causes dear to American leftists: the attacks on the World Trade Center and the Pentagon were not, it seemed, symbolic strikes against U.S. unilateralism with regard to missile defense, post-Kyoto energy policy, land mine treaties, or the rights of children. They were not cosmic payback for our support of Suharto or Pinochet or Marcos or Rios Montt or Mohammed Reza Pahlevi. They were not aimed at Katherine Harris or Kenneth Starr or William Rehnquist. Indeed, the more the West learned about bin Laden, the more we were led down strange narrative byways we hadn't even considered as tangents to the main event: The Somalia expedition convinced him that the United States was a paper tiger? He wants American soldiers, especially women, to stop desecrating the land of the two holy mosques? He speaks of "eighty years" of Arab abasement, harking back to the end of World War I?

Well, that should have given anyone pause for thought. Maybe if bin Laden had denounced the CIA's overthrow of Mossadeq, maybe if he'd jeered at our futile attempts to play Iran off Iraq and vice versa throughout Reagan's presidency, and maybe if he wasn't carrying around one of those theories about the global Jewish conspiracy, he'd have had a shred of credibility with me. But Somalia? Somalia really was an attempt at liberal-internationalist humanitarianism, and as for the eighty-year-old Sykes-Picot agreement divvying up Arab provinces after World War I, there aren't that many American leftists committed to the restoration of the caliphate, so it's hard for me to see the appeal on that count as well. In fact, as Chris Suellentrop of *Slate* observed, the United States doesn't even deserve any grief about the end of the caliphate: "It would be nice," he wrote, "if Bin Laden would note that the United States objected to the Sykes-Picot agreement as a betrayal of the principle of self-determination, but that's probably asking for too much." There's no doubt that our government has committed crimes against humanity in our name, but Somalia and Sykes-Picot aren't among them.

So, faced with an enemy as incomprehensible and as implacable as bin Laden, much of the left checked the man's policy positions on women, homosexuality, secularism, and facial hair, and slowly backed out of the room. They didn't move right, as so many Chomskian leftists have charged; they simply decided that the 11 September attacks were the work of religious fanatics who had no conceivable point of contact with anything identifiable as a "left" project save for a human-rights complaint about the sanctions against Iraq. As Marx himself observed, there are a number of social systems more oppressive than that of capitalism. Al-Qaeda and the Taliban are good cases in point.

For almost a month, the dispute between the Chomsky left and the Hitchens left was largely a theoretical affair, featuring a sweetly pointless debate in the *Nation* over whose condemnation of Clinton's 1998 cruise-missile strike against the al-Shifa pharmaceutical plant in the Sudan was more thorough and/or courageous; then the bombs started dropping on Afghanistan, and the camps hardened into place, with leftists who'd denounced the Taliban steadily for five years now denouncing a military action designed to remove the Taliban from power. This is perhaps the most important episode in the many narratives of 11 September, because it represented the earthquake that had been building along a fault line in the U.S. left dating back to the first Bush administration's operations in Panama and Kuwait, and because it has ramifications for the future of U.S. foreign policy for decades to come.

A large part of the split had to do with the simple fact that bombs were dropping. For U.S. leftists schooled in the lessons of Cambodia, Libya, and the School of the Americas, all U.S. bombing actions are suspect: they are announced by cadaverous white guys with bad hair, they are covered by seven cable channels competing with one another for the catchiest "New War" slogan and Emmy awards for creative flag display, and they invariably kill civilians, the poor, the wretched, the disabled. There is surely much to hate about any bombing campaign.

Yet who would deny that a nation, once attacked, has the right to respond with military force, and who seriously believes that anyone could undertake any "nation-building" enterprise in Afghanistan without first driving the Taliban from power? *Very well,* some of my post-September interlocutors said, *the Taliban must go, but not by force.* A curious answer: Why would any clearthinking leftist believe that the Taliban could be removed by persuasion alone, as if, like Al Gore after the Supreme Court's supremely corrupt decision in *Bush v. Gore,* they would smile wanly into the cameras and say, "It's time for us to go?"

The arguments against military force started flooding the left-leaning listservs. One, the link between the attacks and the Taliban was not strong enough to justify bombing. Two, we had supported bin Laden indirectly back when he was one of the mujahideen fighting the Soviet Union. Three, the terrain and the enemy would quickly lead us into a quagmire. Four, the bombing of Afghanistan was the moral equivalent of the 11 September attacks — or even worse, since the United States was attacking from a position of wealth and strength. Five, there would be no "nation-building" after the ouster of the

Taliban, just more bombing, this time in some other impoverished nation. Six, the United States had been a global aggressor for so long and with such impunity that it had no moral ground from which to operate even after being directly attacked.

These are among the arguments that have insured the Chomskian left's irrelevance to foreign policy debate for the foreseeable future, and I confess I am not always sure why anyone would make them in any case. Arguments three and five are relatively innocuous, being merely predictive, but the rest range from merely illogical (one, two, six) to morally odious (four).[1] For example, the fact that a U.S. government was once foolish enough — or Zbigniew Brzezinski was once cavalier enough — to fund the Arab "Afghanis" in the 1980s does not mean that a U.S. government is barred from opposing any of their progeny now. The Chomskian left has been playing this tune for some time now — *Today's public enemy was yesterday's CIA darling* — and while it does serve a heuristic function, in that it reminds amnesiac Americans that baddies such as Saddam and Noriega and Suharto didn't appear on the world stage out of nowhere, it doesn't serve any substantive function except obfuscation. Would the Chomskian left seriously prefer that the United States stick by its totalitarian ex-clients no matter what, as the cold warriors of the right once urged us to do?

The argument about our past dealings with bin Laden is thus a smokescreen, as was Chomsky's argument in 1999 that our intervention against Milosevic in Kosovo could not be motivated by "humanitarian" concerns because if we were serious about humanitarianism, we would also have intervened in East Timor. Even Chomsky's fans will recall that this argument was not a clarion call for wider U.S. interventions around the world beginning in East Timor; it was an argument designed to obfuscate the issue at hand in Kosovo — namely, allegations that the Serbs were engaged in genocide. Similarly, in addressing the question of whether the United States had the right to respond militarily after 11 September, Chomsky offered more smoke:

> Congress has authorized the use of force against any individuals or countries the President determines to be involved in the attacks, a doctrine that every supporter regards as ultra-criminal. That is easily demonstrated. Simply ask how the same people would have reacted if Nicaragua had adopted this doctrine after the U.S. had rejected the orders of the World Court to terminate its "unlawful use of force" against Nicaragua and had vetoed a Security Council resolution calling on all states to observe international law.

Very well. With regard to Reagan's contra war and the mining of Nicaragua's harbors, Nicaragua and the World Court were in the right, and the United States acted like a rogue nation. How exactly does this prove that "every supporter" regards the use of force as "ultra-criminal" with regard to 11 September?

The fissure on the left that began in 1989 – 90 and became visible in Kosovo is now a chasm. In retrospect, Kosovo didn't have quite the impact on the left it might have, partly because conservatives *also* opposed that operation on the grounds that Clinton had ordered it (by 1999, Clinton could have launched a campaign against childhood diseases and House Republicans would've responded by declaring measles a vegetable and bundling it into school breakfast programs), partly because of Monica, and partly because it was shrouded in murk from Srebrenica to Rambouillet. But many of the most vocal opponents of the U.S.-led NATO intervention in Kosovo are now the most vocal opponents of the U.S.-led intervention in Afghanistan, which suggests two things: first, that the fact of civilian deaths on U.S. soil is in an important sense immaterial to their position on U.S. policy, and second, that on the grounds they offer today, they will never support another American military action of any kind. Permanently alienated by Vietnam, by Chile, by Indonesia, or by Reagan's deadly adventures in Central America, they're gone and they're not coming back, not even if hijackers plow planes into towers in downtown Manhattan.

The right is just gleeful about this, of course, because it needs the Chomskian left for effigies, hate minutes, election-year fund-raising and general vituperation. Christopher Hitchens seems pretty happy as well, since he gets to settle a bunch of old scores and coin acerbic new phrases like "the Milosevic left" and "the Taliban left." But for all my sympathy with Hitchens, I cannot share his sense of exhilaration; instead, as I watch that shard of the left sailing away, I modulate between relief and sorrow. Relief, because the break is decisive and clarifying, highlighting all those who cannot use the word "heroes" without scare quotes, all those who cannot bring themselves to utter anything about freedom and democracy if doing so will make them say words that might also have come from the mouth of a conservative. Sorrow, because there will soon come a time when I am going to miss these people, when I am going to wish they had some clout in domestic politics. Not because I will agree with them, necessarily, but because — unlike liberals — they do not make compromises, and they know how to get mad. Liberals are good at patient deliberation and stress abatement in the Mister Rogers mode, which is why conservatives simply tear them limb from limb whenever anything important — like, say, a presidential election recount in southern Florida — is at stake: while the liberals hold a seminar on the lessons of 1876, Tom DeLay flies in a bunch of goons to stop the recount by force. Liberals like that image of themselves: *So what if those fire-breathing yahoos run the country? At least we've got our sanity and our Birkenstocks.* But for precisely this reason, liberals are not very good at organizing demonstrations and mass protests when the president announces the creation of military tribunals or the abrogation of client-attorney privilege in cases where the client has an al- in his last name. How many liberals stood up and shamed John Ashcroft when he appeared before the Senate on 6 December 2001 and impugned the patriotism of civil libertarians? How many liberals voted against the USA-Patriot Act? How many liberals took to the streets when Bush issued Executive Order 13233, overturning the Presidential Records Act and closing the archives on the Reagan-Bush years? Who's kidding whom? This is just not the kind of thing liberals do these days.

But there's still plenty of mobilizing to do on the domestic front for everyone who prefers democracy to mild totalitarianism, and this should include everyone from William Safire to Katha Pollitt. The narrative of that struggle will doubtless be experimental and self-reflexive and full of postmodern historiographic metafiction in the mode of Ishmael Reed and E. L. Doctorow, but if it's going to be a narrative any of us will want to tell our children at night, first we're going to have to remind liberals how to get good and mad. And we should do it sooner rather than later — that is, before rather than after Ashcroft sets up those new-for-2002 Preventative Detention Camps to keep track of people who show signs of dissenting, demurring, or otherwise disparaging the Department of Justice's good-faith efforts to ensure domestic tranquillity. Because by that time, we won't even be able to tell our stories to our lawyers.

Notes

1. I would go a good deal further than this today and admit that argument five has been borne out spectacularly.

Works Cited

"After Fear" (editorial). *New Republic*, 29 October 2001. Available online at <http://www.tnr.com/102901/editorial102901.html>. Accessed 8 January 2002.
Chomsky, Noam. Interview with Radio B92 (Belgrade). 19 September 2001. Available online at <http://www.b92.net/intervju/eng/2001/0919-chomsky.phtml>. Accessed 8 January 2002.

———. *The New Military Humanism: Lessons from Kosovo*. Monroe, Maine: Common Courage Press, 1999.

———. "Reply to Hitchens." *Nation*, 8 October 2001. Available online at <http://www.thenation.com/doc.mhtml?i=20011015&s=chomsky20011001>. Accessed 9 January 2002.

Coulter, Ann. "This Is War: We Should Invade Their Countries." *National Review*, 13 September 2001. Available online at <http://www.nationalreview.com/coulter/coulter.shtml>. Accessed 7 January 2002.

Foer, Franklin. "Fevered Pitch: Grover Norquist's Strange Alliance with Radical Islam." *New Republic*, 12 November 2001. Available online at <http://www.tnr.com/111201/foer111201.html>. Accessed 7 January 2002.

Goldberg, Jonathan. "L'Affaire Coulter: Goodbye to All That." *National Review Online*, 3 October 2001. Available online at <http://www.nationalreview.com/nr_comment/nr_comment100301.shtml>. Accessed 7 January 2002.

Hall, Stuart. "The Great Moving Right Show." In *The Hard Road to Renewal: Thatcherism and the Crisis of the Left*, 39–56. London: Verso, 1989.

Hitchens, Christopher. "Against Rationalization." *Nation*, 8 October 2001. Available online at <http://www.thenation.com/doc.mhtml?i=20011008&s=hitchens>. Accessed 8 January 2002.

Lowry, Rich. "Against Cruise Missiles: Excuses for Not Taking Serious Action against Our Enemies." *National Review*, 12 September 2001. Available online at <http:www.nationareview.com/lowry/lowry091201.shtml>. Accessed 7 January 2002.

Martin, Jerry L., and Anne D. Neal. *Defending Civilization: How Our Universities Are Failing America and What Can Be Done about It*. Washington, D.C.: American Council of Trustees and Alumni, 2001.

Steele, Shelby. "War of the Worlds: The West Must Stop Apologizing for the Greatness of Our Civilization." *Wall Street Journal Online (Opinion Journal)*, 17 September 2001. Available online at <http://www.opinionjournal.com/extra/?id=95001154>. Accessed 6 January 2002.

Suellentrop, Chris. "What's Osama Talking About?" *Slate*, 8 October 2001. Available online at <http://slate.msn.com/id/1008411>. Accessed 9 January 2002.

Sullivan, Andrew. "Daily Dish." Available online at <http://www.andrewsullivan.com/index.php?dish_inc=archives/2001_09_16_dish_archive.html#5776508>. Accessed 8 January 2002.

Can the Left Get Iraq Right?

[September 2002]

Halfway through George W. Bush's term of office, one year since 9/11, and the ideal of moral clarity in U.S. foreign policy couldn't be murkier. According to Donald Rumsfeld, Paul Wolfowitz, Dick Cheney, and Richard Perle, every moment we postpone war with Iraq damages our credibility; according to Brent Scowcroft, General Anthony Zinni, Lawrence Eagleburger, and James Baker III, nothing would damage our credibility so much as a unilateral, preemptive war on Iraq.

The Bush administration is trying to persuade "allies" like Saudi Arabia to sign up for Gulf War II, but somebody keeps dropping hints to the *Washington Post* that when Iraq goes down, the Rand Corporation will advise the president that the kingdom should go next. On Tuesdays, Thursdays, and Saturdays, administration officials tell the world that they desire nothing more than the liberation of oppressed Iraqis, but on Mondays, Wednesdays, and Fridays, their cheerleaders in the press bellow that what the Islamic world needs now is a crushing, humiliating military defeat that will bring a useful chaos to the part of the world running roughly from the West Bank to Islamabad.

Such is the position of the war party. To gauge by the president's speech to the United Nations last Thursday, the administration actually has a serious case to make against Saddam Hussein's violations of U.N. resolutions, but then again, the administration does not always hold U.N. resolutions in such high regard, and, according to the White House chief of staff, Andrew Card, has waited so long to make its case because August is a bad time for new product placement. And you would think that if the president was having a hard time making his case to the Republican policy elite, let alone the United Nations, it would be a simple matter for the American left to rally popular opposition to the war as well.

You might think that, but you'd be wrong. Most liberals in Congress are either mumbling under their breath or speaking up only to call for a "debate" they themselves are unwilling to begin; the progressive left has been noisier, but the progressive left has its own problems, mired as it is in an Afghanistan quagmire of its own making. It would be a positive service to democracy if left-wing public intellectuals would take the lead where elected liberals cannot or will not, urging their fellow Americans that the war on terrorism requires many things — peace in Israel and Palestine, an end to the long-term U.S. addiction to oil — before it requires any regime change in Iraq. But the left is having some trouble providing that service, because one wing of it actually supports military intervention in Iraq, while another wing opposes all military interventions regardless of their objectives.

The left has been divided before, but rarely has it been at once so vehement and so incoherent as this. On one side are the internationalists who find themselves emboldened by laudable military interventions in Kosovo and Afghanistan, which used U.S. airpower — but not ground troops — to overthrow two of the worst regimes on the planet. Some, like Paul Berman of *Dissent* magazine, have already signed on for another Mission for Good in Iraq, becoming even more hawkish than most of the first Bush administration; others, like Christopher Hitchens, have argued that the United States might do well to consider that "you can't subject the Iraqi people to the cruelty of sanctions for so long while leaving the despot in place." (Hitchens notes that since the United States has intervened on Saddam Hussein's behalf in the past, "there is at least a potential argument that an intervention to cancel such debts would be justifiable." Who could have imagined that Hitchens and his lifelong nemesis Henry Kissinger would wind up sitting on the same fence, each refusing to look at the other?)

On the other side are the anti-imperialists who opposed the war in Afghanistan in stark and unyielding terms. They did not cheer the collapse of the World Trade Center; that is simple slander. But they did argue, to their shame, that the U.S. military response was even more morally odious than the hijackers' deliberate slaughter of civilians. Some antiwar protesters were nineteen-year-old anarchists, some were devout Quakers, and some were Trotskyite diehards, but some were America's most distinguished dissidents at home and abroad, including Howard Zinn and Gore Vidal. And the antiwar left's arguments against war were simply astonishing. As *Z Magazine* contributor Cynthia Peters wrote last October, the operation that wrested control of Afghanistan from al-Qaeda and the Taliban was a "calculated crime against humanity that differs from September 11th only in scale; that is: it is many times larger." Obtuse arguments like these, combined with the paranoid insistence that the United States had long planned strikes against the Taliban to secure an Afghan oil pipeline (a claim thoroughly debunked by Ken Silverstein in *The American Prospect*), have immeasurably damaged the anti-imperialists' cause. The anti-imperialist left correctly believes, for instance, that the American bombing of Kakrak in early July (a massive "intelligence failure" that killed about fifty Afghans attending a wedding party) was an atrocity, but it cannot admit that, on balance, the routing of the Taliban might have struck a blow, however ambiguous and poorly executed, for human freedom.

Accordingly, the *Nation*, the most mainstream of journals on the progressive left, has become remarkably ambivalent about what it means to be a progressive leftist. On one page of its 2 September issue, an unsigned editorial titled "Iraq: The Doubters Grow" asks whether we will leave Iraq in chaos "as we have done in Afghanistan." On the very next page, an editorial by Anthony Borden and John West of the Institute for War and Peace Reporting details the chaos of Kabul yet acknowledges that "conditions are vastly improved from the circumstances of only a few months ago — when the country was plagued by severe persecution and increasing food shortages with seemingly no hope." Perhaps we have not brought disaster to Afghanistan after all; it's hard to tell here. Still further left, the *CounterPunch* and *Z Magazine* stalwarts have kept their self-assurance but have lost their credibility — not with the Bush administration, of course, which had no plans to read Noam Chomsky's complete works before settling on an Iraq policy, but with much of the rest of the progressive left, among whose ranks I include myself.

For leftists like me who had long considered Chomsky as our own beacon of moral clarity, it is hard to say which development is more catastrophic: the fact that Chomsky bashing has become a major political pastime, or the fact that Chomsky has become so very difficult to defend. Chomsky's response to the war in Afghanistan offered a repellent mix of hysteria and hauteur, as in this early interview:

> The U.S. has already demanded that Pakistan terminate the food and other supplies that are keeping at least some of the starving and suffering people of Afghanistan alive. If that demand is implemented, unknown numbers of people who have not the remotest connection to terrorism will die, possibly millions. Let me repeat: the U.S. has demanded that Pakistan kill possibly millions of people who are themselves victims of the Taliban. This has nothing to do even with revenge. It is at a far lower moral level even than that. The significance is heightened by the fact that this is mentioned in passing, with no comment, and probably will hardly be noticed. We can learn a great deal about the moral level of the reigning intellectual culture of the West by observing the reaction to this demand.

By the same token, we can learn a great deal about the moral level of the antiwar left by observing its willingness to debate claims like these; over the past year, unfortunately, Chomsky and his followers have demonstrated rather little capacity for self-criticism. It is apparently not permissible to argue that Chomsky was right about Vietnam, Nicaragua, and East Timor but wrong about Afghanistan; those who fail to acknowledge Chomsky's infallibility about Afghanistan are guilty of thoughtcrime or conservatism, whichever is worse.

The hard left's myopia and intransigence most likely will not matter to most Americans — that is, those who never trusted the judgment of Chomsky or *Z Magazine* in the first place and don't see why it matters now that anti-imperialists have lost a "credibility" they never had in some quarters. But the reason it *should* matter, even in parts of America where there are no campuses, no anti-Sharon rallies, and no subscribers to *CounterPunch*, is that the United States cannot be a beacon of freedom and justice to the world if it conducts itself as an empire. Nor can we fight al-Qaeda networks in sixty countries if we alienate our allies in Europe, who so far seem much more capable of finding and arresting members of al-Qaeda than is our own Justice Department.

The antiwar left once knew well that its anti-imperialism was in fact a form of patriotism — until it lost its bearings in Kosovo and Kabul, insisting beyond all reason that those military campaigns were imperialist wars for oil or regional power. And why does *that* matter? Because in the agora of public opinion, the antiwar left never claimed to speak to pragmatic concerns or political contingencies: for the antiwar left, the moral ground was the only ground there was. So when the antiwar left finds itself on shaky moral ground, it simply collapses.

In foreign affairs, both left and right claim to speak for the conscience of America, but on Iraq the right has no moral clarity and the left has lost its moral compass. This is not a problem for the masters of realpolitik, who have long since inured themselves to the task of doing terrible things to human beings in the course of pursuing the national interest, but it is utterly devastating to those few souls who still dream that the course of human events should be judged — and guided — by principles common to many nations rather than by policies concocted by one. The emergence of the antiwar right, however, may yet hold a lesson for the left, insofar as the antiwar right relies on Brent Scowcroft's internationalism rather than Pat Buchanan's isolationism: the challenge clearly is to learn how to be strenuously anti-imperialist without being indiscriminately antiwar. It is a lesson the American left has never had to learn — until now.[1]

Notes

1. The following week, Noam Chomsky replied to this essay as follows:

> Michael Bérubé condemns my "repellent mix of hysteria and hauteur, as in this early interview: 'The U.S. has already demanded that Pakistan terminate the food and other supplies that are keeping some of the starving and suffering people of Afghanistan alive. If that demand is implemented, unknown numbers of people who have not the remotest connection to terrorism will die.... We can learn a great deal about the moral level of the reigning intellectual culture of the West by observing the reaction to this demand.'" The fact that one might even be willing to debate this outrageous claim illustrates "the hard Left's myopia and intransigence."
>
> He fails to mention, however, that the outrageous claim was not mine. My explicit reference was to *The New York Times*, which reported that Washington "demanded . . . the elimination of truck convoys that provide much of the food and other supplies to Afghanistan's civilian population," and that millions were at risk of starvation, and a month later reported estimates by UN and other aid agencies that "7.5 million Afghans will need food over the winter — 2.5 million more than on Sept. 11."
>
> I don't agree that *The New York Times* and the aid agencies are guilty of a "repellent mix of hysteria and hauteur." And I do think we learn a good deal by the reaction to these reports, then and now.

Note Chomsky's ellipsis in the first paragraph, which, by deleting precisely the language to which I had objected in my essay (about how the war in Afghanistan is at "a far lower moral level" even than revenge for 9/11), is either sly or simply dishonest. Ignoring that ellipsis, however, my reply, which appeared with Chomsky's letter in the *Boston Globe* on 22 September 2002, pointed out that Chomsky had not seen fit to revise his estimate of the millions of Afghan dead to take into account the fact that millions of Afghans were not dead:

> [Chomsky's] most recent essay on the subject, dated July 2002, continues to protest the interruption of the aid convoys, *even after the fall of the Taliban and the resumption of aid to Afghan civilians*. Calling this action "genocide" is precisely the kind of political abuse of language against which Chomsky protested so eloquently 30 years ago.
>
> I count myself among those leftists who were, at first, deeply conflicted about the strikes against Afghanistan, and who remain utterly unconvinced that the Bush administration initiated those strikes out of any concern for Afghan schoolgirls. But the outcome of that war, ambiguous and incomplete as it is, should have provoked many more leftists, including Chomsky, to rethink their willingness to indict the United States of war crimes at the very outset and to consider whether the fall of the Taliban might not have been worth the temporary interruption of aid convoys.

I stand by that reply today.

Works Cited

Borden, Anthony, and John West. "Stirrings in Kabul." *Nation*, 2 September 2002. Available online at <http://www.thenation.com/doc.mhtml?i=20020902&s=borden>. Accessed 6 September 2002.

Chomsky, Noam. Interview with Radio B92 (Belgrade). 19 September 2001. Available online at <http://www.b92.net/intervju/eng/2001/0919-chomsky.phtml>. Accessed 8 January 2002.

———. Letter to the Editor. *Boston Globe*, 22 September 2002, D5.

Hitchens, Christopher. "Macbeth in Mesopotamia." *Nation*, 19 August 2002. Available online at <http://www.thenation.com/doc.mhtml%3Fi=20020819&s=hitchens>. Accessed 4 September 2002.

"Iraq: The Doubters Grow" (editorial). *Nation*, 2 September 2002. Available online at <http://www.thenation.com/doc.mhtml?i=20020902&s=editors>. Accessed 6 September 2002.

Peters, Cynthia. "It's Simple. It's Not So Simple." *Z Magazine Online (ZNet)*, October 2001. Available online at <http://www.zmag.org/peterssimple.htm>. Accessed 24 October 2001.

Ricks, Thomas E. "Briefing Depicted Saudis as Enemies: Ultimatum Urged to Pentagon Board." *Washington Post*, 6 August 2002, A1. Available online at <http://www.washingtonpost.com/ac2/wp-dyn/A47913-2002Aug5?language=printer>. Accessed 18 August 2002.

Silverstein, Ken. "No War for Oil! Is the United States Really after Afghanistan's Resources? Not a Chance." *American Prospect* 13, no. 14 (22 July 2002). Available online at <http://www.prospect.org/print/V13/14/silverstein-k.html>. Accessed 4 August 2002.

For a Better — and Broader — Antiwar Movement

[November 2002]

Now that Iraq has agreed to allow weapons inspectors back into the country, opponents of war with Iraq will have to begin fine-tuning their arguments against invasion. Do we approve of the U.N. Security Council resolution that is sending inspectors in, or do we dismiss the U.N. vote as a mere fig leaf for American hegemony? If we agree that the viability of the United Nations depends in part on its willingness to enforce its resolutions, do we continue to oppose a war if Saddam does not disarm by February? Beneath those questions simmers a debate that has been nagging leftist and liberal intellectuals in recent months: What should we make of recent charges that our largest rallies and demonstrations to date have been led by unreconstructed communist-front groups?

It's an important debate, even if the politics are arcane and the accusations overdrawn; the legitimacy and the direction of the antiwar movement are at stake. To answer the questions is to define what the antiwar movement is *for*.

The charges of communist infiltration give me a poignant sense of déjà vu. One fine spring day in 1982, I was sitting with nearly a million people in New York City's Central Park, demonstrating in favor of a freeze on nuclear weapons. Although I was only twenty at the time, I had a somewhat elaborate position on nuclear policy for my age cohort: I agreed with most antinuclear activists that the MX missile was expensive and useless except as a first-strike weapon, but I departed from antinuke orthodoxy in believing that nuclear weapons launched from submarines were a good deterrent. A Soviet strike could knock out land-based missiles in their silos, I reasoned, and Reagan's plan to deploy Pershing missiles in West Germany would give Moscow only six minutes to respond to an attack — or to determine that their launch-detection systems were in error.

The MX and Pershing missiles, therefore, seemed to me to be destabilizing weapons systems. By contrast, submarine-based weapons were a good deterrent force: too inaccurate to be reliable first-strike weapons but impossible to locate and preempt and, therefore, perfect as retaliatory weapons. If the United States would vow not to initiate a first strike and would maintain a credible submarine deterrent, I thought, that would be good enough for me.

Needless to say, that position put me at odds with many of my fellow demonstrators, who were carrying signs like "One Nuclear Bomb Can Ruin Your Entire Day" and "Arms Are for Hugging." Young thing that I was, I was fairly proud of the fact that my position on nuclear arms couldn't fit on a placard. At the time, however, there was no need to rehearse my differences with anyone on the antinuclear left. The previous year, the Reagan administration had announced that it would consider launching a "warning" nuclear strike in Europe if the Soviet Union invaded West Germany, and defense hawks were arguing that we should embark on an aggressive antisatellite program, even though the United States relied more heavily on satellite information than did the Soviets. The times were urgent, so my friends and I went to Central Park to demonstrate, and we didn't think too much about who was organizing the rally.

Of course, we had read in the *New York Times* that Secretary of Defense Caspar Weinberger had dismissed the demonstration before it had even begun on the grounds that the nuclear-freeze movement was led by Soviet agents and sympathizers. But that dismissal was a source of much amusement in my crowd, which did not, in fact, contain a single Soviet agent or sympathizer. "Caspar, dude," said one of my friends, taking an imaginary hit from an imaginary joint and talking like a stoner trying not to exhale, "like, we're just listening to some Jackson Browne, man."

TWENTY YEARS LATER, the left has begun organizing mass demonstrations against a war in Iraq. But who's doing the organizing? For the 6 October rally in New York, a group called Not in Our Name, behind which one can find Refuse and Resist!, which in turn has ties to the Revolutionary Communist Party. For the 26 October rally in Washington, a group called Act Now to Stop War and End Racism (ANSWER), run out of Ramsey Clark's International Action Center, itself a front for the Workers World Party. The groups involved in the demonstrations thus carry some heavy far left baggage. The Workers World Party was formed in 1959 to support the Soviet invasion of Hungary and protest Khrushchev's revelations of Stalin's crimes. The Revolutionary Communist Party is known for its support of Peru's Shining Path and of the Chinese Communist Party's 1989 massacre of prodemocracy demonstrators in Tiananmen Square. Ramsey Clark himself, of course, has become notable in recent years for being cochair of the International Committee to Defend Slobodan Milosevic, and Clark's International Action Center is a strenuous supporter of North Korea. Suffice it to say that these people aren't just sitting around listening to Jackson Browne.

But does that mean that the anti-war-in-Iraq rallies themselves are tainted by association with groups so bizarrely far left as to be friendly to fascist mass murderers? Most antiwar protesters say that only far right hawks like David Horowitz would think so. All the same, many liberals and progressives I know have refused to have anything to do with any event organized by ANSWER or Not in Our Name; many other liberals and many people farther left have decried the politics of such organizations but have argued either that (1) extremist groups naturally leap to the fore at the outset and then are superseded by more mainstream forces or that (2) in the battle for public opinion, it doesn't matter who organizes a rally so much as who attends it.

Surely, they say, the one hundred thousand people who thronged the National Mall in Washington on 26 October were a more powerful voice against war than the two or three dozen Milosevic/Shining Path fans in their midst. And who else is doing the labor to get one hundred thousand people in one place?

Personally, I find it disingenuous to argue that the politics of a sponsoring organization are immaterial to the nature of the event. Quite apart from the tactical questions of whether a group like the International Action Center or Refuse and Resist! will alienate mainstream Americans who are skeptical about a war in Iraq, and whether the antiwar movement will lack credibility as a result, it is hard to imagine that serious leftists and liberals would make that kind of argument if, say, a group called Nudists against War were sponsoring major rallies (you know, with slogans like "Say NAW to Bush"). Any antiwar demonstration headed by NAW certainly would lack a certain, how shall I say, gravitas — and yet the major difference between the nudists and the Workers World Party, I think, is that the nudists would be rather more benign and, of course, would carry far less baggage.

Then again, antiwar activists don't always have the luxury of waiting around until the right organizing committee comes along. On college campuses, especially, groups such as ANSWER are sometimes the only antiwar game in town, and it's hard to convince twenty-year-old leftists — versions of my younger self — that they should shun their local antiwar organizers because cousins of the great-uncles of the organizers' ancestors supported the Soviet crackdown on Hungary in 1956. Campus leftists thus find themselves caught between two competing and compelling injunctions. On one hand, antiwar veterans such as sociologist Todd Gitlin have argued persuasively that alliances with ANSWER and Not in Our Name will only damage the antiwar cause beyond repair. On the other hand, hard-core leftists including writer Ron Jacobs, in an article in *CounterPunch*, have argued that "Mr. Gitlin and his compatriots, who, whether they like it or not, are today's liberal establishment, are replicating the sins of their fathers in their rebuke of any group with a red tinge in the antiwar movement."

Most of the antiwar advocates I know are patriots who sincerely believe that unilateral war with Iraq is deeply inimical to short-term U.S. economic interests and long-term national security, and none of us want to relive the fate of the fence-sitting social democrats of the 1960s, who divided their time between denouncing the war in Vietnam and denouncing the denouncers of the war in Vietnam. Like Kafka's hunger artist, the anti-antiwar left of the 1960s never did find a food it would deign to eat. We do not want to make the same mistake.

And yet I find that even as I have deep respect for all the tens of thousands of people who have signed a September "Statement of Conscience," put out by Not in Our Name to oppose war in Iraq, I cannot quite join them, even though I, too, oppose the war (and endorse most of the statement). Partly that's because the statement condemns the U.S. strikes in Afghanistan, which killed civilians and failed to capture Osama bin Laden but which also destroyed the al-Qaeda terror camps, brought down the Taliban, and (even more important) slowed down the growing radicalization of Pakistan — a radicalization that, ideally, should be opposed by all secular democrats. It's on these latter grounds that I supported the war in Afghanistan.

But mostly I cannot sign Not in Our Name's statement because it declares, in its third sentence, "We believe that peoples and nations have the right to determine their own destiny, free from military coercion by great powers." It's a euphonious phrase to some ears, but what happens, may I ask, when a "nation" decides that its "destiny" lies in the extermination of a "people?" The sentence reads like a leftover shibboleth from Kosovo, when one wing of the antiwar left devised the argument that the United States and NATO had no business intervening in a matter internal to Serbian affairs. That antiwar faction crafted a new "sovereignty" rationale that, in my opinion, turned its back on decades of left internationalism in order to oppose U.S. military action in Kosovo in whatever terms came most readily to hand.[1]

The appeal to "sovereignty" sounds fine to many leftists when it's a question of defending developing nations from the United States (nations that should be "free from military coercion by great powers"). But should that principle be applied when Saddam Hussein kills Iraqi Kurds? Or when Milosevic kills Kosovar Albanians? Or when Suharto kills the East Timorese, or Rios Montt the indigenous Guatemalan Indians, or Hitler the Jews? Nazi Germany saw the killing of Jews as absolutely central to its "destiny," but one would not want to have seen a sane and serious left defending the enterprise on those grounds. I would prefer to see great powers exercising military coercion to prevent such nations from determining their own destiny (especially in cases like Suharto and Montt, whose regimes the United States had *supported*), and I would be all the happier if the great powers did so in my name.

I HAVE DEAR and trusted friends who tell me that I'm reading the Not in Our Name statement far too closely, that I'm turning into a caricature of a literary theorist parsing the textual resonances and antecedents of a document whose primary purpose is simply to rouse people to action. The charge hits home: perhaps I am just an armchair activist, sitting at home in my study, jawing over the fine points of texts, when I should be organizing teach-ins and rallies. After all, on some accounts, the antiwar movement in the Vietnam era began with a handful of loopy Maoists and did not win the hearts and minds of most Americans until the early 1970s. And we forget all too easily just how courageous it was for Martin Luther King Jr. to declare that he wasn't gonna study war no more at a time when the declaration placed him far to the left of establishment opinion.

But sometimes even armchair activists have their place. I believe the legitimacy of the leading antiwar groups is a real issue, for two crucial reasons. The first is pragmatic: the antiwar movement is never going to be a mass movement if it is led by defenders of Milosevic and the Shining Path. The second is moral: it would be a terrible dereliction of duty if American intellectuals, whether in their studies or on the streets, failed to ask about Americans' rationale for opposing this war.

It is true that, if we set forth everyone's last scruple and caveat about Iraq (just as if we had laid out our positions on nuclear weapons, nuclear deterrence, nuclear power, and nuclear subs twenty years ago), the left would find itself demonstrating in groups of two or three. And it is true that, at the moment, there are powerful temptations to finer and finer parsings of differences internal to the left, whereby some leftists can craft "pure" and/or "pragmatic" positions by criticizing other leftists' excessively "pure" and/or "pragmatic" positions. That seems an especially pointless enterprise today, when the truly significant danger, for any antiwar advocate, isn't the Workers World Party or Revolutionary Communist Party: it's the fact that the Republican Party controls the White House and Congress, while the Democratic Party is rudderless and leaderless — "in its worst shape since 1928," as historian Sean Wilentz wrote in *Salon*, "and there's no FDR even remotely in sight."

But there is also a powerful temptation for leftist-liberal intellectuals and activists, when they are as marginalized as they are today, to become indiscriminate about whom they hang out with. So while there is a crying need for a broad-based antiwar movement that mobilizes against the Bush plan for unilateral preemptive action anywhere in the world, there is also a crying need for a principled, rigorous antiwar rationale that pays Iraqi dissidents in exile the respect of taking seriously their long-standing desire for "regime change" and likewise takes seriously the possibility that Saddam Hussein will not really cooperate with U.N. inspections and will seek to develop and deploy weapons of mass destruction.

Such an antiwar movement would argue against an arrogant and counterproductive U.S. unilateralism. It would distrust U.S. claims to be acting on behalf of oppressed Iraqis on the grounds that the Cheney/Rumsfeld/ Perle axis showed no interest in oppressed Iraqis before now and has already demonstrated its remarkable indifference to nation-building on behalf of oppressed Afghans in Afghanistan. But the movement would base those arguments on an appeal to internationalism rather than on appeals to national sovereignty. Thereby, it would insist that the best alternative to war, an alternative that would accurately and appropriately express international opposition to Saddam Hussein's regime, would consist of the "smart sanctions" that Colin Powell had championed — to little fanfare and less avail — in the early months of the Bush administration. As for those prowar advocates who claim that Saddam cannot be effectively "contained" because he is so much more irrational than Stalin and Mao, my sense is that those critics have far too high an opinion of Stalin and Mao.

The Persian Gulf war sanctions against Saddam have clearly failed on every count, since they have hardened Arab opinion against the United States and killed innocent civilians even as they have allowed the dictator to starve his people and smuggle in military equipment. Just as clearly, the "no war, no sanctions" faction of the antiwar left is operating under the delusion that all of Saddam's past crimes can somehow be laid at the feet of the United States. The ideal antiwar movement, for me, would be one that could answer both the claims of ANSWER, by offering a principled opposition to U.S. hegemony, and the demands of prowar liberals, by insisting that Iraqis would benefit more from peaceful "regime change" than from invasion and bombing. The movement would consist of people who oppose U.S. unilateralism strongly enough to denounce it, and those who oppose Saddam Hussein strongly enough to want to depose him by nonmilitary means. Such an antiwar movement would be, I believe, mature, legitimate, and defensible. And it might just be broadly popular as well.

Notes

1. In response to this point, Ed Herman wrote the following on *ZNet*:

Tapping Bérubé's article on "Toward an Ideal Antiwar Movement," let me enumerate the reasons why it is entirely reasonable to describe Bérubé as a supporter of the imminent war against Iraq. First, he denounces the statement that "we believe that peoples and nations have the right to determine their own destiny free from military coercion by great powers." Bérubé says that the "antiwar faction crafted a new 'sovereignty' rationale . . . that turned its back on decades of left internationalism. . . ." This is complete nonsense, as the "sovereignty rationale" goes back many years and is the basis of international law and the UN (Article 2.1 of the UN Charter says "The organization is based on the principle of the sovereign equality of all its Members.") By "left internationalism" he means cruise missile left and imperial state rejection of that nonintervention principle. Given this rejection, the imperial powers and cruise missile leftists are not disturbed by blatant disregard for the UN Charter and international law in these interventions.

Imagine a mid-1930s "left" organized around the principle that what happens inside Franco's sovereign Spain is none of our business, and you'll have a fair sense of Herman's value as a left intellectual. As for his ham-fisted attempt to construe my opposition to war in Iraq as a form of support for war in Iraq, all I can say is that I am happy that Mr. Herman does not have the power to conduct show trials.

Works Cited

Herman, Edward S. "Much More Severe Problems on the Cruise Missile Left: Herman Responds to Bérubé." *Z Magazine Online (ZNet)*, 9 December 2002. Available online at <http://zmag.org/content/showarticle.cfm?SectionID= 11&ItemID=2722>. Accessed 9 December 2002.

Jacobs, Ron. "Todd Gitlin Does the Bossman's Work: Redbaiting the Antiwar Movement." *CounterPunch*, 17 October 2002. Available online at <http://www .counterpunch.org/jacobs1017.html>. Accessed 4 November 2002.

Wilentz, Sean. "Salon's Exit Poll: What Lamott, Sullivan, Gitlin, Wilentz, and Others Make of the Republican Sweep." Available online at <http://archive .salon.com/politics/feature/2002/11/06/poll>. Accessed 7 November 2002.

I am among the roughly 289.9 million Americans who had never heard of Islamic radical theorist Sayyid Qutb before 11 September 2001. I did not know about the existence of the Muslim Brotherhood or the history of Wahhabism. I was aware of Islamist radicalism only in a kind of loose and scattered way, from the Iranian Revolution to the assassination of Anwar Sadat to the emergence of the mujahideen in Afghanistan to the fatwa issued against the *Satanic Verses* and finally to the al-Qaeda bombings of the late 1990s. In all honesty, though, I had not kept track of Islamist developments in Nigeria, Algeria, Pakistan, Indonesia, and the Sudan.

But in the weeks and months after 11 September, I knew just enough to know this: most of my compatriots on the American left who were urging their fellow citizens to put that day's attacks "in context" didn't know very much about Islamist radicalism either. No one on the left, to my knowledge, truly *blamed* America for the attacks; whereas a few Christian fundamentalists such as Pat Robertson and Jerry Falwell agreed that we'd had it coming, most leftists condemned the murder of innocents on American soil — whether sincerely or furiously or perfunctorily, according to their desires and their degrees of sympathy for the dead and the grieving. Still, when the American left asked about the "root causes" of the attacks, almost without exception, they read from a script with which I was thoroughly familiar: the ugly tale of American imperialism, from the CIA's overthrow of Mossadeq to U.S. support for the Shah and his secret police, the Carter/Reagan arming of the Afghan mujahideen, and the Reagan/Bush arming and whitewashing and then demonizing of Iraq. Many leftists seemed quite sure that the attacks had something to do with the growth of the Israeli right and the steady expansion of the settlements in the Occupied Territories, just as most conservatives were sure that the attacks had something to do with what they called the "appeasement" of Arafat. In short, as far as these critics were concerned, to put 11 September in context, you didn't need to know about the history of political Islam since Kemal Ataturk's dismantling of the caliphate or the arguments mounted in Qutb's *In the Shade of the Qu'ran*. In fact, you didn't need to know very much about at all about the actual beliefs of the people who ordered and carried out the attacks as long as you knew about American and Israeli actions in the Mideast.

Over the course of the following months, I learned that al-Qaeda and its friends were not a ragtag bunch of bomb throwers but rather a deadly serious global network; that their ideological leaders were learned, deeply committed men who wanted to extend sharia law across the globe; that they held liberal democracies beneath contempt and regarded the United States as a paper tiger that would collapse when met with sustained resistance; and that they favored stonings, public executions, and a form of violent, ultrareligious patriarchy so extreme as to outdo even the most vicious and visionary theocrats yet produced by the Bible Belt — that is, the domestic fundamentalists I'd scorned my entire life. These Islamists were freedom fighters, all right, but they were not fighting *for* freedom, seeking to throw off the yoke of Western oppression and establish true democracy; on the contrary, they were fighting *against* freedom, against everything I like about democratic freedoms, and they were doing it worldwide. I gradually decided that people who believe in the promises of liberal democracy should oppose Islamist radicalism just as they would oppose Christian radicalism, and that in the case of the Taliban and its terror-training camps, this opposition should include (but should not be limited to) the use of military force.

In the curious parlance of certain American leftists, my view is not understood as "fighting against violent, ultrareligious patriarchy." It is understood as "moving to the right."

PAUL BERMAN, they say, has moved to the right as well — and judging from his recent reception among the neocons who now run U.S. foreign policy, they may have a point. But the American right is interested in Berman's conclusions, not in his analysis; for the most part, they could not care less about Berman's interpretation of Sayyid Qutb or the way Berman links Islamist radicalism to European totalitarianism. With the exception of a few true believers like Paul Wolfowitz, they don't even really care that Berman has become a warrior for liberal democracy. All they care about is that Berman supported the war on Iraq — and, gauging from a few of the passages in the latter half of *Terror and Liberalism*, might be game for similar wars on Iran and Saudi Arabia as well. Whereas I, from my precarious perch on the plank of the American left that supported war against the Taliban but opposed war on Iraq while acknowledging the desirability of Saddam Hussein's removal, have almost precisely the opposite response to Berman's book: I like his analysis of terrorism but disagree with some of his central conclusions.

Berman deserves praise for his reading of Qutb, which, as many reviewers have already noted, provides *Terror and Liberalism* with its most important and compelling chapters. But more than this, Berman deserves praise for putting the attacks "in context" from the perspective of the attackers — and for refusing to construe Islamism as a form of belief utterly alien to Western thought. Quite the contrary: what makes *Terror and Liberalism* so valuable a contribution to post-9/11 debate is its insistence that the machinery of Islamist terror and its cult of death was first assembled in Europe, and that Islamism must be seen not as a counter to but as a continuation of the strands of antiliberal European thought responsible for the major cataclysms of the twentieth century. I will not pretend to have learned enough in the past two years to be able to determine if Berman is doing justice to the many strands of Islamic thought. Instead, I will briefly paraphrase his argument about Western secular modernity and its discontents, and then proceed to take issue with the conclusions he draws from this argument.

Berman does not rely on the term "modernity," but it is nonetheless central to his argument. Berman prefers "liberalism," which he describes as "the tolerant idea that every sphere of human activity — science, technology, politics, religion, and private life — should operate independently of the others, without trying to yoke everything together under a single guiding hand" (37). Likewise, Berman does not use the word "secularism," but he makes it clear that liberalism begins with the separation of church and state: "The churches, from their place in private life, would be free to bestow blessings and curses. But they would not be able to enforce their blessings and curses by calling out the police. The state, by contrast, would be free to call out the police — but would not have the power to bestow blessings and curses" (80). From these premises follow all those quaint, hopeful nineteenth-century beliefs in the power of human reason, human progress, human emancipation . . . all the beliefs wrecked by the carnage of the First World War, and all the beliefs rejected by the children of modernity who loathed liberalism and devoted themselves instead to what Berman calls "an irrationalist cult of death and murder" (40) that first took hold among Europeans — from dotty Russian anarchists to crazed German chancellors. One of the key features of Western modernity, Berman argues (and he is not alone here), is that it produced its own most virulent opposition. It should come as no surprise that in the wake of the organized slaughter of tens of millions in Europe, some of Western modernity's most irrational and virulent ideas would have found their way to Egypt and points east.

Because Berman's narrative is a history of ideas, and because it insists so strenuously on the Western origins of terrorism and totalitarianism, *Terror and Liberalism* sometimes makes it sound as if Osama bin Laden and Mohammed Atta came to us, via Qutb, by way of D. H. Lawrence and Martin Heidegger. Indeed, readers of Berman could be forgiven for getting the impression that the fate of the world hinges on the outcome of the battle between partisans of Charles Baudelaire and partisans of Walt Whitman. Writing in the *Washington Monthly*, Joshua Micah Marshall suggested that Berman may have given into what Marshall calls the "Orwellian temptation" — that is, the temptation to "take momentous, morally serious questions and make them out to be slightly more momentous and world-historical than they really are." I think it is still much too soon to tell whether Berman is, as Marshall tentatively suggests, "*overstating* the danger of radical Islam." But it might well be the case that Berman is overstating the danger of radical poets and philosophers, or making poets and philosophers more determinative of momentous, morally serious questions than they really are. Call it the Heideggerian temptation.

That, however, is not my principal criticism of *Terror and Liberalism*. I think it makes every kind of sense for Berman to take on the intellectual legacy of Islamist radicalism, and it makes every kind of sense for Berman to dig where the soil seems to be richest, in the writings of Qutb. And of course, ideas do have consequences, particularly when the ideas in question involve stories about a group of people who can regain a lost purity and/or achieve dreams of global hegemony only by purging the globe of unbelievers without and craven accommodationists within. In linking Islamism to Leninism and Nazism, Berman's keen eye and his flair for the counterintuitive are at their best.

Rather, my caveats have to do with the second half of Berman's book, in which Berman turns from being a reliable guide to modernity's discontents to being a less than reliable guide to world events since 11 September. The most problematic of Berman's claims, I think, is his insistence that in 2002 world opinion sided with Palestinians in direct proportion to the frequency and deadliness of Palestinian suicide attacks: according to Berman, "[T]he high tide of the terrorist attacks, in the early months of 2002, proved to be the very moment when, around the world, large numbers of people felt impelled to express their fury at the Israelis" (*Terror* 142). For Berman, this suggests two things: one, that "the titillations of murder and suicide" (*Terror* 143), the allure of the cult of death, called forth a grisly worldwide sympathy vote for suicide bombings. And two, that well-meaning, fuzzy-headed liberals and leftists, not realizing quite what was at stake in the struggle against Islamist terror, were once again replaying the role of the French antiwar socialists in the 1930s, the Paul-Fauristes, who had somehow talked themselves into believing that the "truest danger" came not from Hitler and the Nazis but "from the warmongers and arms manufacturers of France itself, as well as from the other great powers" (*Terror* 125).

That's not the way I remember recent history — and until now I have not written about the question of the Occupied Territories, being one of those depressed American leftists who believe that a fateful corner was turned after 1995 when Israel did not crack down on its own death cultists, the ones who'd just murdered Yitzhak Rabin. Still, I remember Arafat leaving Barak and Clinton twisting at Camp David, I remember the beginning of Intifada II, and I remember world opinion turning sharply against the Palestinian Authority at a result, so much so that by late 2001 it seemed that the remaining members of the land-for-peace Israeli left could fit inside . . . well, not quite inside a phone booth, but perhaps inside an issue of a progressive Jewish bimonthly magazine. Berman remembers the boycotts of Israeli scholars; I remember scholars around the world condemning the boycotts. Berman remembers the world joining in solidarity with Palestinians as they blew up nightclubs and pizza parlors; I remember that the expressions of solidarity with Palestinians depended not on the actions of Palestinians, which were horrifying, but on the actions of Ariel Sharon, which some observers insisted on seeing as still more horrifying. I am not saying that I shared that reaction myself: my own sympathy with the Palestinian cause was deeply damaged by Arafat's refusal to negotiate at Camp David. I believe that both things are true — that Sharon is a war criminal *and* that Arafat helped to elect a war criminal by walking away from Barak (if Arafat did not know he was doing so, he was incompetent; if he did know it, he was something worse). And I agree that 9/11 helped to flush out some serious anti-Semitism, here and in Europe, that had been hiding under the banner of peace and justice. But I believe it is a severe misjudgment to think that half the world is half in love with suicide bombing, and that those of us who still consider the Palestinian cause a just one are secretly thrilled rather than repelled and disgusted by the second Intifada and the tactics of its foot soldiers.

As for those antiwar French socialists, this is a story Berman has told before; indeed, it runs through his work over the past ten years. "Political correctness," on his 1992 account (an account I contested with some bitterness at the time), wasn't simply the work of fussy campus bureaucrats and their foolish speech codes; it was a world historical phenomenon, "the fog that arises from American liberalism's encounter with the iceberg of French cynicism" (*Debating* 24). In *A Tale of Two Utopias*, Berman told a similar story, of the good-hearted, naive kids in SDS (Students for a Democratic Society) unable to realize when their democratic movement had been taken over by a motley assortment of thugs left over from the days of the Third International. In *Terror and Liberalism*, it's the anti-imperialist/neo-isolationist left, unable to imagine any evil greater than that of George W. Bush and his allies at Enron and Halliburton, and unwilling to entertain the possibility that the fight against violent, ultrareligious patriarchy abroad might be tied to the fight against violent, ultrareligious patriarchy in the United States.

In one sense, I'm glad that Berman has found a target worthy of this analysis: the idea that campus PC could be explained by analogy to Stalinism struck me as unserious, whereas I think Berman is right to claim that some addled leftists, in the United States and elsewhere, have no idea what they're dealing with in al-Qaeda — and have taken every opportunity to demonstrate that they have exceptionally poor political judgment as well. My favorite example, among those leftists still taken seriously in campus circles (if nowhere else), is Edward Herman's insistence (in late 2001, no less) that "the idea that the Taliban is a fascist and expansionist threat, and that Islamic fundamentalism more broadly speaking is the same, doesn't hold water."[1] One wonders just how far Islamists would have to reach — beyond, say, Kabul, Lagos, New York, Madrid, London, and Bali — before Herman would consider them "expansionist," and how many more Muslims they would have to kill before Herman would consider them sufficiently dangerous to warrant attention from the left.

But in another sense, oddly enough, Berman's account is unsatisfying not because of its description of liberalism's enemies (which is riveting) or of the softheadedness of certain "hard" leftists (which is overdrawn but all too necessary). Instead, what I find unsatisfying is Berman's account of democracy. Berman tends to confine his discussion of democracy to political institutions — what he rather breezily calls "free elections, political parties, opposition newspapers, a system to defend individual freedom, and that sort of thing" (*Terror* 162) — and an occasional and undetailed invocation of human rights. I'm willing to fight for the ideals of liberal democracy, but I'd like them to be enunciated more carefully and more robustly than this. I'd prefer instead to premise liberalism on the ideal of participatory parity among democratic citizens, and I'd insist that participatory parity cannot be approached, let alone achieved, unless a society first agrees that certain human rights — to food, education, shelter, and health care — are so fundamental to human flourishing that access to them should not be rendered subject to individuals' abilities to pay for them.

It is this conception of democracy that leads me to oppose Islamist radicalism, and to oppose — though in a different register — the conservative and libertarian opponents of democracy in the United States. It is this conception of democracy that leads me to insist that I will not trust those who subvert democracy here (whether by rigging elections in Florida in late 2000 or by rounding up Iranian American émigrés in Los Angeles in late 2002) to bring democracy to the Middle East. And it is this conception of democracy that leads me to suggest that Berman is quite mistaken to argue, in closing, that "we need a new radicalism to press Bush to explain the stakes more clearly and to offer political solutions to people around the world who might otherwise become our enemies" (*Terror* 208). What follows from Berman's muscular analysis of Islamism, I would think, should not be a resolution to render George W. Bush a more eloquent and diplomatic spokesperson for the virtues of liberal modernity; rather, what follows from Berman's analysis should be a resolution to replace Bush — by democratic means — with someone more likely to foster the democratic ideal of participatory parity at home and abroad. My position may still imply a kind of soft, liberal imperialism — a determination, in Berman's spirited closing words, to be "for the freedom of others" (*Terror* 210) regardless of whether those others are currently claiming they want nothing to do with freedom. But it has one important advantage — namely, that it does not put lovers of liberal democracy in the position of resting their hopes on leaders who despise liberals.

Notes

1. Because Herman wrote this passage in the course of a listserv exchange on the Marxism mailing list (see Herman), some readers might get the impression that it is a merely casual utterance, rather than an integral part of Herman's worldview. For those skeptical readers, I want to provide more of the context of Herman's eight-hundred-word letter. The paragraph following the passage I've cited reads as follows:

> The Taliban is a nasty local authoritarian group with very modest power and capabilities — before the U.S. attack, barely able to cope with controlling its own terrain. As I noted, proof of its "transnational designs" by reference to its infiltration of the Pakistan military is laughable — as if every country does not mess around with its neighbors; and no transnational designs are seen by Hitchens in the case of the United States as it buys up Pakistan generals, because its imperial and "humanitarian" service he now applauds, and as an apologist for imperialism he takes its transnational designs as an internalized given. The general ideology of the Taliban and Islamic fundamentalists are no more proof of expansionism than any other ideology, like the Christian, Jewish, or communism [*sic*]. The new

Hitchens, transplanted back into the 1960s and 1970s, would have claimed that communist ideology proved "transnational designs" and he would have supporting the "war against communism" and the "Red fascists."

Herman does not fail to denounce the Taliban as a "nasty local authoritarian group," it is true, but I find remarkable his characterization of the group as "barely able to cope with controlling its own terrain." The picture of the Taliban struggling manfully to achieve sovereignty over "its" terrain is bizarre on its face, but is especially repugnant when one stops to reflect on what Taliban "control" entailed for women, nonbelievers, artists, and innocent statues. And the idea that Taliban interference in Pakistan is to be dismissed on the grounds that every country "mess[es] around with its neighbors" is stunningly insouciant. Here, the prospect of al-Qaeda obtaining access to nuclear weapons is rendered as just a bit of ordinary border-nation jostling and fooling around, like, you know, the way Norway messes with Sweden and Suriname messes with Brazil.

Works Cited

American Civil Liberties Union. "Southern CA Civil Rights Groups Call for End to Misguided 'Special Registration' Program for Non-Immigrant Visa Holders." 19 December 2002. Available online at <http://www.aclu.org/SafeandFree/SafeandFree.cfm?ID=11520&c=206>. Accessed 29 June 2002.

Berman, Paul. *A Tale of Two Utopias: The Political Journey of the Generation of 1968.* New York: Norton, 1996.

———. *Terror and Liberalism.* New York: Norton, 2003.

———, ed. *Debating PC: The Controversy over Political Correctness on College Campuses.* New York: Dell, 1992.

Herman, Edward S. "Edward Herman Replies to David Schweickart's Report on a Meeting for Hitchens." Marxism mailing list, 4 December 2001. Available online at <http://archives.econ.utah.edu/archives/marxism/2002/msg01859.htm>. Accessed 8 June 2003.

Marshall, Joshua Micah. "The Orwell Temptation: Are Intellectuals Overthinking the Middle East?" *Washington Monthly,* May 2003. Available online at <http://www.washingtonmonthly.com/features/2003/0305.marshall.html>. Accessed 22 June 2003.

The Loyalties of American Studies

[June 2004]

In the America of George Bush and John Ashcroft, Fox News television and Clear Channel radio, political dissent has not been criminalized, but it has been widely stigmatized. The master trope of the Bush administration is that of loyalty: criticism and dissent, for this White House, are simply forms of disloyalty and must be punished. This trope governs the Bush administration's approach to governance regardless of whether its critics are former cabinet members and counterterrorism experts such as Paul O'Neill and Richard Clarke, political independents such as Vermont Senator Jim Jeffords, or popular entertainers such as the Dixie Chicks. In the Bush lexicon, it would appear, the phrase "loyal opposition" is filed under "oxymorons," as if the interests of the Bush-Cheney White House were coextensive with the parameters of patriotic political speech in the United States. Accordingly, some dissenters in the United States have given up on the language of patriotism altogether, on the grounds that it is owned by the political right and articulated to discourses of American exceptionalism, religious fundamentalism, and frenetic public flag waving. As an academic field, American studies has long had a productively ambivalent relation to discourses of patriotism. However, in the current political climate, ambivalent relations to discourses of American patriotism, no matter how productive, risk being construed by the state as disloyalty *to* the state. The question of loyalty has thus taken on a new urgency in American studies.

For the past quarter century or more, American studies has been closely identified with the political left in the United States. And for the past quarter century or more, Republican administrations and conservative intellectuals in American civil society have made a point of disparaging and harassing scholarly fields associated with the political left. I need not rehearse that history here, but I do want to note that the harassment of scholarly fields and organizations has taken a variety of forms — for example, the Reagan State Department's refusal to allow Wole Soyinka to attend the 1986 Modern Language Association convention (invoking the McCarthy-era McCarran-Walter Act) and subsequent refusal to recommend MLA members for U.S. Information Agency fellowships abroad after the MLA awarded Soyinka an honorary membership; Lynne Cheney's 1994 – 95 crusade against the National History Standards and the National Endowment for the Humanities, both of which she had overseen prior to 1993; and, most recently, the October 2003 passage by the House of Representatives of the International Studies in Higher Education Act of 2003 (H.R. 3077), one crucial provision of which would establish an "advisory board" that would have the power to investigate individual faculty members and specific classes on campus and, in the language of proposed section 633(d)(2), to "annually monitor, apprise, and evaluate the activities of grant recipients" under Title VI of the Higher Education Act of 1958.

H.R. 3077 never passed the Senate. But regardless of what happens to Title VI programs in the future, it does not take much to imagine that Congress — and freelance right-wing culture warriors such as Stanley Kurtz and Daniel Pipes, who have been instrumental in generating congressional opposition to the work of the Middle Eastern Studies Association and its leadership — might take a similar interest in the "activities" of American studies during the Bush administration's second term and well beyond. We are not yet in the realm of loyalty oaths and mass firings of dissident faculty; at the moment, we are not even close. But there is no question that over the past few years, conservatives in government and in civil society have fostered new initiatives in the academic culture wars. In the case of the attacks on Middle Eastern studies and in David Horowitz's recent calls for "intellectual diversity" among college faculties, such initiatives seek openly to deploy the legislative power of the state in the service of a conservative political platform — and often do so in the language of patriotism and national obligation. The present administration, for its part, has shown itself to be quite willing to interfere in scholarly matters involving "sensitive" areas and languages, and conservative U.S. administrations in the future might very well target American studies scholars as aggressively as the right has targeted Middle Eastern scholars since September 2001.

At one point, for example, it became illegal for U.S. scholars to edit manuscripts from certain countries. In late February 2004, the Bush Treasury Department declared that scholars who edited manuscripts from "disfavored nations" — specifically Iran, but also Cuba, Libya, North Korea, and other nations under U.S. trade embargo (nations with which trade is banned without a government license) — could face "grave legal consequences." As the *New York Times* reported,

> Anyone who publishes material from a country under a trade embargo is forbidden to reorder paragraphs or sentences, correct syntax or gram-

mar, or replace "inappropriate words," according to several advisory letters from the Treasury Department in recent months.

Adding illustrations is prohibited, too. To the baffled dismay of publishers, editors and translators who have been briefed about the policy, only publication of "camera-ready copies of manuscripts" is allowed.…

Nahid Mozaffari, a scholar and editor specializing in literature from Iran, called the implications staggering. "A story, a poem, an article on history, archaeology, linguistics, engineering, physics, mathematics, or any other area of knowledge cannot be translated, and even if submitted in English, cannot be edited in the U.S.," she said.

"This means that the publication of the PEN Anthology of Contemporary Persian Literature that I have been editing for the last three years," she said, "would constitute aiding and abetting the enemy." (A8)

Regulatory edicts this preposterous, like former Secretary of Education Rod Paige's declaration that the National Education Association has behaved like a "terrorist organization" (King), may serve ultimately to outrage reasonable people and damage further the Bush administration's credibility with regard to national security. It is perhaps in part for this reason that the Treasury Department's edict was reversed on 4 April 2004 (but see Givler). But these edicts point also to the contempt with which the current administration regards some of the basic operations of open, democratic societies — even as it claims to be bringing the blessings of democracy to Iraq. Moreover, conservatives' current assaults on scholarly programs and practices do not generate public outrage, partly because previous conservative assaults on academe have largely succeeded in attempting to delegitimate universities as sites of political dissent. In some political circles, it is axiomatic that college faculty are stocked with aging, un-American Yippies who deserve every form of political harassment visited upon them. The actual scholarly needs of translators and Title VI program directors could not matter less to those who guide their lives by that axiom. The possibility of greater governmental "involvement" (though under the present circumstances I prefer to use the word "interference") in scholarly affairs seems to me to provide the occasion for asking just what kind of "American" values American studies might plausibly remain loyal to, if in fact we do not want (as I presume we will not want) to be reconfigured as a scholarly adjunct to a neo-imperialist foreign policy.

THE RANGE OF political positions represented by scholars in American studies is a good deal wider than conservative ideologues in government or in civil society are ordinarily willing to credit; still, it seems safe to say that over the past quarter century, the field has aligned itself with an anti-imperialist intellectual tradition in which U.S. history and culture is viewed critically with regard to its history of conquest in the Western Hemisphere and with regard to its assumption of global power since World War II. Indeed, one wing of American studies has practically devoted itself to exposing the complicity of an earlier generation of American studies scholars — who might have appeared to their contemporaries as liberals, progressives, and socialists — with the ideological machinery of the Cold War.[1] To put this another way, there is to my knowledge no such thing as a pro-imperialist American studies.

But in the years since 11 September, as the Cold War has been superseded by a much more vague and nebulous war on "terror," it has become surprisingly difficult to specify the contours of U.S. anti-imperialism. Opposition to the Bush/Ashcroft/Gonzales domestic agenda with regard to civil liberties, from the USA-Patriot Act to Guantánamo, seems to be nearly universal among liberal, progressive, and leftist scholars in all fields, but with regard to American affairs abroad, there is no similarly near-universal agreement about what constitutes legitimate or productive opposition to U.S. neo-imperialism. To put this another way, the wars in Iraq and Afghanistan have paradoxically confused the terms of anti-imperialism in the United States. On the one hand, the Bush administration has conducted itself arrogantly and appallingly in world affairs, not least in war; on the other hand, not every one of Bush's opponents abroad deserves the support (even the "critical" support) of U.S. anti-imperialists.

To say this is to provoke serious debate among anti-imperialists on the American left and perhaps among many American studies scholars as well — which is, of course, what I mean to do. Even among American progressives who, with varying degrees of reluctance or enthusiasm, supported U.S.-led wars in Kosovo and Afghanistan (many of whom, like myself, are willing to concede that both wars were badly conducted on moral and/or tactical grounds and therefore more easily justified in theory than in practice), there is no support for the neoconservative and explicitly imperialist Project for the New American Century (PNAC). (PNAC, formed in 1997 and chaired by second-generation neoconservative intellectual William Kristol, is dedicated to the proposition "that American leadership is good both for America and for the world; that such leadership requires military strength, diplomatic energy and commitment to moral principle; and that too few political leaders today are making the case for global leadership.")[2]

Rather, such progressives disagree with intellectuals to their left about what constitutes an "imperialist" war. My grounds for supporting a military rather than (or, more accurately, as well as) a police/intelligence response in Afghanistan were that the attacks of 11 September demonstrated that al-Qaeda and the Taliban, as al-Qaeda's ally and state sponsor, had attained a level of global reach that made it imperative that the Taliban be overthrown and its terror training camps destroyed. Similarly, the al-Qaeda attacks in Bali in 2002, Madrid in 2004, and in London in 2005 have demonstrated that the removal of the Taliban was, by itself, not a sufficient means of opposing the spread of al-Qaeda's global reach and that exclusively military responses to terrorism are ineffective and possibly counterproductive.[3] I acknowledge that some critics saw the overthrow of the Taliban as another exercise in American imperialism and therefore as indefensible. Additionally, many critics of the war in Afghanistan have argued that the Taliban have not in fact been routed, and that they are regrouping. But it appears to me that the cogency of the second argument undermines the credibility of the first. What the United States can plausibly be charged with in Afghanistan is not imperialism but a longstanding pattern of criminal negligence: far from propping up a client state of the empire in Afghanistan, we have, by turning to invade Iraq in 2003, allowed Afghanistan to drift back into state failure — precisely the condition that made possible the emergence of the Taliban in the mid-1990s and that made possible the partial Talibanization of Pakistan before 2001. A similar charge of criminal negligence can be made with regard to our more recent conduct in Liberia, whose pleas for U.S. intervention after the fall of Charles Taylor confounded both the Bush regime, bent on invading Iraq, and hard left anti-imperialists, bent on construing all such interventions as illegitimate.

I am well aware that there are those critics for whom no use of U.S. power can be considered legitimate as long as the United States is a global hegemon. Such critics insist that there is no way to remain loyal to the anti-imperialist traditions of American studies while supporting a military operation in Afghanistan that killed some thousands of innocent civilians and extended the global U.S. reach more deeply into Central Asia (entwining us further with unsavory regimes in Pakistan and Uzbekistan in the name of promoting "freedom"). But serious anti-imperialists must, I think, draw a clear line between a legitimate struggle against al-Qaeda and an illegitimate project of remaking the Arab world by force. Those of us who supported the overthrow of the Taliban did not thereby commit ourselves to the idea that the United States can act wherever, whenever, and however it wishes; nor did we commit ourselves to a course of action in which the primary response to al-Qaeda is always and everywhere a military response. On the contrary, *after* the Taliban was overthrown, the best course of action for the United States would have been to pursue international police and intelligence action against al-Qaeda; war in Iraq constituted one of the worst possible courses of action. This position is not inconsistent with condemning the U.S. bombing of the wedding party in Kakrak in July 2002 — an atrocity even if (again, if) unintended — and not inconsistent with arguing that the Bush/Cheney program in Afghanistan since the fall of the Taliban, from the resurgence of Islamism to the creation of a worldwide archipelago of detention-and-torture sites, has proceeded as if it were designed to produce a resurgence of al-Qaeda in that part of the world. On the contrary, it is merely to say that the fight against al-Qaeda is a legitimate fight, pursued by the Bush administration in a dangerously incompetent and counterproductive manner.

The war in Iraq, by contrast, represents a decisive and perhaps irreversible step in U.S. foreign policy: over that threshold, we are explicitly engaged in a preemptive, imperialist, and potentially neocolonialist enterprise, even if, like Paul Wolfowitz or George Packer, one sincerely believes that we are doing it for the good of the planet. To oppose the neoconservative program, as many liberals did, by suggesting that Iraq was a distraction from al-Qaeda and Afghanistan was to miss the point. For Cheney, Wolfowitz, Rumsfeld, and the PNAC crew, it was the other way around: for them, after 11 September, Afghanistan was a distraction from the redrawing of the Middle East beginning with Iraq. Indeed, for PNAC, al-Qaeda itself was not even so much a pretext as a distraction. I want to stress this point, not least because it indicates which war was an imperialist war. Iraq was the priority from the very start, as is made clear by the 1998 PNAC letter to President Clinton calling for the overthrow of Saddam Hussein; for PNAC, Afghanistan was and is a sideshow.[4]

AS I NOTED at the outset, American studies participates in these debates at a time when most of its leading figures are identified with the academic left in the United States, and for this reason, sociologist Alan Wolfe did not restrain himself from calling the field "anti-American," despite the gravity of the charge, in the pages of the *New Republic*. It is possible to narrate the recent history of American studies quite differently, as Amy Kaplan has recently done in noting that the contemporary discourse of American empire "aggressively celebrates the United States as finally revealing its true essence — its manifest destiny — on a global stage" (4): ten years ago, when scholars in American studies spoke of "cultures of United States imperialism," they were made — by critics like Wolfe — to sound as if they were crazed Leninists festooning New York's Upper West Side with wheat-paste posters testifying to the Trilateral Commission's hand in the death of Bruce Lee. Now, however, American studies of the 1990s simply looks like it was ahead of the curve, talking frankly about U.S. imperialism years before anyone else caught on. As *Slate* magazine's Timothy Noah wryly noted in December 2003,

> Within the mainstream of American political discourse, it's perfectly acceptable to criticize pre-emption and unilateralism, but by silent agreement, the word "empire" is understood to be beyond the pale. It's one of those words, like "servant," that Americans refuse to utter because it's too difficult to reconcile with American ideals. The only people rude enough to use the word "empire" to describe the United States are foreigners, hard leftists, and Buchananite conservatives. Oh, and one more: Vice President Dick Cheney.

Noah's column concerned the Cheneys' Christmas card for 2003, which featured Benjamin Franklin's question, "And if a sparrow cannot fall to the ground without His notice, is it probable that an empire can arise without His aid?" (American studies scholars will not be surprised to learn that it was Lynne Cheney, according to her husband, who had selected that line.) In January 2004, in Davos, Dick Cheney was asked about the line by World Economic Forum founder Klaus Schwab, whereupon Cheney replied, "If we were a true empire, we would currently preside over a much greater piece of the Earth's surface than we do" (Schmitt and Landler 10). It may be that Cheney is working with an outmoded, late-nineteenth-century idea of imperialism; it may just as well be that he was expressing not a disavowal but a desire. Either way, American studies, to its credit, can rightfully claim to have been debating the question for two decades and more. The challenge for the field for the foreseeable future is how to oppose imperialism without aligning "imperialism" with every kind of international intervention, such that American studies scholars would wind up in the position of reflexively defending the state sovereignty of every last brutal dictator and mass murderer on the planet if and when that state sovereignty is threatened by the United States.

I do not believe that this form of anti-imperialism would involve a form of disloyalty either to the United States or to American studies. Surely there is nothing "disloyal" about mounting critiques of U.S. imperialism, whether in Cuba, the Philippines, Iraq, or Guantánamo. I think of it, rather, as I think of disloyalty to the Bush regime: as another form of patriotism, of marking the country's betrayals of its democratic ideals precisely in order to affirm those ideals. But there is nothing in the history of the founding of American studies that requires any of its practitioners to understand themselves as loyal Americans. The history of the *funding* of American studies is another matter: as I suggested earlier in this volume in "American Studies without Exceptions," the CIA's past (covert) support for American studies suggests that in the future there might well be forms of official, state-sponsored American studies for which security clearances and loyalty oaths might be prerequisites for participation, particularly with regard to the screening of American studies scholars sent abroad under the auspices of the U.S. Information Agency. Yet those who would exact such loyalty oaths from *all* American studies scholars ought first to reflect that some scholars in the field are not in fact U.S. citizens. Scholars who criticize the United States and its imperialist adventures from the perspective of (for example) Latin American nations that have long been the objects of those adventures surely are not to be expected to profess their love for the United States before they proceed with cultural analysis. Even among U.S. citizens, however, American studies should be understood as an academic discipline and not as a pledge of allegiance; if it is more loyal to the unfinished project of critique than to the unfinished project of America, so be it. American studies does not need to be loyal to the Bush administration, nor need it be loyal to American national interests. For example, it can, while taking "America" as its object, declare a loyalty to liberal internationalism. It can dedicate itself more to the ideal of universal human rights than to the dictates of state sovereignty, and more to a cosmopolitan expression of the ideals of egalitarian democracy and participatory parity than to their defense as uniquely "American" ideals. And it can, if it wishes, do all or none of the above.

Perhaps, to paraphrase a recent essay by Leo Marx, scholars in American studies need not "believe in America" in order to profess a loyalty to the strongest traditions of American dissidence over the past 225 years. As Marx writes,

> [T]he discourse of American studies had been inflected from the beginning by the doctrinal "doubleness" of the adversary culture. That culture evolved to serve the ideological needs of virtually all of the nation's dissident social movements including, for example, the transcendentalist, feminist, and abolitionist movements of the antebellum era; the populist movement of the 1880s and 1890s; the pre – World War I progressive movement and — in the case at hand — the left-labor, anti-fascist movements (and cultural front) of the 1930s; and, to come full circle, the dissident Movement of the Vietnam era. To mobilize opposition to slavery, egregious forms of capitalist exploitation and injustice, and unjust wars, leaders of these dissident movements affirmed their provisional belief in the idea of America. It was a compelling means of exposing the discrepancy between a real and an ideal America or, as Melville put it on the eve of the Civil War, between the world's foulest crime and man's fairest hope.

Marx would leave us in the ambiguous position of Ellison's hibernating invisible man, wondering whether his grandfather meant "to affirm the principle on which the country was built and not the men, or at least not the men who did the violence. . . . Did he mean to affirm the principle, which they themselves had dreamed into being out of the chaos and darkness of the feudal past, and which they had violated and compromised to the point of absurdity even in their own corrupt minds?" (574). While I can profess loyalty to the "principle" — that is, the echo (which resounds throughout Marx's essay) of Lincoln's Gettysburg invocation of the "proposition" to which the nation was dedicated — I must confess that I am not sure what to do with Marx's grandfatherly advice for American studies, any more than the invisible man knew what to do with his grandfather's injunction to live with one's head in the lion's mouth. Over the past twenty-five years, American studies has sometimes been charged with fostering national disunity by critiquing the postwar "consensus" model of American history and developing a multicultural and explicitly conflictual understanding of American society. Scholars in American studies have responded by producing a wave of scholarship that has demonstrated powerfully that the assertion of a "common American culture" is in no way necessary for the cohesion of the American nation-state, and that indeed the conflation of "culture" with "nation" does considerable violence to American history while naturalizing the violence *of* American history (see Kessler-Harris). In retrospect, however, this debate — in which, iconically, I picture liberals like Arthur Schlesinger Jr. and E. D. Hirsch on one side and the past fifteen or twenty presidents of the American Studies Association on the other — looks to me like an overwhelmingly domestic dispute about whether to stress the *pluribus* or the *unum*, and how to defend the relative autonomy of "culture" from "society" within the boundaries of the United States. The post–11 September global landscape, by contrast, would appear to require of American studies scholars that we apply the traditions of American dissidence to new fields of inquiry in which the internationalization(s) of American studies and the new discourses of American empire are understood to be inescapable features of the world our work engages. My provisional — propositional — suggestion is that scholars in American studies reembrace the "doubleness" of U.S. adversary culture, its capacity to denounce and defend, confirm and affirm; that we avoid the mechanical equation in which all who oppose America deserve the name "anti-imperialist"; and that we entertain the possibility that in opposing the Bush regime and its equation of dissent with disloyalty, we cannot but remain loyal to the liberal, egalitarian ideals our current government traduces every time it invokes them.

Notes

1. Joel Pfister's discussion of this flattening out of the history of American studies scholarship is as trenchant today as when it was published in 1991.

2. See the PNAC Web site, <http://www.newamericancentury.org>. In the year between the original publication of this essay and its revision for this book, PNAC dropped the final clause of its mission statement, apparently because it no longer feared that "too few political leaders today are making the case for global leadership." The statement available on the PNAC site now reads, "The Project for the New American Century is a non-profit educational organization dedicated to a few fundamental propositions: that American leadership is good both for America and for the world; and that such leadership requires military strength, diplomatic energy and commitment to moral principle." But you can find the original language preserved at other sites; see, for example, Liu.

3. As to the oft-rehearsed argument that the attacks of 11 September constituted "blowback" for American policies in the Middle East or during the Cold War (with regard to U.S. support for the Afghan mujahideen two decades ago), some populations around the globe have good reason to consider the United States their enemy on the basis of past and present U.S. policy, and some of them would find ready sympathizers within the United States, also for good reason. But by any standard I can credit, al-Qaeda is not one of them.

4. Counterterrorism expert Richard Clarke has offered a dramatic and compelling confirmation of this argument (see Clarke). The 1998 PNAC letter was signed by, among others, Donald Rumsfeld, Paul Wolfowitz, William Kristol, Richard Perle, Richard Armitage, and John Bolton.

Works Cited

Clarke, Richard. *Against All Enemies: Inside America's War on Terror.* New York: Free Press, 2004.

Ellison, Ralph. *Invisible Man.* 2nd ed. New York: Vintage, 1995.

Givler, Peter. "The Defendant Is Charged with Good Editing." *Chronicle Review (Chronicle of Higher Education)*, 21 May 2004, B15. Available online at <http://chronicle.com/prm/weekly/v50/i37/37b01501.htm>. Accessed 5 May 2005.

Kaplan, Amy. "Violent Belongings and the Question of Empire Today: Presidential Address to the American Studies Association, October 17, 2003." *American Quarterly* 56, no. 1 (2004): 1–18.

Kessler-Harris, Alice. "Cultural Locations: Positioning American Studies in the Great Debate." *American Quarterly* 44, no. 3 (1992): 299–312.

King, John. "Paige Calls NEA 'Terrorist Organization.'" Available online at <http://www.cnn.com/2004/EDUCATION/02/23/paige.terrorist.nea>. Accessed 26 February 2004.

Liptak, Adam. "Treasury Department Is Warning Publishers of the Perils of Criminal Editing of the Enemy." *New York Times*, 28 February 2004, A8.

Liu, Henry C. K. "Reaganite Moralists and Hong Kong Security." *Asia Times*, 7 December 2002. Available online at <http://www.atimes.com/atimes/China/DL07Ad01.html>. Accessed 6 May 2005.

Marx, Leo. "Believing in America: An Intellectual Project and a National Ideal." *Boston Review* 28, no. 6 (December 2003 – January 2004). Available online at <http://bostonreview.net/BR28.6/ marx.html>. Accessed 12 December 2003.

Noah, Timothy. "The Imperial Vice Presidency — Dick Cheney Says the E-Word." *Slate*, 17 December 2003. Available online at <http://slate.msn.com/id/2092800/>. Accessed 27 February 2004.

Pfister, Joel. "The Americanization of Cultural Studies." *Yale Journal of Criticism* 4, no. 2 (1991): 199 – 229.

Project for the New American Century. "Letter to President Clinton on Iraq." 26 January 1998. Available online at <http://www.newamericancentury.org./iraqclintonletter.htm>. Accessed 1 March 2004.

Schmitt, Eric, and Mark Landler. "Cheney Calls for More Unity in Fight against Terrorism." *New York Times*, 25 January 2004, I10.

Wolfe, Alan. "Anti-American Studies: The Difference between Criticism and Hate." *New Republic*, 10 February 2003, 25 – 32.

Part Five

POSTS

This final section involves a qualitatively different set of rhetorical occasions: it is composed of short essays written in 2004 – 5 and posted to my blog, <www.michaelberube.com>. But it is not simply a collection of Greatest Blog Hits. Rather, this section seeks to demonstrate the potential discursive and tonal range of academic blog writing while posing the question of whether blog writing can be understood in the terms bequeathed to us by the print culture of the book. For one of the joys and challenges of blog writing — and one of the things that distinguishes it from every other kind of writing — is the plasticity of the hyperlink: on one hand, the hyperlink works as a kind of hyperfootnote, providing not merely the reference to a secondary text but access to the text in its entirety; on the other hand, there is no reason why hyperlinks should always be used so "transparently," and, as I have found in my career as a blogger, they can also be deployed in a more Borgesian or Nabokovian vein to undercut, ironize, or otherwise trouble the protocols of textual reference. Those postmodern intertextual high jinks are impossible to reproduce in print, as is the metonymic skid involved in leaping across Web sites from hyperlink to hyperlink. Accordingly, this section does not attempt to reproduce the textual condition of the blog.

The other distinctive feature of blog writing, of course, is the comments section. Not every blog allows comments, and some blogs' comment sections consist of strings of single-sentence insults and the equivalents of online screams and shouts. But the best, most thought-provoking blogs are renowned not only for the quality of their writing but for the quality of writing they stimulate in response. It is in the daily give-and-take between bloggers and commenters — many of whom, of course, have their own blogs as well — that discursive communities are formed online, and it is in such give-and-take that blogs create the taste by which they are to be enjoyed. (My readers, who currently number roughly eight to nine thousand per day, sometimes leave multiple-paragraph comments that are themselves short-essay responses to short essays.) I mean the allusion to Wordsworth seriously: I believe that blogs render palpable the claims of Jon Klancher's ambitious and powerful book, *The Making of English*

Reading Audiences, 1790 – 1832, which tried to bridge reader-response criticism and reception theory by demonstrating that certain forms of attention and certain groups of "popular" readers were hailed — and created — by the very style and demeanor of print journals in the Romantic era.

I suggested as much one evening to a celebrated husband-and-wife blogging team, Teresa and Patrick Nielsen Hayden, creators of the blog Making Light (< http://nielsenhayden.com/makinglight/ >) and well-known writers and editors in the science fiction community. They replied with a fascinating series of suggestions about how blogs have managed to re-create the zine fandoms and readerships of the 1980s while trying to create readerships and followings in a substantially new medium — just as Klancher had argued with respect to early-nineteenth-century journals. (The Nielsen Haydens were familiar with Klancher's work as well as with the producers of early zines.) The exchanges in blog comments sections, then, can be construed — interestingly enough — in both Habermasian and Lyotardian terms: on one hand, blogs attempt to create a virtual public sphere in which claims can be advanced irrespective of the identity of the claimant (as the cliché has it, on the Internet no one knows you're a dog), but on the other hand, blogs represent a profusion of heterogeneous language games that attempt no orientation toward consensus. (It has recently become common to lament that blogs cater to niche audiences and contribute to the fragmentation of political discourse, as people choose to read only those blogs to which they are broadly sympathetic. The complaint has some merit, of course, but I am left to wonder whether it is really a complaint about blogs qua blogs: to put this another way, I wonder how many people subscribe to the print editions of both the *Nation* and *Commentary*.)

Though it is shorn of both hyperlinks and reader comments, this section attempts to present blog writing as a legitimate vehicle for cultural criticism, occasional essays, extended book reviews, and political satire. Included here are commentaries on J. K. Rowling's *Harry Potter* series, J. M. Coetzee's *Elizabeth Costello*, soccer and French music, and my son Jamie; a revolutionary (if facetious) plan for Democratic electoral success; a response to Peter Beinart and Michael Tomasky on Democrats and national security; and one snippet of a six-part exercise I originally accepted as a dare — nightly blog coverage of the 2004 Republican National Convention in New York City (the premise of which, as you'll see, is that the RNC managed to convert me to a Republican by presenting its "moderate" Giuliani/McCain wing on the first night and then worked me into a proper lather for the remainder of the event).

The section also includes two excerpts from Theory Tuesdays, a series I ran in the latter half of the summer of 2005. The immediate rhetorical occasion for that series was the publication of *Theory's Empire: An Anthology of Dissent*, edited by Daphne Patai and Will H. Corral and offered as a kind of corrective to the *Norton Anthology of Theory and Criticism*, which had appeared four years earlier. More specifically, the occasion for Theory Tuesdays was an online group discussion of *Theory's Empire* conducted by the Valve (<www.thevalve.org>; the group discussion is archived at <http://www.thevalve.org/go/valve/archive_asc/C41>), a literary blog created by the Association of Literary Scholars and Critics. The ALSC's foray into blogging marks, I believe, a generational and tonal shift for the organization, away from the Grouchy Old Men mode of the mid-1990s. For while the academic bloggers at the Valve are critical of critical theory and its excesses, they are young, smart, and exceptionally well informed about varieties of theory and theorists. As a result, the group review of *Theory's Empire* highlighted serious intellectual differences among the participants, but was on the whole a civil and substantive affair in which Theorists did not accuse Anti-Theorists of being troglodytes and Anti-Theorists did not accuse Theorists of destroying Western civilization. (The affair was so civil and substantive, actually, that William Pannapacker, writing in the *Chronicle of Higher Education*, declared himself to be disappointed at the intellectual seriousness of the event: "Some readers, like me, were hoping for an academic donnybrook directly from *Gangs of New York* with Stanley Fish making a cameo appearance as Bill the Butcher" [B8].)

Still, I thought (and think) that 2005 was a very late date for yet another "theory backlash," and I was seriously alarmed by some Patai and Corral's remarks in the introduction to *Theory's Empire*. *Theory's Empire* and the Valve discussion seemed to me to speak not to the moment of Theory's ascendancy but to the moment of its Nortonization. And for Patai and Corral, Theory's Nortonization implies that Theory has now become hardened dogma. Thus, they oddly object to one scholar's remark that students might need help to become familiar with theory and criticism: "[W]hy suggest that students need only become 'familiar' with (and not also critical of) the 'new discourse' they are being taught?" (4). Patai and Corral clearly assume that students who become "familiar" with theory will be somehow prevented from being critical of it as well: "[W]hat the languages of present-day criticism and theory *unmistakably do* is undermine what should be a protected intellectual space — that of classroom teaching and learning — in which ideas can be explored and tried out with an extraordinary measure of freedom and safety" (13; emphasis added). In response to this extraordinary (and irresponsible) claim, I think it's worth insisting that familiarity with a subject should never preclude criticism of it but should always be a prerequisite for it. And since I teach from the *Norton Anthology of Theory and Criticism* in my Introduction to Graduate Study courses, I decided to respond to the Valve review (in which I participated as well) with a series of more extended posts about formalism, structuralism, deconstruction, and Marxism.

I was pleasantly surprised to learn that blog readers were quite willing to make their way through posts of two and three thousand words: my initial post in the Theory Tuesday series, on the *Norton* excerpt from Derrida's "Plato's Pharmacy," drew more than one hundred comments and started a wide-ranging discussion of theory and criticism that then informed my second and third installments in the series (the posts reproduced here). And I have been *very* pleasantly surprised, over the past two years of blogging, to find that the medium — which, even as late as 2003, I associated primarily with mini-editorials and snarky, one-off comments on the news — is a realm that not merely entertains but fosters serious discussions of pragmatism, disability, literary theory, and democracy. Though I cannot reproduce those discussions in full here, I invite you to take them seriously — and, of course, to visit my humble blog now and again to take part in those discussions as they unfold.

Works Cited

Klancher, Jon. *The Making of English Reading Audiences, 1790–1832*. Madison: University of Wisconsin Press, 1987.

Pannapacker, William. "Venting Steam in the Blogosphere." *Chronicle of Higher Education*, 29 July 2005, B8.

Patai, Daphne, and Will H. Corral, eds. *Theory's Empire: An Anthology of Dissent*. New York: Columbia University Press, 2005.

[6 June 2004]

Yes, it's true, I've read all five Harry Potter books, and I know my Flitwick from my Umbridge. I resisted mightily at first, partly for the reasons the *Onion* gestured at in its December 2001 headline, "Children, Creepy Middle-Aged Weirdos Swept Up in Harry Potter Craze." Also partly because of that weird brand of American Anglophilia I associate with PBS, A&E, and Moynihan liberals. Also partly because I thought I'd already read all that stuff back when it was written by Roald Dahl.

I realize that parental reading habits in these matters depend heavily on the age of the children; I believe the last book I read with Nick, actually *with* him, night by night, was the quite wonderful *Racso and the Rats of Nimh*, and that would have been sometime around 1992. From that point on, he was on his own. So when he became one of J. K. Rowling's faithful readers, buying *Goblet of Fire* the day it appeared and devouring it in one all-night reading marathon, I didn't even look over his shoulder.

Then I took Jamie to the first Harry Potter movie, and I was stunned — partly by the story, which was at once darker and more charming than I'd anticipated, but mostly by Jamie, who *completely got it*. I suppose it helped that Jamie was ten at the time and that his glasses look a great deal like Harry's, so that he began talking about attending Hogwarts when he turned eleven and practicing the "Wingardium leviosa" spell now and then. As for me, after we saw the movie, I was curious enough to read the dang book at last, and I was fairly impressed. I've since heard that Harold Bloom, that learned old gasbag and self-designated arbiter of all written words, despises the book and has said so at least once every six months for the past five years. Well, alas, Bloom, my good man — leave aside the sorry spectacle of the world's most famous literary critic spending some of his remaining energies trying to squash J. K. Rowling like a bug, all because of a series of books whose readership extends to *eight-year-olds*, for god's sake (would Lionel Trilling have behaved this way with *A Wrinkle in Time*, do you think?), and let me put it this way: You style yourself after Falstaff, but you have no sense of humor whatsoever. You never did — and your Rowling snits seal the deal. Now, what do we call people who think of themselves as latter-day Falstaffs but who have never uttered a funny thing in their lives? Don't think Shakespeare — think restoration comedy.

Back to Jamie. After Jamie and I had seen *Harry Potter and the Chamber of Secrets* ten or twenty times, I suggested to him that we read the books together. Jamie doesn't really read on his own, unless you count his various coffee-table books about the Beatles, and I wasn't sure that he would be able to follow a narrative of three hundred, four hundred, or seven hundred pages on the basis of nighttime bedside reading, which might cover seven or eight pages on a good night. But then, I didn't think he'd follow the plot of the first movie, so what do I know?

Suffice it to say that the Harry Potter books have extended Jamie's capacity for narrative by powers of ten. We started in early 2003 and we're now a third of the way through *Order of the Phoenix*. I read to him (sometimes Janet does), and I annotate and explain where necessary — not only with regard to unfamiliar words but more important with regard to narrative questions not broached by the films (for example, Harry and the Weasleys' discussion, early in *Chamber of Secrets*, of whether Dobby the house elf might be lying to Harry, since, after all, Dobby works for the Malfoys). Once in a while I ask Jamie questions about things that happened hundreds of pages ago or in other books, and I'm astonished at how much he retains. He's also expanded his emotional repertoire as well, though I really shouldn't say which character he sometimes feels sorry for, or whom he'd like to invite to the Yule Ball, without his permission. But I will say that he's come to understand, via Professors Dumbledore, McGonagall, Sprout, etc. that his own parents are professors too, though without the whole robes-and-hats-and-wands regalia. As the books delve further into the problems associated with the idea of individual autonomy, seriously (via the Imperius Curse, which enables you to control another person) and comically (with Hermione's S.P.E.W., which seeks to liberate house elves despite the fact that they themselves resist their "liberation" mightily and regard Hermione's crusade as a profound insult), we have to stop and discuss what's what and who's who (those of you familiar with the plot twists at the conclusion of *Azkaban* and *Goblet of Fire* know what I mean), and of course Jamie has to protect me from dementors with his patronus every now and then. But for the most part, it's going amazingly well.

So yesterday, he and Janet and I went to see the new movie — a milestone of sorts, since this is the first time Jamie's read the book before seeing the film. I made him promise to hold my hand when the dementors came so that I would not be scared, and he did, but I think even he was a little surprised at how ghastly they are, and didn't have all that much comforting left over for me. I won't bore you with a full review of the film, but I will say that

— The lovely Garman Theater in Bellefonte, Pennsylvania, is a great place to see movies, especially when your tix are taken by a young man who looks exactly like Professor Snape and who has obligingly dressed the part.

— Alfonso Cuarón is a more subtle director than Chris Columbus, but the film nonetheless demands so much compression of the first nine-tenths of the book (in order to do justice to the concluding sequences) that it may be the first movie in the series for which a knowledge of the book is a prerequisite. I know you can't have kids' movies coming in at the length of *Berlin Alexanderplatz*, now, but still, slightly more should have been done with Hermione's inexplicable disappearances, and the Crookshanks-Scabbers subplot, so critical to the novel, is given about eight seconds of screen time.

— We all *love* Alan Rickman.

Kudos to Rowling, by the way, for broaching the issue of having an out gay man — er, I mean, a werewolf, cough cough — teaching at Hogwarts. Note that Hogwarts' only competent Defense against the Dark Arts teacher (over a five-year span!) is chased from his job by a hate campaign mounted by the Malfoys. If I recall correctly (it *was* only yesterday, after all), the film makes matters slightly more explicit than the novel by having Lupin attribute his resignation to the fact that parents will not want "someone like me" teaching their children (he does not use the word "werewolf"). She'd already broached the racism of the Malfoys in *Chamber of Secrets*, and when we get to *Goblet of Fire* we'll come up against the brutal stigma faced by those among us who are half giant. I just gotta love Rowling — she's managed to piss off the insufferable Bloom and the insane fundamentalist right, and she has no patience with *Daily Prophet* reporters who rely lazily and uncritically on sources like the Malfoys or Ministry of Magic apparatchiks. What's not to like?

[29 June 2004]

First off, I should say that although the Bérubé name is originally from Normandy — Damien Bérubé having come to Quebec in 1671 — I've never been to France in my life. In fact I've been to Europe only once as an adult — to Italy in 1999 for ten days. Second, I should note that although trips to France, in the current political climate, would seem to be the exclusive preserve of the treasonous, cosmopolitan, moral-relativist, white-wine-sipping liberal cultural elite, it is actually possible for a family of four to visit Paris and the south of France for under one billion Euros, if you're willing to fly discount (this involves strapping one child to the fuselage of the plane) and stay in hotels into whose rooms one has to be lowered by one's armpits.

No, really, we had a great time, with our moral relativism and our two preternaturally patient, champion-traveler kids and our just-barely-able-to-converse-haltingly-with-the-taxi-driver-about-sports-and-automobiles French. Sure, we underwent what gastroeconomical specialists call a "radical money-ectomy" in our five days in Paris. But it was worth it. And Jamie loved the Métro and the zoo and overcame his fear of heights long enough to accompany me to the top of l'Arc de Triomphe, which, as the plaques at its base will tell you, commemorates French military valor in the Franco-Prussian War, World War I, World War II, la Guerre d'Indochine, and that dustup in Algiers. I would say something properly derisive about this, but on the whole, the French were so nice to us that I just don't have the heart to do the cheese-eating surrender monkeys bit. Apparently they figure that if you're an American in France who can use French verbs in two tenses, you must not be watching Fox News. (Besides, I know perfectly well that the Arc was originally all about Napoleon's victory at Austerlitz, and of course it was great to see the French Resistance commemorated.)

I won't do any serious vacation blogging. Somehow it feels too self-indulgent even for a blog, where one always asks oneself, "Self-indulgent as compared to what, exactly?" Besides, everything you've read about Paris and the south of France is true: no false words have ever been written about these parts of the world. So consult those words if you want the details about what it's like to be there. Here, I'll confine myself to two light observations about cultural matters.

One: it's much fun to turn on the TV and see Jacques Derrida debating Régis Debray, and it's great to see the passages of the Métro festooned with ads for Paul Auster's novel, *La Nuit de l'Oracle*. It's quite true, artists and intellectuals are part of popular media in French life in ways that their American counterparts can only dream about. But it's also quite true, on another front, that French popular music sucks. It actually sucks in so many ways, in so many genres, that I could not keep proper track of its promiscuous modalities of inadequacy. A friend suggested to me that the French never made the categorical distinction between "rock" and "show tunes" that is fundamental to Anglo-American popular music, so that French pop sounds more or less like Barry Manilow. But that doesn't explain the travesty that is French hip-hop. Nor does it explain the curious fact that although experimental French art and literature have in fact rocked almost continuously for the past 175 years, *no French music of any kind* has really mattered to the rest of the world since the mid–thirteenth century, when the hot new musical form known as the motet took Europe by storm. I welcome your theories about this. (Before anybody gets all weird with me about Berlioz and Satie, all I have to say is, two exceptions in 750 years prove the rule. And the incomparable Django Reinhardt wasn't French, he was Manouche.)

Two: I have long thought that soccer — known in some parts of the world (namely, everywhere but here) as football — is almost the perfect sport. It involves intense, explosive large-muscle-group strength, incredible cardiovascular stamina, and stunning small-muscle-group finesse and coordination. It also has nearly ideal combinations of individual virtuosity with team effort, skill with chance, and synoptic strategy with sudden bursts of impromptu brilliance. But unfortunately, the sport has deep structural flaws, the most notorious of which is its offsides rule, which prevents players from sprinting behind defenses. And don't even *try* to defend the inane shootout as a means of deciding games: at the very least, the players should run in from midfield and/or shoot from outside the penalty area. Shooting from eleven meters out is a joke. The main problem, though, is that the scale of soccer is too big. The way I figure it, if soccer would just reduce the size of its field, reduce the number of players on the field, make the ball smaller and harder and flatten it on both ends, make the goal smaller, put up boards and glass around the boundaries, cover the field in ice, and give everybody sticks, *then* you'd have the perfect sport.

But in the course of watching Euro 2004 each night, I learned that (or I should say, Janet pointed out that) "football" does have an indisputable advantage over ice hockey in one key area: soccer players are far more handsome than hockey players—in some cases, astonishingly so. When France tied Croatia 2–2 two weeks ago, you could have told me that the Louis Vuitton house squad was playing the Dolce and Gabbana office team, and I'd have believed you. The next night, Italy played Sweden in the rain, which meant that players had to keep sweeping their hands through their hair (and let's not forget that the international soccer gesture for "I can't believe I missed" is the hands through the hair as well), and I'll be damned if the game didn't look like a two-hour-long Versace ad.

Ah, well, yes, ahem, I did pay attention to the outcomes of the games, even if Janet had her mind on other matters. For those of you following the tournament in other English-speaking nations, there's no question, England was robbed in that game against Portugal. But then, what do you expect from a sport with such severe structural flaws?

Elizabeth Costello is not quite a novel of ideas. It's kind of like a novel of ideas in vignettes — or more accurately, a series of vignettes that stage ideas that don't quite go over. And when I say the ideas don't quite go over, I'm not talking about Coetzee's — I'm talking about Elizabeth Costello's. The fictional Costello, as some of you already know, is an Australian writer of world renown, having "made her name," Coetzee tells us on the first page, "with her fourth novel, *The House on Eccles Street* (1969), whose main character is Marion Bloom, wife of Leopold Bloom, principal character of another novel, *Ulysses* (1922), by James Joyce" (1). OK, for those of you keeping score at home, we've got a fictional character whose career — in her own fiction — consists of rewriting a famous fictional character. But in *this* fiction, she doesn't write any fiction. Instead, she gives an award-acceptance speech at a college in Pennsylvania; a minilecture on a cruise ship; a campus talk and a seminar on animal rights; and a lecture at a conference in Amsterdam, where she plans to speak scathingly about the work of novelist Paul West — and then runs into West at the conference. (She addresses him before her talk, but West does not reply. Nor should he, since he's being addressed by a fictional character, after all.) Here's how the vignettes tend to proceed: Costello's speech/talk/lecture is inappropriate to the occasion and badly received; there is a good question from the audience, and smart, wide-ranging general discussion afterward at faculty dinners, radio interviews, and the like. Costello is old and tired, Coetzee tells us more than more than once, and at times the prose itself is weary too (hers and his), as if it's not entirely sure it's worth the effort to keep going on or as if it's always muttering asides to itself — *No, no, this won't do at all, will it, now?* Franz Kafka's short story, "A Report to an Academy," comes up a few times, beginning with the first chapter, where it is invoked in Costello's trite, tired (and inappropriate-to-the-occasion) speech on "realism." And the final chapter (which gives us Costello in the afterlife), "At the Gate," is very consciously — let's say much too self-consciously — an extended take on Kafka's parable, "Before the Law," but a take in which the text continually complains about its own tired, secondhand artifice: "Is that where she is: not so much in purgatory as in a kind of literary theme park, set up to divert her while she waits, with actors made up to look like writers? But if so, why is the make-up so poor? Why is the whole thing not done better? . . . It is the same with the Kafka business. The wall, the gate, the sentry, are straight out of Kafka. So is the demand for a confession, so is the courtroom with the dozing bailiff and the panel of old men in their crows' robes pretending to pay attention while she thrashes about in the toils of her own words. Kafka, but only the superficies of Kafka; Kafka reduced and flattened to a parody" (208–9).

You get the idea: by this point, the novel is skewering its own remaining devices, presenting us with both the superficies of Kafka and complaints about the presence of all these flattened-Kafka superficies. One wonders (as one is reading — that is, particularly if one is me), *Is it worth the effort to keep going on? No, no, this won't do at all, now.*

And yet the book has a number of high points that have stayed with me over the past couple of weeks. One is the moment in Costello's animal-rights lecture in which she examines cognitive experiments with apes and imagines all the thoughts that apes *might* have about the puzzles they're required to solve, noting that the only "right" thought permitted by the experiment is the narrowly instrumental one that allows the animal to figure out how to eat (72–73). This neat little reversal not only indirectly answers Thomas Nagel's famous question (addressed explicitly by Costello a few pages later) on whether we can know what it is like to be a bat (and Coetzee, in according Costello the ability to imagine simian subjectivity, is of course making that ability available to us), but also makes humans look like the impoverished creatures in the experiment, unable to devise any cognitive tests other than those that measure instrumental reason. It's a shame the rest of Costello's lecture is, as one thoroughly unlikable character points out, so maddeningly incoherent.

Another is the chapter "The Humanities in Africa," which narrates Elizabeth Costello's visit to her sister, Bridget, who is a nun in the Marian Order and a famous person in her own right. Sister Bridget receives an award from an African university and — guess what — gives a difficult and inappropriate acceptance speech. But it is followed by a spirited discussion on the function of the humanities, the German idealization of the Greeks, the role of Christian asceticism in sub-Saharan Africa, the purpose of suffering, and lots, lots more.

This chapter would be good enough in and of itself, and it is, but what made it especially enjoyable for me is that I had the experience, four years ago, of hearing Coetzee read part of it at a symposium on Global Humanities 2000 held by the Leslie Humanities Center at Dartmouth. (This item occupies its own file drawer in my office, marked "Conferences to Which Both J. M. Coetzee and I Have Been Invited." No, I'm kidding. The other featured speaker, by the way, was Samuel Delany, and I got a chance to talk to him briefly about his novel, *Hogg*.) I was slated to deliver a paper that eventually became "The Utility of the Arts and Humanities" (the fourth essay in this book), in which I argue — ecumenically but not, I hope, contentlessly — for the centrality of interpretation in the disciplines of the humanities while noting the sublime uselessness of some branches of the theoretical sciences. But the day before I gave my talk, Coetzee did his reading — and in that chapter, Sister Bridget basically dismisses my argument like so: "That man at lunch was arguing for the humanities as a set of techniques, the human sciences. Dry as dust. What young man or woman with blood in their veins would want to spend their life scratching around in the archives or doing *explication de texte* without end?" (132).

Gulp, I thought, *and now I have to get up and give a paper that argues for* explication de texte *without end*. Well, I figured I might as well directly address Sister Bridget and her chapter, so that night I stayed up and rewrote parts of my talk so that they engaged what I'd heard from Coetzee's characters. The next day, I gave my paper with Coetzee in the audience maybe fifty feet away in an amphitheater room, looking down at me impassively but not quite expressionlessly. ("Bemusedly," I think, would be le mot juste.) It was a little like Elizabeth Costello addressing Paul West (except that I was not fictional at the time and I was not arguing that Coetzee had given voice to evil, as Costello charges West with doing), because Coetzee did not say a word in reply, either after my talk or at any point in the symposium. *That's all right*, I thought, *it is the prerogative of world-famous novelists*. After all, though he spoke in propositions about the topic at hand, he himself did not propose anything, as Sir Philip Sidney might have pointed out; his characters did all the proposing, and Coetzee was somewhere behind or above them, paring his fingernails. I admit that I did have a moment of terror — *I hope he's not thinking we're all abject fools around here*, a thought that quickly took its real shape, *I hope he doesn't think I'm a complete idiot or a presumptuous asshole for tweaking my talk so that it responds to his reading* — but mostly I was worried that my talk would sound, to quote Sister Bridget, dry as dust.

After all, the "man at lunch" whose argument earns Sister Bridget's scorn had actually come up with a much better example of the centrality of interpretation than anything I had at my disposal:

> "But," says the young man seated next to Mrs. Godwin, "surely that is precisely what humanism stood for, and the Renaissance too: for humankind as humankind is capable of being. For the ascent of man. The humanists

were not crypto-atheists. They were not even Lutherans in disguise. They were Catholic Christians like yourself, Sister. Think of Lorenzo Valla. Valla had nothing against the Church, he just happened to know Greek better than Jerome did, and pointed out some of the mistakes Jerome made in translating the New Testament. If the Church had accepted the principle that Jerome's Vulgate was a human production, and therefore capable of being improved, rather than being the word of God itself, perhaps the whole history of the West would have been different." (128–29)

Damn, I wish I'd thought of that. *Explication de texte* without end as a rebuke to authoritarianism, theocracy, and terror. So that's my borrowed Thought for the Day. You are hereby invited to read the rest of the book for yourselves.

Works Cited

Coetzee, J. M. *Elizabeth Costello*. New York: Viking, 2003.

Republican National Convention, Second Night

[31 August 2004]

First, folks, a few words about irony. I have employed irony on this site before, back when I was a few miles left of the DemocRATS — that is, a couple of days ago. But irony is an ill wind that bites the hand that feeds our country's fashionable liberal cynicism. So you are now entering the no-irony zone. You have been warned.

Well, Day 2 at the RNC was a mixed bag. On the one hand, we showcased our diversity. We did tolerance and moderation last night, and in so doing we opened a six-pack of tall-boy whoop-ass on those French-speaking Democrats and their "intimate friends" in the theater industry and the anti-Christian media. When we do tolerance and moderation, we take no mother-lovin' prisoners! But tonight it was all about diversity. Michael Steele himself was incredibly diverse. The liberal media won't admit it, but black Republicans are actually much more diverse than black Democrats. You see, since most African Americans are Democrats, black Democrats are basically just party-line groupthinkers. Black Republicans, by contrast, think for themselves in a way that truly diversifies diversity. And that's why we put them front and center when we have our conventions — because, unlike the Rats, we respect African Americans as individuals rather than as members of a group.

And then the highlight of the night, the man we all came to see, Arnold Schwarzenegger. Schwarzenegger spells "diversity." For while the Democrats think Hollywood is the heart and soul of America, Republicans know that the heart and soul of America is someplace else, like a small town in a swing state or a quiet, modest house in the country where immigrants are working hard to better themselves by farming the land or pumping iron or something. Arnold Schwarzenegger symbolizes that heart and soul, having risen from humble immigrant iron-pumping origins to fame and success and announcing his candidacy for governor of California on the *Tonight Show* — the classic American immigrant's dream. And as Arnold put it so eloquently tonight, immigrants don't have to fear the Republican Party — the Republican Party loves them. And they don't have to agree with everything in the Republican

Party, like, for example, the part of the party that doesn't love immigrants at all, because we "can respectfully disagree and still be good Republicans." Now that's diversity — and tolerance too!

How do you know you're a Republican, Arnold asked? If you believe that government should be accountable to the people instead of the people being accountable to the government, you're a Republican. Well, no kidding! Again, you won't hear this from the liberal media, but independent studies have proven that the Bush presidency has been the most accountable presidency ever — and more than twice as accountable as Clinton's. In fact, you could say that the "W" in George W. Bush stands for "We Have Been Extremely Accountable."

Also, Arnold said, if you think your family knows how to spend money better than the government does, you're a Republican. Damn straight, Kindergarten Cop! In the past year, my family has initiated a bold new spending program designed to bolster the alternative-rock industry, and next year we're unveiling our plan to provide health care for all Americans except the ones who don't live with us. Also, don't forget to check out the new Bérubé Turnpike we'll be building in a town near you. It'll be a toll road, so that we can raise the funds for the light rail system we're working on for 2009.

Some of you might doubt that my family can pull this off. Well, some of you might just be *economic girlie-men*! The kind who get their panties in a bunch about a little deficit here and a little job loss there! You people don't have health care? You can't afford a visit to the dentist, you say, and you've got this inflammation that you're worried about? You're a bunch of fags!! Why not just go to Hollywood and become DemocRATS, you lily-livered gum-inflamed liberal whiners?

Enough about you. This night wasn't about you. It was about a president who knows how to *terminate terrorism*. That's right, you wanted to know if Arnold would say "terminate," and you got your answer — we will terminate terrorism. Terrorism will come at us in a big truck carrying crude oil or liquid nitrogen or something, and we'll crush it in a drill press or maybe shoot it and shatter it into a million pieces, but then the terrorists' metal forearm will survive and provide scientists with the basis for creating a whole new kind of artificial intelligence, or the liquid-metal terrorist will re-form and we'll have to shoot it with one of those huge exploding bullets and make it fall backward into a vat of molten steel, and then we'll have to send ourselves back into the past (that is, to the present) to protect ourselves from the terrorists who want to start a global thermonuclear war, but then it'll turn out that the war happens anyway, which is kind of complicated, because we thought we'd avoided it when we shot the liquid-metal terrorist with the huge exploding bullet and he fell . . . *Never mind*, that's not the point, the point is that leadership is all about "making decisions you think are right and then standing behind those decisions." Even when it looks like your decision to invade Iraq was based on the advice of a notorious kleptomaniac who was possibly serving as a double agent for Iranian mullahs, *you stand behind your decision*, because leadership is all about making decisions you think are right and then standing behind them. Um, I said that already. But that's all right, because it makes it even more true!! And I stand firm in repeating what I said about leadership!!

I do have two quibbles with Arnold's speech. One, he said, "You don't reason with terrorists, you defeat them." Maybe this is one of those moments where he's respectfully disagreeing with the president, who recently told us (and I'm paraphrasing from memory here) that we can't win a war on terrorism in a way that winnably defeats terrorists because this is a different kind of conflict than the kind of conflict in which you win a war, but that doesn't mean we won't win. But I think Schwarzenegger should have consulted the president about this. And two, he said that "we do not fight for imperialism, we fight for human rights." I know I've only been a Republican for twenty-four hours now, but I have to press the "respectful disagreement" button here. Screw human rights — I'm in it for the imperialism. You may be happy right where you are in Sacramento, Arnold, but me, I want one of those no-bid contracts.

Next up were the twins, Barbara and Jenna. And here, I think, is where my new party revealed a genius I didn't know it had. For years, progressive left literary types like me used to taunt Republicans: "Nyah nyah, nyah nyah," we suggested, "you don't know anything about surrealism, nyah nyah, never heard of the European avant-garde, la la la la la la." We thought we were the last word in urbane sophistication, and that Republicans could not begin to comprehend — or even catch — our allusions to figures like Bréton and Bataille. But then along come the Bush twins, and ooh la la, surrealism is born anew! "My dad already had a chief of staff — and his name is Andy!" said Jenna. It is beyond humor, it is beyond your petty-ironic Democrat understanding. "Our parents' favorite term of endearment for each other is Bushy," they said, following this with, "We had a hamster too, but our hamster didn't make it." *What does this mean?* you ask. Foolish liberal Democrats, fretting about "What does this mean, this strange talk of bushes and lost hamsters." It is not about meaning. It is about the irruption of the unconscious into the very fabric of everyday life, where the eye becomes an egg *and the hamster disappears into the bushy undergrowth, there to be transformed into the heart and soul of America*. Hah! Now we find that Republican diversity is even more diverse than Michael Steele and Arnold Schwarzenegger — it extends even to the domain of live performance art, where Barbara and Jenna Bush evoke Bréton and Bataille and Beavis and Butthead in an intertextual performance that leaves you girlie-men cultural-studies Democrats gasping for air. I especially liked the bit about how their parents taught them to respect everyone. *Except the people we run against — them we slime!* Heh. Heh heh. Heh.

After Arnold and the twins, Laura was a serious letdown, I have to say. She was not very diverse, and she was not very surrealist either. She *did* manage to point out that her husband was the very first president to support stem cell research, slapping down that liberal-media Big Lie about how Bush declared a moratorium on it, and she *did* manage to be strong and emphatic, not at all shrill and smug like Hitlery, but why did she have to go and mention Vaclav Havel? He's a foreign leader, and as Rudy G. told us last night, foreign leaders suck eggs. "Democracy requires the participation of everyone," Havel told Laura. Screw that participatory shit! We have an election to win here. No wonder nobody clapped at that line! Diebold their lame asses, I say, and if there's a black DemocRAT in Florida who wants to vote, he (or she!) better be ready to recite the Constitution backward and prove that his (or her!) grandfather wasn't a Democrat (or a felon, assuming you make the distinction!). And then we have to hear about the president shedding tears as he's hugged families who've lost loved ones? What the hell is this, Oprah? First of all, George Bush would have to have *really long arms* to hug entire families. And second of all, let's leave this sensitive, family-hugging crap to John Kerry, whose campaign is based entirely on hugging, nuancing, and reasoning with terrorists. From my leaders I want to hear more about terminating terrorism with huge exploding bullets and time travel, and that's why I can't wait to hear Dick Cheney speak tomorrow night.

America moves ahead! And this blog will follow.

More Plans for Democrats in Distress

[5 December 2004]

E ver since the election, I've been hearing a lot about the South. In fact, even before the election, liberals were knocking themselves out about the South. It's occurred to us, of course, that the last nonsouthern Democratic nominee to be elected president was Kennedy, and we know that even Kennedy wouldn't have squeaked in if not for the overwhelming last-minute turnout of dead people in Chicago. The problem is that whenever one of us talks about appeasing the South politically — when a liberal says he follows NASCAR, for example, or says he wants the support of guys with Confederate flags in their pickups, or suggests that Democrats should interpret the Bible more literally and treat evolutionary "theory" more skeptically — we all go batshit insane in response. Some of us have even suggested that the Civil War was a bad idea — that we should've let the South secede back in 1861 and waited around 130-something years for a NATO "humanitarian intervention" to end slavery. In response, southern liberals have raised hell, accusing their blue-state colleagues of every kind of regionalist elitism and moral hauteur; one of them (I forget who, or I'd provide the link) reminded us that even in a blood-red state like South Carolina, more than 40 percent of the voters went for Kerry.

I haven't weighed in on this debate until now. And I have only two words for y'all: *Stop it*. That's right, *Stop it*. And I get to say "y'all" because I lived in the South for six years — not deep in the South, but indelibly in the South nonetheless (you know, where people use "right" as an intensifier, as in "I'll bring that over right quick"), and I can tell you that although the region is profoundly conservative in every sense of the word, it's also responsible for some of the best music and literature produced in this nation. We need the South culturally, even though it's way beyond problematic politically. And there's no use going into all the reasons why it's so problematic politically, because (1) we already know perfectly well what those are and (2) we are forbidden from speaking about them, lest the media portray us as mandarin, green-tea-sipping elitists.

Besides, we need to focus our attention on jettisoning an even more problematic region — a belt of Even Redder States that have none of the cultural advantages or storied charm of the South. That's right, I'm talking about nullifying the Louisiana Purchase.

That's really where things went wrong, folks. Jefferson's Folly (as it should hereafter be known) gave us what is now Louisiana, Arkansas, Missouri, Iowa, half of Minnesota (we'll keep some of Minnesota, thanks), North Dakota, South Dakota, Nebraska, Kansas, Oklahoma, most of Montana and Wyoming, small chunks of New Mexico and Texas, and the conservative eastern half of Colorado to boot. And while everyone's been obsessing about the land of Dixie and its peculiar institutions, the good people living on this windswept, culturally barren swath of land have been dragging the country to the right, to the right, to the right — and right off the cliff. It's time to cut them loose.

"Holy Heartland, Michael," you say. "Have you lost your mind? You can't undo a real estate deal from two centuries ago — there's no precedent for it, no protocols! What are you saying, we give all those half-billion acres of land back to the Sioux and the Pawnee? And on what legal reasoning, may I ask?"

What legal reasoning are you talking about here? What kind of ignorant imaginary interlocutor are you? Haven't you ever read the text of the Louisiana Purchase? The final sentence of the document reads, "Done at Paris the tenth day of Floreal in the eleventh year of the French Republic; and the 30th of April 1803." Don't you see? *There is no month of Floreal.* That was a reference to some weird-ass, short-lived "French Revolution" calendar that doesn't exist anymore, full of dates like "le dix-huitième Brumaire" and "le vingtième Fromage." That contract isn't binding, any more than your lease would be if it said you had to pay the rent on the thirty-ninth day of each month. "Eleventh year of the French Republic," indeed. It might as well say "Year Zed in Organic Time."

And no, I'm not talking about giving the land back to the Native American tribes who lived on it. It's not theirs, after all — it belongs to the French. Thus, when we void the Purchase and return the territory to France, all those red-state voters will become French citizens, and the fair cities of Baton Rouge, Pierre, Des Moines, and Cape Girardeau will — at long last — be repatriated. Of course, we'll have to ask for our $15,000,000 back, prorated for inflation since 1803 (or "year eleven," ha ha ha). I suggest we set a reasonable price of $10,000 per acre, which brings the total cost to $5,299,116,800,000, or enough to reduce the federal debt by almost 75 percent, knocking it down under the $2,000,000,000,000 mark.

So the United States will be close to solvent again, and the upstanding, God-fearing people of Nebraska and Wyoming and Oklahoma will join together in singing "La Marseillaise."

I can't think of a more satisfying outcome.

In my characteristically belated, catching-up kind of way, I've finally decided what I think of that 6 March *New York Times* roundtable on liberalism featuring Peter Beinart, Michael Tomasky, and Katrina vanden
Heuvel. Yes, I know — I'll be weighing in on the significance of the French
Revolution next (though personally, I think it's too soon to tell on that one).
Most of what I've read so far among liberals/progressives/lefties takes Beinart
to task for repeating one of the ripest items in the RNC bag of chestnuts: "It's
remarkable to me how many people still mention the fact that [anti-abortion
Pennsylvania governor] Bob Casey was denied the right to speak at the 1992
Democratic Convention." Yeah, well, it's really remarkable to me too, since, as
everyone and her brother has pointed out, Casey was actually denied a speaking slot because he hadn't endorsed the damn Clinton/Gore ticket. Listen.
Anyone who repeats this canard again is a GOP android. You don't have to
go to all the trouble of giving them the Voigt-Kampff empathy test from *Do
Androids Dream of Electric Sheep?* — just ask them if the Democrats are so
stridently pro-abortion that they wouldn't even let poor Bob Casey speak at
the 1992 convention. If they say yes, you may feel free to "retire" them.

And then there's Beinart's last-gasp defense of the thing that has been killing Democrats for the past three years, the item on which Kerry was so spectacularly, extravagantly incoherent. Iraq. Beinart is no longer prowar, but,

> Let me say a couple of things as someone who did support the war in Iraq.
> There is no question that the war is going very, very badly. But I think
> two things remain even if we do end up deciding that Iraq was a terrible
> disaster. The first is that there is an important connection between dic-
> tatorship and the rise of Islamic fundamentalism. Secular dictators like
> Saddam Hussein or secular autocrats like Hosni Mubarak create a politi-
> cal dynamic in which liberalism gets weakened and weakened. And the
> only alternative becomes Islamic fundamentalism.

I happen to think he's right that there is such a connection and that its roots
go all the way back to the CIA's Original Sin of overthrowing Mossadeq in

Iran and installing the Shah in 1953. (Though I don't mean this to suggest that I think we're to blame for everything that's happened in the region since; nor do I think that we "created" Islamism by means of our foreign policy. I think Islamists did that pretty much on their own.) I also think that liberals and leftists should be at one in opposing dictatorships *regardless* of whether they involve any Islamic fundamentalism. But this is not, not, not a justification for preemptive invasion and war. Saying — or even implying — that the connection between dictatorship and Islamic fundamentalism is a legitimate reason for war in Iraq is tantamount to signing on for the entire century-long PNAC package of wars in the Middle East as one dictatorship after another is toppled in Syria, Iran, Jordan, and then we have to decide just how we're going to tell our secular autocratic friends in Egypt and Saudi Arabia that we're coming to clear them out.

But, folks, I know you know all this already. So I'm going to focus not on Beinart himself but on the Beinart Effect. His clarion call in last December's essay, "A Fighting Faith" — as Mark Schmitt put it last month, "apparently soon to be a major motion picture perhaps starring John Cusack as the late Senator Henry M. Jackson" — for Democrats to repudiate Michael Moore and MoveOn.org contained a tiny but crucial grain of truth: Michael Moore does indeed go around saying that terrorism is a phantom menace. "For Moore," Beinart wrote, "terrorism is an opiate whipped up by corporate bosses. In *Dude, Where's My Country?*, he says it plainly: 'There is no terrorist threat.' And he wonders, 'Why has our government gone to such absurd lengths to convince us our lives are in danger?'" The closing minutes of *Fahrenheit 9/11* strike a similar note as well.

Now, it's one thing to ridicule the color-coded terror alerts and Tom Ridge's special sales on duct tape. That ridicule is entirely appropriate, especially when you take into account the *very curious timing* of those orange alerts. It's quite another thing to say, as Ed Herman did in December 2001, "The idea that the Taliban is a fascist and expansionist threat, and that Islamic fundamentalism more broadly speaking is the same, doesn't hold water." Remarks like these suggest that one wing of the American left just doesn't take Islamic fundamentalism or al-Qaeda very seriously, and they (that is, the remarks and the people who've made them) have now become the source of both Paul Berman's and Peter Beinart's analogies between what they see as the naive, trusting fools who were soft on communism in 1947 and the naive, trusting fools who are soft on Islamism today.

The problem, then, is that this determined underestimation of political Islam and groups like al-Qaeda produces a compensatory overestimation of political Islam and groups like al-Qaeda. Josh Marshall — no shrinking violet he, and no lefter-than-thou guy either — called Berman on this phenomenon almost two years ago in his review of the book, suggesting that *Terror and Liberalism* had given in to what he called the "Orwell Temptation," the tendency to "take momentous, morally serious questions and make them out to be slightly more momentous and world-historical than they really are." The Beinart Effect is a closely related phenomenon; it is not, however, a question of how the "soft" left has affected Beinart so much as a question of how Beinart's insistence on "a fighting faith" has affected other liberals.

And here, this blog is looking at you, Michael Tomasky. Don't get me wrong — I love you like a brother or maybe a cousin; I didn't much care for your argument in *Left for Dead*, ten years ago, that the academic left bore some responsibility for the Gingrich Revolution (you remember that line about how we "sit around debating the canon at a handful of elite universities and arguing over Fish's and Jameson's influence on the academy"), but I've thoroughly enjoyed most of your work since, and I cite you all the time, really I do. But you've got to stop saying things like this (from that *Times* roundtable): "First, terrorism is a threat. It threatened our shores more directly than the Soviet Union ever did. And it must be the focus of a foreign policy." The "threatened our shores more directly than the Soviet Union" line is just asking to be kicked, and (as I'm sure you're aware), the sharp-toed Tom Tomorrow delivered precisely that kick two weeks ago. Quite apart of whether it's accurate (and it's not), it plays right into Beinart's thesis in "A Fighting Faith" and promises to fight even *harder* to combat the *most serious threat we have ever faced, ever.*

Likewise, you really shouldn't have announced your "principled realism" in the March 2005 issue of *The American Prospect* by way of that banner cover headline, "Between Chomsky and Cheney." Look, I know what this really means: it means Chomsky supports no international interventions led by the United States or its allies, military or otherwise, and Cheney supports international intervention twenty-four/seven, preferably unilateral, military and otherwise, whereas principled realists support *some* international interventions (Liberia and Darfur as well as Afghanistan, say), maybe led by the United States, maybe not, and preferably (though not dogmatically) not military. And I realize that you can't fit all that on a magazine cover. But if you really split the difference between Chomsky and Cheney, you wind up with Scoop Jackson or Joe Lieberman, and trust me, you don't want that.

Besides, as Rick Perlstein pointed out to me a few days ago, there's something very, very troubling about the whole Beinart analogy between anti-Islamism and anticommunism, and "principled realists" ought to be much more wary of it than they are. Yes, the Americans for Democratic Action met at the Willard Hotel in 1947. Yes, they announced their opposition to communism "because the interests of the United States are the interests of free men everywhere" and America should support "democratic and freedom-loving peoples the world over." (Beinart quotes their statement accurately, for what that's worth.) And yes, they had a better sense of totalitarianism than did their critics on the left at the time. *But it doesn't seem, in retrospect, that this managed to inoculate American liberals and progressives against McCarthyism over the course of the ensuing decade.* A fat lot of good it did, actually. When the shock troops of the right broke down your door fifty-odd years ago, searching for spies and softies and fellow travelers and people who'd voted for Norman Thomas in 1932 and people who knew someone who'd just denounced the Taft-Hartley Act, and when you insisted, as you were being led away, that you were in fact an anticommunist, you remember what the reply was: they didn't care what kind of communist you were.

So yes, let's have a fighting liberalism: let us oppose violent, fundamentalist, patriarchal, homophobic, and theocratic forces abroad, just as we do at home. But let's not give in to the Orwell Temptation, or its corollary, the Beinart Effect. And let's not delude ourselves into thinking that adopting a "fighting liberalism" will keep the wolves of the right at bay.

Works Cited

Beinart, Peter. "A Fighting Faith." *New Republic*, 19 December 2004. Available online at <http://www.tnr.com/doc.mhtml?pt=whKP5U%2BbbaxbirV9FQh Quh%3D%3D>. Accessed 18 March 2005.

Beinart, Peter, Michael Tomasky, and Katrina vanden Heuvel. "Left Behind." Roundtable with Barry Gewen. *New York Times Book Review*, 6 March 2005. Available online at <http://www.nytimes.com/2005/03/06/books/review/006LIBERA.html?ex=1137301200&en=898029e539dd1b82&ei=5070>. Accessed 18 March 2005.

Berman, Paul. *Terror and Liberalism*. New York: Norton, 2003.

Marshall, Joshua Micah. "The Orwell Temptation: Are Intellectuals Overthinking the Middle East?" *Washington Monthly*, May 2003. Available online at <http://www.washingtonmonthly.com/features/2003/0305.marshall.html>. Accessed 22 June 2003.

Schmitt, Mark. "More on Peter Beinart's 'Fighting Faith.'" *Decembrist* (blog), 7 February 2005. Available online at <http://markschmitt.typepad.com/decembrist/2005/02/more_on_peter_b.html>. Accessed 18 March 2005.

[19 July 2005]

OK, so I'm a few hours late with today's Theory Tuesday. That's because I left my copy of *Russian Formalist Criticism: Four Essays* on top of the refrigerator last night and spent way too much time this morning running around looking for it. (I don't write these blog entries in advance, folks — they come to you fresh from the keyboard, handcrafted on the very day they go up. How do I post a twenty-two-hundred-word theory thing in one day? It's simple: I type really, really fast.)

Now to Viktor Shklovsky, as I promised last week. Why Shklovsky, why now? Because long ago in 1986, my dissertation director, Michael Levenson (about whom more in a future installment), taught an introduction-to-theory class in which he suggested not only that modern literary theory begins with the Russian Formalists but more specifically that Shklovsky's idea of "defamiliarization" (or deautomatization, or more precisely, for those of you who speak Russian, *ostranenie*) runs throughout twentieth-century literature and literary theory, even (or especially) where it doesn't declare itself by name. The more I read, the more I came to think that Michael was right on both counts. The world of "Theory" began to seem to me like an *ostranenie*-o-rama: if there was one thing that feminist critics, psychoanalytic critics, Marxist critics, and deconstructionists wanted to do to me, it was to make me see things anew, to make the familiar strange. Whether they sought to reveal the workings of patriarchy, of ideology, of the unconscious, or of language itself, they were engaged in the Shklovskian task of *laying bare the device*. Even Hans Robert Jauss's "reception aesthetics" depends on the idea of defamiliarization, when it claims that the value of a work is a function of the degree to which it violates the "horizon of expectations" of its readership. And then four years after I took that course, Judith Butler published *Gender Trouble*, with its now-famous analysis of gender performativity and the meaning of drag, and I thought to myself, *Wow, still more defamiliarization! Drag denaturalizes, disidentifies, and defamiliarizes! Hey, Michael was right!*

So if you want a handy entry point into Theory, you can hardly do better than Shklovsky, for all kinds of reasons. Not only because he devises a theory of "poetic" as opposed to "ordinary" language, thereby setting the terms for another six or seven decades of debate, but because he names a project that, taking its motive from the aesthetics of modernism, became part of the armature of theory itself. Here's what I mean: many of the successes *and* many of the excesses of theory can be traced to its desire (yes, it has desires) to defamiliarize, to make strange. I think this is where much of the energy of theory, and much of the frustration and hostility it's aroused, ultimately comes from: whereas just-plain-vanilla literary criticism usually tries to explicate a text, or to take it apart and put it back together, or simply to describe what's going on in this or that difficult passage, literary theory's ambitions (for better and worse) are grander. When theory works — when it leads you to see things about texts and textuality that you'd never seen before — it's a remarkable thing: you come away thinking, *Well, I'll never look at rhetorical questions quite the same way again*, or *I'll never look at drag the same way again*, or (for you Raymond Williams fans out there) *I'll never think of the word "culture" in the same way again*. When it doesn't work, well, that's when it looks more like a bunch of people dressing up banal or insane propositions in ornate and/or ungainly and/or neologistic language. That's when you get people like Baudrillard saying, "[B]y the orbital establishment of a system of control like peaceful coexistence, all terrestrial microsystems are satellized and lose their autonomy" (277), at which point you should decide to move away from the guy who's *clearly been in the coffee shop too long* and has been slipping absinthe into his espresso since noon. (I note in passing that very few people bother to read — or even anthologize — Baudrillard's "The Precession of Simulacra" all the way through. There's a good reason for that.)

Now, I imagine that some of you are already thinking of this or that objection to the preceding paragraph, because you're just that way. For one thing, Shklovsky's theory of "defamiliarization" isn't supposed to be a theory about theory; it's supposed to be a theory of *literariness* (not of "literature": this is a crucial distinction, the very foundation of Formalism). Fair enough. Let's go to the text: "Art as Technique," also translated as "Art as Device." It was published in 1917, a very busy year for most of Russia.

Shklovsky opens by taking issue with people who claim that "a satisfactory style is precisely that style which delivers the greatest amount of thought in the fewest words"; he calls this kind of stylistic efficiency and compression "algebrization" (12), since it tends toward the reduction of concepts into handy single-letter symbols (through which "we see the object as though it were enveloped in a sack" [12]). And in this searing passage, he denounces the "habitualization" to which it inevitably leads:

And so life is reckoned as nothing. Habitualization devours works, clothes, furniture, one's wife, and the fear of war. . . . And art exists that one may recover the sensation of life; it exists to make one feel things, to make the stone stony. The purpose of art is to impart the sensation of things as they are perceived and not as they are known. The technique of art is to make objects "unfamiliar," to make forms difficult, to increase the difficulty and length of perception because the process of perception is an aesthetic end in itself and must be prolonged. *Art is a way of experiencing the artfulness of an object; the object is not important.* (12)

A bit later on, the Marxists will have at Shklovsky for that last line; Bakhtin and Medvedev, for instance, will insist that Shklovsky "radically distorts the meaning of the device, interpreting it as an abstraction from semantic ideological significance. But, in fact, the whole meaning of the device is in the latter" (61). They have a point: if you bracket the object altogether, you wind up unable to say just what it is that's being made strange. But Shklovsky is also making the entirely necessary (and very modernist) point that the aesthetic is not a function of objects-in-themselves: it is not the case, he says, that some objects are naturally aesthetic and some aren't. It is a question of technique, of device: where you find *ostranenie*, there you find art. A few pages later, Shklovsky says this in so many words: "I personally feel that defamiliarization is found almost everywhere form is found" (18).

This is great stuff, and I bet most of us believe some version of it. In fact, it's become kind of (ulp) familiar, and you can find versions of this argument not only in literature departments but in arts-foundation rhetoric and museum brochures (and other places, too, as you'll see if you keep reading). Art renews perception, art is a way of seeing, art deepens the spirit, art renders the world anew. All of which can be quite true, you know — or else I wouldn't bother with art myself.

But it's obvious that this is a modernist theory of art. A neoclassical theorist like Nicolas Boileau would insist instead that art involves the correct presentation of the unities; a straight-up classical theorist like Horace would suggest that the function of art is to delight and instruct; and legions of readers in every era might say (I'm thinking especially of you medievalists) that the function of art is to make the unfamiliar *familiar*, so that we can better understand our place in God's creation.

In one way, to call Shklovsky's a "modernist" theory is simply to remark that Russian Formalism went hand in hand with Russian Futurism, which, in the person of Vladimir Mayakovsky, partook eagerly in the Russian Revolution:

the new society would have a new literature and a new literary criticism and theory (now *that's* excitement). For Russia, of course, the period was marked not only by the aesthetic turbulence of international modernism but by the radical (and violent) change from feudalism to communism, and as a result, there was some really intense and energetic theorizing going on until Stalin shut down the whole show in 1928 (after which some of its participants packed up and moved to Prague, where they were permitted another two decades of speculative thought before the Iron Curtain fell on that stage as well). Boris Eichenbaum's account of the time in "The Theory of the 'Formal Method'" sometimes makes it sound as if the revolution were fought not by Bolsheviks and Mensheviks against czarists but by rival schools of poets and theorists:

> The historical battle between the two generations — a battle which was fought over principles and was extraordinarily intense — was therefore resolved in the journals, and the battle line was drawn over Symbolist theory and Impressionistic criticism rather than over any work being done by the Academicians. We entered the fight against the Symbolists in order to wrest poetics from their hands — to free it from its ties with their subjective philosophical and aesthetic theories and to direct it toward the scientific investigation of facts. We were raised on their works, and we saw their errors with the greatest clarity. At this time, the struggle became even more urgent because the Futurists (Khlebnikov, Kruchenykh, and Mayakovsky), who were on the rise, opposed the Symbolist poetics and supported the Formalists. (1064 – 65)

It sounds almost like a Monty Python bit; you expect to hear next that Alexander Kerensky was defeated by the experimental poetics of the Opoyaz group, and that the Battle of the Journals set the terms for the Second Congress of Soviets in October 1917. But Eichenbaum's not kidding: some of the polemical energy of the Formalists was drawn from the sense that they were fighting the old society in the name of the new, just as Lenin and Trotsky were. Of course, Trotsky himself repeatedly weighed in on Formalist and post-Formalist debates in the 1920s and 1930s, so that sense was not all that delusional.

But the theory's debt to modernism is also its undoing. Part of the problem, as I've already noted, is that the idea of defamiliarization sets at a discount every earlier form of art whose purpose it was to put things in their proper place. But another part of the problem is that defamiliarization is contingent on the existence of the familiar, and the "familiar" is (guess what) historically and culturally variable, as Shklovsky inadvertently demonstrates (and as Michael Levenson pointed out to his class almost twenty years ago):

Tolstoy makes the familiar seem strange by not naming the familiar object. He describes an object as if he were seeing it for the first time, an event as if it were happening for the first time. . . . For example, in "Shame" Tolstoy "defamiliarizes" the idea of flogging in this way: "to strip people who have broken the law, to hurl them to the floor, and to rap on their bottoms with switches," and, after a few lines, "to lash about on the naked buttocks." . . . The familiar act of flogging is made unfamiliar both by the description and by the proposal to change its form without changing its nature. (13)

Over the years, most of my students, up until the Era of Guantánamo and Abu Ghraib, have responded to this passage by saying, "Huh? The familiar act of flogging?" (I suppose we should stop here and thank George Bush and Alberto Gonzales for making this aspect of Shklovsky's work more teachable today. Thanks, guys.) And once you pull that thread, the whole fabric of the theory starts to unravel. First you start to realize that defamiliarization is a modernist/avant-garde defense of art, and then you realize that the idea itself has to be historicized. Then you have to start taking account of which times and places might have found flogging to be so habitual that their artists needed to "defamiliarize" it in order to renew perception, and before you know it, you're asking about the social and cultural norms that art seeks to illuminate or violate, and presto, *you're not a Formalist anymore.*

And then you start thinking, *Hell, what if defamiliarization isn't specific to "the literary" in the first place? What if the pictures of Abu Ghraib, rather than the short stories of Leo Tolstoy, render the world unfamiliar and strange? What if theory, rather than literature, makes the stone stony?* Or if you still don't like "theory," try this: once upon a time I was reading an airline magazine when I came across an ad for an ad agency. The agency promised its potential clients that its innovative campaigns would "defamiliarize" products and companies, leading consumers to see them in a wholly new way. This ad made my head hurt. It was as if *Entertainment Weekly* were quoting Walter Benjamin's line about how "the bourgeois apparatus of production and publication can assimilate astonishing quantities of revolutionary themes, indeed, can propagate them without calling its own existence, and the existence of the class that owns it, seriously into question" (229). I half expected to read "We've got *ostranenie* and we can make it work for you."

Of course, there's a way around this problem, but it's a circular way: you can say that defamiliarization is a property of the literary and that (as Shklovsky suggests) the literary is found wherever you find defamiliarization — in an advertisement, in *Gender Trouble*, in Abu Ghraib. But that's not a very satisfying argument, is it now? What do you do?

Tune in to find out the chilling answer in next week's Theory Tuesday!

Works Cited

Bakhtin, M. M., and P. N. Medvedev. *The Formal Method in Literary Scholarship: A Critical Introduction to Sociological Poetics.* Translated by Albert J. Wehrle. Baltimore: Johns Hopkins University Press, 1978.

Baudrillard, Jean. "The Precession of Simulacra." In *Art after Modernism: Rethinking Representation*, edited by Brian Wallis, 253 – 81. New York: New Museum of Contemporary Art in association with David R. Godine, 1984.

Benjamin, Walter. "The Author as Producer." In *Reflections: Essays, Aphorisms, Autobiographical Writings*, edited and introduction by Peter Demetz, translated by Edmund Jephcott, 220 – 38. New York: Schocken, 1986.

Butler, Judith. *Gender Trouble: Feminism and the Subversion of Identity.* New York: Routledge, 1990.

Eichenbaum, Boris. "The Theory of the 'Formal Method.'" In *The Norton Anthology of Theory and Criticism*, edited by Vincent B. Leitch, William E. Cain, Laurie A. Finke, Barbara E. Johnson, John McGowan, and Jeffrey J. Williams, 1062 – 87. New York: Norton, 2001.

Shklovsky, Viktor. "Art as Technique." In *Russian Formalist Criticism: Four Essays*, translated and introduction by Lee T. Lemon and Marion J. Reis, 3 – 24. Lincoln: University of Nebraska Press, 1965.

I learned over the weekend that the esteemed R. J. Eskow has called me the Al Jackson Jr. of literary theory. I am more honored and humbled than I can say, being a huge Al Jackson fan who still hasn't quite mastered the master's playing on songs like Al Green's "Still in Love with You." But it raises the stakes considerably for Theory Tuesdays, which now, I suppose, are expected to be funky as well as informative. Sad to say, I'm just not up to funky today. Besides, we're doing structuralism, which is damn near guaranteed to defunkify any atmosphere.

The early returns on Theory Tuesdays appear to be a mixed bag. The academics who read this blog tend to like these installments, even (or especially) when they take issue with them; everybody else seems willing (more or less) to wait them out in the hopes that someday this blog will be funny again. I should explain that these posts were originally meant (for those of who you believe in "intentionality") as an extended reply to the *Theory's Empire* challenge: because I teach Intro to Graduate Study with the help of the *Norton Anthology of Theory and Criticism* (I'm not one of the editors, as my occasional guest blogger John McGowan is, but I did provide a big long blurb on the back cover, so you might as well consider this blog Norton Central), a couple of photocopied essays, and guest appearances from my colleagues (who come in to describe the past twenty years of work in their various fields), I thought it might be a good idea to offer some of my course notes on this blog.

The course itself — which, before I arrived at Penn State, some students disliked so much they called it boot camp — is also a mixed bag. (And that's why the department head asked me to teach it: I'm the Mixed Bag Guy.) The idea is to introduce first-year graduate students to the various workings of the profession, which means (1) research methods and materials, online resources, rare books, and the like; (2) learning about the recent histories of the various subfields, from medieval to postmodern; (3) acquiring the rudiments of what people call theory; and (4) learning how various conferences and scholarly journals work. I decided to approach (3) not by instructing students on What's Hot Now (which is, I fear, what theory caricaturists tend to think) but by filling them in on the background that most theory-literate people take for granted. I've never forgotten the graduate student who once complained to me that no one explained Mikhail Bakhtin to her when she was an undergraduate, but nonetheless a number of her professors in graduate school assumed that she would be familiar with Bakhtin. "What, was I absent on Bakhtin Day?" she asked. "I think a lot of people were absent that day," I replied. Besides, I think that to "get" Bakhtin, you need to go back and replay those early debates between formalism and Marxism, just as you need to go back and catch up on your *ostranenie* to get a handle on literature since the Romantics and theory since the Russian Formalists.

So today I'm going to say a few words about structuralism, staying with the Old School for now. But before I get to Roman Jakobson and (very briefly) Claude Lévi-Strauss, I want to bring up two side issues raised by the crew at the Valve (<www.thevalve.org>).

The first one is minor: you would think, from reading the posts of the past month, that no one questioned people like Derrida until John Searle came along. That sounds strange to me, because when I read the 1985 *Against Theory* volume inspired by Walter Benn Michaels's and Steven Knapp's bizarrely reductive argument for a form of intentionalism that even intentionalists don't recognize, I came across Richard Rorty writing about how "Derrida looks bad whenever he attempts argument on his opponents' turf; those are the passages in which he becomes a patsy for John Searle" (135). I don't know why this doesn't count when Rorty says it, but it should. Or is it that for some people, Rorty is too identified with the Theory camp? And likewise, I've gotten the impression once or twice that people imagine that all this Theory arrived to say nothing more complicated than "The sign is multivalent," to which the Theory detractors can, of course, reply, "Yes, we knew that already." Well, we knew that too, and we knew you knew it; even Robert Plant knew it when he wrote, in *On Certainty*, "You know sometimes words have two meanings." I'll get back to this at the very end of this post, folks, but for now let it suffice to say that the devil is in the details: the *real* fun lies in finding out just how multivalent that sign can be, and what its multivalences can mean in various contexts. The current anti-Theory camp is quite right not to call for a return to a prelapsarian past or a faux-naïf future. (*This just in: sign not multivalent after all!*) But there's more to theory than a little ambiguity here and a little undecidability there, and again, the important thing lies in learning how "multivalence" and "multiaccentuality" (V. N. Volosinov's term, not mine) actually work.

The second side issue is more important, and I think was best represented by Sean McCann's complaint (<http://www.thevalve.org/go/valve/article/

theorys_empire_its_the_institution_stupid/ >) that some of the *TE* discussion was deflected onto the institutional status of theory rather than the merits of specific theories. Sean acknowledges that this was understandable and not entirely regrettable, either; but I still think the complaint misrecognizes its occasion. *TE*'s publication is a response (as the editors say) not to theory but to *its institutionalization* in the form of the *Norton*, and it was meant to provide critiques of theories and theorists that the *Norton* does not. In other words, the discussion was always already institutional, which is why I considered it entirely within bounds to point out that some of Theory got a free pass twenty or thirty years ago precisely because it seemed to be associated with the most exciting and prolific people in the humanities, whereas the anti-Theory crew seemed to be composed chiefly of cranks and curmudgeons. Theory acquired some of its authority for institutional reasons, and Sean's account of one of the consequences sounds about right to me: distinguishing theory-institutionalization from institutionalization in general, he writes,

> [T]his situation is particularly toxic in literary academia because of a historic professional self-image that cast literature as the anti-disciplinary discipline. As a special kind of knowledge, or rather experience, literature was understood to rise above and cast into doubt the authority of other fields — especially mere "science." To look back over the grand moments of Theory — in its Deconstructive, or New Historicist, or Cult Stud moments — is, I think, to see renewed and intensified versions of that attitude. Not literature, but Theory now is the special kind of expertise that challenges all other expertise, the unique kind of training that subverts all other discipline.

Contrast this account of theory with Brad DeLong's narrative (< http://www.j-bradford-delong.net/movable_type/2005-3_archives/001282.html >) of How He Came to Grips with Foucault: for DeLong, a Foucauldian account of the history of economics brought him to see some things and take issue with others. And that's all I would ever ask a theory to do, myself. That's all I ever ask students to ask for, too.

As for the ancillary complaint (John Ellis's, I believe) that theory has encouraged a kind of amnesia about intellectual history: this strikes me as precisely the kind of complaint that has more bearing on the institutional setting of theory than on theory itself. I mean, seriously, theory is responsible for quite a few revivals and recoveries here and there: the recent Spinoza boomlet is largely the doing of Gilles Deleuze, just as queer theory got some of us (belatedly) reading Sylvan Tompkins and Erving Goffman. The posthumous, three-decades-delayed explosions of interest in the idiosyncratic Marxist work of Antonio Gramsci and Walter Benjamin? Those, too, were brought to you by Theory Productions Worldwide.

All of which reminds me of how very fortunate I was to have, as a theory mentor and dissertation director, Michael Levenson. At a time when the Theory Wings of some departments included a few poseurs and provocateurs and even flaneurs (!), Michael presented the theory division of the intellectual history of the twentieth century with real rigor — and without fanfare. Virginia wasn't a theory hotbed in those days; quite the contrary. When that *New York Times Magazine* piece on the Yale critics appeared in 1986 (see Campbell), all of us in Charlottesville said "Grrrrrrr" (and not much more) because we'd had a thing about Yale ever since they beat us 23 – 21 in the 1983 Aporia Bowl on de Man's last-second field goal. Likewise, just down south of us, Duke was amassing a queer theory/cultural studies team that would win three consecutive NCAA championships; they were building toward the glory years of Bobby Hurley, Eve Sedgwick, Stanley Fish, and Christian Laettner. So dear old U.Va. sometimes behaved as if it had a kind of theory chip on its shoulder. But not Michael: Michael was all theory all the time, with no time for institutional politics. I don't think I've acknowledged my debt to him sufficiently in print, so — as I'm about to repeat much of what he taught me about Jakobson and Lévi-Strauss and much of what I teach my students — here's to him. Thanks, Michael.

The Jakobson excerpts in the *Norton* are short but sufficient to the purpose. From "Linguistics and Poetics," we have the six functions of language and the famous formula (which I suggest my students tattoo onto their arms), "[T]he poetic function projects the principle of equivalence from the axis of selection into the axis of combination" (1265). If you've got the formula, the six functions, the distinction between metaphor and metonymy (in "Two Aspects of Language and Two Types of Aphasic Disturbances"), and the brief discussion of "Hiawatha" and "I Like Ike," you've got your Jakobson in a nutshell. And if you have your Jakobson in a nutshell, you've got your structuralism in a nutshell; and (here's the best thing) if you've got your structuralism in a nutshell, then you could be bounded in that nutshell and count yourself a king of infinite space, were it not that you would have bad poststructuralist dreams. Because if there's one thing you can't say about structuralism, you can't charge it with being insufficiently ambitious.

OK, explanations are in order. Let's take the six functions of language first. Every message has six components: an addresser and an addressee, of course; a context; a message; a contact; and a code. The context is the setting, the contact is the physical or psychological channel of connection, the code is the shared language, and the message is the message. To each component there is a corresponding function:

Messages that focus on the code — "What do you mean by that?" — are called *metalingual*.

Messages that focus on the context — "The cat is on the mat" (a hypothetical sentence popular among philosophers, even though, curiously enough, no cat has ever been on a mat anywhere in the world) — are called *referential*.

Messages that focus on the contact — "Can you hear me?" — are called *phatic*.

Messages that focus on the addressee — "Please take that cat off the mat!" — are called *conative*.

Messages that focus on the addresser — "A slumber did my spirit seal" — are called *emotive*.

Messages that focus on the message — "A slumber did my spirit seal" — are called *poetic*.

You can already see my thumb on the scales with those last two examples, but you get the idea. This really isn't a bad way to classify utterances, and what's even better, Jakobson insists that most utterances are mixtures, with one "dominant" feature among several. This gets him out of the Formalist Impasse, insofar as he's not required to adduce examples of utterances that are "purely" poetic and to distinguish them categorically from merely "practical" or "ordinary" speech. On the contrary, he insists that "any attempt to reduce the sphere of the poetic function to poetry or to confine poetry to the poetic function would be a delusive oversimplification. The poetic function is not the sole function of verbal art but only its dominant, determining function, whereas in all other verbal activities it acts as a subsidiary, accessory constituent" (1264). Jakobson thus deftly refigures the difference between the poetic and other modes of speech as a difference in degree rather than in kind, and disarms wiseguys like me who like to open class with poems such as

Unbelted occupants
Are not able to resist
The tremendous forces of impact by holding tight
Or bracing themselves. Their impact
With the vehicle interior
Has all the energy they had
Just before the collision.

It is a compelling piece of work. I want particularly to draw your attention to the reiteration and personalization of "impact," as the impact is no longer that of "tremendous forces" but of the "occupants" themselves, and the way this process is repeated in line 6, where we find that their impact "has all the energy they had." That abrupt modulation into the past tense is, I think, understated and powerful. We need not say any more about why these occupants are now spoken of only in terms of the energy they have lost. And that's why, if you want an account of a car crash that is at once clinically precise and strangely moving, I recommend the 2003 VW Passat owner's manual.

Jakobson's response to this (and all such Fishy endeavors) is simply, *What did you expect?* Of course you can find elements of the poetic even in the most utilitarian of utterances, even campaign slogans. Here's Roman on "I Like Ike": "[B]oth cola alliterate with each other, and the first of the two alliterating words is included in the second: /ay/-/ayk/, a paronomastic image of the loving subject enveloped by the beloved object. The secondary, poetic function of this campaign slogan reinforces its impressiveness and efficacy" (1264).

And you thought jargon-laden overreading was invented in 1991!

Really, the notion of the "dominant" solves all kinds of problems . . . except one. How do you know that the emphasis on the message itself is the dominant feature of the utterance? Uh, because the utterance is poetic. OK, then how do you know the utterance is poetic? Uh, because the emphasis on the message itself is the dominant . . . ooooooh (cue Yosemite Sam voice here), *ya varmint, it's circularity all over again!* What, after all, is the difference between citing Wordsworth's "A Slumber Did My Spirit Seal" as an emotive utterance and citing it as a poetic utterance? Aren't poetic utterances, particularly in lyric, likely to be emotive as well, whereas in epic (or pastoral, or georgic) they might be referential as well?

Yes, but (and here comes the bromide) it all depends on how you look at it. It all depends on who or what historical epoch or what cultural formation is doing the looking. Where Jakobson goes wrong is just here: he insists that "Hiawatha" (for example) retains its dominant poetic function even when it's being read on the Senate floor by a filibustering senator, whereas I (because I'm of a more pragmatist bent) would suggest that any filibuster is at once phatic (a message about Senate procedure itself) and referential (in its attempt to forestall a vote), regardless of whether it involves a poem or a telephone book or a car owner's manual. Jakobson thus backs into one of two uncomfortable positions: either an utterance carries the designs of its utterer through all space and time, so that "Hiawatha"'s dominant is whatever Longfellow originally intended it to be, or certain utterances have intrinsic features that render them indelibly poetic, referential, metalingual, etc. Since Jakobson's inquiry set out partly to obviate the problems of postulating "intrinsic" features and original intentions, you can see that this makes for a bit of a mess. One is left with the conclusion that Jakobson has defined not six types of utterances but six ways of *attending to* utterances and that the determination of which utterances have a dominant "poetic" function (and how, and why) is left profoundly up for grabs.

But, as I said earlier, that's where the real fun is.

Jakobson argues nonetheless that "the indispensable feature inherent in any piece of poetry" (1265) is that it messes with the principles of metaphor and metonymy. Metaphor, you know, expresses likeness or equivalence; metonymy expresses contiguity and/or combination. "My love is like a red red rose" is metaphor; "The White House said today" is metonymy. Now go back and plug this into that formula I mentioned earlier: *The poetic function projects the principle of equivalence from the axis of selection into the axis of combination.* Jakobson adds, "Equivalence is promoted to the constitutive device of the sequence" (1265). Basically, the poetic function treats metonymic relations as if they were metaphoric. It sounds cool, and it is, particularly when you're trying to figure out why the only emperor is the emperor of ice cream. But this is a description of only certain kinds of poetry, and surely we want to escape the conclusion that very few poems contain a dominant poetic function. We also want to know just *who* is promoting equivalence to the constitutive device of the sequence: Does the poet — or the poetic function — do this at the outset? Or do we (whoever "we" are) do it whenever we stop reading the owner's manual for content and start looking at the language *as language*?

Just to be clear about this: I don't teach Jakobson to trash him for not being pragmatist enough. Neither did Michael Levenson. Jakobson's work was hugely influential for quite some time, and for good reason: those six functions of language, together with the idea of metaphor and metonymy as "poles" corresponding to axes of selection (equivalence) and combination (contiguity), will get you pretty far in the world. At one point in "Two Aspects of Language," Jakobson writes, "Similarity connects a metaphorical term with the term for which it is substituted. Consequently, when constructing a metalanguage to interpret tropes, the researcher possesses more homogeneous means to handle metaphor, whereas metonymy, based on a different principle, easily defies interpretation. Therefore nothing comparable to the rich literature on metaphor can be cited for the theory of metonymy" (1269). *Ha ha!*, I tell my students. *We fixed that!* If you root around in Lacan-inflected theory of the 1970s and 1980s, you'll find that *it's all about the metonymy*. In fact, the more intensely Lacanian you get, the more likely it is that you'll wind up speaking about metaphor as if it were the vehicle for Evil Incarnate (because it asserts a likeness between two things, a Dreaded Dyad), whereas metonymy disrupts all systems of likeness, initiates that exciting, never-ending Metonymic Skid, and ushers us into the way language (and therefore the world) really works. "The unconscious is structured like a language," said the Lacanians, and suddenly metaphor was out and metonymy was the shit. But if you take a step back, you'll realize that we were still working with the terms more or less as Jakobson left them to us.

Borrowing yet one more page from Michael Levenson, though, I hasten to point out to my students that there are two very annoying things about structuralism. One, it is constitutionally grandiose. No sooner does Jakobson discover two types of aphasia than he's off to the races, carving up genres (from lyric to epic), artistic schools, and even entire historical periods according to whether they are predominantly metaphorical or metonymic. (Romanticism and symbolism are metaphorical; realism is metonymic; cubism is metonymic, but surrealism is metaphorical. Bob, you and Kathy are metaphorical. . . .) And there's no reason to stop at literary and cultural history, oh no!

> A careful analysis and comparison of these phenomena with the whole syndrome of the corresponding type of aphasia is an imperative task for joint research by experts in psychopathology, psychology, linguistics, poetics, and semiotics, the general science of signs. The dichotomy discussed here *appears to be of primal significance and consequence for all verbal behavior and for human behavior in general.* (1267; emphasis added)

As Levenson paraphrased this twenty years ago: *Today an investigation of two types of aphasic disturbances — tomorrow, ze universe!*

Two, even though (or, more precisely, because) structuralism wanted to be a theory of everything, it did not want to be a mere theory of "meaning" — especially in the hands of Lévi-Strauss, for whom meaning was "epiphenomenal." I'll spare you the full-dress analysis of Lévi-Strauss, since this post is already past the three-thousand-word mark, but basically, the man insisted that meaning is to structure as the taste of sugar is to the chemical composition of sugar. And Lévi-Strauss could not have cared less about the taste of sugar: he was after the structure, which was somehow "deeper" than mere meaning and antecedent to it. It is stunning, I think, how un- or antihermeneutic a position this really is. (That's one reason why Jonathan Culler's mid-1970s structuralist dream of amassing all possible interpretive modes that can generate all possible textual interpretations was so mistaken. The other reason is that it was mad — mad, I say.) In his remarkable essay, "Structure and Hermeneutics," Paul Ricoeur objected to the idea that structuralist interpretation could escape the boundaries of all human forms of interpretation (these would be the boundaries marked by the hermeneutic circle) and was willing to credit structuralist anthropology with being a kind of science while noting that "the passage from a structural science to a structuralist philosophy seems to me to be not very satisfying and not even very coherent" (45). Suffice it to say, for now, that I'm with Ricoeur on this.

Oh, one last thing. In the course of composing this post I came across this comprehensive "Semiotics for Beginners" site: <http://www.aber.ac.uk/media/Documents/S4B/sem-gloss.html>. Just in case you're looking for (a lot) more of where this came from.

Works Cited

Campbell, Colin. "The Tyranny of the Yale Critics." *New York Times Magazine*, 9 February 1986, 20 – 26, 28, 43, 47 – 48.

Jakobson, Roman. "Linguistics and Poetics." In *The Norton Anthology of Theory and Criticism*, edited by Vincent B. Leitch, William E. Cain, Laurie A. Finke, Barbara E. Johnson, John McGowan, and Jeffrey J. Williams, 1258 – 65. New York: Norton, 2001.

———. "Two Aspects of Language and Two Types of Aphasic Disturbances." In *The Norton Anthology of Theory and Criticism*, edited by Vincent B. Leitch, William E. Cain, Laurie A. Finke, Barbara E. Johnson, John McGowan, and Jeffrey J. Williams, 1265 – 69. New York: Norton, 2001.

Patai, Daphne, and Will H. Corral, eds. *Theory's Empire: An Anthology of Dissent.* New York: Columbia University Press, 2005.

Ricoeur, Paul. "Structure and Hermeneutics." Translated by Kathleen McLoughlin. In *The Conflict of Interpretations*, edited by Don Ihde, 27 – 61. Evanston, Ill.: Northwestern University Press, 1974.

Rorty, Richard. "Philosophy without Principles." In *Against Theory: Literary Studies and the New Pragmatism*, edited by W. J. T. Mitchell, 132 – 38. Chicago: University of Chicago Press, 1985.

[13 April 2005]

In the opening pages of *Life as We Know It*, I wrote that most of my time with Jamie — that is, when I'm actually with him, doing stuff — is lived pretty much moment by moment. And I wrote this specific passage just under ten years ago:

> Occasionally it will occur to Janet or to me that Jamie will always be "disabled," that his adult and adolescent years will undoubtedly be more difficult emotionally — for him and for us — than his early childhood, that we will never *not* worry about his future, his quality of life, whether we're doing enough for him. But usually these moments occur in the relative comfort of abstraction, when Janet and I are lying in bed at night and wondering what will become of us all. When I'm *with* Jamie, by contrast, I'm almost always fully occupied by taking care of his present needs rather than by worrying about his future. When he asks to hear the Beatles because he loves their cover of Little Richard's "Long Tall Sally," I just play the song, sing along, and watch him dance with delight; I do not concern myself with extraneous questions such as whether he'll ever distinguish early Beatles from late Beatles, Paul's songs from John's, originals from covers. These questions are now central to Nick's enjoyment of the Beatles, but that's Nick for you. Jamie is entirely sui generis, and as long as I'm with him I can't think of him as anything but Jamie. (xi)

The clear implication here — and you don't have to be a literature Ph.D. to see it — is that a child with Down syndrome will never have the intellectual capacity to understand the Beatles' oeuvre, or even to understand that some songs preceded others, were written by different band members, and so forth.

Well, this is long, long overdue, but I owe Jamie one enormous apology: I couldn't have been more wrong. Over the past ten years, Jamie has become so fascinated with the Beatles that he's memorized almost the entire songbook. He still has trouble identifying late Harrisonian ephemera like "The Inner Light," "Old Brown Shoe," and "Only a Northern Song" (all of which suck anyway), and he's not crazy about *Abbey Road* (with good reason). But in every other respect, his knowledge of Beatles music verges on the preternatural.

It started a couple of years ago, when he was fascinated with "Being for the Benefit of Mr. Kite," and "Come Together" (he still gets a kick out of "juju eyeball"), whereupon I explained to him that John had written those songs and that John liked to play games with words. Well, Jamie was so thrilled with this news that he demanded to know what else John had written. So I went back over the corpus, so to speak, and found to my surprise that John had written almost three-quarters of the originals on the Beatles' first four records. (My tally is twenty-five Lennons, ten McCartneys — though I'm counting "Hard Day's Night" under John even though Paul wrote the middle eight. I attribute "I Wanna Be Your Man" to both of them. As for songs after 1964, I attribute "We Can Work It Out" to Paul even though John wrote the middle eight. If anyone knows which of them wrote "Tell Me What You See," let me know — I'm inclined to Paul, because it sounds to me like a rewrite of "Things We Said Today," but I'm not sure.) I revisited a mess of other things about John's early work as well, like his fondness for melisma (as in the final verse of "Not a Second Time," which gets positively silly in this respect) and his felicity with pop musical genres we ordinarily associate more with Paul (not only the remarkable "This Boy" and "Yes It Is" but the relatively obscure "Ask Me Why," which is way too complicated for its own good but a hell of an effort nonetheless).

Before I knew it, Jamie had memorized "the Johns," as he puts it, and proceeded to master the other three as well (for Ringo, we go by the songs he sang, not just the two he wrote). Then Jamie wanted to know who wrote "Bad Boy" or "Roll over Beethoven" or "Anna." Then he began to understand (as we made him presents of each CD) which records contained which songs. Then, as he began to ask which came first, I bought him one of my favorite extended pieces of rock criticism, Roy Carr and Tony Tyler's *The Beatles: An Illustrated Record*. By now, Jamie had a sense of the year-by-year, record-by-record trajectory, and an astonishing memory for other things as well.

"Remember when the Beatles were in the Bahamas?" he asked one day.

"Uh," I said, trying to think of Beatles' world tours, "I don't think they ever played in the Bahamas."

"No, in *Help!*," he insisted, and proceeded to show me one of the pictures in yet another Beatles coffee-table book we'd gotten him. Yep, there were the Beatles in the Bahamas. Score one for Jamie. Now Jamie has a whole quiver of such questions. Remember when the Beatles had a pillow fight? Remember when John disappeared in the bathtub? Remember when Ringo was combing his hair?

So when he's bored, or when we're trying to kill time in long lines or on long trips, Jamie will now ask me to "do all Pauls" or whomever, and I will proceed to pick random tunes from here, there, and everywhere. I'll sing about two bars — "Close your eyes, and . . ." and Jamie will immediately jump in and say *"With the Beatles.* 1963. Next!" And I'll say, "Let me think," and he will mock me, and I'll sing "Martha, my dear . . ." and he'll say *"White Beatles.* 1968. Next!" — and this can go on, as you might imagine, for some time, until *my* memory is exhausted. When we came back from Houston last month and waited fifteen minutes by the baggage carousel, we got through about sixty or seventy of these, much to the amusement and/or annoyance of our fellow travelers, one of whom asked, "Did you already do 'Norwegian Wood'?"

What makes this especially curious to me is that he's not just cataloging information and spewing it back; he's got everything cross-referenced somehow, and he never fails to name songs I've forgotten. For example, by the time we'd gotten on the shuttle bus to Extremely Remote Parking at BWI, Jamie was chortling in the back seat at the fact that I'd forgotten "Rain," "Any Time at All," and even "Don't Let Me Down" from the list of Johns. I never, never manage to remember the whole damn song list, and I always forget different songs each time (though for some reason I have particular trouble with "Paperback Writer" and "Drive My Car" among the Pauls). And Jamie never fails to catch the omissions. It's astonishing.

Equally astonishing is his ability to remember where we'd left off three or four days ago, and to pick up from there. "More Johns," he said one day last summer as we were tooling around Paris; "If I fell in love with you . . ." I replied, only to be met with, "We did that already. Next!"

But even more astonishing is his ability to associate specific words with specific songs. One night we were doing the words on his spelling list, and when he came to "through" he sang, "Through thick and thin she will always be my friend." The word "you're" was met with "You're gonna lose that girl"; "picture" with "Picture yourself in a boat on a river." On certain days he has to use his spelling words in complete sentences, and we've told him that he can't always just place them in Beatles songs, that he has to think up his *own* sentences. But if you'd asked me ten years ago whether I imagined that I would ever have to issue Jamie an injunction like that — *Stop quoting Beatles lyrics in your spelling-word sentences* — I probably would have given you a very dirty look.

And so, Jamie, I admit it. Even when I was trying to represent you to the best of my ability ten years ago, I underestimated you. I was wrong, and I apologize. And through thick and thin, I will always be your friend.

Works Cited

Bérubé, Michael. *Life as We Know It: A Father, a Family, and an Exceptional Child.* New York: Vintage, 1998.

Carr, Roy, and Tony Tyler. *The Beatles: An Illustrated Record.* New York: Crown, 1975.

Index

Abrams, M. H., 107

Abu Ghraib, 234, 317, 318

Academic freedom, 206, 276–77

Academic left: and conflation of natural and social reality, 10; and Sokal Hoax, 15, 16, 20; as politically counterproductive, 29; and relativism, 35; and truth, 46–47; and Lyotard, 121; and cultural studies, 144; and cultural justice, 231–32; rise of, 236; and schism in left, 237; and patriotism, 246; and American studies, 280; and Gingrich, 311. *See also* Cultural left

Academic life: and public time, 5; and working conditions of scholars, 151, 169, 185, 186–87, 194–98; and anxiety dreams, 190–93; and parenting, 194–98; and speaking engagements, 199–203

Academic territorialism, 152, 160, 164

Academic writing, 3–4, 6 (n. 1), 167, 168

Acker, Kathy, 27

Act Now to Stop War and End Racism (ANSWER), 234, 261, 262–63, 265

Adjunct teaching positions, 151, 159, 160

Afghanistan: nation building in, 249–50; and mujahideen, 267; U.S. negligence of, 279

Afghanistan, war in: and Chomsky, 232, 234, 256, 257, 258 (n. 1); and left, 232, 233, 234, 249, 251, 254–56, 257, 258 (n. 1), 311; and liberal internationalists, 255; and antiwar movement, 263;

and al-Qaeda, 263, 280; and anti-imperialism, 278; and progressives, 278, 279

African American literature, 138 (n. 1), 179, 188 (n. 1)

African American studies, 114, 115

Agamben, Giorgio, 151, 154, 163

Albert, David, 29–30, 32

Alberti, John, 169

Algeria, 267

Ali, Tariq, 231

Al-Qaeda: and progressivism, 232; nonviolent opposition to, 233; and right, 246; and left, 248, 255, 257, 279, 310–11; oppression of, 249; and war in Afghanistan, 263, 280; bombings of late 1990s, 267; as global network, 268; Herman on, 274 (n. 1); and Iraq war, 279–80

Alterman, Eric, 231, 237

American Association of University Professors, 197

American Council of Trustees and Alumni, 246

American exceptionalism, 130, 133, 275

American left. *See* Left

Americanness: and nation-state, 125

Americans for Democratic Action, 311–12

American studies: and relation to state, 94–95, 124, 127, 132–34, 135, 136–37, 275, 283; and corporate multiversity, 124–26, 133, 134; and internation-

Corporations: and "conquest of cool," 143, 144

Corral, Will H., 291

Coulter, Ann, 203, 245

Cowen, Tyler, 145

Creationism, 31, 62 – 63, 64, 67

Crick, Francis, 42

Croly, Herbert, 241

Crosman, Inge, 97

Cuba, 276, 281

Culler, Jonathan, 97, 98, 99, 326

Cultural journalists, 9, 12, 176 – 77, 223

Cultural left: and utility of science, 75; and utility of arts and humanities, 80; and E. O. Wilson, 84; and state, 131; and schism in left, 232, 236, 237; and social stigma, 238. *See also* Academic left

Cultural right, 75, 80

Cultural studies: and rhetoric of utility, 12; Gross/Levitt critique of, 15; and Sokal Hoax, 16, 20, 29, 30, 32 – 33 (n. 2), 145; and science studies, 17 – 18, 30, 32 – 33 (n. 2); and utility of humanities, 76; and Frank, 95, 144 – 46, 148; and reader-response theory, 98; and interpretive communities, 106; and discourses of popular evaluation, 152, 217, 218; as established subfield, 154

Culture wars, 129, 138 (n. 3), 223, 246, 276

Dahl, Roald, 293

Damrosch, David, 170 – 71

Darfur, 311

Dawkins, Richard, 44

Dean, Tim, 69 (n. 1), 170

Death penalty, 35 – 36

Debray, Régis, 297

Deconstructionism, 97, 118, 119, 154, 163

Defense of Marriage Act (1996), 197

Dehumanization, 238

DeLay, Tom, 80, 252

Delbanco, Andrew, 155, 156, 157, 158, 171

Deleuze, Gilles, 55, 151, 163, 321

DeLillo, Don, 172, 174 – 75, 222, 226

DeLong, Brad, 321

De Man, Paul, 57

Democracy: and Nussbaum, 116; and Congress for Cultural Freedom, 128; and market populism, 141; and Frank, 146 – 47, 148; and mobilization, 252; and al-Qaeda, 268; Berman on, 272; and conservatism, 273; and Bush administration, 277; and American studies, 281, 282; and blog writing, 292

Democratic Party, 264, 290, 307 – 8, 309, 310

Denby, David, 83

Denning, Michael, 130, 145

Derrida, Jacques, 11 – 12, 26 – 27, 29, 49, 56, 118 – 19, 163, 292, 297, 320

Desmond, Jane C., 138 (n. 2)

Determinacy/indeterminacy distinction, 100 – 104, 107 – 8

Dewey, John, 50, 236, 237

Diamond, Jared, 62

Diggins, John Patrick, 232

Dirac, Paul, 21, 22 – 23, 27

Disability studies, 154 – 55, 179, 188 (n. 1), 292

Discursive knowledge, 50

Dissent: and American studies, 128 – 29, 131, 133, 134 – 35, 138 (n. 3), 282; stigmatization of, 275 – 76, 277, 283

Doctorow, E. L., 252

Dodd, Philip, 129 – 30

Dolomieu, Déodat de, 67

Domínguez, Virginia R., 138 (n. 2)

Down syndrome, 41 – 42, 43

D'Souza, Dinesh, 105, 138 (n. 3), 169

Dworkin, Ronald, 105

Kamuf, Peggy, 6 (n. 1), 118
Kant, Immanuel, 87, 117
Kaplan, Amy, 280
Kaplan, Lawrence F., 247
Kennan, George, 131–32
Kennedy, John F., 307
Kernan, Alvin, 155, 157, 158
Kerouac, Jack, 172, 173
Kerr, Clark, 117
Kerry, John, 306, 307, 309
Khrushchev, Nikita, 132, 261
Kimball, Roger, 28, 221–22, 223
King, Martin Luther, Jr., 264
Kipnis, Laura, 4
Kissinger, Henry, 255
Klancher, Jon, 98, 289–90
Knapp, Steven, 320
Knowledge: social character of, 10, 64;
    development of patentable forms
    of, 12; discursive knowledge, 50; as
    observer independent, 59; objective
    knowledge, 76; creation of, 81
Komar, Vitaly, 2, 129, 203
Kornheiser, Tony, 210
Kosovo, 250, 251, 255, 257, 263, 278
Kristeva, Julia, 11, 55, 56, 57
Kristol, William, 244, 278, 284 (n. 4)
Kuenzli, Rudolf, 99–100
Kuhn, Thomas, 12, 31–32, 60, 93, 101,
    102, 103, 108, 109
Kurtz, Stanley, 276
Kushner, Tony, 129

Lacan, Jacques, 11, 12, 19, 55–56, 57, 58,
    325–26
Laettner, Christian, 322
Language games: and Sokal, 16–17,
    33 (n. 3); and Lyotard, 119, 121; and
    blogs, 290
Large Numbers Hypothesis, 22–23, 27
Latour, Bruno, 15, 55, 67
Lauterbur, Paul, 74
Leavis, F. R., 76

Left: and post-9/11 political landscape,
    5, 231; and conflation of natural and
    social reality, 10; and links between
    scientists and military, 26; and
    academic left as politically counter-
    productive, 29; irrationalist wing
    of, 30; and postmodernism's politi-
    cally reactionary consequences, 31;
    identification with science, 35; Sokal
    on, 35; and social justice, 35, 43, 231,
    241; and biological determinism,
    42–43; schisms in, 47, 232, 236, 237,
    251, 255, 264; and pro-Sokal/anti-
    Sokal camps, 54; and relativism, 54;
    French psychoanalytic left, 55–56,
    58; cogency of, 75; New Left, 94, 239;
    and world citizenship, 117; noncom-
    munist left, 131, 133; and relation to
    state, 137; and market populism,
    148; two lefts, 231, 236, 237, 238, 241,
    242; far left, 232, 234; and Rorty, 231,
    236–42; and war in Afghanistan,
    232, 233, 234, 249, 251, 254–56, 257,
    258 (n. 1), 311; reformist left, 232, 236,
    237, 241; and Iraq war, 233, 234, 254,
    268; renewal of, 236; sectarianism of,
    236; and coalitions with progressives
    and liberals, 237, 240; leftist thought
    as zero-sum game, 237, 240; history
    of, 239; and politics of recognition,
    240; and politics of redistribution,
    240, 241; Old Left, 241; and imperi-
    alism, 247, 255–56, 257, 267, 272, 278,
    279; and terrorist attacks, 247–52,
    267; and antiwar movement, 255,
    257, 260, 261, 262, 265, 270–71;
    and prowar liberals, 268, 272; and
    Islamic fundamentalism, 272, 310;
    and American studies, 275. *See also*
    Academic left; Cultural left
Lejeune, Jerome, 41
Lekson, Steve, 62
Leninism, 270, 280

world citizenship, 111, 112, 113, 115, 116 – 17, 118, 122; and missions of higher education, 111 – 12, 122 – 23; and conflict between authority and reason, 112, 121 – 22; and curricular reform, 113, 114, 115, 116

Objectivism, 47, 48 – 49
Observer independence, 11, 59
Occupied Territories, 267, 271
Ohmann, Richard, 145
Oil, 255, 257
Oklahoma City bombings, 246
Old Left, 241
Ondaatje, Michael, 222
O'Neill, Paul, 245, 275
Orwell, George, 134
Other, 43
Owsley, Douglas, 62

Packer, George, 280
Paglia, Camille, 19
Paige, Rod, 277
Pakistan, 256, 258 (n. 1), 263, 267, 273 – 74 (n. 1), 279
Palestine, 255, 270, 271
Pannapacker, William, 291
Parenting, 194 – 98, 293 – 94, 328 – 30
Patai, Daphne, 291
Patriotism, 246, 275, 276, 281
Pattullo, E. L., 121
Pennsylvania State University, 163, 166, 169 – 70
Penzias, Arno, 22
Perle, Richard, 254, 265, 284 (n. 4)
Perlstein, Rick, 311
Persian Gulf war, 265
Peru, 261
Peters, Cynthia, 233, 255
Peters, Tom, 142, 147
Pfister, Joel, 284 (n. 1)
Philippines, 281
Phillips, William, 127

Physical sciences, 11, 158
Physics: and Sokal Hoax, 16, 20 – 21, 24, 28; recent theories of, 21 – 23; and Aronowitz, 25; and Republican Party, 31
Pickering, Andrew, 75
Pinsker, Sanford, 221 – 22, 223
Pipes, Daniel, 276
Plant, Robert, 320
Plutocracy, 237
Political correctness, 238, 271 – 72
Political left. *See* Left
Political protests: and invited speakers, 202 – 3
Political right. *See* Right
Politics of recognition, 238, 240, 242
Politics of redistribution, 238, 240, 241, 242
Pollitt, Katha, 252
Pollock, Jackson, 128
Poniewozik, James, 218 – 19
Pope, Alexander, 213
Popper, Karl, 59
Popular culture, 5, 152, 213 – 26 passim, 297
Popular writing, 3 – 4, 6 (n. 1), 168
Postcolonial theory, 98, 154, 163
Postmodernism: Gross/Levitt critique of, 15; and Sokal Hoax, 16, 20, 31; and quantum mechanics, 24; and multiplicity of viewpoints, 25; politically reactionary consequences of, 31; and Nussbaum, 94, 112, 115, 118 – 19; and decline in literary study, 157; and popular culture, 224, 225
Poststructuralism, 10, 12, 163
Poststructuralist psychoanalysis, 56
Poulet, Georges, 97
Powell, Colin, 247, 265
Pragmatism, 10, 45 – 46, 48 – 51, 292, 325
Pratt, Mary Louise, 2
Presidential Records Act, 252

Index | 343

Rorty, Richard: and contingency, 36; on antifoundationalism, 45, 49 – 50, 55; and pragmatism, 46, 51; and interpretive communities, 109; and cultural cosmopolitanism, 134; and paid political class, 137; and left, 231, 236 – 42; and literary theory, 320

Rosenberg, Ethel, 129

Rosenberg, Julius, 129

Rosenblatt, Louise, 98

Ross, Andrew, 12 – 13 (n. 1), 15, 17 – 20, 28, 29, 75, 144, 145

Rothko, Mark, 128

Rowe, John Carlos, 126

Rowling, J. K., 290, 293 – 95

Rumsfeld, Donald, 245, 254, 265, 280, 284 (n. 4)

Rustin, Bayard, 241, 242

Sadat, Anwar, 267

Safire, William, 252

Same-sex couples, 197 – 98

Sánchez, George, 132

Sartre, Jean-Paul, 45, 51 – 52 (n. 3)

Sassure, Nicolas-Theodor von, 67

Saudi Arabia, 248, 254, 268, 310

Saunders, Frances Stonor, 127, 128, 129 – 31, 138 (n. 3)

Schlesinger, Arthur, 130 – 31, 283

Schmitt, Mark, 310

Schoenberg, Arnold, 128

Schwab, Klaus, 281

Schwarzenegger, Arnold, 303 – 5

Sciences: exchanges with humanities, 10, 58, 74 – 75, 84 – 85; democratic practice of, 12 – 13 (n. 1); Sokal on, 15 – 16, 30 – 31, 32, 55, 69 (n. 2); popularization of, 24; science studies contrasted with, 30; and relativism, 31; left identified with, 35; and social facts vs. brute facts, 40; and falsification of theories, 59 – 60; and symmetry of beliefs, 67 – 68; and rhetoric of util-

ity, 72 – 73, 74, 75 – 76; and Fish/Iser debate, 107 – 8; applied sciences, 125, 126, 167

Science studies: and Sokal Hoax, 9, 15, 54; Sokal on, 12; and cultural studies, 17 – 18, 30, 32 – 33 (n. 2); and religious right, 31; social goals of, 45; post-Sokal debate on, 57; and facts, 59; Boghossian on, 65 – 66; critics of, 75

Scott, Janny, 28 – 29

Scowcroft, Brent, 254, 257

SDS (Students for a Democratic Society), 272

Searle, John, 11, 38, 39 – 40, 107 – 8, 320

Secularism, 48 – 49, 50, 248

Sedgwick, Eve, 98, 163, 322

Senge, Peter, 142

Serrano, Andres, 129

Sexuality: and Nussbaum, 118, 120 – 21

Shakespeare, William, 78, 125, 164, 206, 207 – 8 (n. 2)

Sharon, Ariel, 247, 271

Sheldrake, Rupert, 26

Shining Path, 261, 264

Shklovsky, Viktor, 79, 163, 164, 313 – 17

Silverstein, Ken, 255

Smith, Anna Deavere, 129

Smith, Barbara Herrnstein, 46 – 47, 55, 106, 217

Smith, Henry Nash, 125 – 26

Smith, Zadie, 222

Snow, C. P., 74 – 75

Snyder, Dan, 205

Soccer, 297 – 98

Social constructionism, 10, 11, 40 – 41, 43, 44, 59, 60, 63 – 64

Social Darwinism, 42, 43

Social justice: and left, 35, 43, 231, 241; and social constructionism, 44; trans-historical grounds for, 45, 48; and realism, 48; prospects for, 237

Social sciences, 124, 135, 158

Sokal, Alan: comments on hoax, 9, 11,

The following is the original publication information for the essays in this book that have been reprinted:

"The Return of Realism and the Future of Contingency" originally appeared in *What's Left of Theory?: New Work on the Politics of Literary Theory*, edited by Judith Butler, John Guillory, and Kendall Thomas, 137–56. New York: Routledge, 2000.

"Of Fine Clothes and Naked Emperors" originally appeared in *Tikkun*, March–April 1999, 73–76.

"The Utility of the Arts and Humanities" originally appeared in *Arts and Humanities in Higher Education* 2, no. 1 (2003): 23–40.

"There Is Nothing inside the Text; or, Why No One's Heard of Wolfgang Iser" originally appeared in *Postmodern Sophistry: Stanley Fish and the Critical Enterprise*, edited by Gary A. Olson and Lynn Worsham, 11–26. Albany: State University of New York Press, 2004.

"Citizens of the World, Unite: Martha Nussbaum's Plan for Cultivating Humanity" originally appeared as "Citizens of the World, Unite," *Lingua Franca* 7, no. 7 (September 1997): 54–61.

"American Studies without Exceptions" originally appeared in *PMLA* 118, no. 1 (2003): 103–13.

"Idolatries of the Marketplace: Thomas Frank, Cultural Studies, and the Voice of the People" originally appeared as "Idolatries of the Marketplace," *Common Review* 1, no. 1 (2001): 51–57.

"Days of Future Past" originally appeared in *ADE [Association of Departments of English] Bulletin* 131 (2002): 20–26.

"Teaching to the Six" originally appeared in *Pedagogy* 2, no. 1 (2002): 3–15.

"Working for the U: On the Rhetoric of 'Affiliation'" originally appeared as "Working for the U.," in *Affiliations: Identity in Academic Culture*, edited by Jeffrey R. Di Leo, 33–43. Lincoln: University of Nebraska Press, 2003.

"Dream a Little Dream" originally appeared in the *Chronicle of Higher Education*, 21 September 2001, A48.

"Professing and Parenting" originally appeared as "Professors Can Be Parents, Too," *Chronicle of Higher Education*, 12 April 2002, B12–13.

"Speaking of Speakers" originally appeared as "Travels and Travails as a Guest Speaker and Host," *Chronicle of Higher Education*, 21 March 2003, B5.

"Universities Should Be Open for Business" originally appeared as "A Shakespeare Department and Other Business Ideas for Colleges Everywhere," *Chronicle of Higher Education*, 28 January 2000, A64.

"Analyze, Don't Summarize" originally appeared in the *Chronicle of Higher Education*, 1 October 2004, B5.

"The Top 10 Contradictory Things about Popular Culture" originally appeared as "Pop Culture's Lists, Rankings, and Critics," *Chronicle of Higher Education*, 17 November 2000, B7–9.

"The Elvis Costello Problem" originally appeared as "The 'Elvis Costello Problem' in Teaching Popular Culture," *Chronicle of Higher Education*, 13 August 1999, B4–5.

"The Lefts before 11 September" originally appeared as "Achieving a United Left," *Tikkun*, July–August 1999, 67–70.

"Nation and Narration" originally appeared in *Context: A Forum for Literary Arts and Culture* 10 (2002): 15–17.

"Can the Left Get Iraq Right?" originally appeared as "Peace Puzzle: Why the Left Can't Get Iraq Right," *Boston Globe*, 15 September 2002, E1–2.

"For a Better — and Broader — Antiwar Movement" originally appeared as "Toward an Ideal Antiwar Movement: Mature, Legitimate, and Popular," *Chronicle of Higher Education*, 29 November 2002, B12–13.

"Fighting Liberals" originally appeared in *Tikkun*, July–August 2003, 76–79.

"The Loyalties of American Studies" originally appeared in *American Quarterly* 56, no. 2 (2004): 223–33.

Blog Posts

"Azkaban Blogging," 6 June 2004: <http://www.michaelberube.com/index.php/weblog/azkaban_blogging/>

"Back in Les États-Unis," 29 June 2004: <http://www.michaelberube.com/index.php/weblog/back_in_les_tats_unis/>

"Vacation Reading II," 7 July 2004: <http://www.michaelberube.com/index.php/weblog/vacation_reading_ii/>

"Republican National Convention, Second Night," 31 August 2004: <http://www.michaelberube.com/index.php/weblog/second_night/>

"More Plans for Democrats in Distress," 5 December 2004: <http://www.michaelberube.com/index.php/weblog/more_plans_for_democrats_in_distress/>

"The Beinart Effect," 18 March 2005: <http://www.michaelberube.com/index.php/weblog/the_beinart_effect/>

"Theory Tuesday II," 19 July 2005: <http://www.michaelberube.com/index.php/weblog/theory_tuesday_ii/>

"Theory Tuesday III," 26 July 2005: <http://www.michaelberube.com/index.php/weblog/theory_tuesday_iii/>

"Was I Ever Wrong," 13 April 2005: <http://www.michaelberube.com/index.php/weblog/was_i_ever_wrong/>